MEDIEVAL TRAV.

READINGS IN MEDIEVAL CIVILIZATIONS AND CULTURES: XXII
series editor: Paul Edward Dutton

MEDIEVAL TRAVEL AND TRAVELERS

A READER

edited by

JOHN F. ROMANO

UNIVERSITY OF TORONTO PRESS
Toronto Buffalo London

© University of Toronto Press 2020
Toronto Buffalo London
utorontopress.com

ISBN 978-1-4875-8803-8 (cloth)   ISBN 978-1-4875-8804-5 (EPUB)
ISBN 978-1-4875-8802-1 (paper)   ISBN 978-1-4875-8805-2 (PDF)

LIBRARY AND ARCHIVES CANADA CATALOGUING IN PUBLICATION

Title: Medieval travel and travelers : a reader / edited by John F. Romano.
Names: Romano, John F., editor.
Series: Readings in medieval civilizations and cultures ; 22.
Description: Series statement: Readings in medieval civilizations and cultures ; XXII | Includes bibliographical references and index.
Identifiers: Canadiana (print) 20190222905 | Canadiana (ebook) 20190223022 | ISBN 9781487588038 (cloth) | ISBN 9781487588021 (paper) | ISBN 9781487588045 (EPUB) | ISBN 9781487588052 (PDF)
Subjects: LCSH: Travel, Medieval—Sources. | LCSH: Voyages and travels—Sources. | LCSH: Travelers—Arab countries—Sources. | LCSH: Travelers—Europe, Western—Sources. | LCSH: Travelers—East Asia—Sources.
Classification: LCC G89 .M43 2020 | DDC 910.409/02—dc23

We welcome comments and suggestions regarding any aspect of our publications—please feel free to contact us at news@utorontopress.com or visit us at utorontopress.com.

Every effort has been made to contact copyright holders; in the event of an error or omission, please notify the publisher.

University of Toronto Press acknowledges the financial assistance to its publishing program of the Canada Council for the Arts and the Ontario Arts Council, an agency of the Government of Ontario.

**Canada Council
for the Arts**   **Conseil des Arts
du Canada**

ONTARIO ARTS COUNCIL
CONSEIL DES ARTS DE L'ONTARIO
an Ontario government agency
un organisme du gouvernement de l'Ontario

Funded by the   Financé par le
Government   gouvernement
of Canada   du Canada

For my wife, Julie, whose presence by my side has considerably brightened my travels.

CONTENTS

ACKNOWLEDGMENTS

In the course of compiling such an eclectic group of sources, I have incurred many debts. I would like to thank Paul Dutton, who enthusiastically responded to my initial queries and renewed his welcome to my project several years after I first contacted him; his gentle suggestions greatly shaped the final product. The staff at the University of Toronto Press have been wonderful to work with. In particular, Natalie Fingerhut has guided me through the process of producing the book, and Emily Reiner's keen editorial eye has saved me from countless errors. My wife, Julie, was the original impetus for this volume, and in addition to having ideas bounced off her, she carefully read the manuscript. The librarians at Benedictine College, and in particular Jane Schuele and Lois Farrell, have supplied me with a constant stream of obscure books. Four undergraduates of exceptional talent—Elise Huntley, Lucy Leighton, Sarah Salter, and Allison Segura—sampled and transcribed texts, and I thank my dean, Kimberly Shankman, for the financial support to hire them as my student assistants. Vedran Sulovsky generously critiqued my translation of the *Life of St. Christopher*, suggesting several improvements. The final editing of the project was completed at the American Academy in Rome, and its unique environment was ideal for working through these texts. Although I had many helpful conversations about medieval travel at the Academy, I want to thank especially Victoria Steele, who read and commented on several chapters. I also consulted with my good friend Evan Dawley on several points. Finally, I would like to extend my gratitude to the students who took my seminars on Medieval Travelers, and who unwittingly served as guinea pigs as I determined which works should find their way into the pages of this book.

INTRODUCTION

Travel is fatal to prejudice, bigotry, and narrow-mindedness, and many of our people need it sorely on these accounts. Broad, wholesome, charitable views of men and things can not be acquired by vegetating in one little corner of the earth all one's lifetime.

Mark Twain, *The Innocents Abroad* (1869)

This volume seems doomed at the outset. The popular conception is that medieval people traveled little, and as a result, there was little chance to develop the broad, wholesome, and charitable views that Mark Twain hoped would be its byproduct (instead of the prejudice, bigotry, and narrow-mindedness that often appeared instead). Yet evaluating the degree to which people in the Middle Ages undertook travel has proved difficult, because no reader dedicated to the experience of journeying in this period exists. While they may have heard of no other medieval traveler, everyone knows Marco Polo. However, reading the book of his famous travels in isolation can give the reader a limited or inaccurate notion of how he fits into a broader landscape. As I hope the reader will see, Polo must rather be seen as one of many travelers during a time in which people were on the move for a variety of different reasons.

This volume is intended to allow students and the general reader to examine for themselves the words of men and women who have traveled in the past, and it assumes no previous knowledge of medieval civilization. It is through the sources from the period that one comes to a deep understanding of the past and feels the excitement of discovery. The chronological boundaries of this volume will be broadly "medieval"—that is, from c. 500 to c. 1475. I do not incorporate early modern travelers who discovered the "New World," in part because there are already readers available that do so and in part because it would make the volume impossibly broad. Geographically speaking, I wanted to survey an extensive swathe of territory, drawing upon sources that touch on western Europe, the Byzantine Empire, the Muslim world, and East Asia. Several of these sources focus on the Mediterranean Sea. A few of them venture beyond these boundaries, with Vikings traveling to North America and Ibn Battuta making his way to West Africa. Although several derive from Christian sources, both eastern and western, one will also find Jewish and Muslim voices in these pages. Although these travelers are still only the tip of the iceberg, they will provide an idea of the broad range of experiences on the road.

While most of the sources are written, some are images, which are intended as opportunities for further reflection about what medieval people expected to find in foreign locales. Whenever possible, I have included complete sources, but in some cases I provide excerpts of the most important passages or those that preserve the flavor of a larger source. It has been impossible to be exhaustive in the sources included here. For instance, Benedict the Pole must serve as the sole representative of near-contemporary mendicant friars who journeyed further east. There is a broader literature of imaginary travel, which in turn helped to inspire genuine voyages, but the emphasis in this volume is on the lived experience of travel. It can only be hoped that the selections here will spark the reader's curiosity to locate the many other medieval travelers who left traces of their journeys.

These sources have much to teach scholars and students alike. I have intentionally cast as wide a net as I was able in selecting these sources, with some being obscure or largely inaccessible. The result is that some will be new even to those who have previously studied aspects of medieval travel, and the juxtaposition of documents that have never been published together will cast new light on all of them. It is to be greatly desired that this volume will help to advance discussion of aspects of medieval travel, medieval mentalities, interactions with the "other," and postcolonial studies. These journeys take place at a time before western Europeans took center stage in the world of travel: I wish to show an interchange among different civilizations, not only travelers coming from the "west" into the "east."

I would like to think that the readings expand students' worldviews to help give perspective to our contemporary era of globalization. Travel is ideal for cross-cultural comparison, and in fact travel can help to crystallize the identities of those who partake in it. These sources on travel lend themselves to a host of questions: What did cultural interaction mean in the premodern world? What were the different purposes and experiences of travel? How did religion inform travelers' observations? To what extent are these accounts realistic? I should add that this compilation is somewhat artificial in that there existed across these civilizations nothing like the modern genre of "travel literature." As a few of my students have reminded me, some of these sources would not qualify as modern pieces of travel writing, and others do not pretend to be narratives in the first place. The question of genre should not impede our appreciation of what we do have in these sources: when read carefully, they can inform us about what travel was like in an earlier age and how people thought about it, however one might classify the selections.

It is inevitable that there are certain limitations in the primary sources available to discuss medieval travel, and these limitations shape the story that is told about it. Travel in this period was expensive, which limited who could undertake it. Generally speaking, one had to be at least in the middle class to have some access to writing because of the expense involved in producing texts. So we tend to hear less about the journeys of poor travelers. The sources that discuss travel skew overwhelmingly male and represent a male viewpoint. Margery Kempe is the lone female representative of travelers here. Certain locations such as India and sub-Saharan Africa are normally destinations rather than the origin of travelers. The writers often display bias toward those who are different from them, in some cases with offensive language. In all of these examples, the sourcebook reflects the characteristics of the sources that scholars have at their disposal.

There were many ways in which I might have organized the sources in this volume, with the most natural candidates being chronologically or geographically. I have opted instead for a broadly thematic arrangement, with the selections in each chapter arranged in a roughly chronological order. The advantage of this organization is that it allows the reader to compare and contrast sources that describe similar aspects of travel, however separated by time and place. The categories are not airtight, and attentive readers will see that religion appears frequently even in those journeys in which it is not the main impetus. Rabban Sauma may have been a diplomat, but he also took the time to examine relics and attend worship services while he was in Rome. Naturally, the sources can be read independently of the section in which they appear, or in concert with a source from another chapter.

A special caveat is necessary about the translations that appear here. Putting together a volume that encompasses such disparate peoples and traditions has meant that the original sources were in a variety of languages. Translation necessarily flattens the initial linguistic range, removing the particular characteristics of individual languages, and makes it hazardous to base arguments on phrasing that may at first glance appear similar in more than one source. It has also meant that I have had to be dependent on older translations for most sources, though I have checked the translations against editions of the sources that appear in the languages that I know. At the same time, I have updated the phrasing to reflect modern American usage. In cases in which a brief explanation or point of clarification was necessary, I have put these in square brackets. In making sense of the sources and in writing the brief introductions to the sources, I have been aided considerably by two encyclopedias: *Trade, Travel, and Exploration in the Middle Ages: An Encyclopedia*, edited by John Block Friedman and Kristen Mossler Figg (New York: Garland, 2000), and *Literature of Travel and Exploration: An Encyclopedia*, edited by Jennifer Speake (New York: Fitzroy Dearborn, 2003); the reader is directed to these works for further detail and bibliography. Following each source are questions that are meant to suggest the main themes or subjects for further reflection, but these can be modified or passed over completely.

It has been a great source of pleasure for me to discover and pore over new accounts of medieval travelers, and I hope that the reader will share the enjoyment that I have experienced in piecing together this volume. I have often vegetated in my corner of the world, as Mark Twain lamented, but reading travelogues has allowed me to wander to destinations far from home. Surely Twain's statement that people need travel and the understanding derived from it is as true today as it was in the nineteenth century, or more to the point, in the Middle Ages.

A NOTE ON CURRENCIES, PLACE NAMES, AND WEIGHTS AND MEASURES

Due to the nature of a sourcebook on medieval travel, which encompasses travelers from several different civilizations, the reader will encounter a bewildering array of currencies, place names, and weights and measures. It will be useful to explain at the outset how I have dealt with each of these categories.

Nearly all of the currencies included in these sources are metal, although there are a few references to paper money. I have given the form of metal of a particular currency, although I have refrained from including anything about its purchasing power. In most cases it would be difficult to formulate a standard value, although in some cases, one can figure out how much a unit of currency could buy in the context of the narrative.

The proper names of places in both modern scholarship and older translations are confusing and inconsistent. My overriding concern in the present volume was to provide versions that were easily identifiable (when possible) and that could be found in standard reference works. As a result, I have in some cases silently changed the spellings of place names for the convenience of the reader. When the version of the name provided in a source deviated too much from the modern spelling, I provided the correct spelling or modern version of a name in brackets. In cases in which an identification is uncertain, I have added a question mark in brackets. In cases in which there is only a question mark in brackets, the identity of the place remains uncertain.

I have declined to convert weights and measures within sources, which in some cases rendered the reading of the texts difficult and added little to their comprehension. Instead I provide a brief chart here that summarizes the major weights and measures used, with both modern US and metric equivalents; with these, the numbers in the sources can be easily converted. A note of caution applies, however: we have only a rough idea of the equivalencies for most weights and measures. Even in the original sources, some were at best guesses while others were completely fictional. All of these numbers should be used with caution.

batman = 8.8 pounds or 4 kilograms

cantar/kantar/qintar = 100 pounds or 45.4 kilograms

cubit = a unit measured from the tip of the middle finger to the bottom of the elbow. The biblical cubit (operative in some medieval texts) is 18 inches or 45.7 centimeters.

ell = a unit equivalent to the cubit. Both terms are used synonymously in the work by Nasir-i Khusraw.

farsakh/farsang/parasang = 3–4 miles or 4.8–6.4 kilometers

fathom = 6 feet or 1.8 meters

German mile = 4.6 miles or 7.4 kilometers

kharvar = 350 pounds or 158.8 kilograms

kos = 6.5 miles or 10.5 kilometers

league = the distance one can travel in an hour. It varied considerably, from 7,500 to 15,000 feet or 2.3 to 4.6 kilometers.

mann/maund = 2.2 pounds or 1 kilogram

marrah = 3.5 miles or 5.6 kilometers

mithqal = 0.5 ounce or 14.2 grams

palm = 10 inches or 25.4 centimeters

picco = 1 yard or 0.9 meter

saggio (*plural* saggi) = 0.15 ounce or 4.3 grams

seer = 5.6 ounces or 158.8 grams

span = a unit that is the distance of a human hand, from the tip of the thumb to the tip of the little finger. It equals half a cubit, 9 inches or 22.9 centimeters.

CHAPTER ONE

MAPPING OUT JOURNEYS

The sources in this chapter are grouped together under the subject of "mapping out journeys," although only the first few are maps, and only one of these may seem similar to a modern map. It is intended as a whole to give some idea of how a medieval traveler would have oriented himself or herself more broadly. How were foreign places and peoples imagined? What did the earth as a whole look like? How did one navigate a city? Or speak to strangers? What did a traveler hope to find in exotic locations? Which challenges hampered arrival at one's destination, and how were they overcome? The reader is left to puzzle out to what degree the information provided by these sources was practical and to what extent it was symbolic or an exercise in wish fulfillment. With the maps in particular it may be possible to make out a progression from a wholly symbolic format to something more practical. Some of the texts have ready parallels in modern maps, phrase books, and guidebooks, but the surface similarity may give way to strangeness upon further examination. For instance, those who conceive of paradise as an incorporeal spiritual realm may be surprised to see that for medieval people, heaven was a place on earth. Several gazetteers (geographical dictionaries) listed destinations for travel along with their goods and wonders, and perhaps no place so often as India, and so the last two items in this chapter are a taste of a widespread tradition.

1. MAPS

(a) T-O World Map

This map, named after the shape of the T in its center and the circular O that surrounds it, was one of the most common representations in medieval Europe of inhabited parts of the globe. The Latin text on the map shows that east is at the top, followed clockwise by south, west, and north. The Mediterranean Sea in the middle divides the landmass into three continents—Asia at the top, Europe in the lower left, and Africa in the lower right—all of which are encircled by the ocean. On each continent is the name of one of Noah's sons, each of whom was thought to have populated an area of the world after the biblical flood (see Genesis 10).

Source: Isidorus Hispalensis, *Etymologiae* (Augsburg: Günther Zainer, 1472), p. 360. Latin.

Questions: How does this map differ from modern maps? Does it permit the viewer to gain an idea of the size and position of the continents? Which continents were western Europeans aware of and which were they ignorant of? How does the map reflect the religious beliefs of those who made it?

Figure 1.1 T-O World Map

(b) Osma Beatus World Map

This eleventh-century map came from a Spanish commentary on the Book of Revelation. It displays Asia at the top, with Europe in the lower left-hand corner and Africa (also referred to as Libia) in the lower right-hand corner. It also has a separate southern continent, with an inhabitant—a one-footed monster known as a monopod or skiapod. In addition to providing place names, the designer also placed the twelve apostles where they were said to have preached. Paradise is at the top in the east, with its four rivers (see Genesis 2).

Source: Konrad Miller, *Mappaemundi: Die ältesten Weltkarten*, vol. 1: *Die Weltkarte des Beatus* (776 n. Chr.) (Stuttgart: J. Roth, 1895–98), p. 35. Latin.

Questions: Can this map be considered a T-O map (see doc. 1a)? Which people, geographical features, or buildings did the creator of this map choose to include, and what do they show about his or her priorities? Which of the place names can you identify?

Figure 1.2 Osma Beatus World Map

(c) Sawley (or Henry of Mainz) World Map

This map from the twelfth century once illustrated a chronicle by Henry, a priest of Mainz Cathedral, but the only extant copy derives from Sawley Abbey in England. East is at the top, followed clockwise by south, west, and north. Asia is at the top, with Europe in the lower left and Africa in the lower right hand. Paradise appears as an island at the top center. The eight winds are shown as blank half-circles around the outer part of the globe. Two of the islands are surrounded by smaller islands. A mythical creature known as a basilisk is depicted in Africa.

Source: Konrad Miller, *Mappaemundi: Die ältesten Weltkarten*, vol. 3: *Die kleineren Weltkarten* (Stuttgart: J. Roth, 1895–98), Table II. Latin.

Questions: How is this map similar or dissimilar to the previous map? Is it a T-O map (see doc. 1a)? Which geographical features or buildings did the creator of this map incorporate? Can you identify any place names? How did religion play a part in the choice of illustrations?

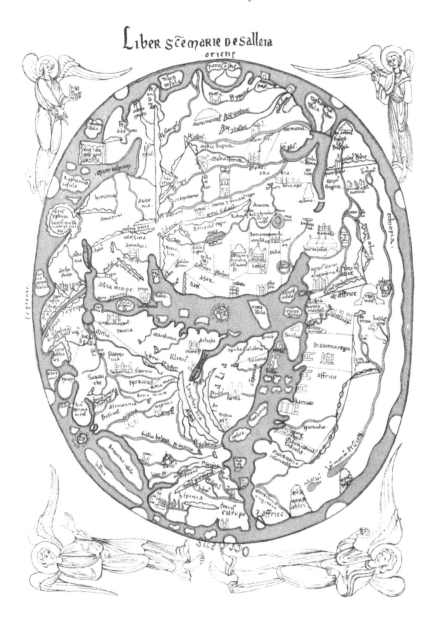

Figure 1.3 Sawley (or Henry of Mainz) World Map

(d) Al-Idrisi World Map

Al-Idrisi (1100–1165) was a renowned Arabic geographer, who would frequently illustrate his books with maps; his work borrows both from Muslim and European cartographic knowledge. Al-Idrisi thought the globe was round but only described the inhabited part. He divided the world up latitudinally (with lines to separate the regions) and longitudinally, with numbers to show what he referred to as climates, further described in his books. Prominent in his map are mountain ranges.

Source: William Vincent, *The Commerce and Navigation of the Ancients in the Indian Ocean* (London: T. Cadell and W. Davies, 1807), p. 617. Arabic.

Questions: Which areas of the world can you identify in this map, and how do they differ from how they would be depicted in a modern map? Can this map have had a practical value for a traveler who needed to locate a place? How does this map differ from the other maps in this section? Did religion play any part in how the world is shown in this map?

Figure 1.4 Al-Idrisi World Map

(e) Carte pisane

Carte pisane or portolan charts, that is, maps related to ports, were maps of the Mediterranean. They first appeared in the thirteenth century. Striking here are what are called rhumb lines, which connect points on two large circles; these were used to help sailors get their bearings. These maps emphasize the coastal regions, with less detail given the further one goes inland. Carte pisane were taken to sea for navigation, and due to wear and tear, normally only copies found in libraries survive.

Source: M. Jomard, *Les monuments de la géographie; ou Recueil d'anciennes cartes européennes et orientales* (Paris: M. Duprat, 1862), pp. 47–48. Latin.

Questions: How were the data for this map collected? Which features of this map make it well suited to practical use? Does it have inaccurate aspects? Why are the coastal regions detailed? How does this map differ from the other maps in this section? Did its creators have a different set of values than the creators of the other maps?

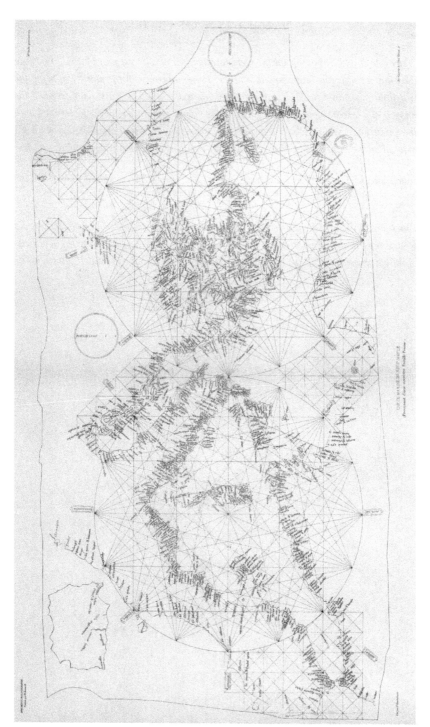

Figure 1.5 Carte pisane

2. WOODCUTS OF CITIES

The book in which these woodcuts were incorporated was an account of a pilgrimage to the Holy Land in the late fifteenth century. Perhaps because of the novelty of being the first illustrated travel book, it quickly became a best seller. The artist who designed the images, and who also published the work, was named Erhard Reuwich; he traveled with the priest from Mainz who wrote the text accompanying the images. Other than his place of origin—the city of Utrecht—scholars know virtually nothing about Reuwich.

Source: Bernhard von Breydenbach, *Peregrinatio in terram sanctam* (Mainz: Erhard Reuwich, 1486), pp. 36–37 (Parens [Poreč]); 41–42 (Corfu); 48 (Modon [Methoni]). Latin.

Questions: What do the illustrations of these cities hold in common? Which features did Reuwich particularly call attention to, and why do you think he did so? Do the depictions of the cities appear realistic? If not, why not? What aspects of cities did Reuwich omit?

Figure 1.6 Parens [Poreč]

Figure 1.7 Corfu

Figure 1.8 Modon [Methoni]

3. WOODCUTS OF PEOPLE

(a) "Exotic" People

Included in the same work on pilgrimage to the Holy Land (see doc. 2) were illustrations of the local inhabitants that the author encountered along the way. Scholars tend to doubt that the artist had actually seen the people that he depicted here. In addition to the images, each group was described, often in highly negative terms.

Source: Bernhard von Breydenbach, *Peregrinatio in terram sanctam* (Mainz: Erhard Reuwich, 1486), pp. 167 (Saracens [Muslims]); 168 (Jews); 172 (Greeks); 176 (Syrians); 184 (Ethiopians); 287 (Turks). Latin.

Questions: How are the various groups depicted? Why might the audience have viewed them as "exotic"? What commonalities are there across the different categories of people? Where do women appear, and how are they depicted? How do the items that appear with people reveal something about their character? Does the illustrator dislike some peoples or view them as enemies?

Figure 1.9 Saracens [Muslims]

Figure 1.10 Jews

Figure 1.11 Greeks

Figure 1.12 Syrians

Figure 1.13 Ethiopians

Figure 1.14 Turks

(b) Monsters

These woodcuts were incorporated into the Nuremberg Chronicle, *printed in 1493, which was one of the most successful early printed books. The volume as a whole provided the history of the world as based on the Bible, but it also incorporated numerous illustrations, often of contemporary cities. After the initial printing, the images were sometimes colored, and some were even sold separately from the text. The monsters depicted here are part of a long tradition of medieval art showing the distinctive peoples who supposedly lived in faraway lands.*

Source: Hartmann Schedel, *Liber chronicarum* (Nuremberg: Anton Koberger, 1493), fol. XIIr and XIIv. Latin.

Questions: Which of the human monsters have some kind of physical abnormality, and what are those abnormalities? Which of them are a mixture between human and animal, and with which animals are the humans combined? Are any of the monsters depicted here familiar from other sources? Why do you think that people were so fascinated by all of these variations on human bodies? Can these images suggest what readers thought was a "normal" human body?

Figure 1.15 Woodcuts from fol. XIIr: Cynocephalus (dog-headed man); cyclops; blemmya (man with no head); antipod (man with twisted legs); hermaphrodite; monopod or skiapod (one-footed man); parocita (man with narrow mouth); man with no nose; man with big lower lip; panothius (man with big ears); satyr; hippopod (man with hooves); pygmy fighting against cranes

Figure 1.16 Woodcuts from fol. XIIv: Six-armed man; hairy woman; man with twelve fingers; centaur; four-eyed man; man with long neck and birdlike face

4. COSMAS INDIKOPLEUSTES, *THE CHRISTIAN TOPOGRAPHY OF COSMAS*

This sixth-century author is traditionally known as Cosmas Indikopleustes (Cosmas the Indian Sea Traveler), although his real name was Constantine of Antioch; he was a merchant living in the city of Alexandria. In this work Cosmas rejected the geographical ideas of other Christian groups, some of whom he felt were too wedded to ancient Greek, "pagan" science. Cosmas sketched his own geography of the world with words, but also with diagrams (though no reliable copies of these diagrams exist today). Despite the popular misconception, most medieval thinkers did not think that the earth was flat, making Cosmas an unusual case.

Source: trans. John W. McCrindle, Cosmas Indicopleustes, *The Christian Topography of Cosmas, an Egyptian Monk* (London: Hakluyt Society, 1897), pp. 129–37. Greek. Revised.

A summary recapitulation and description of the figures of the world; also the refutation of the sphere.

It is written:"In the beginning God made the heaven and the earth" [Genesis 1:1]. We therefore first depict, along with the earth, the heaven that is vaulted and which has its extremities bound together with the extremities of the earth. To the best of our ability we have endeavored to delineate it on its western side and its eastern; for these two sides are walls, extending from below to the vault above. There is also the firmament [a vault] which, in the middle, is bound together with the first heaven, and which, on its upper side, has the waters according to divine scripture itself. The position and figure are such as here sketched. To the extremities on the four sides of the earth the heaven is fastened at its own four extremities, making the figure of a cube, that is to say, a quadrangular figure, while up above it curves round in the form of an oblong vault and becomes as it were a vast canopy. And in the middle the firmament is made fast to it, and thus two places are formed.

From the earth to the firmament is the first place, this world, namely, in which are the angels and men and all the present state of existence. From the firmament again to the vault above is the second place—the kingdom of heaven, into which Christ, first of all, entered, after his ascension, having prepared for us a new and living way.

On the western side and the eastern the outline presented is short, as in the case of an oblong vault, but on its north and south sides it shows its length. Its figure is therefore something such as this.

This is the first heaven, shaped like a vaulted chamber, which was created on the first day along with the earth, and of it Isaiah speaks thus: "He that has established the heaven as a vaulted chamber" [Isaiah 40:22]. But the heaven, which is bound to the first at the middle, is that which was created on the second day, to which Isaiah refers when he says: "And having stretched it out as a tent to dwell in" [Isaiah 40:22]. David also says concerning it: "Stretching out the heaven as a curtain" [Psalm 104:2–3], and indicating it still more clearly he says: "Who lays the beams of his chambers in the waters" [Isaiah 40:22]. Now, when scripture speaks of the extremities of heaven and earth, this cannot be understood as applicable to a sphere. Isaiah again says: "Thus says the Lord, he that made the heaven and pitched it" [Isaiah 42:5], and the apostle [Paul] in like manner says: "Of the true Tabernacle which the Lord pitched and not man" [Hebrews 8:2]. They both speak of the heaven as standing on and fixed on the earth, and not as revolving round it. What is more, the extremities of the heaven are bound together with the extremities of the earth, and on both sides, and concerning this it is written in Job: "And he inclined heaven to earth, and the earth is poured out as dust, and I have fastened it as a square block to a stone" [Job 38:38]. And with regard to the earth it is again written in Job: "He that hangs the earth on nothing" [Job 25:7]; meaning, that it had nothing underneath it. And David in harmony with this, when he could discover nothing on which it was founded, says: "He that has founded the earth on its own stability" [Psalm 104:5], as if he said, it has been founded by you upon itself, and not upon anything else.

To the best of our ability we have endeavored to depict heaven having the firmament within it and the mountain peaks in the middle of the earth which we now inhabit, and the ocean surrounding it, and the four navigable gulfs which run into it—the Roman, the Arabian, the Persian, and the Caspian or Hyrcanian. The ocean again we have depicted as surrounded by the land on its farther side, where also paradise lies in the east. Then again we depict the breadth of the earth and of the ocean, and of the gulfs, and of the earth beyond, and paradise, leaving out for the present the peaks, in order that a comprehensive view may be more readily gained by those who examine the delineation. Now the figure of the whole earth, with respect to this surface and to the breadth, is such as has been indicated.

With that earth which is situated beyond the ocean, the first heaven, which is like a vaulted chamber, is bound together at its extremities on all sides, and at its west and at its east side a wall is found rising straight upward, but at the south and at the north side there is a wall equal at the base until it takes what has evidently the form of a vaulted chamber, while at the top it rolls itself into a very lofty arch, like the spacious roof over a bath, with an arena-like floor below, so that the wall itself forms a vaulted roof. Then, as we have just stated over and over again, the firmament which is spread out in the middle is at a certain height bound together with the heaven itself in order that two places may be formed—an upper place and a lower. Now one of these places, namely, the lower, comprising the earth and the water and the other elements and the heavenly bodies, is this world which extends from the earth to the firmament, having the earth for its floor, the walls reaching down from the first heaven for its sides, and the firmament for its roof. The other place again which extends from the firmament to the vault of the first heaven is, that is to say, the kingdom of heaven into which the Lord Christ, after he had risen from the dead, ascended, and into which the righteous will also afterward ascend, and has for its floor the firmament or second heaven, and the first heaven itself for its walls and its vaulted roof. We further again depict the altitude and figure of this earth in which we humans dwell, and which is encircled by the ocean, and contains the four navigable gulfs. Its eastern and its southern parts are low and depressed, while its northern and western are of very great elevation, but slope so gradually that the inequality is not perceived. The earth has therefore in its northern and western parts an elevation equivalent to its breadth. We therefore thus depict its figure according to the best of our ability.

The earth taken as a whole is quadrangular according to the delineation already given. We have also indicated the altitude of its most central part and the heights in its northern and western parts. Hence we have delineated it as placed in the center surrounded by the ocean and also by the earth on the opposite side of the ocean, with the heavenly bodies circling round it, so that the conical mountain can project a shadow according even to the pagans, while in accordance with this figure eclipses can occur, as well as the vicissitudes of night and day. Divine scripture confirms the truth of this, saying: "The sun rises and the sun goes down, and draws to its own place. On its rising it goes then to the south and rotates its circles, and turns around the air on its circles" [Ecclesiastes 1:6–7]; meaning that in circling through the air it comes back again to its own place.

In this view the inhabited parts of the earth are thus represented. In accordance with this, the sun rising in the east, and running through the south in the course of its revolutions, always, when giving light to the summit of the earth, or even to the earth itself, makes night to the ocean and the earth beyond it. Then again, when it is in the west and the north beyond the summit of the earth, it leaves us here in darkness, until in making its circuit it again appears in the east where the earth is depressed, and mounting the sky in the south again illuminates all this side. The eclipses of the moon therefore, even according to this delineation, if at any rate what the pagans say is true, can occur when either the sun or the moon is hidden by the summit of the earth; for they say that a solar eclipse is not produced by the shadow of the earth, but because in a perpendicular line the moon is directly below the sun, so that it is illuminated on that side which the sun sees, but not on that which it does not see—yes, rather, it [the moon] prevents it [the sun] from being visible by running under it, at the occurrence at all events of the lunar new month, when the moon is not enlightened on that side which is visible to us. The opinion therefore which we hold is in no way adverse to such views, except only with respect to the motion and revolution of the heaven—a theory subversive alike of all divine scripture both of the Old and the New Testament, and of Christian doctrine. But to inquire further into these matters we have no leisure; for such knowledge is unprofitable to us who have access to a more profitable knowledge, which imparts to our soul a good and beneficent hope which God has promised he will give to those who believe in him, while those who act unjustly he has doomed to perdition. But with God's help we will delineate the figure of the earth on the reverse side in its northern portion, that we may be able again in turn to delineate the circuit of the heavenly bodies—and it is like this.

When therefore the setting sun runs from here by the ministration of the invisible powers, according to the views of divine scripture, it makes night in the other part—that namely which is inhabited; but when he runs to the opposite side he makes darkness there. But we will now concisely, according to our ability, delineate the heaven and the earth, and we do so like this.

This part of the earth situated beyond the north, where the luminaries pursue their course from the west through the north toward the east is uninhabited, and this stands upright like a wall, and when the sun comes to it, it leaves in darkness the other part which is inhabited. The earth therefore is found to have in this part, from the ocean beneath up to its summit, an altitude according with the measure of the breadth of its inhabited parts. Hence as it intercepts midway the light of the heavenly bodies, the nights and all the rest follow.

It is necessary for those who wish to be considered Christians to inquire into which of these eight or nine heavens Christ has ascended, and into which they themselves hope to ascend, and what is the use of the other seven or eight heavens. For having already delineated the world in accordance with the scriptural view, we assert that two places were created, one adapted to the present state of existence, and the other to that which is to come, since we have such a hope, one that is better than the life here. And you, if as Christians you hold such a hope, will of necessity be asked what is the use of the seven or eight other heavens. For the pagans who hold the theory of the sphere, if consistent with themselves, neither entertain such a hope, nor allow that there are waters above the heaven, nor are found to acknowledge that the heavenly bodies and the world will come to an end; but expect that the world in the state of corruption will continue forever. If the sphere which has motion forces the others to revolve along with it from east to west, from where is produced the motion, in the contrary direction, of the seven planets? Is it the spheres that have the contrary motion, or the stars themselves? If the spheres, how can they at one and the same time move both westward and eastward? And if the stars, how do the planets cut their way through the heavenly bodies? Is it not evident that a heavenly body cannot be cut apart? For unless it were corruptible, it could not be cut through. How then do you make such suppositions?

Since beyond this sphere neither place, nor body, nor element, nor any of their parts anywhere exists, how do you say it is moved? Tell us, do not begrudge us an answer. For, except in some place or in space at large, it cannot possibly be moved. Show us therefore by what instrument—naming any one you please—it can be moved without place or body, or element or space. And do not, because you are experts in the science of nature, jauntily treat us to nothing but empty phrases. But since some insist that the sphere rotates like a lathe by the shaft, or like a wagon or a machine by the axle, let these show on what support the shaft and the axle rest, and then again on what this support rests, and so on to infinity. How then do you reason with respect to the natural world? And how does an axis not also pass through the earth, which is in the middle, and turn it round? And again tell me, you who follow these men and yet wish to be Christians, into what place of the eight spheres, or of the ninth which is called by some the starless, has Christ entered, or will we ourselves enter? Or how can water be contained on a rotating sphere? Or how when the stars fall at the final consummation can such spheres as yours be preserved? Or what can be the use of them? Is it not evident that you argue against the hope held out by the Christian doctrine? For these views cannot be consistently held except by pagans, who have no hope of another and better state, and who consequently suppose that the world is eternal, in order that the rich abundance of the spheres in which the planets will accomplish their courses may be preserved for them—while in another sphere are the fixed stars—and their error has some show of reason in its favor. But you advance arguments altogether incredible, and will have it that there is a multitude of spheres, and that there is no final consummation of the world since you are unable to tell what is the necessity of these things. And in like manner you will have it that the waters above the spheres rotate—a most ridiculous idea and altogether idiotic, and you advance arguments which are self-contradictory and opposed to the nature of things. And though you allow that the universe was created in six days, yet you find no mention of the making of a third heaven, and far less of the eight or nine which you venture to affirm. How great is your knowledge! How great your wisdom! How great your intelligence! How great your inconsistency! "No man can serve two masters" [Matthew 6:24], as has well been said by the Lord, but if one will serve God, let him serve him, or if money, then money. And again he says, through Paul: "You cannot be partakers of the table of the Lord, and of the table of devils" [1 Corinthians 10:21]. And again: "Do not be unequally yoked together with unbelievers; for what fellowship does righteousness have with lawlessness, and what communion does light have with darkness? And what concord does Christ have with Belial? Or what part does he that believes have with an infidel? And what agreement does the temple of God have with idols?" [2 Corinthians 6:14, 16].

And how again was it possible for the earth, which according to you is placed in the very middle of the universe, to have been submerged by the deluge in the time of Noah? Or how can it be believed that on the first and the second day it was covered by the waters, and on the third, when the waters were gathered together, that it made its appearance, as is recorded in Genesis? But with even greater wisdom you suppose that there are men walking all the earth over with their feet opposite the feet of other men. We therefore depict according to your view the earth and the Antipodes, and let each one of you who has sound vision and the power of reasoning justly turn the earth round whatever way he pleases, and let him say whether the Antipodes can be all standing upright in the same sense of the expression. But this they will not show even should they speak unrestrained by shame. Such then is our reply to your fictitious and false theories and to the conclusions of your reasonings which are capricious, self-contradictory, inconsistent, doomed to be utterly confounded, and to be whirled round and round even more than that unstable and revolving mythical sphere of yours. Therefore, O Christ-loving Father, since I have in this way brought to an end the fourth book with a delineation of the Antipodes, I will begin the fifth book, as I promised at your pious desire, and it will contain a description of the Tabernacle prepared by Moses in the wilderness, if God wills, who is the savior of us all.

Questions: How does the author describe the appearance of the earth? What would a diagram of his vision of the world look like? What were the sources of authority for the author's assertions about the shape of the earth? Which views was the author arguing against, and what flaws did he find with their model? How did the author refer to his intellectual opponents?

5. EINSIEDELN ITINERARY

As numerous pilgrims traveled from throughout the Christian world to the city of Rome, written itineraries emerged to guide them; this is the most famous of them. It was written either in the late eighth or early ninth century. It derives its title from the name of the Swiss monastery that holds the only surviving copy. The itinerary names ten routes that go across the city of Rome, mostly inside its walls. The eleventh and last route lists some of the holy sites of the city outside the walls. For each of the first ten routes, the first and last point are named in the title, and then the author gives things that the pilgrim would see on the left or right, and in some cases, in the middle of the road. The author was less systematic with the last route.

Source: trans. John F. Romano, *Roma in età carolingia e gli scritti dell'Anonimo augiense*, ed. Stefano Del Lungo (Rome: Presso la Società alla biblioteca Vallicelliana, 2004), pp. 66–73. Latin.

(1) From the Gate of St-Peter to the Church of St-Lucia in Orthea

LEFT	*RIGHT*
Circus Flaminius	Church of St-Lawrence in Damaso
The Pantheon	Theater of Pompey, Cypress tree
The Baths of Commodus	Church of St-Lawrence. Capitoline Hill
The Forum of Trajan and his column	Church of St-Sergius, where the center of Rome is

ARCH OF SEPTIMIUS SEVERUS

The Tiber River	Equestrian statue of Constantine
Church of St-Hadrian	
Church of St-Cyriacus	

ROMAN FORUM

Church of St-Agatha, where there are
images of Saints Paul and Mary

SUBURA

Baths of Constantine	Church of St-Pudenziana on the Patrician Road
Church of St-Vitale on the Long Road, where there are great horses	Church of St-Lawrence in Formoso, where he was roasted
	Again through the Subura
	Baths of Trajan
Church of St-Eufemia on the Patrician Road	Church of St-Peter in Chains

(2) From the Gate of St-Peter to the Salerian Gate

LEFT	*RIGHT*

THROUGH THE ARCH [of Arcadius, Honorius, and Theodosius]

Church of St-Apollinaris	Circus Flaminius, where the Church of St-Agnes is
	Baths of Alexander and Church of St-Eustachius
Church of St-Lawrence in Lucina	The Pantheon and Baths of Commodus

AQUEDUCT OF THE VIRGIN

Obelisk	The Antonine column
Church of St-Sylvester, where there is a fountain	Church of St-Susanna and the Lateran aqueduct
Church of St-Felix in Pincis	
	Baths of Sallust and the pyramid

(3) From the Numentine Gate to the Roman Forum

LEFT	RIGHT
Baths of Diocletian	Baths of Sallust
Church of St-Cyriacus. Church of St-Vitale	Church of St-Susanna and marble statues of horses
Church of St-Agatha with a charitable distribution center	Church of St-Marcellus
Monastery of St-Agatha	Church of the Holy Apostles
Baths of Constantine	Trajan Forum
	Church of St-Hadrian

On the Numentine Road outside the wall

Church of St-Agnes	Church of St-Nicomedes

(4) From the Flaminean Gate to the Lateran Road

LEFT	RIGHT
Sacristy [?]	Church of St-Lawrence in Lucina
Church of St-Sylvester and from here through the portico to the Antonine column	Obelisk
Ruins of the Aqueduct of the Virgin	
Church of St-Marcellus	Antonine Column

Again through the portico to the Lateran Road

Church of the Holy Apostles	Baths of Alexander
	Church of St-Eustachius and the Pantheon
	Baths of Commodus
	Temple of Minerva and Church of St-Mark

(5) From the Tiburtine Gate to the Subura

LEFT	RIGHT
Church of St-Isidore	Claudian aqueduct

Under the Hill Road

Church of St-Eusebius	Baths of Diocletian
Church of St-Vitus	Church of St-Agatha
Church of St-Mary with the crèche	Church of St-Vitale
	Church of St-Pudenziana
Again the church of St-Vitus	Church of St-Lawrence in Formoso, where he was roasted
Church of St-Eufemia	Monastery of St-Agatha

(6) Another road from the Tiburtine Road to the Church of St-Vitus

LEFT	RIGHT

THROUGH THE ARCH

Claudian aqueduct	Church of St-Agatha
Church of St-Bibiana	Church of St-Eusebius
Nymph Fountain	

On the Tiburtine Road outside the wall

| Church of St-Hippolytus | Church of St-Lawrence |

(7) From the Aurelian Gate to the Praenestinian Gate

LEFT	RIGHT
Fountain of St-Peter, where his prison is	Mills, *Mica aurea* [ancient building]
	Church of St-Mary [in Trastevere]
Church of Sts-John and Paul	Church of St-Chrysogonus and church of St-Cecilia

Across the Greater Bridge

| Church of St-George, Church of St-Sergius | Palatine Hill, Church of St-Theodore |

Through the arch

Capitoline Hill, the center of Rome	Church of St-Mary Antiqua
	Equestrian statue of Constantine
Church of St-Hadrian	Church of Sts-Cosmas and Damian

Roman Forum

| Church of St-Cyriacus and Baths of Constantine | Palace of Trajan, where the Church of St-Peter in Chains is |
| Monastery of St-Agatha | |

SUBURA

Church of St-Lawrence in Formoso	Church of St-Lucia in Orthea
Church of St-Vitale	Church of Sts-Sylvester and Martin
Church of St-Pudenziana and Church of St-Eufemia	
Church of St-Mary Major	Palace of Pilate at Holy Cross in Jerusalem
Church of St-Vitus, nymph fountain	Amphitheater [Castrense]
Church of St-Bibiana	Lateran aqueduct, monastery of Honorius
Claudian aqueduct	

Praenestinian Gate

On the Praenestinian Road outside the wall

| Claudian aqueduct | Church of St-Helen, church of Sts-Marcellinus and Peter |

(8) From the Gate of St-Peter to the Asinarian Gate

LEFT	RIGHT

Through the arch

Circus Flaminius, where St-Agnes is	Church of St-Lawrence in Damaso
Baths of Alexander	Theater of Pompey
Church of St-Eustachius, the Pantheon	Cypress tree
Baths of Commodus	Church of St-Lawrence at the Temple of Minerva
The Temple of Minerva, where the church of St-Mary is	Capitoline Hill
Church of St-Mark	Church of St-Sergius, where the center of Rome is

Forum of Trajan and his column
Tiber River   Church of St-George

THROUGH THE ARCH OF SEPTIMIUS SEVERUS, Roman Forum
Church of St-Hadrian
Church of Sts-Cosmas and Damian   Church of St-Mary Antiqua
Palace of Nero   Church of St-Theodore
Church of St-Peter   Palatine Hill
Church of St-Peter in Chains
Arch of Titus and Vespasian   *Testamentum* [Monument (?)]
Baths of Trajan   Arch of Constantine
Amphitheater [Colosseum]   *Meta Sudans* [Large, cone-shaped
                                                           fountain]

Church of St-Clement
Monastery of Honorius   Head of Africa Road
Claudian aqueduct   Church of the Four Crowned Martyrs
Lateran Palace   Church of St-John Lateran

Asinarian Gate

(9) From the Seven Roads to the Metrovian Gate

LEFT   *RIGHT*

Church of Sts-John and Paul   Clivus Scaurus [Scaurus Incline]
Lateran aqueduct   Church of St-Stephen on the
                                                          Caelian Hill
Church of St-Erasmus
                                                     Church of St-Mary in Domnica
                                                     Again, another street through the
                                                          Metrovian Gate
                                                     Church of St-Sixtus
On the Latin Road within the city
Church of St-John

Outside the city
                                                     Church of St-Januarius
Oratory of St-Mary   Oratory of St-Sixtus
Church of St-Gordian   Church of St-Eugenia, Church of
                                                          St-Theodore

(10) From the Appian Gate to the Greek Bank on the Appian Road

LEFT   *RIGHT*

Marcian aqueduct   Arch of Drusus
Coclea Fracta [Mausoleum (?)]   Church of St-Sixtus
Baths of Caracalla   Through the Seven Roads
Church of Sts-Nereus and Achilleus   Septizodium [Pagan Temple to Seven
                                                          Suns], Palatine Hill
From here along the portico to the
   aqueduct

Circus Maximus	Church of St-Lucia
Aventine Hill	

And like this along the portico to the church of St-Anastasia
Again on the same road outside the city

Church of St-Januarius	Church of St-Petronilla, Church of Nereus and Achilleus
Where Sixtus was martyred	Church of Sts-Mark and Marcellinus, Church of St-Soter
Church of St-Eugenia	Church of Sts-Cornelius, Sixtus, Fabian, Anterus, and Miltiades
Church of St-Theodore	Church of St-Sebastian

(11) [Roads outside the city]

On the Portensian Road outside the city on the right. Church of Sts-Abdon and Sennen.

On the Aurelian Road outside the city on the right. Church of Sts-Pancras, Processus, and Martinian.

On the Salerian Road outside the city on the right. Church of St-Saturninus, Church of St-Felicity and her Seven Sons.

On the Pincian Road outside the city on the right. Church of St-Basilissa, Church of St-Pamphilius. Church of Sts-Protus and Hyacinth. Church of St-Hermes, Church of the Head of St-John.

Questions: What is the main goal of this source? Can it be considered a kind of map? Why are there so many churches listed in this itinerary? What other kinds of sites appear here, and why might some of these be surprising? Which of the locations listed are associated with the ancient city of Rome, and why do you think they were included? Why do certain names on the itinerary appear more than once?

6. EINHARD, *THE TRANSLATION AND MIRACLES OF MARCELLINUS AND PETER*

Einhard (c. 770–840) was a scholar from modern-day Germany. He attached himself to the court of the Frankish ruler Charlemagne (r. 768–814) and served the Carolingian royal house in a variety of capacities including explaining ancient books, directing the construction of buildings, and representing them as an ambassador. Einhard arranged to have the relics (physical remains) of the martyr saints Marcellinus and Peter transferred from the city of Rome and wrote this work to describe their transport and the miracles associated with them. Eventually they would be deposited in the monastery at Seligenstadt, which was founded by Einhard.

Source: ed. and trans. Paul Edward Dutton, Einhard, "The Translation and Miracles of Marcellinus and Peter," in *Charlemagne's Courtier* (Peterborough, ON: Broadview Press, 1998), pp. 107–08. Latin.

Book 3

19. Now when necessity forced me, as usual, to travel to the king's court in the month of December on the Kalends [1 December 829], if I recall correctly, I left the place of the martyrs [at Seligenstadt] and on the next day reached the fortified city that is today called Wiesbaden where I could rest [for the night]. Since that place is surrounded by a forest, in order to pass through it more easily we had arisen earlier than normal. The servants who were assigned to precede us with the baggage started out first. But after they had departed and had started to travel away from the town where we remained, such an immense cloud of darkness enshrouded them that they could not determine where they ought to turn. On top of that, it was dreadfully cold and the earth was so covered with frost that they could not see the road. As well the mountain peaks by which they had to travel were [so] socked in with a blanket of clouds that it could not [even] be determined how far or how close they were. A thick fog lying in the valleys rose up those [mountain tops] and blocked their sight, [thus] delaying those who wanted to continue their journey. When they realized that they were hindered by all these difficulties and that it was not clear what they should do, they got off their horses and attempted to find the road by touch, since they could not see it. But when this didn't really work, they once again mounted their horses and decided it would be better to get lost, a prospect that horrified them, rather than to delay. Therefore, they carried on for a short time in the dark and came to a cross in honor of blessed Marcellinus that had been erected along the road they were traveling. Now, the reason that cross had been placed there was that two years before when I had been returning from the palace the residents of the town where I had spent the night had come out to meet me at that spot, since I was carrying the relics of the blessed martyr Marcellinus, which had just been returned to me. To mark this meeting, they took the trouble to erect a [cross] as if in place of an inscription or monument in veneration of the blessed martyr. After those servants had arrived there more by accident than by carefully planned journey, they decided to wait there for their companions who were on the way. So that they might not [also] get lost, they assembled everyone by blowing a horn. Once they were all together, they called upon the blessed martyrs to help them and they raised their voices and loudly chanted the *Kyrie eleison* [Lord, have mercy] three times.

After this, a great flash of light shone upon them, shimmering forth from the heavens for so long that it matched the brightness of daylight. That lightning was of such great help to them in continuing their journey, that once the cloud had lifted, the darkness had been dispelled, and their way forward was clear, they continued their journey without getting lost throughout the night, although they were traveling through woods and mountains darkened by forests. In fact, such a great amount of heat had been produced by that first flash [of lightning] and by [all] that light, that they said they felt that it was like the heat of a furnace. By that blast not only the cloud, but also the frost that was then covering the mountains and the entire forest was so burned off that by the time a third flash [of lightning] happened almost no trace of the [previous] cold could be detected. Those who saw and experienced these things reported them to me on the evening of the same day after we stopped for the night. I believed their account and praised and gave thanks for the mercy of the almighty God, because he had deigned to help and console us in our time of need because of the merits of his saints.

Questions: Which obstacles did Einhard and his party face in their attempt to arrive at the king's court? In what way did the cross they encountered have special meaning for Einhard? How did Einhard's servants call on the help of the saints? What allowed the servants to find the road again, and what did Einhard believe truly saved them?

7. PARIS CONVERSATIONS

Although commonly referred to as a series of "conversations," this source is best described as a phrase book. It was likely written in the tenth century by someone living in what is today France in order to help him communicate with Germans in the course of his travels. It is only so reliable as a guide: in some cases, it only provides the German without a translation, and the term in no. 6 is mistranslated. In three cases (nos. 88, 100, 102) the terms in the manuscript are so difficult to make sense of that I have omitted them. The author has indicated how to say certain expressions both formally and informally, depending on the addressee.

Source: trans. John F. Romano, *Althochdeutsches Lesebuch: Zusammengestellt und mit Wörterbuch versehen,* 17th ed., ed. Wilhelm Braune, Karl Helm, and Ernst A. Ebbinghaus (Tübingen: Max Niemeyer Verlag, 1994), pp. 9–11. Old High German/Latin.

1. Head
2. Hair
3. Ear
4. Eyes
5. Mouth
6. Tongues = Teeth [!]
7. Beard
8. Hand
9. Glove
10. Breast

11. Stomach
12. Full stomach
13. Help!
14. My lord
15. Where have you found lodging tonight, companion [*or* buddy]?
16. At the count's house.
17. Where are you coming from, brother?
18. From my godfather's house.
19. *or* From my lord's house.
20. What homeland do you come from?
21. I was in that Frankland.
22. What did you do there?
23. I dined there.
24. Were you at matins last night? [Given only in German]
25. Faithfully yes. [Given only in German]
26. I didn't see you [informal] there.
27. *or* I didn't see you [formal] there.
28. Did you see my lord at matins?
29. Faithfully no.
30. What do you want?
31. Where is your lord?
32. I don't know.
33. *or* He is with his lord.
34. Good-looking vassal [that is, a subordinate]!
35. Quick vassal!
36. Bad vassal, my faith!
37. Where is he?
38. Hit him in the neck.
39. Watch out for yours! [Given only in German]
40. Get out of here!
41. Very frequently. [Given only in German]
42. A dog's ass up your nose!
43. My lord wants to speak with you.
44. Lord, I want that too.
45. Saddle my horse.
46. I want to ride out of here.
47. By my faith, I don't care what you say!
48. So help me God, I have nothing at all.
49. Lord, go to sleep.
50. It's time.
51. Give me my horse.

52. Give me my shield.

53. Give me my spear, sword. [Given only in German]

54. Give me my sword. [Given only in German]

55. Give me my gloves.

56. Give me my walking-stick.

57. Give me my knife.

58. Give me a candle.

59. Where is your wife?

60. Why didn't you go to matins?

61. I don't know.

62. You were asleep with your wife in your bed.

63. If your lord knew that you had been sleeping with this woman, he would faithfully be angry, on my head.

64. What did you [formal] say?

65. Listen, fool!

66. Do you want to feel the hide of your horse on your back?

67. The fool, he likes to screw!

68. Good man.

69. I have enough.

70. Not enough.

71. Lord, I want to drink.

72. Do you have grain for my horses?

73. Yes, I have it, lord.

74. I don't have a drop, I have enough/not enough.

75. Lord, do you want to drink good wine?

76. Yes, I want it faithfully.

77. What is that?

78. I don't know.

79. Mend my shoe.

80. Have you seen my lord today?

81. By God, I didn't see your lord yesterday or today.

82. In what place did you learn this?

83. How many times did you screw?

84. Faithfully I don't know [?]. [Given only in German.]

85. May God give you salvation.

86. May God give you success.

87. When are you going? [Given only in German]

89. Where are you going?

90. By God, I don't know a thing about that.

91. Go on that road.

92. Where is your wife?

93. Where is your husband?
94. Do you want some apples?
95. Faithfully I want them.
96. Did you dine today?
97. I ate bread today. [Given only in German]
98. I ate meat today. [Given only in German]
99. I drank wine. [Given only in German]
101. Darling, let me screw. [Given only in German]
103. To another village.
104. What did you do there?
105. I was sent there.
106. Drink in God's love, in all God's sanctity, in the love of Saint Mary and all those belonging to her.
[Unnumbered] Drink, brother. [Given only in German]
[Unnumbered] I don't want to enter your house.
[Unnumbered] I don't want to ask my brother for his sword.

Questions: According to this phrase book, which words or phrases were considered most necessary for the traveler? What can they tell us about what a traveler would need or want? Which dangers or insults might a traveler encounter? How might they inform a historian about human relationships? Are there any words and phrases that you would have expected in a phrase book that did not appear here?

8. RICHER OF ST-RÉMI, *HISTORIES*

The author of this passage was a late-tenth-century chronicler and monk at the abbey of St-Rémi in France. The work as a whole sheds light on an otherwise obscure period in French history that saw a new royal family come into power, as well as the devotion to learning displayed by its author. This excerpt describes his journey in 991 to Chartres, demonstrating several practical obstacles that medieval travelers encountered.

Source: ed. and trans. Justin Lake, Richer of Saint-Rémi, *Histories*, vol. 2 (Cambridge, MA: Harvard University Press, 2011), pp. 304–11 [English pages only]. Latin.

Book 4

50. On the Difficulty of the Author's Journey from Reims to Chartres

One day . . . when I was thinking often and at length about the liberal arts out of a desire to learn Hippocrates of Cos's logical [approach to medicine, which formulated cures by reason], I encountered a knight from Chartres while I was in the city of Reims. When I asked him who he was and who had sent him, and why and from where he had come, he said that he was a messenger sent from Heribrand, a cleric of Chartres, and that he wished to speak with Richer, a monk of St-Rémi. Recognizing right away the name of my friend and the reason for which he had been sent, I told him that I was the one he was looking for, and after bestowing a kiss upon him, we withdrew in private. He immediately produced a letter urging me to come read the *Aphorisms* [of Hippocrates of Cos]. I was delighted at this, and taking a boy along with me, I arranged to make the journey to Chartres with the knight. Upon setting out, however, the only help I received from my abbot was a single horse. Lacking in money, a change of clothes, and other necessities, I arrived in Orbais, a place known for its great hospitality. There I was refreshed by the conversation of the lord abbot D [?] and sustained by his generosity, and on the next day I undertook to travel as far as Meaux.

But when my two companions and I entered the winding paths of the woods, we were not spared the vicissitudes of ill fortune. For we chose the wrong path at a crossroads and wandered six leagues out of our way. Then, after we had passed Château-Thierry, the horse that up to now had seemed like Bucephalus [Alexander the Great's horse] became slower than a reluctant little donkey. The sun had already passed midday and was edging into dusk when the whole sky dissolved into a downpour, and that hardy Bucephalus, done in by his final exertions, succumbed and collapsed beneath the legs of the boy who was riding him, dropping dead at the sixth milestone from the city as if he had been struck by lightning. Those who have ever suffered similar misfortunes can judge from their own experiences how great my agitation and anxiety were at that moment. After the loss of his horse, the boy, who was not accustomed to the rigors of such a long journey, lay down, completely exhausted. The baggage sat there without anyone to carry it. Rain was coming down in a tremendous downpour. Clouds filled the sky. The sun was already setting and casting threatening shadows. Yet amid all of this, God's counsel was not lacking to one in doubt. And so I left the boy there with the baggage. After telling him what to say if he was questioned by a passerby, and urging him not to fall asleep, I arrived at Meaux accompanied only by the knight of Chartres. I started out across the bridge, which I could scarcely make out in the dim light, and as I inspected it carefully I was tormented once more by new misfortunes. For it was riddled with so many and such large gaps that it was scarcely possible that those connected with the townsmen [of Reims] could have crossed over it on the same day. The intrepid Chartrain, who showed considerable foresight during the course of the journey, looked around everywhere for a boat, but finding none, he returned to the perils of the bridge, and with God's help saw to it that the horses crossed safely. Sometimes putting a shield down under the horses' feet in the gaping holes and sometimes joining together discarded planks, sometimes bending down and sometimes standing up straight, sometimes coming forward and sometimes running back, he successfully made it all the way across the bridge with the horses, while I accompanied him. Gloomy night had fallen and covered the world in foul darkness when I arrived at the Church of St-Faro, where the brothers were still preparing the fraternal libation. On that day they had celebrated a solemn feast, and the chapter [of the *Rule* of Saint Benedict] concerning the cellarer of the monastery had been read aloud, which was the reason they were taking their drink so late. I was received by them as a brother and refreshed with pleasing conversation and ample food.

I sent the knight of Chartres back with some horses to try the perils of the bridge (which we had escaped) once more and find the boy. He crossed the bridge in the manner previously described, and in the course of his wandering he came across the boy during the second watch of the night [around midnight]. Despite calling out to him many times, he was barely able to find him. He took the boy along with him, and when he arrived at the city and considered the perils of the bridge (which he knew from experience to be exceedingly dangerous), he turned aside and took the boy and the horses to someone's cottage instead. Although they had eaten nothing the whole day, they stopped there that night only to rest and not to eat. Those who have ever been compelled to stay awake at night because they are worried about those dear to them can imagine how sleeplessly I passed the night, and with what great torments I was afflicted.

Shortly after the longed-for light of day had returned, they arrived, weak from their great hunger. Food was brought to them, and fodder and straw were set before the horses. After sending the boy away on foot to the abbot, I hastened to Chartres accompanied only by the knight. Then, after sending back the horses, I recalled the boy from Meaux. After he had returned and all my worries had been put to rest, I applied myself diligently to the *Aphorisms* of Hippocrates with master Heribrand, a man of great generosity and learning. But since I only learned about the prognosis of disease in this work and a basic understanding of illnesses would not satisfy my desire, I also asked to read one of his books entitled *On the Concordance of Hippocrates, Galen, and Soranus*. This I obtained, since the powers of pharmacology, botany, and surgery were not hidden from one so skilled in medicine.

Questions: Which difficulties did Richer run into in his journey to Chartres, and how did he react to them? Who accompanied him, and what role did the other travelers play? How did the travelers adapt to the unexpected obstacles? According to the author, how did God enter into the events on the road? What was the reward for Richer's exertions?

9. JORDANUS OF SEVERAC, *MIRABILIA DESCRIPTA*

The author was a fourteenth-century Dominican missionary who traveled widely in India, the Middle East, and China. Toward the end of his life, the pope named him the bishop of the southern part of India, but it is uncertain to what degree he actually served in this position. The major goal of the book was to introduce western European readers to the wonders that a traveler would find in the east. Although this particular work did not circulate widely in the Middle Ages, it is emblematic of the exotic life imagined for the eastern world. This excerpt focuses on "India the Lesser" or "First India," which is to say the northernmost part of India.

Source: trans. Henry Yule, Friar Jordanus, *Mirabilia descripta or the Wonders of the East* (London: Hakluyt Society, 1863), pp. 11–25. Latin. Revised.

Concerning India the Lesser

At the entrance to India the Lesser are date palms, giving a very great quantity of the sweetest fruit; but further on in India they are not found.

In the lesser India are many things worthy to be noted with wonder; for there are no springs, no rivers, no ponds; nor does it ever rain, except during three months, that is, between the middle of May and the middle of August; and (wonderful!) notwithstanding this, the soil is most kindly and fertile, and during the nine months of the year in which it does not rain, so much dew is found every day upon the ground that it is not dried up by the sun's rays until the middle of the third hour of the day.

Here are many and boundless marvels; and in this First India begins, as it were, another world; for the men and women are all black, and they have for covering nothing but a strip of cotton tied round the loins, and the end of it flung over the naked back. Wheaten bread is there not eaten by the natives, although wheat they have in plenty; but rice is eaten with its seasoning, only boiled in water. And they have milk and butter and oil, which they often eat uncooked. In this India there are no horses, nor mules, nor camels, nor elephants; but only cows, with which they do all their doings that they have to do, whether it be riding, or carrying, or field labor. The asses are few in number and very small, and not worth much.

The days and nights do not vary there more than by two hours at the most.

There are always fruits and flowers there, diverse trees, and fruits of diverse kinds; for example there are some trees which bear very big fruit, called *chaqui*; and the fruit is of such size that one is enough for five persons.

There is another tree which has fruit like that just named, and it is called *bloqui*, quite as big and as sweet, but not of the same species. These fruits never grow on the twigs, for these are not able to bear their weight, but only from the main branches, and even from the trunk of the tree itself, down to the very roots.

There is another tree which has fruit like a plum, but a very big one, which is called *aniba*. This is a fruit so sweet and delicious as it is impossible to utter in words.

There are many other fruit trees of diverse kinds, which it would be tedious to describe in detail.

I will only say this much, that this India, as regards fruit and other things, is entirely different from Christendom; except, indeed, that there are lemons there, in some places, as sweet as sugar, while there are other lemons sour like ours. There are also pomegranates, but very poor and small. There are but few vines, and they make from them no wine, but eat the fresh grapes; albeit there are a number of other trees whose sap they collect, and it stands in place of wine to them.

First of these is a certain tree called *nargil* [coconut palm], which every month in the year sends out a beautiful frond like that of a date palm tree, the frond or branch of which produces very large fruit, as big as a man's head. There often grow on one such stem thirty of those fruits as big as I have said. And both flowers and fruits are produced at the same time, beginning with the first month and going up gradually to the twelfth; so that there are flowers and fruit in eleven stages of growth to be seen together. A wonder! And a thing which cannot be well understood without being witnessed. From these branches and fruits is drawn a very sweet water. The kernel at first is very tender and pleasant to eat; afterward it becomes harder, and a milk is drawn from it as good as milk of almonds; and when the kernel becomes harder still, an oil is made from it of great medicinal power. And if anyone does not care to have fruit, when the fruit-bearing stem is one or two months old, he makes a cut in it, and binds a pot to this incision; and so the sap, which would have been converted into fruit, drops in; and it is white like milk, and sweet like must, and makes one drunk like wine, so that the natives drink it for wine; and those who do not wish to drink it like this boil it down to one-third of its bulk, and then it becomes thick, like honey; and it is sweet, and fit for making preserves, like honey and the honeycomb. One branch gives one potful in the day and one in the night, on the average throughout the year: so five or six pots may be found hung upon the same tree at once. With the leaves of this tree they cover their houses during the rainy season. The fruit is that which we call nuts of India; and from the rind of that fruit is made the twine with which they stitch their boats together in those parts.

There is another tree of different species, which like that gives all the year round a white liquor pleasant to drink, which tree is called *tari*. There is also another, called *belluri,* giving a liquor of the same kind, but better. There are also many other trees, and wonderful ones; among which is one which sends forth roots from high up, which gradually grow down to the ground and enter it, and then grow into trunks like the main trunk, forming as it were an arch; and by this kind of multiplication one tree will have at once as many as twenty or thirty trunks beside one another, and all connected together. It is marvelous! And truly this which I have seen with my eyes, it is hard to utter with my tongue. The fruit of this tree is not useful, but poisonous and deadly. There is also a tree harder than all, which the strongest arrows can scarcely pierce. The trees in this India, and also in India the Greater, never shed their leaves until the new ones come. To write about the other trees would be too long a business, and tedious beyond measure; seeing that they are many and diverse, and beyond the comprehension of humans.

But about wild beasts of the forest I say this: there are lions, leopards, snow leopards, and another kind something like a greyhound, having only the ears black and the whole body perfectly white, which among those people is called *siagois* [caracal]. This animal, whatever it catches, never lets go, even to death. There is also another animal, which is called rhinoceros, as big as a horse, having one horn long and twisted, but it is not the unicorn. There are also venomous animals, such as many serpents, big beyond bounds, and of diverse colors, black, red, white, and green, and multicolored; two-headed also, three-headed, and five-headed. Admirable marvels.

There are also crocodiles, which are vulgarly called *calcatix,* some of them are so big that they are bigger than the biggest horse. These animals are like lizards, and have a tail stretched over all, like a lizard's and have a head like a pig's, and rows of teeth so powerful and horrible that no animal can escape their force, particularly in the water. This animal has, as it were, a coat of mail; and there is no sword, nor lance, nor arrow, which can in any way hurt him, on account of the hardness of his scales. In the water, in short, there is nothing so strong, nothing so evil, as this wonderful animal. There are also many other reptiles, whose names, to speak plainly, I do not know.

As for birds, I say plainly that they are of quite different kinds from what are found on this side of the world; except, indeed, crows and sparrows; for there are parrots and popinjays in very great numbers, so that a thousand or more may be seen in a flock. These birds, when tamed and kept in cages, speak so that you would take them for rational beings. There are also bats really and truly as big as kites. These birds fly nowhere by day, but only when the sun sets. Wonderful! By day they hang themselves up on trees by the feet, with their bodies downwards, and in the daytime they look just like big fruit on the tree.

There are also other birds, such as peacocks, quails, Indian fowls, and others, diverse in kind; some white as white can be, some green as green can be, some multicolored, of such beauty as is past telling.

In this India, when men go to the wars, and when they act as guards to their lords, they go naked, with a round shield—a frail and paltry affair—and holding a kind of a sword in their hands; and, truly, their fighting seems like child's play.

In this India are many and diverse precious stones, among which are the best diamonds under heaven. These stones never can be dressed or shaped by any art, except what nature has given. But I omit the properties of these stones, not to be verbose. In this India are many other precious stones, endowed with excellent virtues, which may be gathered by anybody; nor is anyone hindered.

In this India, on the death of a noble, or of any people of substance, their bodies are burned: and also their wives follow them alive to the fire, and, for the sake of worldly glory, and for the love of their husbands, and for eternal life, burn along with them, with as much joy as if they were going to be wedded; and those who do this have the higher repute for virtue and perfection among the rest. Wonderful! I have sometimes seen, for one dead man, who was burnt, five living women take their places on the fire with him, and die with their dead.

There are also other pagans in this India who worship fire; they do not bury their dead, neither do they burn them, but cast them into the middle of a certain roofless tower, and there expose them totally uncovered to the fowls of heaven. These people believe in two First Principles, to wit, of Evil and of Good, of Darkness and of Light, matters which at present I do not intend to discuss. There are also certain others who are called *dumbri*, who eat carrion and carcasses; who have absolutely no object of worship; and who have to do the drudgeries of other people, and carry loads.

In this India there is green ginger, and it grows there in great abundance. There is also a multitude of sugarcane; carobs also, of such size and bigness that it is something stupendous. I could tell very wonderful things of this India; but I am not able to detail them for lack of time. *Cassia fistula* [golden rain tree] is in some parts of this India extremely abundant.

The people of this India are very clean in their feeding; true in speech, and eminent in justice, maintaining carefully the privileges of every man according to his degree, as they have come down from old times.

The heat there is perfectly horrible, and more intolerable to strangers than it is possible to say.

In this India there does not exist, nor is found, any metal but what comes from abroad, except gold, iron, and electrum. There is no pepper there, nor any kind of spice except ginger.

In this India the greater part of the people worship idols, although a great share of the sovereignty is in the hands of the Turkish Saracens [Muslims], who came forth from Multan [a province of Pendjab, Pakistan], and conquered and usurped dominion to themselves not long since, and destroyed an infinity of idol temples, and likewise many churches, of which they made mosques for Muhammad, taking possession of their endowments of property. It is a grief to hear, and a woe to see!

The pagans of this India have prophecies of their own that we Latins are to subjugate the whole world.

In this India there is a scattered people, one here, another there, who call themselves Christians, but they are not so, nor do they have baptism, nor do they know anything else about the faith. On the contrary, they believe Saint Thomas the Great to be Christ!

There, in the India I speak of, I baptized and brought into the faith about three hundred souls, of whom many were idolaters and Saracens.

And let me tell you that among the idolaters a man may with safety expound the word of the Lord; nor is anyone from among the idolaters hindered from being baptized throughout all the east, whether they be Tartars [Mongols], or Indians, or others.

These idolaters sacrifice to their gods in this manner; that is, there is one man who is priest to the idol, and he wears a long alb, down to the ground almost, and above this a white surplice in our fashion; and he has a clergyman with an alb who goes after him, and carries a footstool, which he sets before the priest. And upon this the priest kneels, and so begins to advance from a distance, like one performing his stations; and he carries upon his bent arms a tray of two cubits long, all full of edible things of different sorts, with lit candles at top; and praying he comes up to the altar where the idol is, and deposits the offering before it after their manner; and he pours a libation, and places part of the offering in the hands of the idol, and then divides the leftover, and himself eats a part of it.

They make idols after the likeness of almost all living things of the idolaters; and they have moreover their god according to his likeness. It is true that over all gods they place One God, the Almighty Creator of all those. They hold also that the world has existed now 28,000 years.

The Indians, both of this India, and of the other Indies, never kill an ox, but rather honor him like a father; and some, even perhaps the majority, worship him. They will more readily spare him who has slain five men than him who has slain one ox, saying that it is no more lawful to kill an ox than to kill one's father. This is because oxen do all their services, and moreover furnish them with milk and butter, and all sorts of good things. The great lords among the idolaters, every morning when they rise, and before they go anywhere, make the fattest cows come before them, and lay their hands upon them, and then rub their own faces, believing that after this they can have no ailment.

Let this be enough about Lesser India; for were I to set forth particulars of everything down to worms and the like, a year would not suffice for the description.

Truly, as for the women and men, the blacker they are, the more beautiful they are.

Questions: What does Jordanus consider to be strange or exotic about northern India? Which of the wonders are according to him the most positive and which are the most negative? What did Jordanus think about the customs and beliefs of the Indians he observed? According to the author, what role did Turkish Saracens (Muslims) play in India at this time, and how did he react to them? Should we trust Jordanus as a reporter of India in his time? Why or why not?

10. BOOK OF THE KNOWLEDGE OF ALL KINGDOMS, LANDS, AND LORDSHIPS THAT ARE IN THE WORLD

This collection of geographical knowledge from the fourteenth century was written by an anonymous Franciscan friar who was born in Spain. Several of its sections are important; it is for instance one of the earliest detailed accounts of sub-Saharan Africa. The geographical sections vary greatly in quality, with some of them providing inexact or confused information, or even biblical places like Gog and Magog (Ezekiel 38–39; Revelation 20:8); this explains the several doubtful identifications of place-names. Although the author claimed to have visited all of the locations he described, historians debate whether he traveled only to a limited number of areas or relied entirely on textual sources to fabricate an imaginary journey—or some combination of these two possibilities. Throughout the work the author demonstrates an unusual interest in flags.

Source: trans. Clements Markham, *Book of the Knowledge of All the Kingdoms, Lands, and Lordships That Are in the World, and the Arms and Devices of Each Land and Lordship, or of the Kings and Lords Who Possess Them* (London: Hakluyt Society, 1912), pp. 5–6, 10–11, 29–38, 46–48. Spanish. Revised.

Cologne

From there I went along the coast to a city which they call Zeeland and from there to another called Maxa [Maastricht?], and to another [called] Lübeck which are cities of Germany. From there I passed to the great and rich city of Dordrecht, crossing a great river which they call the Rhine, having its origin in the German Alps. This river passes by Cologne, a great city of Germany. In this city they say that the three Magi Kings are interred, who worshipped Jesus

Christ in Bethlehem. But when I traveled in the empire of Cathay [northern China] I was in a city called Solin [Saba?] and they showed me three highly revered monuments and they were in honor of the three Magi Kings who adored Jesus Christ, and they said that they were natives of that city. In this Germany there are some very high mountains which they call the German Alps. Two rivers rise in them, one called the Rhône, which flows by a city called Lyons and unites with another very large river coming from the Alps of Alsace. They flow past Lyons and Avignon, a city where the pope resides, and enter the Mediterranean Sea near a city they call Arles. These cities are in the kingdom of Provence. They call the other river the Rhine and it flows by the city of Cologne which I have already referred to, and enters the German Sea. The other river is called the Danube. It traverses all Germany and enters the middle of the kingdom of Hungary, forming ten large islands. Further on I will relate how they make a great lake of sweet water in the province of Bavaria, which they call the Lake of Donaueschingen, near a city called Ratisbon, and [the Danube] enters the province of Germany near a city they call Donaustauf. Afterward the Danube enters the province of Pannonia, and goes by Passau and Innsbruck and Vienna and Hédervár, and afterward enters the kingdom of Hungary and, crossing the whole of it, enters the greater sea by a city which they call Widdin. After that it forms a very large island. The emperor of Germany has for his coat of arms a flag—yellow with a black eagle crowned.

Norway

I departed from Gotland and went to a province which is between Sweden and Norway called Gothia [modern southern Sweden]. There I found three great cities, the first Stockholm, another Calmar, and another Söderköping. This city of Stockholm faces the German Sea, a great gulf on the shores of which there are many cities. The water of this gulf gets frozen from the cold of the Tramontane [northern wind]. The people of this Gothia conquered Spain and were the lords of it for a long time. The coat of arms of this kingdom are a yellow flag with two red lions facing each other as for Sweden.

I departed from Gothia and ascended the lofty mountains of Norway which is a very strong kingdom containing three great cities. They call the largest Bergen where they crown the kings, another is called Nidaros, another Trondheim, and another Tonsberg. In the mountains of this Norway they breed many birds, gyrfalcons, goshawks, and falcons; also many fierce beasts, white wild boars, and white bears. They say that a prince, son of the king of Norway, conquered the country of Flanders in the time of King Arthur of Britain. And be it known that this Norway toward the north is uninhabited, and that the year makes one day for six months, and another six months night, and there are men who have their heads fixed on their breasts with no necks whatever, but I did not see them. This king of this Norway has for his coat of arms a flag—gold with a black lion.

I departed from Norway in a ship of the English, and we shaped a course to the west, and came to an island called Oland, then to one called Listerby and then we came to another called Bornholm, and then another very large Zealand which is at the entrance of the Gulf of Frisa [Smålandsfarvandet?] already mentioned. This island of Zealand is very populous and has four great cities called Copenhagen, Ringsted, Stor Hedding, Leland. The king of this island has for his coat of arms a flag—gold with a black lion, as in Norway.

Africa

I returned to Cape Bojador from where I had started, and went by the Sahara with some Moors who were taking gold to the king of Guinea on camels. We came to some very great and high mountains in the middle of the Sahara which they call Saguia el-Hamra and afterward we traveled a very great distance over the Sahara until we came to another mountain called Isfurent [?]. Here I parted from those Moors, and joined some others who came to Algarve. I went with them, over the Sahara, until we reached Mascarota [Tamegroute?], a town of the king of Morocco which is at the foot of the Atlas Mountains. There I stayed for some time, and then went to Sijilmasa [modern Tafilat], a rich city in the Sahara, near a river which comes from the Shining Mountains [Atlas Mountains]. The king of it has for his coat of arms a white flag with the root of a green palm tree, in this manner.

I departed from Sijilmasa and went six days' journey, over an inhabited country to the Draa River. The country is well peopled and supplied with provisions in spite of being in the Sahara. And I left the Draa River with some Moors who were going to Guinea. I went with them over the Sahara until we arrived at Tocoron [?] which is a city among some mountains. The inhabitants are black and the king of Tocoron has for his coat of arms a white flag with a black mountain in the middle, like that of the king of Guinea.

From there I went to Tibalbert, a city on some very high mountains, from there to another mountain called Sidan [?], which is under the king of Guinea, and from there to Buda, a well-supplied city, also on the top of a mountain. Know that the city was peopled by a king of Tlemcen. For he was bad and did evil things, and the people wanted to kill him. So he fled, with his treasure, to this place, and founded this city of Buda. Its flag is white with a red moon.

Afterward I departed from Buda and went, by the Sahara, to another mountain called Ghana in which there is a rich, well-supplied city of the same name.

It is the head of the kingdom where they crown the kings. And the king of Guinea has a gold flag with a black mountain in the middle.

I left Ghana and went to Crima [?], another city in the Sahara, and from there to Mesça [?], a rich city by which a river flows which rises in the Shining Mountains. Know that in this river ends the river of Guinea which is very wide and very long and along which there are many lands both desert and inhabited. It is 65 days' journey in length, and 40 wide. Of Guinea there is much to say. It contains seven mountains well peopled, and land yielding abundantly as long as there are mountains, elsewhere it is all Sahara. Two ranges of mountains extend to the Niger River, and there they collect the ivory teeth, and the gold in the ant hills which the ants make on the river banks. The ants are as big as cats, and dig out much earth. This kingdom is bound by the kingdom of Organa in which also there is much desert, and on another side with the branch of the Nile which they call the Niger River. And further out, in the Sahara there are three very high mountains, which are very populous. The first mountain is called Organ [?] where is the head of the kingdom where the king is crowned. The second is called Tamar [?] because there are in it many palm trees. The third is called Timer [?] because here the people on the river banks collect much gold; we cannot give the quantity but there is much. The king of Organa has for his coat of arms a white flag with a green palm tree and two keys.

I departed from the kingdom of Organa and passed on to the kingdom of Tauser [Tozeur?] which also consists of extensive deserts, all lifeless Sahara, but it has six mountains inhabited by black people. The first is where the king always resides, and where he is crowned. Some call it Almena [?], others Albertara [?], others Merma [?], others Catifi el Quibir [?], others Saploya [?]. The king of this kingdom of Tauser is always at war with the Moorish Arabs who live in the Sahara. He has for his coat of arms a flag of yellow with a black mountain, like the king of Guinea.

I departed from Tauser and traveled for a very long distance on camels, until I arrived at the kingdom they call Tlemcen which borders on the Niger River. They live always at war with the Christians of Nubia [modern Sudan] and Ethiopia. There are in this kingdom five large places inhabited by blacks. They are Trimisin [?], Oadac [?], Manola [?], Orzia [?], and Palola [?]. Know that these inhabitants of this kingdom of Tlemcen peopled it from North Africa. The king has for his coat of arms a purple flag with a white moon.

From there I went to another kingdom called Dongola, bound by the deserts of Egypt and the Nile River. The river forms two courses, the greater, flowing to the westward, called the Niger River. On its banks is the kingdom of Guinea. The other part flows through the deserts of Egypt and enters the Mediterranean Sea at Damietta. Between these two branches of the river is the kingdom of Dongola, a country well peopled with Christians from Nubia, but they are black. It is a rich land and very well supplied, and with many fruit trees. The land has a very hot climate. The king of Dongola has for his coat of arms a white flag with a cross like this [a cross with two horizontal beams].

In this kingdom of Dongola I found Christians, Genoese merchants. I joined with them and we took the road to the Nile River traveling 60 days' journey over the deserts of Egypt until we arrived at the city of Cairo which is the head of the kingdom of Egypt where they crown their kings as I have already related. I left Cairo and went to Damietta, where I found a ship of Christians and went on board. I sailed in that ship until I disembarked at Ceuta already mentioned, and went from there by land to Marrakech again, then crossed the Shining Mountains to Gazula. I remained there for some time as it is pleasant. Then some Moors equipped a galley to go to the Niger River, for there they make great profits. I went with them on account of something they said to me, so we left Gazula in that galley. Always keeping along the shores of the western sea we passed Capes Non and Saubrun and Bojador, all an uninhabited coast, and came to the Niger River already mentioned, which is a branch of the Nile rising in the lofty mountains of the Antarctic Pole, where, it is said, is the terrestrial paradise. It traverses the whole land of Nubia and Ethiopia and divides into two branches, one flowing through Egypt to Damietta, the other larger branch flowing westward to the occidental sea, and called the Niger River. We went on after leaving this river for a very long distance, always keeping in sight of the coast, leaving behind us the Canary Islands, and came to an island inhabited by many people. They call this island Galpis. It is a well-supplied island, but the people are idolaters. They took us all before their king, and wondered much at us and our language and customs. The merchants who armed the galley made much profit. The king's coat of arms is a white flag with the figure of his idol.

We left the island of Galpis and shaped an eastern course toward the southern sea until we found another island called Quible [?]. This island Quible is in the southern sea and is peopled by blacks. We left it on the right hand, keeping along the coast, and came in sight of a very high mountain called Sierra Leone. We went there and found it inhabited by many people. There rises from it a river which becomes very large and flows through a fine country. Here the galley turned back, and I remained for some time. Afterward I departed from Sierra Leone with some people and went to another mountain called Lirri [?]. A river rises from it called Kamaranka. I left this kingdom called Lirri, and went to another called Gotonie [?] consisting of some very high mountains. They say there are no others so high in the world. They are called the Mountains of the Moon. Others give them the name of the Mountains of Gold, and

five rivers flow from them which are the biggest in the world. They all fall
into the Niger River; and they form a lake so large that it is 20 days' journey in
length and 10 in width. In the middle of it there is a large island called Palola [?]
inhabited by blacks, but most of the land is uninhabited, owing to the intense
heat and it is all dead sand. There are six mountains in this land, the largest
being the Mountain of Gold, others Lirri, Sierra Leone, Burga [?], Elbahac
[?], Elmolac [Marrah Mountains?]. Know that this kingdom of Gotonie is not
very populous, except in these mountains. But it has extensive lands bounded
by the Niger River, the ocean, and a gulf which enters for 15 days' journey
from the ocean. So that it is one of the largest kingdoms in the world. Its coat
of arms is some yellow sashes on a spear.

Be it known that this land we are describing is very hot, but it abounds in
many delights, and there are many camels. On the banks of this Niger River
they breed the great beasts yielding ivory, and from here the merchants bring
the teeth. On the banks of this river they collect gold in the ant hills and collect
the ambergris, and for this reason the country is very rich. I departed from this
kingdom of Gotonie and arrived at a gulf connected with the sea, and in the
gulf there were three islands, called Zanon [?], Azeuean [?], and Malicun [?].
I crossed this gulf until I came to a great city called Amenuan [?]. It is a very
great and populous kingdom with a land supplying all that is good, but the
people are heathens and believe in idols. The kingdom contains eight great cities, called Amenuan [?], where the king always resides and is crowned, Goran
[?], Asçida [?], Cologane [?], Benateo [?], Vnda [?], Gaona [?] and Canben [?].
The king has a white flag with an idol.

In this kingdom of Amenuan there enters a branch of the river Euphrates
which rises in the lofty mountains of the Antarctic Pole, where they say that the
terrestrial paradise is. This river Euphrates forms three branches, one entering
the middle of the kingdom of Amenuan and the other branches flowing round
the whole kingdom, the width, in some places, being two days' journey. When
I crossed this great river I first made a long journey along its banks which are
very populous. I came to a great city called Graçiona [?] which is the head of
the empire of Abdeselib, a word meaning "Servant of the Cross." The Abdeselib is defender of the church of Nubia and Ethiopia, and he defends Prester
John who is patriarch of Nubia and Abyssinia, and rules over very great lands
and many cities of Christians. But they are blacks as to their skins and burn
the sign of the cross with fire in recognition of baptism. But although these
men are blacks, they are still men of intelligence with good brains, and they
have understanding and knowledge. Their land is well supplied with all good
things, and excellent water of that which comes from the Antarctic Pole where,
it is said, is the earthly paradise. They told me that the Genoese whose galley
was wrecked at Amenuan, and who were saved, were brought here. It was

never known what became of the other galley which escaped. The Emperor Abdeselib has for his coat of arms a white flag with a black cross like this.

I departed from the city of Graçiona, for the cities of this empire had names which I could not obtain, and traveled over many lands and through many cities arriving at the city of Malsa [?] where Prester John always resides. He is the patriarch of Nubia and Ethiopia, and at his coming he always goes along the banks of the river Euphrates. This is a well-peopled and well-supplied land. From the time I came to Malsa I saw and heard marvelous things every day. I inquired what the terrestrial paradise was like, and wise men told me that it consisted of mountains so high that they came near to the circuit of the moon. No man has been able to see it all, for of twenty men who went, not more than three ever saw it, and they had never heard tell of any man who had ascended the mountains. There are men who say that they saw it from the east, and others that they saw it from the west. They say that when the sun is in Gemini they see it to the south, and when the sun is in Capricorn they see it from the east. They further told me that these mountains were surrounded by very deep seas, and that from the water of those seas come four rivers which are the largest in the world. They call them Tigris, Euphrates, Gihon [?], and Pishon. These four rivers irrigate all Nubia and Ethiopia. The waters which descend by these rivers make so great a noise that it can be heard at a distance of two days' journey. All the men who live near it are deaf, and cannot hear each other owing to the great noise of the waters. At all times the sun in those mountains is there day and night either on one side or the other. This is because half those mountains are above the horizon, and the other half are beneath the horizon, so that, on the top of the mountains, it is never either cold nor dark, nor hot nor dry, nor moist, but a stable temperature. All things, whether animal or vegetable, can never decay nor die. They told me many other secrets of the stars both as regards judgments and magical powers, also concerning herbs, plants, and minerals, and I saw several marvelous things. The Greeks call this place *ortodoxis*, and the Jews *ganheden*, and the Latins the terrestrial paradise, because there is always a good temperature. The coat of arms of Prester John is a white flag with a black cross having two crooks, one on each side. For in Nubia and Ethiopia there are two emperors, one being emperor of Graçiona and the other emperor of Magdasor [?].

I departed from the city of Malsa, the residence of Prester John, and took an eastern route, crossing the Nile River and finding many cities called Amoc [?], Araoc [?], Sarma [?], Oça [?], Morania [?], Vyma [?], Gabencolic [?], Glaoc [?], and many other towns. Twice I crossed the river Gihon [?] and finally reached a great city called Magdasor. It is a very great empire in which there are many cities, towns, castles, villages, and a populous land of Nubian Christians. This empire of Magdasor is all surrounded by two of the rivers that come from the deep seas encircling the terrestrial paradise, one Gihon the other Pishon. On another side it is bounded by a gulf of the Sea of Judaea which enters into the land 40 days' journey. In this city of Magdasor they told me of a Genoese whom they called Sor Leonis, who went in search of his father, who came in two galleys already mentioned. They treated him honorably. This Sor Leonis wanted to go on to the empire of Graçiona in search of his father, but the emperor of Magdasor would not consent, because the way was doubtful and the road dangerous. Know that in this land of Nubia and Abyssinia there are 154 regions, lands desert and lands inhabited insomuch that it embraces a fourth part of the whole face of the earth. The emperor of Magdasor has for a coat of arms a white flag with a black cross.

Gog and Magog

I departed from the empire of Cathay toward the north, up the course of the river Magog and traveled for 65 days. I did not find town nor city. The land is entirely inhabited by tribes with flocks. It is all a plain country and has no stones, no trees, nor people who eat bread, but only meat and milk. Yet they sow a seed which they call *monos* [black gram], something like sesame seeds. It is sown at any time of the year, presently sprouts, and is reaped after 30 days. This is raised in great quantity. It is cooked with milk, and makes very good food, which the people eat and give to travelers. These tribes have many horses without a number. They do not eat barley because there is none, but only hay. They are so numerous because the climate is suitable. From there I reached the Caspian Mountains of Magog. Know that these mountains are of immeasurable height, and surround Mongolia from sea to sea, and there is only one very narrow pass. Here there is a castle built of magnet iron throughout; for nature made it in this manner, and it reaches to the clouds. At its foot rises the river Magog. On the other side there is another castle which is as high, and built of the same stone, called Gog. The castles are very high on the top, so that 10,000 men can reside in each of them. Between the two are the Iron Gates which shut the entrance to Mongolia. Within these mountains all the land is plain without stones or trees, and with a temperate climate, and left to many flocks. It is 100 days' journey long and 70 broad, all closed in by these Caspian Mountains. To the east it is all bounded by the sea, and also there are very great rocky dales.

Within this Mongolia there are countless tribes who do not observe any of the commandments of God, except that they do no evil to one another. They are very confident, and great fighters both on foot and on horseback, insomuch that Alexander was unable to conquer them, or to enter their country by the mountains for they shut and fastened those iron gates by placing great rocks against them, and they were closed for a long time. Eventually they removed the obstruction, coming out and conquering a great part of the world them-selves. For from that lineage came all those of the empire of Cathay. From that lineage also came those of the empires of Bengal, Arabia, and Mesopotamia, all the Persians, those of the empire of Sarra [the Golden Horde?], both Turks and Tartars [Mongols], Saracens [Muslims], and Goths. Some of them turned to the law of Abraham [Judaism?] and others turned Moors. The wise men of Mongolia say that when 7,000 years of the era of Adam are completed, they will be lords of the whole face of the earth, and will make all peoples conform to their law and to their freedom. But certainly they observe no law whatever, and keep no commandments of God except not doing evil to one another.

This enclosed Mongolia forms a fourth part of the whole earth. In the middle of this land there is a great lake which they called Lake Lob. The people of this land are called Mongols and the land is known as Mongolia, the land of Tagojar [?], the land of Gog and Magog. With these mountains the empire of Cathay is bounded. I lived for some time in that castle of Magog because I saw and heard marvelous things every day. On the north side Mongolia is bounded by the lands of Albizibi [part of central Asia?] which are desert and uninhabited, though there are people in some places who are vile and eaters of raw flesh and fish. They have long faces like dogs, but they are white and do anything they see to do. They are called cynocephali. I saw one of them in the city of Norgancio [?].

Questions: Why does the author not deal with the logistics of daily travel? Which infor-mation did he think important to preserve about the locations he included, and do you trust the author's observations? Is there a difference in the kind of information he gives about each place? What do we learn about the people who populated these places? Where is it most difficult to identify the names of the places, and why do you think that this is so?

CHAPTER TWO

RELIGIOUS JOURNEYS

Religion is often described as one of the most pervasive features of medieval life. It should come as no surprise, then, that many of the journeys that people undertook were motivated by religion. But just as religion came in many forms, so did travel that involved religion. People invoke the help of God and the saints before undertaking a journey. They travel to convert others to their faith or to compare various religious options before deciding which belief and practice is right for them. Across a period of centuries they go on pilgrimages to see the holy city of Jerusalem, where Jesus was believed to have suffered, died, and been resurrected. Journeys could give unmediated access to the divine through mystical visions that took the travelers to heaven and hell, but then back to Earth to share their view of the afterlife. As students read through the selections in this chapter, they should analyze them both for the commonalities and differences in religious journeys. Did the experience of pilgrimage change over time, or did the experience depend on the personality of the traveler? What determined whether a missionary found success in converting people? Did heaven look the same to a Christian and a Muslim? What was the nature of the religious knowledge or experience gained through travel? And how did everyday life intrude on higher spiritual aims?

11. TRAVEL PRAYERS IN THE *GREGORIAN SACRAMENTARY*

The Gregorian Sacramentary *is a book that contained prayers for public worship. At its core, it was a papal production compiled in the seventh century, but it was exported to Charlemagne's kingdom in the eighth century and supplemented by several additional prayers in the ninth. Some of the prayers could be said in any appropriate context, whereas others were designed for use in the Mass, the central act of worship in western Europe, during which it was believed that bread and wine were transformed into the body and blood of Jesus Christ. Certain prayers allotted space to insert a specific traveler's name.*

Source: trans. John F. Romano, *Le sacramentaire grégorien: Ses principales formes d'après les plus anciens manuscrits*, ed. Jean Deshusses, vol. 1 (Fribourg: Éditions universitaires, 1971–82), pp. 343 (no. 999), 437–39 (nos. 1313–22). Latin.

Prayer for Those Who Are Making a Journey

Hear us, O Lord, and may the journey of your servant [supply name] always be guided among the dangers of this life with your help.

Prayers for Brothers Setting Out on a Journey

O God, you who always dispense your mercy on those who love you, and you who are in no region distant from those who serve you, guide the journey of your servant [supply name] in your will, so that by your protection and your leading the way, he may walk through the paths of justice without accident. Through Christ our Lord, who lives and reigns forever and ever.

Another prayer on the same theme. Hear, O Lord, our prayers, and accompany the journey of your servant [supply name] favorably, and grant your mercy everywhere just as you are everywhere, inasmuch as he is defended from all adversities by the deliverance of your aid, he may obtain the execution of his just desires.

Prayer for Those Returning from a Journey

Oh all-powerful eternal God, you who arrange our seasons and life, grant the help of continual tranquility to your servant [supply name], so that he whom you have returned unharmed by your own labors, you may make secure in your protection.

At the Coming of Arriving Brothers

Oh God, visitor of the humble, you who console us with fraternal love, extend your grace to our community, so that for those in whom you dwell, we may experience your coming in us.

Mass for Those Making a Journey

Hear, O Lord, our prayers, and arrange the road of your servant [supply name] in the prosperity of your salvation, so that among all the varieties of the road and this life, he may always be protected by your help. Through Christ our Lord, who lives and reigns forever and ever.

Prayer over the gifts [bread and wine]. Look favorably, O Lord, on our prayers, and kindly receive these offerings that we offer to you for your servant [supply name], so that you both may guide his path going before him in your grace, and that you may also deign to accompany him by following after him, so that we may rejoice from your action and his unharmed state according to the protection of your mercy. Through Christ our Lord, who lives and reigns forever and ever.

Final prayer. Oh God of infinite mercy and of immense majesty, whom neither the spaces of places nor the intervals of time separate from those whom you protect, listen to your servants [supply names] who trust everywhere in you, and through every road on which they will go, deign to be a guide and companion to them: let no adversity harm them, no difficulty stand in their way, let all things be beneficial for them, let all things be prosperous, and whatever they ask for as a just request, let them attain by a quick execution. Through Christ our Lord, who lives and reigns forever and ever.

Mass for Sailors

Oh God, you who conveyed our fathers through the Red Sea and transported them through the greater water singing praises of your name, we entreat in prayers that after having driven away their adversities, you protect your servants in this ship with a desirable port and a tranquil course. Through Christ our Lord, who lives and reigns forever and ever.

Prayer over the gifts. Receive, we seek, O Lord, the prayers of your servants with the offerings of sacrifices, and celebrating your mysteries, defend us from all dangers. Through Christ our Lord, who lives and reigns forever and ever.

Final prayer. Through the divine mystery of the consecration, we entreat humbly and beg your majesty, O Lord, so that for those whose presence you came through the heavenly gifts, you may by the wood of the holy cross both remove their sins, and in your compassion rescue them from all dangers.

Questions: What did travelers seek from God as they set out on a journey? Were all of the requests made for physical things, and if not, what spiritual gifts did they ask for? According to the prayers, which characteristics allowed God to deliver aid to travelers? Which biblical precedent for God's assistance to travelers did the prayers reference?

12. *THE VISION OF ADAMNÁN*

Medieval accounts of travel through the afterlife did not start with the Divine Comedy *of Dante. One such earlier account of hell and heaven was falsely attributed to the seventh-century Irish abbot and writer Adamnán. It was actually written by unknown authors, some of it in the tenth century and the rest of it in the eleventh century, who drew on a wealth of biblical, theological, and native Irish literature. It is a good example of the Irish belief in the spiritual trials that one would have to overcome during travel. It reflects a time before the topography of the Christian afterlife had been securely mapped out.*

Source: trans. Charles Stuart Boswell, *An Irish Precursor of Dante* (London: D. Nutt, 1908), pp. 28–44. Irish. Revised.

1. Noble and wonderful is the Lord of the elements, and great and marvelous are his might and his power. For he calls to himself in heaven the charitable and merciful, the meek and considerate; but he relegates and casts down to hell the impious and unprofitable host of the children of the curse. For on the blessed he bestows the hidden treasures and the manifold wages of heaven, while he inflicts a diversity of torments, in many kinds, upon the sons of death.

2. Now there are multitudes of the saints and righteous ones of the Lord of Creation, and of the apostles and disciples of Jesus Christ, to whom have been revealed the secrets and the mysteries of the heavenly kingdom, and the golden wages of the righteous; likewise the diverse pains of hell, with them that are put in their presence. For to the apostle Peter was shown the four-cornered vessel, let down from heaven, with four cords to it, and they with sound as sweet as any music. Also, the apostle Paul was caught up to heaven, and heard the ineffable words of the angels, and the speech of them that dwell in heaven. Moreover, on the day of Mary's death, all the apostles were brought to look upon the pains and miserable punishments of the unblessed; for the Lord commanded the angels of the west to open up the earth before the face of the apostles, that they might see and consider hell with all its torments, even as he himself had told them, a long time before his passion.

3. Finally, to Adamnán ua Thinne, the high scholar of the western world, were revealed the things which are here recorded; for his soul departed from out his body on the feast of John the Baptist, and was conveyed to the celestial realm, where the heavenly angels are, and to hell, with its rabble crowd. For no sooner had the soul issued from out the body, than there appeared to it the angel that had been its guardian while in the flesh, and bore it away with him to view, firstly, the kingdom of heaven.

4. Now the first land to which they come is the land of saints. A bright land of fair weather is that country. In it are diverse and wondrous companies, clad in cassocks of white linen, with hoods of radiant white upon their heads. The saints of the eastern world form a company apart in the east of the land of saints; the saints of the western world are to the west of the same land; the saints of the northern world and of the south, in their great concourse, are to the south and north. For every one that is in the land of saints may freely listen to the music, and may contemplate the vault, in which are the nine classes of heaven, according to their rank and order.

5. For one spell, then, the saints keep singing marvelous music in praise of God; for another, they are listening to the music of the heavenly host; for the saints have no other need than to listen to the music that they hear, and to contemplate the radiance that they see, and to sate themselves with the fragrance that there is in that land. The wonderful Lord is face to face with them, in the southeast, and a crystal veil between; to the south is a golden portico, and through it they discern the form and adumbration of the people of heaven. No veil, however, nor cloud is between the host of heaven and the host of the saints, but those are ever manifest and present to these, in a place that is over against them. A circle of fire surrounds this place, yet do they all pass in and out, and it harms none.

6. Now, the twelve apostles and Mary the pure Virgin form a band apart, around the mighty Lord. Next to the apostles are the patriarchs and prophets, and the disciples of Jesus. On the other side are holy virgins, at Mary's right hand, and with no great space between. Babies and the young are about them on every side, and the bird-choirs of the heavenly folk, making their music. And among these companies, bands of angels, guardians of the souls, do perpetual attendance in the royal presence. No man is there in this present life who may describe those assemblies, or who may tell of the very manner of them. And the bands and companies which are in the land of saints abide continually in even such great glory as aforesaid, until the great parliament of doom, when the righteous judge, on the day of judgment, will dispose them in their stations and abiding places where they will contemplate God's countenance, with no veil nor shadow between, through ages everlasting.

7. But great and vast as are the splendor and the radiance in the land of saints, even as has been said, more vast, a thousand times, the splendor which is in the region of the heavenly host, around the Lord's own throne. This throne is fashioned like a canopied chair, and beneath it are four columns of precious stone. Though one should have no music at all, save the harmonious music of those four columns, yet would he have his fill of melody and delight. Three stately birds are perched upon that chair, in front of the king, their minds intent upon the creator throughout all ages, for that is their vocation. They celebrate the eight canonical hours, praising and adoring the Lord, and the archangels accompany them. For the birds and the archangels lead the music, and then the heavenly host, with the saints and virgins, make response.

8. Over the head of the glorious one that sits upon the royal throne is a great arch, like a wrought helmet, or a regal diadem: and the eye which should behold it would immediately melt away. Three circles are round about it, separating it from the host, and by no explanation may the nature of them be known. Six thousand thousands, in guise of horses and of birds, surround the fiery chair, which still burns on, without end or term.

9. Now to describe the mighty Lord who is on that throne is not for any, unless he himself should do so, or should so direct the heavenly dignitaries. For none could tell of his vehemence and might, his glow and splendor, his brightness and loveliness, his liberality and steadfastness, nor of the multitude of his angels and archangels, which chant their songs to him. His messengers keep going to and from him, forever and ever, with brief messages to each assemblage, telling to the one host of his mildness and mercy, and to the other of his sternness and harshness.

10. Whoever should stand facing him, east and west, south and north, would behold on each side of him a majestic countenance, seven times as radiant as the sun. No human form there, with head or foot, may be discerned, but a fiery mass, burning on forever, while one and all are filled with awe and trembling before him. Heaven and earth are filled full with the light of him, and a radiance as of a royal star encircles him. Three thousand different songs are chanted by each several choir about him, and sweeter than all the varied music of the world is each individual song of them.

11. Furthermore, in this way is the fashion of that city, in which that throne is set. Seven crystal walls of various hue surround it, each wall higher than the wall that is before it. The floor, moreover, and the lowest base of that city, is of fair crystal, with the sun's countenance upon it, shot through with blue, and purple, and green, and every hue beside.

12. A gentle folk, most mild, most kind, lacking in no good quality, are they that dwell within that city; for none come there, and none abide there ever, save holy youths, and pilgrims zealous for God. But as for their array and

ordinance, hard is it to understand how it is arranged, for none turns back nor side to another, but the unspeakable power of God has set, and keeps, them face to face, in ranks and lofty columns, all round the throne, circling it in brightness and bliss, their faces all toward God.

13. There is a chancel rail of silver between each two choirs, cunningly worked with red gold and silver, and choice rows of precious stones, variegated with diverse gems, and against that lattice are seats and canopies of carbuncle. Between every two chief companies are three precious stones, softly vocal with sweet melody, and the upper halves of them are lit lamps. Seven thousand angels, as it were great candles, shine and illumine that city round about; seven thousand others within it are aflame forever, throughout the royal city. The men of all the world, if gathered into one place, many as they are, would derive sustenance enough from the sweet savor of any one of those candles.

14. Now, such of the world's inhabitants who do not arrive at that city after their life is over, and to whom a dwelling place within is not allotted after the words of doom will have been spoken, find a restless and unstable habitation, until the coming of judgment, on heights and hilltops, and in marshy places. Just so journey those hordes and companies, with the guardian angel of every soul among them, serving and tending them. In the main doorway of the city they are confronted by a veil of fire and a veil of ice, hitting perpetually one against the other. The noise and din of these veils, as they clash together, are heard throughout the world, and the seed of Adam, should they hear that din, would be seized because of that with trembling and intolerable dismay. Faint and dazed are the wicked at that din; though, on the side of the heavenly host, nothing is heard of that rude discord, save a very little only, and that sweeter than any music.

15. Awful is that city, and wonderful to describe; for a little out of much is that which we have told concerning its various orders, and the wonders of it. Seldom indeed may a spirit, after its communion and dwelling with the body, in slumber and repose, in freedom and luxury, succeed in getting to the throne of the creator, unguided by the angels; for the seven heavens are a difficult trial, nor is any one of them easier than the rest. Six guarded doors confront all those of mortal race who reach the kingdom. There sits a porter and warder of the heavenly host, keeping guard over each door. At the door of that heaven which is nearest on the closer side sits the archangel Michael, and with him two youths, with iron rods in their laps to whip and hit the sinners as they pass through this the first grief and torment of the path they have to tread.

16. At the door of the next heaven, the archangel Ariel is guardian, and with him two youths, with fiery whips in their hands, wherewith they whip the wicked across the face and eyes. A river of fire, its surface an ever-burning flame, lies before that door. Abersetus is the angel's name who keeps watch

over that river, and purges the souls of the righteous, and washes them in the stream, according to the amount of guilt that clings to them, until they become pure and shining as is the radiance of the stars. Close by is a pleasant spring, flowery and fragrant, to cleanse and solace the souls of the righteous, though it annoys and scalds the souls of the guilty, and takes nothing from them, but it is increase of pain and torment that comes upon them there. Sinners arise from out of it in grief and immeasurable sadness, but the righteous proceed with joy and great delight to the door of the third heaven.

17. Above this, a fiery furnace keeps forever burning, its flames reaching a height of twelve thousand cubits; through it the righteous pass in the twinkling of an eye, but the souls of sinners are baked and scorched within it for twelve years, and then their guardian angel carries them to the fourth door. About the entrance door of the fourth heaven is a fiery stream, like the preceding. It is surrounded by a wall of fire, in breadth twelve thousand measured cubits, through which the souls of the righteous pass as though it were not there, while the souls of the sinful stay within it, amid pain and tribulation, for another twelve years, until their guardian angel bears them to the door of the fifth heaven.

18. In that place is a fiery river, which is unlike all rivers, for in its middle is a strange kind of whirlpool, in which the souls of the wicked keep turning round and round, and there they abide for the space of sixteen years; the righteous, however, succeed at it right away, without any hindrance. So soon as the due time comes for the sinners to be released from there, the angel strikes the water with a rod, hard as though it were of stone, and uplifts the spirits with the end of that rod. Then Michael bears them up to the door of the sixth heaven; but no pain nor torment is dispensed to the spirits at that door, but there they are illumined with the luster and brilliancy of precious stones. Then Michael comes to the angel of the Trinity, and one on either side they usher the soul into the presence of God.

19. Infinite and beyond telling is the welcome with which the Lord and the heavenly host then receive the soul, if he be a pure and righteous soul; if, however, he be an unrighteous and unprofitable soul, harsh and ungentle is the reception of him by the mighty Lord. For he says to the heavenly angels, "Take, O heavenly angels, this unprofitable soul, and deliver him into the hand of Lucifer, that he may plunge him and utterly extinguish him in hell's abyss, through ages everlasting."

20. Thereupon that wretched soul is parted, fearfully, sternly, awfully, from sight of the heavenly kingdom, and of God's countenance. Then he utters a groan, heavier than any groan, as he comes into the devil's presence, after beholding the bliss of the kingdom of heaven. He is then deprived of the guidance of the archangels, in whose company he had come into heaven. Twelve fiery dragons swallow up every spirit, one after the other, until the lowest

dragon lands him in the devil's mouth. There he experiences the consummation of all evil, in the devil's own presence, throughout all ages.

21. After that his guardian angel had revealed to Adamnán's spirit these visions of the heavenly kingdom, and of the first progress of every soul after parting from its body, he brought him to visit the lowest hell, with all its pains, and its crosses, and its torments. Now, the first region to which he came was a land burnt black, waste and scorched, but with no punishment at all in it. A glen, filled with fire, was on the further side of it; huge the flame of it, extending beyond the margin on either hand. Black its base, red the middle, and the upper part of it. Eight serpents were in it, with eyes like coals of fire.

22. An enormous bridge spans the glen, reaching from one bank to the other; high the middle of it, but lower its two extremities. Three companies seek to pass over it, but not all succeed. One company finds the bridge to be of ample width, from beginning to end, until they succeed in crossing the fiery glen, safe and sound, fearless and undismayed. The second company, when entering upon it, finds it narrow at first, but broad afterward, until they, in the same fashion, journey across that same glen, with great peril behind. But to the last company the bridge is broad at first, but cramped and narrow afterward, until they fall from it into that same perilous glen, into the throats of those eight red-hot serpents, that have their dwelling place in the glen.

23. Now the folk to whom that path was easy were the chaste, the penitent, the diligent, they who had zealously borne a bloody testimony to God. The band who found the path narrow at first, but afterward broad, were they who had hardly been constrained to do God's will, but had afterward converted their constraint into the willing service of God. They, however, to whom this way was broad at first, but narrow afterward, were sinners who had listened to the precepts in God's word, and after having heard, did not fulfill them.

24. Furthermore, vast multitudes abide beyond, feeble and powerless, on the shore of perpetual pain, in the land of utter darkness. Every other hour the pain ebbs away from them, and the next hour it returns to them again. Now these are they in whom good and evil were equally balanced, and on the day of doom, judgment will be passed between them, and their good will quench their evil on that day; and then will they be brought to the haven of life, in God's own presence, through ages everlasting.

25. Another great company is there, near to the last-named group, and monstrous their torment. And this is their plight: they are chained to fiery columns, a sea of fire about them up to their chins, and about their middle fiery chains, in the shape of vipers. Their faces are aflame with agony. They who are tormented thus are sinners, fratricides, ravagers of God's Church, and merciless wardens, who, in presence of the relics of the saints, had been set

over the Church's tithes and offerings, and had alienated these riches to their private store, away from the Lord's guests and needy ones.

26. Great multitudes there are, standing in blackest mire up to their waists. Short hoods of ice are on them. Without rest or intermission, through all time, everything below their waist is perpetually scorched with alternating cold and heat. Demon hosts surround them, with fiery clubs in their hands, striking them over the head, though they struggle against them continually. These wretches all have their foreheads to the north, and a rough, sharp wind blowing full on their foreheads in addition to every other woe. Red showers of fire are raining on them, every night and every day, and they cannot ward them off, but must endure them throughout all ages, wailing and moaning.

27. Some of them have streams of fire in the hollows of their faces; some, fiery nails through their tongues; others, through their heads, from side to side. They who are so punished are thieves and liars, and they who have practiced treachery, abusive robbery, and rapine; judges of false judgment and contentious persons; women who have dealt in poison and spells, witches, and learned men who have practiced heresy. Another great throng is set on islands, in the middle of the fiery sea. About them is a silver wall built of the clothing and the alms which they had bestowed. These are they who have practiced mercy without zeal, and have remained in loose living, and in the bonds of their sin, until the hour of their death; but their alms are a defensive wall for them, in the fiery sea, until the judgment, and after judgment they will be brought into the haven of life.

28. Another great multitude is there, clad in red and fiery mantles down to their middle. Their trembling and their outcries make themselves heard, even to the firmament. An unspeakable throng of demons is throttling them, holding by the leash half-skinned, stinking hounds, which they incite to devour and consume them. Red glowing chains are constantly ablaze around their necks. Every alternate hour they are borne up to the firmament, and the next hour they are dashed down into hell's abyss. Now they that are punished in this way are the ordained who have broken their vows, and become haters of piety; also, impostors who have deceived and seduced the multitude, and have undertaken miracles and wonders that they are not able to perform. Moreover, the children that are tearing the men in orders are they who were committed to them for improvement, but they did not improve them, neither did they reprimand them for their sins.

29. After that is another vast company; they go east and west, unresting, across the fiery flagstones, at war with the demon hosts. Innumerable showers of red-hot arrows are rained on them by the demons. Running, they go on without stop or delay, making for a black lake and a black river, that they may extinguish those arrows in them. A weeping and wailing, truly miserable and

piteous, the sinners make in those waters, for in them they only meet with an increase of their pain. Now they that are punished in this way are cheating craftsmen, weavers, and merchants; judges that judged falsely, both Jews, and others similarly; impious kings, wardens of lewd and crooked ways, adulterous women, and the pimps that destroyed them by their evil practices.

Beyond the land of torment is a fiery wall; seven times more horrible and cruel is it than the land of pain itself. However, no soul dwells therein until judgment, but it is the province of the demons only, until the day of judgment.

30. At that time, woe to him that will dwell in those pains, in company with the devil's own tribe! Woe to him that is not cautious of that tribe! Woe to him over whom a vile and savage demon is set in dominion! Woe to him that will be listening to the spirits, moaning and complaining to the Lord, for the speedy coming of the day of judgment, that they may know whether they will find any remission of their doom; for they get no respite ever, save only for three hours on every Sunday. Woe to him for whom that land will be for a lasting inheritance, even forever and ever! For this is the nature of it: mountains, caverns, and thorny bushes; plains, bare and parched, with stagnant, serpent-haunted lakes. The soil is rough and sandy, very rugged, icebound. Broad fiery flagstones are strewn on the plain. Great seas are there, with horrible abysses, wherein is the devil's constant habitation and dwelling place. Four mighty rivers cross the middle of it: a river of fire, a river of snow, a river of poison, a river of black, murky water. In these wallow eager hosts of demons, after making their holiday and their delight in tormenting the souls.

31. What time the holy companies of the heavenly host are singing the eight hours with harmonious melody, praising the Lord with cheerfulness and great gladness, then do the souls of the wicked utter piteous and weary wailings, as they are buffeted unceasingly by the demon hordes.

Such then are the pains and torments which his guardian angel revealed to the spirit of Adamnán, after his journey toward the heavenly kingdom. After which he was borne in the twinkling of an eye through the golden forecourt, and through the crystal veil, to the land of saints, to where he had been brought at first, after his departure from the body. But when he intended to rest and delay in that land, he heard, through the veil, the angel's voice enjoining him to return again into that body from where he had departed, and to rehearse in courts and assemblies, and in the great congregations of laymen and of clerics, the rewards of heaven and the pains of hell, just as his guardian angel had revealed them to him.

Questions: What role does the supposed author Adamnán play in this document? How are heaven and hell described in the vision? What arguments could be made that rather than being a realistic narrative, this is a literary work and should be read as such? Which dispositions or behaviors would allow one entrance to heaven or condemn one to hell? What kind of effect do you think the writer wanted to have on his audience? What are some of the non-human residents of the afterlife, and what are they shown doing?

13. LIFE OF ANSKAR

The following is an excerpt from the saint's life of Anskar (801–865), a Benedictine monk, scholar, and eventually the bishop of Hamburg. Anskar is often regarded as an "Apostle to the North," since he was one of the first missionaries to travel into Scandinavia and preach Christianity there. The Christianization of the northern parts of Europe would take centuries. While the purpose of a saint's life is to convince readers of the subject's holiness, this biography also preserves some precious glimpses into life in ninth-century Sweden and Denmark, which were a world apart from the rest of western Europe.

Source: ed. and trans. Paul Edward Dutton, *Carolingian Civilization: A Reader*, 2nd ed. (Peterborough, ON: Broadview Press, 2004), pp. 410–12, 415–16, 429–34. Latin.

9. Meanwhile it happened that Swedish ambassadors had come to the emperor Louis [the Pious, r. 813–840], and, among other matters which they had been ordered to bring to the attention of the emperor, they informed him that there were many belonging to their people who desired to embrace the Christian religion and that their king so far favored this suggestion that he would permit God's priests to reside there, provided that they might be deemed worthy of such a favor and that the emperor would send suitable preachers. When the God-fearing emperor heard this he was greatly delighted, and a second time he endeavored to find men whom he might send into those districts, who might discover whether this people was prepared to accept the faith, as the ambassadors had assured him, and might begin to inculcate the observance of the Christian religion. So it came about that his serene majesty began once again to discuss the matter with your [Adalhard's] abbot and asked him whether by chance he could find one of his monks who, for the name of Christ, was willing to go into those parts; or who would go and stay with [King] Harald [of Denmark, r. 812–813, 819–827] while God's servant Anskar, who was with him, undertook this mission. Thus it was that Anskar was summoned by royal command to the palace, and was told that he should not even stop to shave himself before coming into the royal presence.

The man of God, who knew clearly beforehand for what purpose he was being summoned, burned with fervor and love toward God and esteemed it a special joy if he might be allowed to press forward in the work of winning souls for him. If in a journey of this kind any harm or misfortune should befall him, he was resolved to bear it patiently for Christ's sake; and he had no hesitation in undertaking this task, as he was comforted by the heavenly vision which he had previously seen. At the time to which we refer, when he was staying with you and had already been divinely enlightened by two visions it seemed to him one night that he had come to a house in which were standing many preachers who had been prepared for their task of preaching. In their presence he was suddenly transported and he saw shining around him a light from heaven which excelled the brightness of the sun; and, as he marveled what this might be, a voice like that which he declared that he had heard in his first vision said to him: "Your sin is forgiven." In answer to that voice, being, as we believe, divinely inspired, he said: "Lord, what would you have me do?" Again the voice was heard saying: "Go and declare the word of God to the nations." As God's servant thought upon this vision he rejoiced in the Lord greatly, for he perceived that what he had been commanded [to do] was in part accomplished and he desired to add to his labors by preaching the word of God to the Swedes. When, after that, he was brought into the presence of the emperor and was asked by him whether he was willing to undertake this mission, he replied readily that he was prepared to undertake any task which the emperor might decide to place upon him for the name of Christ.

10. Then, by the good providence of God, the venerable abbot [Wala] found for him among your fraternity a companion, namely the prior Witmar, who was both worthy and willing to undertake this great task. He further arranged that the good Father Gislemar, a man approved by faith and good works, and by his fervent zeal for God, should stay with Harald. Anskar then undertook the mission committed to him by the emperor, who desired that he should go to the Swedes and discover whether that people was prepared to accept the faith as their messengers had declared. How great and serious were the calamities which he suffered while engaged in this mission, Father Witmar, who himself shared them, can best tell. It may suffice for me to say that while they were in the midst of their journey they fell into the hands of pirates. The merchants with whom they were traveling defended themselves vigorously and for a time successfully, but eventually they were conquered and overcome by the pirates, who took from them their ships and all that they possessed, while they themselves barely escaped on foot to land. They lost then the royal gifts which they should have delivered there, together with all their other possessions, save only what they were able to take away and carry with them as they left the ship. They were plundered, moreover, of nearly forty books which they had accumulated for the service of God. When this happened some were disposed to turn and go back, but no argument could divert God's servant from the journey which he had undertaken. On the contrary, he submitted everything that might happen to him to God's will and was by no means disposed to return

until, with God's help, he could ascertain whether he would be allowed to preach the Gospel in those parts.

11. With great difficulty they accomplished their long journey on foot, traversing also the intervening seas, where it was possible, by ship, and eventually arrived at the Swedish port called Birka. They were kindly received in that place by the king, who was called Björn [II, r. early ninth century], whose messengers had informed him of the reason for which they had come. When he understood the object of their mission and had discussed the matter with his men, with the approval and consent of all, he granted them permission to remain there and to preach the Gospel of Christ and offered liberty to any who desired it to accept their teaching.

Accordingly the servants of God, when they saw that matters had turned out propitiously as they had desired, began eagerly to preach the word of salvation to the people of that place. There were many who were well disposed toward their mission and who willingly listened to the teaching of the Lord. There were also many Christians who were held captive among them, and who rejoiced that now at last they were able to participate in the divine mysteries. It was thus made clear that everything was as their messengers had declared to the emperor, and some of them desired earnestly to receive the grace of baptism. These included the prefect of this town named Herigar, who was a counselor of the king and much loved by him. He received the gift of holy baptism and was strengthened in the Catholic faith. A little later he built a church on his own ancestral property and served God with the utmost devotion. Several remarkable deeds were accomplished by this man who afforded many proofs of his invincible faith. . . .

16. While these events, which brought praise and honor to God, were taking place in both directions, pirates suddenly arrived and surrounded the town of Hamburg. As this happened suddenly and unexpectedly, there was no time to collect the people in the villages; moreover, the count who at this time was the prefect of the place, namely the illustrious Bernhar, was absent. The bishop who was there and those who remained in the city and its suburbs, when the first news of their [the pirates'] coming arrived, desired to hold the place until further help might reach them. But when the country people put pressure upon him and the town was already besieged, he perceived that resistance was impossible and accordingly made preparations to carry away the sacred relics. As for himself, when his clergy had been scattered and had fled in various directions, he with difficulty escaped without even a cloak to cover his body. The people left the town and wandered here and there; and, while most fled, some were caught and of these the greater part was killed. The enemy then seized the town and plundered it and its immediate neighborhood. They had come in the evening and they remained that night and the next day and night.

When everything had been burned and destroyed they departed. The church there, which had been built in a wonderful manner under the guidance of the bishop, and the monastery, which was also of marvelous construction, were reduced to ashes. The Bible that the emperor had given to our father and which was beautifully transcribed, together with many other books, was lost in the fire. Everything which was used in the services of the church and all his treasures and possessions were lost by pillage or by fire during the enemy attack. This attack left him practically naked as nothing had previously been taken away, nor was anything removed at the time except that which each fugitive was able to carry away. By none of these things was our holy father distressed, nor did he sin with his lips, but when in a moment of time he lost almost everything that he had been able to gather together or to collect for purposes of building, he repeated again and again the words of Job: "The Lord gave, the Lord has taken away; the Lord's will has been done. Blessed be the name of the Lord" [Job 1:21].

17. After these occurrences the bishop continued with his people in their distress and misfortune, while the brothers belonging to his order traversed various districts and wandered here and there taking with them the holy relics; and nowhere did they find rest, owing to the devices of the wicked one.

It happened, too, at this time, at the instigation of the devil, that the Swedish people were inflamed with zeal and fury, and began by insidious means to persecute Bishop Gautbert. Thus it came about that some of the people, moved by a common impulse, made a sudden attack upon the house in which he was staying with the object of destroying it; and in their hatred of the Christian name they killed Nithard and made him, in our opinion, a true martyr. Gautbert himself and those of his companions who were present they bound and, after plundering everything that they could find in their house, they drove them from their territory with insults and abuse. This was not done by command of the king, but was brought about by a plot devised by the people. . . .

25. Meanwhile our lord and master Anskar, being greatly distressed on behalf of the Swedish race because it was at that time without a priest, begged King Horik [I, r. 813–854], who was his intimate friend, to help him make an effort to reach this kingdom. The king received this request with the utmost good will and promised that he would do everything to help. Accordingly the bishop began to negotiate with Bishop Gautbert saying that a further attempt must be made to discover whether this race, having been divinely admonished, would permit priests to dwell among them, so that the Christian faith, which had been established in those parts, might not perish in consequence of their neglect. Bishop Gautbert, who is also called Simon, replied that, as he had been expelled from that country, he would not venture to go there again and that the attempt

could not be advantageous, but would on the contrary be dangerous, should those who remembered what happened before raise a disturbance about him. He said that it seemed to him to be more fitting that he [Anskar] should go who was the first to undertake this mission and who had been kindly treated there, and that he would send with him his nephew [Erimbert] who might remain there, should he find an opportunity for preaching, and might perform the duties of a priest among the people. When they had so decided, they came to King Louis and told him the reason for their action and begged that he would permit them to do this. He asked whether they themselves had come to an agreement, whereupon the venerable Bishop Gautbert replied: "We are in the service of God and always have been united and it is our unanimous desire that this should be done." Accordingly, the king, who was ever ready to further God's work, enjoined this mission upon our holy father in accordance with the terms they had agreed among themselves and, on his part, entrusted to the bishop injunctions addressed to the king of Sweden as his father had done previously.

Our good father then began to prepare for this journey and became the more eager to accomplish it with the utmost speed. Moreover he believed that he was commanded by heaven to undertake it, as he was influenced by a vision which he had seen earlier. For in that vision he thought that he was anxious in view of this very journey and it seemed to him that he came to a place where there were large buildings and dwellings of different kinds. A certain man met him there and said:

> Do not be too distressed about the journey over which you are anxious, for there is a certain prophet in this place who will inform you concerning all these matters. And that in regard to this matter no hesitation should take possession of your mind, I will tell you who this prophet is: Adalhard, the once famous abbot, is the prophet whom the Lord has sent to you to tell you the things that are to come to pass.

Being greatly encouraged by what he heard in this vision, Anskar replied: "Where will I find him, O Lord?" "You will find him," was the reply, "by your own effort; and no one may bring him to you." Then it seemed to him that he passed round the dwellings seeking for him and at the same time he said to himself, "If without my asking him he will tell me what is in my mind, then I will be satisfied that he is a true prophet." He went on then to a bright and beautiful dwelling and saw him sitting on his chair and recognized him without delay. He [the prophet] looked upon him and said immediately:

> Hear, O islands, and give ear to your peoples from afar. The Lord has called you from the womb and from your mother's belly; he has remembered

your name, and he has made your mouth as a sharp sword and has covered you with the shadow of his hand and has made you like a choice arrow. He has hidden you in his quiver, and has said to you, "You are my servant, for in you I will be glorified."

Having said this he stretched out his arm and lifted his right hand to him. When Anskar saw this he advanced to his knees hoping that he would be willing to bless him. But he added these words:

Now says the Lord that formed you in the womb to be his servant, I have given you to be a light to the gentiles that you may be present to them for salvation even to the ends of the earth. Kings will see and princes will rise up together and they will worship the Lord your God, even the holy one of Israel, for he will glorify you [cf. Isaiah 66:18–20].

God's servant, having beheld this vision long before he set out on his journey, was assured that he was summoned by divine command to go to those parts, and specially by the word that had been spoken "Hear, O islands," because almost all that country consisted of islands; and by that which had been added, "You will be present to them for salvation even to the ends of the earth," because in the north the end of the world lay in Swedish territory. Finally the word quoted from the end of Jeremiah's prophecy: "For he will glorify you," encouraged his eager desire, as he thought that this referred to the crown of martyrdom that had once been promised to him.

26. As he was then about to set out on this journey he took with him the message and the token given him by King Horik, who directed him to give the message to the Swedish king named Olof [I] and to say that the messenger whom King Louis had sent to his kingdom was well known to him and that he had never before in his life seen so good a man, nor had he ever found any other human being so trustworthy. In recognition of his goodness he had allowed him to do whatever he wished in his kingdom in the interests of the Christian religion and King Louis begged that he would permit him to establish the Christian religion in his own kingdom, as he desired, for he would do nothing that would not be good and right.

Anskar accomplished the journey on which he had set out and after spending nearly twenty days in a ship, he arrived at Birka where he found that the king and many of the people were perplexed by grievous errors. It happened, at the instigation of the devil, who knew beforehand of the coming of this good man, that someone had come there and said that he had been present at a meeting of the gods, who were believed to be the owners of this land,

and had been sent by them to make this announcement to the king and the people:

> You, I say, have long enjoyed our good will, and under our protection the land in which you dwell has long been fertile and has had peace and prosperity. You have also duly sacrificed and performed the vows made to us, and your worship has been very pleasing to us. But now you are keeping back the usual sacrifices and are slothful in paying your voluntary offerings; you are, moreover, displeasing us greatly by introducing a foreign god in order to supplant us. If you want to enjoy our good will, offer the sacrifices that have been omitted and give greater vows. And do not receive the worship of any other god, who teaches that which is opposed to our teaching, nor pay any attention to his service. Furthermore, if you desire to have more gods and we do not suffice, we will agree to summon your former king, Eric [III], to join us so that he may be one of the gods.

This devilish announcement, which was publicly made on the arrival of the bishop, disturbed the minds of all and their hearts were deceived and disquieted. For they had resolved to have a temple in honor of the late king and had begun to render votive offerings and sacrifices to him as to a god. When, then, the bishop came there, he asked his friends, the ones he had formerly known there, how he might speak to the king on this matter. They all, with one accord, disagreed with him doing so and said that for the time being this mission could effect nothing, and that if he had anything of value with him he should give it to the king so that he might escape with his life. He replied, "For the saving of my life I would give nothing, for, if my Lord will so ordain, I am ready to submit to torments and to suffer death for his name." Being in great uncertainty in regard to this matter, he acted on the advice that he received, and invited the king to partake of his hospitality. Then, as a fellow guest, he offered what gifts he could and gave him the things with which he had been entrusted, for the cause of his coming had already been explained to the king by Horik's messenger and by the bishop's friends who resided there. The king was delighted with his kindness and liberality, and said that he gladly agreed to what he had proposed. He said:

> In former times there have been clergy who have been driven out by a rising of the people and not by the command of the king. On this account I have not the power, nor do I dare, to approve the objects of your mission until I can consult our gods by the casting of lots and until I can determine the will of the people in regard to this matter. Let your messenger attend with me the next assembly and I will speak to the people on your behalf. And if they approve your desire and the gods consent, that which you have

asked will be successfully carried out, but if it should turn out otherwise, I will let you know. It is our custom that the control of public business of every kind should rest with the whole people and not with the king.

When our good pastor received the king's reply he turned to the Lord for refuge, gave up his time to fasting and prayer, and with heartfelt contrition he humbled himself before God.

27. While he was in this difficult position and the time for the assembly drew near, he was one day engaged in the service of the Mass and, while the priest was standing by the altar and was blessing the sacred mysteries, a divine inspiration came upon him as he prostrated himself on the ground. Strengthened, then, by the gift of the Holy Spirit and adorned with the most complete confidence, he recognized that all would turn out as he desired. Accordingly, when the Mass was finished, he declared to this same priest, who was his most intimate associate, that he ought to have no fear, for God himself would be his helper. When the priest asked how he knew this he replied that his knowledge was divinely inspired. The brother was able to recognize this divine illumination, as he knew that he had been divinely inspired in many previous instances, and the result quickly justified his confidence.

As soon as his chiefs were assembled the king began to discuss with them the mission on which our father had come. They determined that an inquiry should be made by the casting of lots in order to discover the will of the gods. They went out, therefore, to the plain, in accordance with their custom, and the lot decided that it was the will of God that the Christian religion should be established there. When this happened, one of the chief men, who was a friend of the bishop, told him at once and advised him to be comforted, and said, "Be strong and act with vigor, for God has not denied your wish nor rejected your mission." He was then full of courage and rejoicing in spirit exulted in the Lord. When the day for the assembly which was held in the town of Birka drew near, in accordance with their national custom the king caused a proclamation to be made to the people by a voice of a herald, in order that they might be informed concerning the object of their mission. On hearing this, those who had before been led astray into error, held discordant and confused opinions. In the midst of the noise and confusion one of the older men among them said:

Listen to me, O king and people. In regard to the worship of this God it is well known to many of us that he can afford much help to those who place their hope in him. For many of us have proved this to be the case on several occasions when in peril from sea and in other crises. Why, then, do we reject that which we know to be both needful and useful? Some of us who have on various occasions been to Dorestad have of our own accord adopted this form of religion, believing it to be beneficial. Our way there is now beset by those who lie in wait for us and is rendered dangerous by the attacks of pirates. Why then do we not take that which is brought to us and which, when it was at a distance, we sought eagerly to obtain? We have frequently proved that the help afforded by this God can be useful to us. Why should we not gladly agree to continue as his servants? Consider carefully, O people, and do not cast away that which will be to your advantage. For, inasmuch as we cannot be sure that our gods will be favorably disposed, it is good for us to have the help of this God who is always and under all circumstances able and willing to succor those who cry out to him.

When he had finished speaking all the people unanimously decided that the priests should remain with them and that everything that pertained to the performance of the Christian mysteries should be done without objection or hindrance. The king then rose up from among the assembly and without delay directed one of his own messengers to accompany the bishop's messenger and to tell him that the people were unanimously inclined to accept his proposal and at the same time to tell him that, while their action was entirely agreeable to him, he could not give his full consent until, in another assembly, which was to be held in another part of his kingdom, he could announce this resolution to the people who lived in that district.

Once again, then, our good father sought, as was his custom, for divine assistance, and eagerly besought God's mercy. When the time for the assembly came and the king had caused to be proclaimed by the voice of a herald the object for which the bishop had come and all that had been said and done at the previous assembly by divine providence, the hearts of all became as one, so that they too would give their entire and complete assent.

Questions: How did political rulers play a part in Anskar's missionary efforts? What kind of visions did Anskar receive and in what way were they, too, a kind of journey? What were the dangers that Anskar encountered in traveling to the north? Did he also face supernatural foes? Why did Anskar's brother monks worry about him traveling alone? Based on this source, what can we say about the pagan religion that Sweden previously had? What would ultimately cause the Swedes to decide to convert to Christianity?

14. THE WESTERN EUROPEAN MONK BERNARD'S JOURNEY TO JERUSALEM

The Holy Land was considered the prime destination for Christian pilgrims throughout the Middle Ages, especially because of its connection with the earthly career of Jesus. The

French monk Bernard, who departed on his journey in 867, should be seen as one example of this very popular tradition, although most pilgrims did not leave a written account. Rather than just describe his particular experience, Bernard wished to provide a guide for future monks who wanted to follow in his steps. The first paragraph of the travelogue was tacked on by an editor in the tenth century, whereas the rest is by Bernard himself.

Source: ed. and trans. Paul Edward Dutton, *Carolingian Civilization: A Reader*, 2nd ed. (Peterborough, ON: Broadview Press, 2004), pp. 472–79. Latin.

Here starts the account of the journey of three monks, namely Bernard and his companions, and of the holy places [they visited] and of Babylon [Old Cairo]. [It contains] a description of the places that the wise Bernard saw when he went to Jerusalem and returned, and of Jerusalem itself and the places around it. We learned of these things in the 970th year of the incarnation of our Lord Jesus Christ.

1. Wishing in the name of the Lord to see the places of the holy ones which are in Jerusalem, I, Bernard, joined together in affectionate esteem with two monks. One's name was Theudemund [and he came] from the monastery of St-Vincent of Benevento [San Vincenzo al Volturno]; the other, a Spaniard, was named Stephen. Thus we approached Nicholas [I, r. 858–867], the pontiff, in Rome [and] obtained with his blessing and also his help the desired permission to proceed [with our journey].

2. From there we traveled to Monte Gargano [near modern-day Foggia] in which is [found] the Church of St-Michael under solid stone [a cave] upon which there are acorn-bearing oak trees. The archangel himself is said to have dedicated that [shrine], whose entrance is from the north and can admit 60 people in it [at a time]. Inside on the east [wall] there is an image of that angel; to the south there is an altar upon which the Mass is offered and no other offering except that is placed there. However, in front of the altar a certain vessel is suspended in which offerings are dropped. [That vessel] also has other altars near it. The abbot of that place is called Benignatus, who rules over many monks.

3. Leaving Monte Gargano, after [traveling] 150 miles we came to the city of the Saracens [Muslims] called Bari, which for a long time was subject to the Beneventans. This city situated on the sea is protected by two very broad walls on the south, but juts out exposed to the sea on the north. And so here we sought out the ruler [the emir] of that city, [who] was named Sawdan, [and] we arranged the entire business of sailing by obtaining two letters. The text of these [two] letters for the ruler of Alexandria and also [the ruler] of Babylon set out a description of our appearance [for the purposes of identification] and journey. For those rulers are under the rule of the caliph who lives

in Baghdad and Axinarri [Samarra], which lie beyond Jerusalem, and he rules all the Saracens.

4. Departing from Bari, we walked south for 90 miles until [we came] to the port of the city Taranto where we found six ships, in which there were 9,000 Christian Beneventans held captive. In two ships which left first for Africa there were 3,000 captives; the next two departing ships similarly carried away 3,000 to Tripoli.

5. Entering the two remaining ships, on which there was also the same number of captives, we were taken to the port of Alexandria [after] sailing for 30 days. We wished to proceed onto the shore, [but] were stopped by the captain who was [in command] of more than 60 sailors. We paid him six gold coins to give us the opportunity to leave.

6. Once we left [the boat], we traveled to the ruler of Alexandria, to whom we showed the letter which Sawdan gave us, [but] it did us no good, although he stated that he was familiar with everything in that letter. At his request each one of us on his own behalf paid him 13 *denarii* [silver coins] and he drew up a letter for us [to give] to the ruler of Babylon. Such is the custom of that people that only [that currency] which can be weighed is taken [as payment] at its weight and not in some other way. [Thus] six *solidi* [gold coins] and six *denarii* for us make three *solidi* and three *denarii* for them.

This Alexandria lies on the sea; in it Saint Mark proclaim[ed] the Gospel and carried out his episcopal office. Outside the eastern gate of this city is the monastery of St-Mark, in which there are monks beside the church in which he [that is, his body] formerly rested. But Venetians coming by boat secretly removed his body from its guardians and transported him to their island. Outside the western gate is a monastery which is dedicated to the Forty Saints where monks also reside. On the north is the port of that city; on the south there enters the Gihon [?] or Nile, which waters Egypt and runs through the middle of the city, entering the [Mediterranean] sea at that port.

7. Embarking upon a ship we sailed south for six days and came to the city of Babylon of Egypt where pharaoh, the king, once reigned, under whom Joseph built seven granaries which still stand [the pyramids]. While we were going forth into Babylon, the guards of the city led us to the ruler, who is called Adelacham, a Saracen, and he inquired of us the full nature of our journey and from which rulers we had letters. For that reason we showed him the letters from Sawdan and from the ruler of Alexandria. But that did not help us [and] we were sent to prison by him until, after six days had passed [and] with the help of God, a plan took shape. Each of us on his own behalf paid 13 *denarii*, just as [I described] above. He also gave us a letter [so that] whoever saw it thereafter in whatever city or place would not dare to compel anything from us. For he was the second [most powerful person] in the empire of the caliph.

But after we entered the cities named below we were not allowed to leave before receiving a charter or the impression of a seal, which we obtained for either one or two *denarii*.

In this city the lord patriarch is Michael and by the grace of God he sets the order for all the bishops, monks, and Christians all over Egypt. Those Christians, however, live under such a law among the pagans [Muslims] that on their own behalf each one pays a tribute each year to that ruler so that he might live securely and freely. He exacts a tribute of either three, two, or one gold *aureus* or from a lower class person of 12 *denarii*. Nevertheless, if it is the case that either a resident or foreign Christian cannot pay those 13 *denarii*, he is cast into prison until either by the mercy of God he is freed by his angel or he is redeemed by other good Christians.

8. With those maintaining themselves in this way, we returned back by way of the river Gihon for three days and we came to the city of Sitinuth. From Sitinuth we proceeded to Maalla; from Maalla we passed over to Damietta, which has the sea on the north, but the Nile river on all [other] sides with the exception of a little land. From there we sailed to the city of Tanis in which there are very pious Christians committed to providing great hospitality. This city, however, has no land without churches and the plain of Zoan is found there. In it in the likeness of three walls lie the bodies of those who were slaughtered in the time of Moses.

9. From Tanis we came to the city of Ferama [Tell el Farama] where there is a church in honor of the blessed Mary at the place to which, after the angel's warning, Joseph fled with the boy and mother. In this city there is a multitude of camels which foreigners rent for a price from the inhabitants of that area to carry loads for them through the desert, which is a journey of six days. The entrance to the desert begins at this city and it is fittingly called a desert since it supports neither grass nor produce from any seed with the exception of palm trees. Rather all is as white as Champagne is when it snows. In the middle of the journey there are two hospices, one called Albara [al-Warrada], the other called Albachara [al-Bakkara]. In them the business of procuring the things necessary to those making [such] a journey is conducted by Christians and pagans [Muslims]. Between [those two hospices] the earth produces nothing, except what was stated [palm trees]. After Albachara the land is soon found to be fertile until the city of Gaza, which was the city of Samson; it is extremely rich in all things.

10. From there we came to Alariza [el-Arish]. From Alariza we entered Ramla near which is the monastery of the martyr, Saint George, where [the saint's body] rests. From Ramla we hurried on to the fortress of Emmaus. From Emmaus we passed on to the holy city of Jerusalem and were received in the hospice of the most glorious emperor Charles where all who come to

that place for the sake of devotion [and who] speak the Roman tongue are welcome. Beside this [hospice] lies a church in honor of Saint Mary which possesses, from the devotion of the emperor [Charlemagne, r. 768–814], an extremely fine library [or Bible] along with 12 buildings, fields, vines, and a garden in the valley of Jehoshaphat. [Situated] before that hospice is a market for [the use of] which each one conducting business there pays two gold coins per year to the one who oversees that [market].

11. Within that city [of Jerusalem], with other churches left aside [here], four churches stand out [and] share common walls with each other. One, which lies to the east, contains Mount Calvary and the place where the cross of the Lord was found and it is called the Basilica of Constantine. Another [lies] to the south; a third to the west, in the middle of which is the Sepulcher of the Lord which has nine columns around it, between which stand walls made of the finest stones. Four of the nine columns are before the face of that monument; with their walls they enclose the [tomb]stone placed before the sepulcher, which the angel rolled back and on which he sat after the resurrection of the Lord was brought about. It is not necessary to say more about this sepulcher, since Bede in his history says enough about it.

This, however, should be said: that on the holy Sabbath that is the vigil of Easter the morning service begins in this church and after the service is completed the *Kyrie eleison* [Lord, have mercy] is sung until, when the angel comes, the light in the lamps hung above the sepulcher is set aflame. From it the patriarch supplies [flame] to the bishops and the rest of the people in order that each might light [a candle] for himself at his own place [in the church]. This patriarch is called Theodosius, who on account of the merit of his devotion was seized by Christians from his own monastery, which lies 15 miles from Jerusalem. And he was established as the patriarch over all Christians who are in the Promised Land. Between these four churches is a park [paradise] without a roof whose walls shine with gold; the floor is arranged with the most precious stone, having in its middle a border of four chains which come from the four churches. The middle of the world is said to be in that spot.

12. Moreover, there is in that city another church to the south on Mount Sion which is called [the Church] of St-Simeon where the Lord washed the feet of his disciples. In that church hangs the Lord's crown of thorns and [also] in it one of the dead is reported to be Saint Mary. Near it toward the east is a church in honor of Saint Stephen in the place where he was brought to be stoned. In a straight [line] to the east is the church in honor of Saint Peter in the place where he denied the Lord. To the north is the Temple of Solomon [now] containing the synagogue [mosque] of the Saracens. To the south are the iron gates through which the angel of the Lord led Peter forth from prison which afterward were not open.

13. Departing from Jerusalem, we descended into the valley of Jehoshaphat, which is a mile from the city, and contains the villa of Gethsemane with the place of the birth of Saint Mary. In the place there is a very large church in her honor. Also in the villa itself is the round Church of St-Mary where her sepulcher is [located]; it does not have a roof above it, [but] suffers little rain. There is also a church in honor of Saint Leontius where, it is said, the Lord will come to judge.

14. From there we proceeded to the Mount of Olives on whose slope is displayed the place of the Lord's prayer to [God] the Father. Also on the side of the same mountain is displayed the place where the Pharisees brought forth to the Lord the woman caught in adultery; it has a church in honor of Saint John in which is preserved in marble the writing that the Lord wrote on the ground.

15. At the peak, however, of that Mount [of Olives], a mile from the valley of Jehoshaphat, is the place of the Lord's ascension to [God] the Father. It possesses a roofless round church in the middle of which, that is on the spot of the Lord's ascension, is contained an altar in open air at which the solemnities of the Mass are celebrated.

16. From there we passed over to Bethany, which is to the south, at a distance of a mile from the Mount of Olives. On the way down from that mountain there is a monastery whose church displays the sepulcher of Lazarus. Near it there is a pond on the north, where by the Lord's order the revived Lazarus washed himself. It is said that afterward he had continued as the bishop of Ephesus for 40 years. Also on the way down from the Mount of Olives to the western sea a marble slab is displayed from which the Lord mounted the foal of an ass. Among these [sights] to the south in the valley of Jehoshaphat is the pool of Siloam.

17. Besides [those sights], when we went out of Jerusalem, we crossed over to Bethlehem where the Lord was born, which was six miles [away]. A field was shown to us in which Habakkuk was working when the angel of the Lord ordered him to carry lunch to Daniel in Babylon, which is to the south, where Nebuchadnezzar rules [and] which serpents and beasts now inhabit. Bethlehem has a great church in honor of Saint Mary in the middle of which is a crypt under a solid stone [a cave]. The entrance to it lies to the south, but its exit [lies] to the east. In it on the west [side] of that crypt is displayed the manger of the Lord. However, the place where the Lord [first] cried out is to the east and has an altar at which Mass is celebrated. Near this church to the south is the Church of the Blessed Innocents, the martyrs. Next, one mile from Bethlehem, is the monastery of the Holy Shepherds to whom the angel appeared at the Lord's nativity.

18. At last, 30 miles from Jerusalem is the [river] Jordan to the east, beside which is the monastery of St-John the Baptist. In those places there also stand many [other] monasteries.

19. There is, among these [sights] to the western part of the city of Jerusalem at [a distance of] one mile, the Church of St-Mamilla. In it are [to be found] the many bodies of the martyrs who were killed by the Saracens. They were carefully buried there by that [saint].

20. Thus, returning from the holy city of Jerusalem we came to the sea. Entering onto the sea [on a ship], we sailed for 60 days with the greatest difficulty, [as we] lacked a good wind. At last, leaving the sea we came to the Golden Mountain [Monte Olevano near Salerno] where there is a crypt [a cave] possessing seven altars [and] also having above it a sizable forest. No one can enter into that crypt because of its darkness without torches. Valentinus was the lord abbot in that same place [when we passed there].

21. Traveling from the Golden Mountain we came to Rome. Within that city on the eastern part, in the place which is called the Lateran, there is a church well built in honor of Saint John the Baptist, which is the permanent abode of the popes. Besides, in that same place each night the keys of the universal city are brought to the pope. But on the western part [of the city of Rome] is the Church of St-Peter, prince of the apostles, in which he himself rests in this body. In size there is no comparable church in the whole world to [St-Peter]. It also contains an array of decorations. In that city rest the countless bodies of saints.

22. In this city we separated from each other. But I afterward traveled to the Mont-Saint-Michel, which is a place situated on a mountain that extends in the sea for two leagues. On the summit of that mountain is a church in honor of Saint Michael and the sea flows around that mountain twice daily, that is in the morning and at night, and no person can approach the mountain until the sea recedes. However, on the feast of Saint Michael [16 October] the sea is connected in flowing around the mountain, but stands in the likeness of walls on the right and left. And on that solemn day all, [that is,] whoever comes for [the purpose of] prayer, can approach the mountain at any hour, which however cannot be done on other days. The abbot there is the Breton Phinimontius.

23. At last I will tell you how Christians keep God's law in Jerusalem or in Egypt. The Christians, however, and pagans [Muslims] have such a peace placed between them there that if I, who exhibit great poverty, was making a journey [there] and on that journey my camel or donkey was to die and I left there all my possessions without a guard and I went to another city nearby, when I returned I would find all my possessions safe and sound. Such is the peace there! But if they find a person in transit either during the day or at night in a city or on the sea or on some journey without some document [a license to travel] or the seal of some king or that land's ruler, he is immediately ordered to be shut up in a prison until the day arrives when he can furnish a reason as to whether [or not] he is a spy or some such thing.

24. The Beneventans in their pride killed their own ruler, Sichard [in 839], and so greatly overthrew the law of the Christians. Then they had quarrels and disputes among themselves until Louis [II, co-emperor 844–855, emperor 855–875], the brother of Lothar [II, d. 869] and Charles [of Provence, r. 855–863], with those Beneventans inviting him, received power over them. But in the Roman lands many evils occurred and there men are evil thieves and bandits. And, therefore, people who wish to go to St-Peter cannot pass through there unless there are many of them and they are armed. In Lombardy, with that Louis ruling, a good enough peace exists. The Bretons also maintain peace among themselves. They even keep the law such as I [will] describe to you. Thus, if someone should injure another, a third [party], whoever it is who sees this [crime], will immediately come [to his aid] and he will avenge him as if he were his own relative. And if they find someone guilty of theft beyond four *denarii* they either kill him or suspend him on a pillory.

25. Finally [let me say that] in the valley of Gethsemane we saw squared marble stones of such refinement that on them one could catch sight of all the things a person might possibly wish to see as if on a mirror.

Questions: Which holy sites did Bernard see on his pilgrimage? What opportunities for worship does he mention? Which kinds of observations does he have about non-religious things? What aspects of his report might prove useful to a future traveler? Does the reader learn anything about Bernard's personal reaction to travel? What can this travelogue tell us about interaction between Muslims and Bernard's party, or Christians more generally?

15. AL-TABARI, *THE PROPHET ASCENDS TO THE SEVENTH HEAVEN*

Al-Tabari (839–923) was a noted Muslim religious scholar and historian who spent most of his career in Baghdad. He wrote voluminously on the Muslim holy book the Qur'an, the law, and the history of the Prophet Muhammad. The following is an excerpt from that history, describing the miraculous journey of Muhammad into heaven while he was still alive, which traditionally was said to have happened in 621. While earlier versions of the event seem to depict it as a spiritual journey, by Al-Tabari's time it was seen as a physical ascension. It has in time become one of the most important Muslim feasts.

Source: trans. W. Montgomery Watt and M. V. McDonald, Al-Tabari, *The History of Al-Ṭabarī*, vol. 6: *Muḥammad at Mecca* (Albany, NY: State University of New York Press, 1987), pp. 78–80. Arabic.

Ibn Humayd-Harun b. al-Mughirah and Hakkam b. Salm–'Anbasah–Abu Hashim al-Wasiti–Mayumun b. Siyah–Anas b. Malik [Muslim authorities responsible for this tale]: At the time when the Prophet [Muhammad] became a prophet, he used to sleep around the Kaaba [in Mecca] as did the Quraysh [tribe]. On one occasion two angels, Gabriel and Michael, came to him and said, "Which of the Quraysh were we ordered to come to?" Then they said, "We were ordered to come to their chief," and went away. After this they came from the Qibla [the place to which prayer is directed] and there were three of them. They came upon him as he slept, turned him on his back, and opened his breast. Then they brought water from Zamzam and washed away the doubt, or polytheism, or pre-Islamic beliefs, or error, which was in his breast. Then they brought a golden basin full of faith and wisdom, and his breast and belly were filled with faith and wisdom.

Then he was taken up to the earthly heaven. Gabriel asked for admittance, and they said, "Who is it?" "Gabriel," he said. "Who is with you?" they said. "Muhammad," he answered. "Has his mission commenced?" they asked. "Yes," he said. "Welcome," they said, and called down God's blessings on him. When he went in, he saw before him a huge and handsome man. "Who is this, Gabriel?" he asked. "This is your father, Adam," he replied. Then they took him to the second heaven. Gabriel asked for admission, and they said the same as before. Indeed, the same questions were asked and the same answers given in all the heavens. When Muhammad went in to the second heaven he saw before him two men. "Who are these, Gabriel?" he asked. "John and Jesus, the two maternal cousins," he replied. Then he was taken to the third heaven, and when he went in he saw before him a man. "Who is this, Gabriel?" he asked. He replied, "Your brother Joseph who was given preeminence in beauty over other men as is the full moon over the stars at night." Then he was taken to the fourth heaven, and he saw before him a man and said, "Who is this, Gabriel?" "This is Idris [Enoch]," he said, and recited: "And we raised him to high station."

Then he was taken to the fifth heaven, and he saw before him a man and said, "Who is this, Gabriel?" "This is Aaron," he said. Then he was taken to the sixth heaven, and he saw before him a man and said, "Who is this, Gabriel?" "This is Moses," he said. Then he was taken to the seventh heaven, and he saw before him a man and said, "Who is this, Gabriel?" "This is your father Abraham," he said.

Then he took him to paradise, and there before him was a river whiter than milk and sweeter than honey, with pearly domes on either side of it. "What is this, Gabriel?" he asked. Gabriel replied, "This is al-Kawthar [a chapter of the Qur'an], which your Lord has given to you, and these are your dwellings." Then Gabriel took a handful of its earth and see! it was fragrant musk. Then he went out to the Sidrat al-Muntaha, which was a lote tree bearing fruits the largest of which were like earthenware jars and the smallest like eggs. Then his Lord drew near, "until he was distant two bows' length or nearer." Because of the nearness of its Lord the lote tree became covered by the like of such jewels as pearls, rubies, chrysolites, and colored pearls. God made revelation to his servant, caused him to understand and know, and prescribed for him fifty prayers [daily].

Then he went back past Moses, who said to him, "What did he impose [on] your community?" "Fifty prayers," he said. "Go back to your Lord," said Moses, "and ask him to lighten the burden for your community, for your community is the weakest in strength and the shortest-lived." Then he told Muhammad what he himself had suffered at the hands of the Children of Israel. The Messenger of God went back, and God reduced the number by ten. Then he passed Moses again, who said, "Go back to your Lord and ask him to lighten the burden further." This continued until he had gone back five times. One more Moses said, "Go back to your Lord and ask him to lighten the burden," but the Messenger of God said, "I am not going back, although I do not wish to disobey you," for it had been put into his heart that he should not go back. God said, "My speech is not to be changed, and my decision and precept is not to be reversed, but he [Muhammad] lightened the burden of prayer on my community to a tenth of what it was at first."

Anas [a companion of Muhammad]: I never encountered any scent, not even the scent of a bride, more fragrant than the skin of the Messenger of God. I pressed my skin to his and smelt it.

Questions: Who made Muhammad's journey possible? What was necessary to do to Muhammad before he was ready to ascend to heaven? How did heaven appear to Muhammad? Whom did Muhammad meet in heaven, and what was the conversation with them like? How did the journey change Muhammad?

16. *THE SEAFARER*

The Seafarer is an anonymous poem found in the Exeter Book, a manuscript preserved in Exeter Cathedral in England that contains some of the oldest Old English poetry. The manuscript was copied in the second half of the tenth century, although its contents might be considerably older. Scholars have debated several aspects of this work. The first half of the poem seems to be a lament while the second seems to provide moral teaching, leading some to think that it may have originally been two independent poems. Some see it as describing the literal travels of a sailor, while others see it as an allegory for the travel of the Christian through the world to his or her destination in heaven.

Source: trans. R. K. Gordon, *Anglo-Saxon Poetry* (London: J. M. Dent & Sons, 1926), pp. 76–78. Old English.

I can utter a true song about myself, tell of my travels, how in toilsome days I often suffered a time of hardship, how I have borne bitter sorrow in my breast, made trial of many sorrowful abodes on ships; dread was the rolling of the waves. There the hard night watch at the boat's prow was often my task, when it tossed by the cliffs. Afflicted with cold, my feet were fettered by frost, chill bonds. There my sorrows, hot round my heart, were sighed forth; hunger within rent the mind of the sea-weary man. The man who fares most prosperously on land knows not how I, careworn, have spent a winter as an exile on the ice-cold sea, cut off from kinsmen, hung round with icicles. The hail flew in showers, I heard naught there save the sea booming, the ice-cold billow, at times the song of the swan. I took my gladness in the cry of the gannet and the sound of the curlew instead of the laughter of men, in the screaming of gull instead of the drink of mead. There the storms beat against the rocky cliffs; there the tern with icy feathers answered them; full often the dewy-winged eagle screamed around. No protector could comfort the heart in its need. And yet he who has the bliss of life, who, proud and flushed with wine, suffers few hardships in the city, little believes how I often in weariness had to dwell on the ocean path. The shadow of night grew dark, snow came from the north, frost bound the earth; hail fell on the ground, coldest of grain. And yet the thoughts of my heart are now stirred that I myself should make trial of the high streams, of the tossing of the salt waves; the desire of the heart always exhorts to venture forth that I may visit the land of strange people far from here. And yet there is no man on earth so proud, nor so generous of his gifts, nor so bold in youth, nor so daring in his deeds, nor with a lord so gracious to him, that he has not always anxiety about his seafaring, as to what the Lord will bestow on him. His thoughts are not of the harp, nor of receiving rings, nor of delight in a woman, nor of joy in the world, not of aught else save the rolling of the waves; but he who sets out on the waters ever feels longing. The groves put forth blossoms; cities grow beautiful; the fields are fair; the world revives; all these urge the heart of the eager-minded man to a journey, him who thus purposes to fare far on the ways of the flood. Likewise the cuckoo exhorts with sad voice; the harbinger of summer sings, bodes bitter sorrow to the heart. The man knows not, the prosperous being, what some of those endure who most widely pace the paths of exile. And yet my heart is now restless in my breast, my mind is with the sea flood over the whale's domain; it fares widely over the face of the earth, comes again to me eager and unsatisfied; the lone flier screams, resistlessly urges the heart to the whale-way over the stretch of seas.

Wherefore the joys of the Lord are more inspiring for me than this dead fleeting life on earth. I have no faith that earthly riches will abide forever. Each one of three things is ever uncertain before its time comes; illness or age or hostility will take life away from a man doomed and dying. Wherefore the praise of living men who will speak after he is gone, the best of fame after death for every man is that he should strive before he must depart, work on earth with bold deeds against the malice of fiends, against the devil, so that the children of men may later exalt him and his praise live afterward among the angels for ever and ever, the joy of life eternal, delight amid angels.

The days have departed, all the pomps of earth's kingdom; kings, or emperors, or givers of gold, are not as of yore when they wrought among themselves greatest deeds of glory, and lived in most lordly splendor. This host has fallen, the delights have departed; weaklings live on and possess this world, enjoy it by their toil. Glory is laid low; the nobleness of the earth ages and withers, as now every man does throughout the world. Old age comes on him; his face grows pale; grey-haired he laments; he knows that his former friends, the sons of princes, have been laid in the earth. Then, when life leaves him, his body can neither taste sweetness, nor feel pain, nor stir a hand, nor ponder in thought. Though he will strew the grave with gold, bury his brother with various treasures beside dead kinsmen, that will not go with him. To the soul full of sins the gold which it hoards while it lives here gives no help in the face of God's wrath. Great is the fear of God, whereby the earth turns; he established the mighty plains, the face of the earth, and the sky above. Foolish is he who fears not his Lord; death comes to him unexpected. Blessed is he who lives humbly; mercy comes to him from heaven; God establishes that heart in him because he trusts in his strength.

One must check a violent mind and control it with firmness, and be trustworthy to men, pure in ways of life.

Every man should show moderation in love toward a friend and enmity toward a foe. . . . Fate is more strong, God more mighty than any man's thought. Let us consider where we possess our home, and then think how we may come thither, and let us then also attempt to win there, to the eternal bliss, where life springs from God's love, joy in heaven. Thanks be forever to the holy one because he, the prince of glory, the Lord everlasting, has honored us. Amen.

Questions: How does the narrator describe winter seafaring? Does it have any positive aspects? What role do animals play in the poem? In light of the challenges the author faced, why does he still venture out on the sea? What does he hope that the suffering will lead to? Is the narrator despairing of the state of the world? What kind of religious advice does he offer his reader? If the poem is by one author, why is there no mention of seafaring in the second half of the poem?

17. *THE RUSSIAN PRIMARY CHRONICLE*

This source is a history of the eastern Slavic peoples known as Kievan Rus' from c. 850 to 1110. It is sometimes attributed to a monk of Kiev named Nestor (c. 1056–c. 1114). It is the main narrative source we have for the early history of eastern Slavic peoples. The goal of the source was to insert the eastern Slavs into universal history. Among its precious pieces of information is this account of their conversion to Christianity under Vladimir I of Kiev (r. 980–1015), however idealized it may be. The "Greeks" of the anecdote are the residents of the Byzantine Empire.

Source: ed. and trans. Samuel Hazzard Cross and Olgerd P. Sherbowitz-Wetzor, *The Russian Primary Chronicle: Laurentian Text* (Cambridge, MA: Medieval Academy of America, 1953), pp. 96–98, 110–13. Old East Slavic. Revised.

983. Vladimir [I] marched on the Yatvingians, conquered them, and seized their territory. He returned to Kiev, and together with his people made sacrifice to the idols. The elders and the boyars [nobles] then proposed that they should cast lots for a youth and a maiden, and sacrifice to the gods whomsoever the lot should fall upon.

Now there was a certain Varangian whose house was situated by the spot where now stands the Church of the Holy Virgin which Vladimir built. This Varangian had immigrated from Greece. He adhered to the Christian faith, and he had a son, fair in face and in heart, on whom, through the devil's hatred, the lot fell. For the devil, though he had dominion over all the rest, could not suffer this youth. He was like a thorn in the devil's heart, and the accursed one was eager to destroy him, and even aroused the people to that. Messengers thus came and said to the father, "Since the lot has fallen upon your son, the gods have claimed him as their own. Let us therefore make sacrifices to the gods." But the Varangian replied, "These are not gods, but only idols of wood. Today it is, and tomorrow it will rot away. These gods do not eat, or drink, or speak; they are fashioned by hand out of wood. But the God whom the Greeks serve and worship is one; it is he who has made heaven and earth, the stars, the moon, the sun, and mankind, and has granted him life upon earth. But what have these gods created? They are themselves manufactured. I will not give up my son to devils." So the messengers went back and reported to the people. The latter took up arms, marched against the Varangian and his son, and on breaking down the stockade about his house, found him standing with his son upon the porch. They then called upon him to surrender his son that they might offer him to the gods. But he replied, "If they be gods, they will send one of their number to take my son. What need have you of him?" They straightaway raised a shout, and broke up the structure under them. Thus the people killed them, and no one knows where they are buried.

For at this time the Russes were ignorant pagans. The devil rejoiced at that, for he did not know that his ruin was approaching. He was so eager to destroy the Christian people, yet he was expelled by the true cross even from these very lands. The accursed one thought to himself, "This is my habitation, a land where the apostles have not taught nor the prophets prophesied." He knew not that the prophet had said, "I will call those my people who are not my people" [Hosea 2:23]. Likewise it is written of the apostles, "Their message has gone out into all the earth and their words to the end of the world" [Psalm 19:5]. Though the apostles have not been there in person, their teachings resound like trumpets in the churches throughout the world. Through their instruction we overcome the hostile adversary, and trample him under our feet. For likewise did the holy fathers trample upon him, and they have received the heavenly crown in company with the holy martyrs and the just.

984. Vladimir attacked the Radimichians. His general was named Wolf's Tail, and Vladimir sent him on ahead. He met the Radimichians by the river Pishchan', and overcame them. Therefore the Russes ridiculed the Radimichians, saying that the men on the Pishchan' fled in the presence of a wolf's tail. Now the Radimichians belong to the race of the Lyakhs. They had come and settled in these regions, and pay tribute to the Russes, an obligation which they maintain to the present day.

985. Accompanied by his uncle Dobrynya, Vladimir set out by boat to attack the Bulgars. He also brought Turks overland on horseback, and conquered the Bulgars. Dobrynya remarked to Vladimir, "I have seen the prisoners, who all wear boots. They will not pay us tribute. Let us rather look for foes with bast shoes [made from tree bark]." So Vladimir made peace with the Bulgars, and they confirmed it by oath. The Bulgars declared, "May peace prevail between us until stone floats and straw sinks." Then Vladimir returned to Kiev.

986. Vladimir was visited by Bulgars of Muslim faith, who said, "Though you are a wise and prudent prince, you have no religion. Adopt our faith, and revere Muhammad." Vladimir inquired what was the nature of their religion. They replied that they believed in God, and that Muhammad instructed them to practice circumcision, to eat no pork, to drink no wine, and, after death, promised them complete fulfillment of their carnal desires. "Muhammad," they asserted, "will give each man seventy fair women. He may choose one fair one, and upon that woman will Muhammad confer the charms of them all, and she will be his wife. Muhammad promises that one may then satisfy every desire, but whoever is poor in this world will be no different in the next." They also spoke other false things which out of modesty may not be written down. Vladimir listened to them, for he was fond of women and indulgence, regarding which he heard with pleasure. But circumcision and abstinence from

pork and wine were disagreeable to him. "Drinking," said he, "is the joy of the Russes. We cannot exist without that pleasure."

Then came the Germans, asserting that they had come as emissaries of the pope. They added, "Thus says the pope: 'Your country is like our country, but your faith is not as ours. For our faith is the light. We worship God, who has made heaven and earth, the stars, the moon, and every creature, while your gods are only wood.'" Vladimir inquired what their teaching was. They replied, "Fasting according to one's strength. But whatever one eats or drinks is all to the glory of God, as our teacher Paul has said." Then Vladimir answered, "Depart from here; our fathers accepted no such principle."

The Jewish Khazars heard of these missions, and came themselves, saying, "We have learned that Bulgars and Christians came to here to instruct you in their faiths. The Christians believe in him whom we crucified, but we believe in the one God of Abraham, Isaac, and Jacob." Then Vladimir inquired what their religion was. They replied that its tenets included circumcision and not eating pork or hare, and observing the Sabbath. The prince then asked where their native land was, and they replied that it was in Jerusalem. When Vladimir inquired where that was, they made answer, "God was angry at our forefathers, and scattered us among the gentiles on account of our sins. Our land was then given to the Christians." The prince then demanded, "How can you hope to teach others while you yourselves are cast out and scattered abroad by the hand of God? If God loved you and your faith, you would not be thus dispersed in foreign lands. Do you expect us to accept that faith also?"

Then the Greeks sent to Vladimir a scholar, who spoke thus: "We have heard that the Bulgarians came and urged you to adopt their faith, which pollutes heaven and earth. They are accursed above all men, like Sodom and Gomorrah, upon which the Lord let fall burning stone, and which he buried and submerged. The day of destruction likewise awaits these men, on which the Lord will come to judge the earth, and to destroy all those who do evil and abomination. For they moisten their excrement, and pour the water into their mouths, and anoint their beards with it, remembering Muhammad. The women also perform this abomination, and even worse ones." Vladimir, upon hearing their statements, spat upon the earth, saying, "This is a vile thing."

Then the scholar said, "We have likewise heard how men came from Rome to convert you to their faith. It differs but little from ours, for they commune with wafers, called *oplatki*, which God did not give them, for he ordained that we should commune with bread. For when he had taken bread, the Lord gave it to his disciples, saying, 'This is my body broken for you.' Likewise he took the cup, and said, 'This is my blood of the New Testament.' They do not so act, for they have modified the faith." Then Vladimir remarked that the Jews had come into his presence and had stated that the Germans and the

Greeks believe in him whom they crucified. To this the scholar replied, "In truth we believe in him. For some of the prophets foretold that God should be incarnate, and others that he should be crucified and buried, but arise on the third day and ascend into heaven. For the Jews killed the prophets, and still others they persecuted. When their prophecy was fulfilled, our Lord came to earth, was crucified, rose again, and ascended into heaven. He awaited their repentance for forty-six years, but they did not repent, so that the Lord let loose the Romans upon them. Their cities were destroyed, and they were scattered among the gentiles, under whom they are now in servitude."

Vladimir then inquired why God should have descended to earth and should have endured such pain. The scholar answered and said, "If you are desirous of hearing the story, I will tell you from the beginning why God descended to earth." Vladimir replied, "Gladly would I hear it." Afterward the scholar thus began his narrative: "In the beginning, God created heaven and earth on the first day. . . ."

As he spoke thus, he exhibited to Vladimir a canvas on which was depicted the judgment day of the Lord, and showed him, on the right, the righteous going to their bliss in paradise, and on the left, the sinners on their way to torment. Then Vladimir sighed and said, "Happy are they on the right, but woe to those on the left!" The scholar replied, "If you desire to take your place on the right with the just, then accept baptism!" Vladimir took this counsel to heart, saying, "I will wait yet a little while longer," for he wished to inquire about all the faiths. Vladimir then gave the scholar many gifts, and dismissed him with great honor.

987. Vladimir then summoned together his boyars and the city elders and said to them, "Behold, the Bulgars came before me urging me to accept their religion. Then came the Germans and praised their own faith; and after them came the Jews. Finally the Greeks appeared, criticizing all other faiths but commending their own, and they spoke at length, telling the history of the whole world from its beginning. Their words were artful, and it was wondrous to listen and pleasant to hear them. They preach the existence of another world. 'Whoever adopts our religion and then dies will arise and live forever. But whosoever embraces another faith, will be consumed with fire in the next world.' What is your opinion on this subject, and what do you answer?" The boyars and the elders replied, "You know, oh Prince, that no man condemns his own possessions, but praises them instead. If you desire to make certain, you have servants at your disposal. Send them to inquire about the ritual of each and how he worships God."

Their counsel pleased the prince and all the people, so that they chose good and wise men to the number of ten, and directed them to go first among the Bulgars and inspect their faith. The emissaries went their way, and when they arrived at their destination they beheld the disgraceful actions of the Bulgars and their worship in the mosque; then they returned to their country. Vladimir then instructed them to go likewise among the Germans, and examine their faith, and finally to go visit the Greeks. Thus they went into Germany, and after viewing the German ceremonial, they proceeded to Tsar'grad, where they appeared before the emperor. He inquired on what mission they had come, and they reported to him all that had occurred. When the emperor heard their words, he rejoiced, and did them great honor on that very day.

On the next day, the emperor sent a message to the patriarch to inform him that a Russian delegation had arrived to examine the Greek faith, and directed him to prepare the church and the clergy, and to array himself in his sacerdotal robes, so that the Russes might behold the glory of the God of the Greeks. When the patriarch received these commands, he bade the clergy assemble, and they performed the customary rites. They burned incense, and the choirs sang hymns. The emperor accompanied the Russes to the church, and placed them in a wide space, calling their attention to the beauty of the edifice, the chanting, and the pontifical services and the ministry of the deacons, while he explained to them the worship of his God. The Russes were astonished, and in their wonder praised the Greek ceremonial. Then the emperors Basil [II, r. 976–1025] and Constantine [VIII, r. 962–1028] invited the envoys to their presence and said, "Go from here to your native country," and dismissed them with valuable presents and great honor.

Thus they returned to their own country, and the prince called together his boyars and the elders. Vladimir then announced the return of the envoys who had been sent out, and suggested that their report be heard. He thus commanded them to speak out before his retinue. The envoys reported, "When we journeyed among the Bulgars, we beheld how they worship in their temple, called a mosque, while they stand ungirt. The Bulgar bows, sits down, looks from one place to another like one possessed, and there is no happiness among them, but instead only sorrow and a dreadful stench. Their religion is not good. Then we went among the Germans, and saw them performing many ceremonies in their temples; but we beheld no glory there. Then we went to Greece, and the Greeks led us to the edifices where they worship their God, and we knew not whether we were in heaven or on earth. For on earth there is no such splendor or such beauty, and we are at a loss how to describe it. We know only that God dwells there among men, and their service is fairer than the ceremonies of other nations. For we cannot forget that beauty. Every man, after tasting something sweet, is unwilling to accept that which is bitter, and therefore we cannot dwell longer here." Then the boyars spoke and said, "If the Greek faith were evil, it would not have been adopted by your grandmother Olga [r. 945–960] who was wiser than all other men." Vladimir then inquired where they should all accept baptism, and they replied that the decision rested with him.

After a year had passed, in 6496 [988], Vladimir proceeded with an armed force against Cherson, a Greek city, and the people of Cherson barricaded themselves within. Vladimir halted at a farther side of the city beside the harbor, a bowshot from the town, and the inhabitants resisted energetically while Vladimir besieged the town. Eventually, however, they became exhausted, and Vladimir warned them that if they did not surrender, he would remain on the spot for three years. When they failed to heed this threat, Vladimir marshalled his troops and ordered the construction of an earthwork in the direction of the city. While this work was under construction, the inhabitants dug a tunnel under the city wall, stole the heaped-up earth, and carried it into the city, where they piled it up in the center of the town. But the soldiers kept on building, and Vladimir persisted. Then a man of Cherson, Anastasius by name, shot into the Russ camp an arrow on which he had written, "There are springs behind you to the east, from which water flows in pipes. Dig down and cut them off." When Vladimir received this information, he raised his eyes to heaven and vowed that if this hope was realized, he would be baptized. He gave orders straightaway to dig down above the pipes, and the water supply was thus cut off. The inhabitants were accordingly overcome by thirst, and surrendered.

Vladimir and his retinue entered the city, and he sent messages to the emperors Basil and Constantine, saying, "Behold, I have captured your glorious city. I have also heard that you have an unwedded sister. Unless you give her to me as a wife, I will deal with your own city as I have with Cherson." When the emperors heard this message, they were troubled, and replied, "It is not fitting for Christians to 'give' in marriage to pagans. If you are baptized, you will have her as a wife, inherit the kingdom of God, and be our companion in the faith. Unless you do so, however, we cannot give you our sister in marriage."

When Vladimir learned their response, he directed the envoys of the emperors to report to the latter that he was willing to accept baptism, having already given some study to their religion, and that the Greek faith and ritual, as described by the emissaries sent to examine it, had pleased him well. When the emperors heard this report, they rejoiced, and persuaded their sister Anna to consent to the match. They then requested Vladimir to submit to baptism before they should send their sister to him, but Vladimir desired that the princess should herself bring priests to baptize him. The emperors complied with his request, and sent forth their sister, accompanied by some dignitaries and priests. Anna, however, departed with reluctance. "It is as if I were setting out into captivity," she lamented; "better were it for me to die at home." But her brothers protested, "Through your agency God turns the land of Rus' to repentance, and you will relieve Greece from the danger of grievous war. Do you not see how much harm the Russes have already brought upon the Greeks? If you do not set out, they may bring on us the same misfortunes." It was thus that they overcame her hesitation only with great difficulty. The princess embarked upon a ship, and after tearfully embracing her kinfolk, she set forth across the sea and arrived at Cherson. The natives came forth to greet her, and conducted her into the city, where they settled her in the palace.

By divine agency, Vladimir was suffering at that moment from a disease of the eyes, and could see nothing, being in great distress. The princess declared to him that if he desired to be relieved of this disease, he should be baptized with all due speed, otherwise it could not be cured. When Vladimir heard her message, he said, "If this proves true, then surely is the God of the Christians great," and gave order that he should be baptized. The bishop of Cherson, together with the princess's priests, after announcing the tidings, baptized Vladimir, and as the bishop laid his hand upon him, he straightaway received his sight. Upon experiencing this miraculous cure, Vladimir glorified God, saying, "I have now perceived the one true God." When his followers beheld this miracle, many of them were also baptized.

Questions: What was the attitude of eastern Slavic peoples to Christianity at the beginning of the story? How do the various missionaries who come to Vladimir I attempt to pitch their religions to him, and what did he find disagreeable about what he heard? How did the emissaries that Vladimir I sent out inform them about their religious options? What finally convinced the eastern Slavs to convert to the Byzantine form of Christianity? How did military expeditions and conquest figure into the story as a whole?

18. *LIFE OF SAINT CHRISTOPHER*

This saint's life was included in The Golden Legend, *a vast compendium of biographies of holy Christians completed in c. 1265, and one of the best sellers of the Middle Ages. The subject of this life is Saint Christopher, whom medieval Christians venerated as a third-century martyr; however, serious doubts have now been raised as to whether he existed at all. Saint Christopher was said to protect people against an untimely death. Because this fate was particularly relevant to travelers, he would in time become the patron saint of travelers, and his image was reproduced popularly so that people could pray to him.*

Source: trans. John F. Romano, Jacobus de Voragine, *Legenda aurea: Vulgo historia Lombardica dicta*, ed. Johann Georg Theodor Graesse (Dresden; Leipzig: Arnold, 1846), pp. 430–34. Latin.

Before his baptism Christopher was called Reprobus [the reject], but afterward he was called Christopher, as it were "the one bearing Christ," which applied to him because he carried Christ in four ways—that is, on his shoulders by transporting [him], in his body by mortification, in his mind by devotion, in his mouth by his confession and preaching.

Christopher by birth was a Canaanite; he was of very great size and he had a dreadful face and he measured twelve cubits in height. In some accounts of his deeds it is told that when he was with a certain king of the Canaanites, the idea came to him to look for the greatest ruler who was in the world and to become his servant to reside with him. So he came to a great king, who enjoyed widespread fame, so that the world had no greater ruler. The king upon seeing him received him willingly and had him stay at his court.

But one day a jester in the presence of the king sang a song, in which the devil was frequently named. As the king was a Christian, whenever he heard the devil named, immediately he made the sign of the cross on his forehead. Seeing this, Christopher marveled greatly at why the king had made it and what this kind of sign meant.

When, however, he questioned the king about this matter, and he did not want to explain it to him, Christopher responded: "Unless you tell me, I won't stay with you any longer." Compelled, the king told him: "Whenever I hear the devil named, by this sign I protect myself, fearing that he may gain power over me and harm me." To this Christopher [responded]: "If you fear that the devil may harm you, then it is exposed that he is greater and more powerful than you, since it has been shown that you dread him so! So I am frustrated in my hope, thinking that I had found the greatest and most powerful lord in the world. But now farewell, because I want to look for this devil to take him as a lord and to become his servant."

So he withdrew from the king and rushed to look for the devil. And when he traveled through a wilderness, he saw a great multitude of knights. One savage and dreadful knight came to him and asked where he was traveling. To which Christopher responded: "I'm going around to look for the lord devil, so that I may take him as a lord." To which he [the devil] responded: "I'm the one you are looking for." Rejoicing, Christopher committed himself to his perpetual service and accepted him as his lord.

When they both were traveling together on a common road, they found a cross standing upright. As soon as the devil saw the cross, he fled in terror. He left the road, led Christopher through a harsh wilderness, and afterward led him back to the road. Christopher saw this and marveled, and asked him why was he afraid enough to leave the level road and to take a long detour through such a harsh wilderness. When he absolutely did not wish to disclose this, Christopher said: "Unless you tell me, I will at once withdraw from you." Thus compelled, the devil said to him: "A man called Christ was crucified. When I see his sign of the cross, I am petrified and I flee in terror." To this

Christopher [responded]: "So this Christ, whose sign you dread so much, is greater and more powerful than you? So I have labored in vain and I still have not found the greatest ruler in the world. Now farewell, because I want to leave you and search for Christ himself."

So when he had long looked for someone to make Christ known to him, he finally came upon a hermit who preached Christ. And he [the hermit] instructed him diligently in his faith and the hermit said to Christopher: "This king whom you wish to serve requires this service: you must fast frequently." To this Christopher [responded]: "Let him ask for another service from me, because I can't do that thing." The hermit again: "You must also say many prayers." To this Christopher [responded]: "I don't know what that is, and I can't perform that kind of service." To this the hermit [responded]: "Do you know that notorious river where many people put their lives in danger and perish while crossing?" To which Christopher [responded]: "I know [it]." And he [the hermit]: "Since you are of great size and you have a strong body, if you stay next to that river and help everyone across, it will be something very pleasing to the king Christ, whom you desire to serve. And I hope that he will reveal himself there." To this Christopher [responded]: "Certainly I am able to do this service and I promise to serve him in this way."

So he arrived at the aforementioned river and there he built a house. And he carried in his hands a long pole instead of a walking stick, which held him up in the water. And he carried all people across without ceasing. When, after many days had passed, he was resting in his little house, he heard the voice of a child calling to him and saying: "Christopher, come out and bring me across." Christopher leapt up in a rush, but he found no one, and returning to his aforementioned little house, he heard again the voice calling for him. He again ran out and found no one. The third time, after having been called by the same one as before, he went out and found a child next to the riverbank, and he asked Christopher resolutely to carry him across. So Christopher, lifting the child on his shoulders and taking up his staff, entered the river to cross it. And see! the water of the river swelled gradually and the weight of the child became oppressive like lead, and however further he went on, the greater the waves grew and the child pressed down more and more with an intolerable weight on Christopher's shoulders, to the point that he found himself in great anguish and dreaded that his life was in danger.

Having barely evaded [death] and crossed the river, he set the child on the bank and said to him: "Child, you put me in great danger, and you weighed so much that if I had the entire world on me, it could hardly have felt like a greater weight." To which the child responded: "Do not marvel, Christopher, because you have not only had the entire world on you, but you also carried him who created the world on your shoulders. I am Christ your king, whom you serve in this work, and to show that I am telling the truth, when you cross over, plant your staff in the ground next to your little house, and in the morning you will see that it already flourished and bore fruit." And at once he vanished from sight. So coming [there], Christopher planted his staff in the ground, and rising in the morning, he found it bearing fronds and dates like a palm tree.

Now after this he came to Samos, a city of Lycia, where since he did not understand the language, he prayed to the Lord that he might be granted understanding of their language. When he was immersed in prayer, the judges left him alone, thinking him insane. But when he attained what he asked for, he, covering his face, came to "the place of battle" [1 Samuel 14:20, 17:22], and he comforted the Christians and those who were being tortured in the [name of the] Lord. Then one of the judges struck him in his face, at which Christopher, uncovering his face, said: "If I were not a Christian, I would immediately avenge my injury." Then Christopher planted his rod into the ground and he prayed to the Lord that it grow leaves to cause the conversion of the people. When this immediately came to pass, eight thousand men believed [in Jesus]. But the king sent two hundred knights to bring him [Christopher] to him, and when they found him praying and they were afraid to inform him [Christopher] of this. Again he sent just as many, and they also immediately prayed with the one in prayer. Getting up, Christopher said to them: "Who are you looking for?" Upon seeing his face, they said: "The king sent us to bring you chained to him." To them Christopher [responded]: "If I did [not] want [to go], you would not be able to take [me], either free or bound." They said to him: "So if you don't want to, go free, wherever you want, and we will tell the king that we didn't find you." "Let's not," he said, "but I'll go with you." Now he converted them to the faith and had them bind his hands behind his back and brought him before the king chained.

When the king saw him he was terrified and immediately fell from his throne. Then having been lifted up by his servants, he questioned him about his name and his homeland. To which Christopher [responded]: "Before my baptism, I was called Reprobus, but now I am called Christopher." To this the king [responded]: "You have been given a stupid name, that is of Christ crucified, who neither helped himself nor will he be able to help you. So now, damned Canaanite, why don't you sacrifice to our gods?" To this Christopher [responded]: "Rightly you are called 'Dagnus,' because you are the death of the world, the devil's companion. Your gods are the works of human hands." To which the king [responded]: "You were raised among wild animals and you can only [do] savage works and speak strange things to men. So now if you will sacrifice, you will attain great honors from me, but if you do not, you will be destroyed by tortures!"

So with [Christopher] not wanting to sacrifice, [the king] commanded that he be put in jail. And he had the knights who had been sent to Christopher beheaded because of the name of Christ. Then he had two beautiful young women, one of whom was named Nicaea and the other Aquilina, shut up with him in the jail, promising them many gifts if they lured him [Christopher] into sin. Upon seeing this Christopher immediately devoted himself to prayer. But when he was threatened by their groping and embraces, he rose and said to them: "What are you looking for and for what reason were you sent in here?" But they, terrified by the brightness of his face, said: "Have mercy on us, saint of God, so we may be able to believe in the God you preach."

Upon hearing this, the king had them brought to him and he said: "So you have been seduced too? I swear by the gods, that, unless you sacrifice to the gods, you will perish by an evil death." They responded: "If you want us to sacrifice, command the streets to be cleaned and that everyone assemble at the temple." After this was done, they entered the temple, and loosening their belts, they put them around the necks of the gods, and dragging them shamefully to the ground, they shattered into dust. And they said to the witnesses: "Go and call doctors to heal your gods." Then at the command of the king Aquilina was hanged and a huge stone was tied to her feet so that all her limbs were broken. After she departed to the Lord, her sister Nicaea was thrown into the fire, but she emerged from it unscathed; immediately she was beheaded.

So afterward Christopher was brought before the king, who commanded that he be beaten with iron rods and a fiery hot iron helmet be placed on his head. Then he had an iron seat made and Christopher was bound to it, and it was set on fire by throwing pitch on it. But the seat crumbled like wax and Christopher emerged unscathed. Then he ordered that he be bound to a stake and shot with arrows by four hundred soldiers. But all of the arrows were suspended in midair and none of them could hit him. But when the king, thinking that he had been shot with the arrows by the soldiers, mocked him, right away one of the arrows came from midair and turned itself around. It hit the king in the eye and immediately blinded him. To this Christopher [responded]: "Tomorrow my time will be at an end. So you, tyrant, may make paste from my blood and rub it on your eyes, and you will recover your health." Then at the command of the king he was led off to be beheaded and while he was pouring out prayers there, he was beheaded. But the king took a little of his blood and put it on his eye, and he said: "In the name of God and of Saint Christopher," and instantly he was healed. Then the king believed, issuing the command that if anyone blasphemed against Saint Christopher, instantly he would be killed with the sword.

Now Ambrose in his preface had this to say about this martyr: "Lord, you bestowed such a great amount of virtue and the grace of teaching on Christopher so that by heavenly miracles you revived forty-eight thousand men from the error of paganism to the reverence of Christian doctrine. He also encouraged Nicaea and Aquilina who for a long time were working at a public brothel in filthy prostitution to a way of life of chastity and taught them to receive the crown [of martyrdom]. Because of this, having been restrained in an iron seat among funerary flames, he did not fear the excessive heat and for an entire day he could not be pierced by the arrows of all of the soldiers. Another one of them struck the eye of the executioner, who however having mixed the blood of the martyr with earth, restored his sight. And having removed the blindness of the body, it also gave light to his mind. For he was granted grace in your sight and he humbly obtained the ability to drive away sicknesses and weaknesses."

Questions: What different kinds of missions does Christopher have in this biography, and why is travel an important aspect of his story? Which of his journeys shaped the holy person he would become? Is it fair to say that Christopher's form of religiosity was more physical than intellectual? Why or why not? To what degree do you think this account is more mythical than historical?

19. BENEDICT THE POLE, *NARRATIVE*

Benedict (c. 1200–1280) was a Franciscan friar who from 1245 to 1247 accompanied a fellow Franciscan, John of Plano Carpini, on an extensive journey to the court of the great khan of the Mongols. The two were emissaries of Pope Innocent IV, who held out hope of converting the Mongols to Christianity and enlisting them as allies. Historians know little about Benedict aside from what he reveals in this travelogue. Franciscans and other late-medieval religious orders such as Dominicans were not bound to monasteries and were accustomed to making journeys to serve as diplomats or preach Christianity, among other reasons.

Source: Benedict the Pole, "Narrative," in *The Mission to Asia: Narratives and Letters of the Franciscan Missionaries in Mongolia and China in the Thirteenth and Fourteenth Centuries*, ed. Christopher Dawson (London: Sheed & Ward, 1980), pp. 79–84. Latin. Revised.

In the year of our Lord 1245 Brother John of the Order of Friars Minor [Franciscans], named of Plano Carpini, was sent to the Tartars [Mongols] by the lord pope, with another brother of the same order, and leaving Lyons in Gaul where the pope was, he went to Poland and there at Vratislavia [modern Wrocław] took a third brother of the same order, named Benedict, a Pole by race, to be his interpreter and the companion of his labor and cares.

With the help of Conrad, duke of the Poles, they reached Kiev, a city of Russia, which is now under the Tartar yoke, and the rulers of the city gave them guides for six days' journey to the Tartar frontier guard on the borders of the Coman country.

When the captains of this frontier guard heard that they were envoys of the pope, they asked and received presents, and the two friars John and Benedict left their companion, who was sick, with the horses and servants that they had brought with them, and were taken on horses provided by the Tartars with their baggage to the second camp.

And so by many camps and changes of horses, they came on the third day to the general of an army, who was in command of 8,000 troops, and when his servants had asked and received gifts they took them to their commander, Corenza. He inquired of them the cause of their journey and the nature of their business, and on learning this, he sent them three Tartars from his following so that they should have horses and provisions from one army to another until they came to Batu [Khan, r. 1227–1255], who is one of the great princes of the Tartars and the one who laid waste Hungary.

On their way they crossed the rivers Nepere [Dnieper] and Don, and they spent five weeks and more on this journey—that is, from the first Sunday in Lent [5 March] to Maundy Thursday [13 April], when they reached Batu, finding him on the great river Ethil which the Russians call the Volga, and which is supposed to be the Thanais.

And when the servants of Batu received the presents that they demanded, namely 40 beaver skins and 80 badger skins, they carried them between the two sacred fires, and the friars were obliged to do likewise, since it is the custom of the Tartars to purify envoys and presents by fire. Beyond the fires there stood a chariot bearing a golden statue of the emperor, which also it is their custom to worship. But as the friars utterly refused to do so they were only compelled to bow their heads.

When Batu had heard the pope's letters and examined them word by word, after five days, that is, on the Tuesday after Easter [18 April], he sent the friars with his own litters and the same Tartar guides as before to the son of the great emperor, whose name is Güyük Khan [r. 1246–1248], in the native land of the Tartars.

And so they were dismissed by Prince Batu and, binding their limbs with bandages to bear the strain of continual riding, they left the land of the Comans after two weeks. This is the land which was once named Pontus and in it there is a great deal of wormwood, as Ovid remarks in his epistles: "The bitter wormwood shivers in the endless plains."

Now as the friars traversed Comania they had on their right the land of the Saxi, whom we believe to be Goths and who are Christians: next the Alans who are Christians and then the Guzari [Khazars] who are likewise Christian.

In their country is situated Ornas, a rich city which the Tartars captured by flooding it with water. After, the Circassians, and they are Christians. And finally the Georgians, also Christians.

Before this in Russia, they had the Mordvins, who are pagans and have the greater part of the back of their heads shorn. Then the Bylers who are pagan, then the Bascards [Bashkirs] who are the ancient Hungarians, then the dog-headed cynocephali, then the parocitae, who have such small and narrow mouths that they cannot chew anything solid but take liquids, and inhale the steam of meat and fruit.

On the frontier of Comania, they crossed a river named Yaralk [Yaik or Ural] where the land of the Kangites begins. Through this country they rode for 20 days, finding few men, but many marshes and saltings and salt rivers, which we believe to be the Meotide swamps; moreover, for eight days they traversed a vast desert sandy and parched with drought.

After the land of the Kangites they reached Turkey [Turkestan] where they found for the first time a large city—Yankint—and they traveled through Turkey for about ten days. Now Turkey follows the law of Muhammad. After Turkey they entered a land which is called Kara Kitai—that is to say Black Cathay—and the inhabitants are pagans and they found no city there, but they found a sea on their left hand which we believe to be the Caspian. After this they entered the land of the Naimans who were once lords of the Tartars and here also they found no villages or cities. Finally they entered the land of the Tartars on the Feast of Mary Magdalene [22 July], when they found the emperor at a great encampment which is called Syra Orda. Here they stayed four months and were present at the election of Güyük Khan their emperor.

And the same Brother Benedict the Pole related to us by word of mouth how they had both seen about 5,000 princes and great men who were all clad in cloth of gold on the first day when they assembled for the election of the king. But neither on that day, nor on the next when they appeared in white samite, did they come to an agreement. But on the third day, when they wore red samite, they reached agreement and made the election. Moreover, the same brother affirms that there were about 3,000 ambassador envoys from different parts of the world present, bringing letters, answers, and every kind of tribute and gifts to the court. And among them were the aforesaid friars who wore brocade over their habit as needs must, for no envoy is allowed to see the face of the elect and crowned king, unless he is correctly dressed.

Accordingly they were admitted to the Syra Orda which is the emperor's abode, and saw him wearing his crown and shining in splendid robes. He was sitting in the midst of the tent on a dais richly ornamented with gold and silver and with a canopy over it. There were four separate sets of steps leading up to this dais. Three of them were in front, one in the middle by which the emperor alone went up and down, and two at the sides for the grandees and lesser men, while by the fourth flight, which was at the back, his mother and his wife and family used to ascend. Likewise, the Syra Orda had three entrances, like doors, and the one in the middle, which is the largest and far exceeds the others, always stands open without any guard, for the king alone goes in and out by it, and if anyone else were to enter by it he would be slain without mercy. But the two side doors were closed with bars, and have most severe guards keeping watch with arms, and through these, men enter with awe for fear of the appointed penalty.

On the third day the mission of the lord pope was heard after discussion and deliberation through the official and interpreters, and afterward the friars were sent to the emperor's mother whom they found in another place, also sitting in a great and very fair tent. And she treated them with great courtesy and friendliness and sent them back to her son.

While they were staying there they often met Georgians who lived among the Tartars and were highly respected by them as brave and warlike men. These people are called Georgians because they invoke Saint George in their wars and have him as patron and honor him beyond all other saints. They use the Greek version of holy scripture and have crosses on their camps and their carts. They follow the Greek rites in divine worship among the Tartars.

And so when the business on which they had come had been completed the friars were sent back by the emperor to carry letters to the lord pope signed under his own seal. They set out westwards with the envoys of the sultan of Babylon [Baghdad], and when they had traveled together for 15 days, the envoys turned southwards and left them. But the friars traveled on to the west, and after crossing the Rhine at Cologne they returned to the lord pope at Lyons and presented to him the letters of the emperor of the Tartars, the purport of which according to the Latin translation that was made is as follows:

The Strength of God, the Emperor of All Men, to the Great Pope, Authentic and True Letters

Having taken counsel for making peace with us, you pope and all Christians have sent an envoy to us, as we have heard from him and as your letters declare. Therefore, if you wish to have peace with us, you pope and all kings and potentates, in no way delay to come to me and make terms of peace and then you will hear alike our answer and our will. The contents of your letters stated that we ought to be baptized and become Christians. To this we answer briefly that we do not understand in what way we ought to do this. To the rest of the contents of your letters, that is: that you wonder at so great a slaughter of men, especially of Christians and in particular Poles, Moravians, and Hungarians, we reply likewise that this also we do not understand. However, that we may not seem to pass it over in silence altogether, we give you this for our answer.

Because they did not obey the word of God and the command of Genghis Khan [r. 1206–1227] and the khan, but took council to slay our envoys, therefore God ordered us to destroy them and gave them up into our hands. For otherwise if God had not done this, what could man do to man? But you men of the west believe that you alone are Christians and despise others. But how can you know to whom God deigns to confer his grace? But we worshipping God have destroyed the whole earth from the east to the west in the power of God. And if this were not the power of God, what could men have done? Therefore if you accept peace and are willing to surrender your fortresses to us, you pope and Christian princes, in no way delay coming to me to conclude peace and then we will know that you wish to have peace with us. But if you should not believe our letters and the command of God nor hearken to our counsel then we will know for certain that you wish to have war. After that we do not know what will happen, God alone knows.

Genghis Khan, first Emperor, second Ögedei Khan [r. 1229–1241], third Güyük Khan.

Questions: How would you describe the reception by the Mongols of Benedict and his companion? How dependent were they on presenting gifts to continue their travel? What hints about Benedict's feelings about this journey do we get in his report? What can this source tell us about the Mongols and other people of central Asia at the time when it was written? What kind of response did the pope receive when he invited the Mongol leader to convert to Christianity?

20. PASCAL DE VITORIA, *LETTER*

Like Benedict the Pole, Pascal (late thirteenth century—c. 1339/40) was also a Franciscan friar who traveled deep into the territory dominated by Mongols, although Pascal was more singularly devoted to missionary labors. Virtually nothing about his life is known apart from what is preserved in this letter. He may have originated from Spain, where he sent this letter. He would be killed around a year after having composed this letter. Here Pascal referred alternatively to Muslims as "Saracens" and "Hagarenes," both intended as negative terms.

Source: trans. Henry Yule, Pascal de Vitoria, "Letter," in *Cathay and the Way Thither*, vol. 1 (London: Hakluyt Society, 1866), pp. 231–37. Latin. Revised.

Letter from Pascal de Vitoria, a missionary Franciscan in Mongolia, to his brethren of the Convent of Vitoria [in Spain], 1338.

Dearly beloved fathers, your sanctities are aware that when I left you I proceeded to Avignon in company with the dear father Friar Gonsalvo Transtorna. From there we went, with the blessing of the reverend the general, to get the benefit of the indulgence at Assisi; and after that we embarked at Venice on board a certain carrack, and sailed down the Adriatic Sea. We next sailed through the sea of Portus, leaving Sclavonia to the left and Turkey to the right, and landed in Greece at Galata near Constantinople, where we found the father vicar of Cathay [northern China] in the vicariat of the east. Then, embarking on another vessel, we sailed across the Black Sea, whose depth is unfathomable, to Gazaria in the vicariat of the north, and in the empire of the Tartars [the Mongol empire]. Then traversing another sea which has no bottom, we landed at Tana [modern Azov].

And having got there sooner than my comrade, I found my way with some Greeks by wagons as far as Sarai; while my comrade, with some other friars, was carried on further to Urghandj [modern Khiva]. I was willing enough to go with him, but after taking counsel on the matter, I determined first to learn the language of the country. And by God's help I did learn the Chamanian [Cuman] language, and the Uigurian [Uyghur] character; which language and character are commonly used throughout all those kingdoms or empires of the Tartars, Persians, Chaldaeans, Medes, and of Cathay. My comrade turned back from Urghandj and went to you again. But I could not bear to return, like a dog to his vomit, and I was desirous to obtain the grace conceded by his holiness the pope, so I would not turn back. For you must know that all of us friars who come into these parts have the same privileges as those who go with license to Jerusalem; that is to say, the fullest indulgence both from punishment and from guilt, and those who persevere to the end, a crown of life.

Therefore, my fathers, from the time when I had acquired the language, by the grace of God I often preached without an interpreter both to the Saracens and to the schismatic and heretical Christians. I then received a mandate from my vicar to the effect that on receipt of his letter I should in salutary obedience to him, as in duty bound, proceed to finish the journey which I had commenced.

I had now been staying more than a year in the aforesaid Sarai, a city of the Saracens of the Tartar empire, in the vicariat of the north, where three years before a certain friar of ours, Stephen by name, suffered honorable martyrdom at the hands of the Saracens. Embarking on a certain vessel with some Armenians, I departed from there by the river called the Volga, and then along the shore of the sea which is called the Caspian, until I came in twelve days' travel to Saray-Jük. From that place I got on a cart drawn by camels (for to ride those animals is something terrible), and on the fiftieth day reached Urghanj, which

is a city at the extremity of the empire of the Tartars and the Persians. The city
is otherwise called Hus, and the body of the blessed Job is there.

From there I again mounted a camel cart, and traveled with a party of
accursed Hagarenes and followers of Muhammad, I being the only Christian
among them, with a certain servant called Zinguo, until by God's grace we
reached the empire of the Medes [Transoxiana]. What my sufferings have
been there, how many and how great, God himself knows, and it would be
a long story to tell in a letter. However, the emperor of the Tartars had been
slain by his natural brother, and the caravan of Saracens with which I traveled was detained by the way in the cities of the Saracens, for fear of war and
plunder.

Hence I was long tarrying among the Saracens, and I preached to them
for several days openly and publicly the name of Jesus Christ and his Gospel.
I opened out and laid bare the cheats, falsehoods, and blunders of their false
prophet [Muhammad]; with a loud voice, and in public, I did confound their
barkings; and trusting in our Lord Jesus Christ I was not much afraid of them,
but received from the Holy Spirit comfort and light. They treated me civilly
and set me in front of their mosque during their Easter [Eid al-Fitr]; at which
mosque, on account of its being their Easter, there were assembled from diverse
quarters a number of their *cadini*, that is, of their bishops [really judges], and of
their *talisimani*, that is, of their priests [scholars?]. And guided by the teaching
of the Holy Spirit I disputed with them in that same place before the mosque,
on theology, and regarding their false Alchoran [Qur'an] and its doctrine, for
five-and-twenty days; and in fact I was barely able once a day to snatch a meal
of bread and water.

But by the grace of God the doctrine of the holy Trinity was disclosed
and preached to them, and at last even they, in spite of their reluctance, had
to admit its truth; and, thanks be to the almighty God, I carried off the victory on all points, to the praise and honor of Jesus Christ and of holy mother
Church. And then these children of the devil tried to tempt and pervert me
with bribes, promising me wives and handmaidens, gold and silver and lands,
horses and cattle, and other delights of this world. But when in every way I
rejected their promises with scorn, then for two days together they pelted me
with stones, besides putting fire to my face and my feet, plucking out my beard,
and heaping upon me for a length of time all kinds of insult and abuse. God,
who is blessed, through whom I am poor, rejoicing and exulting in our Lord
Jesus Christ, knows that it is by his marvelous compassion alone I have been
judged worthy to bear such things for his name.

And now I have been graciously brought to Alimali [modern Korgas], a
city in the midst of the land of the Medes, in the vicariat of Cathay. And thus,
beginning at Urghandj, which is the last city of the Persians and Tartars, all the

way to Alimali, I was constantly alone among the Saracens, but by word and act and dress, publicly bore the name of the Lord Jesus Christ. And by those Saracens I have often been offered poison; I have been cast into the water; I have suffered blows and other injuries more than I can tell in a letter. But I give thanks to God for all things, because I expect to suffer still greater things for his name, for the forgiveness of my sins, and that I may safely reach the kingdom of heaven through his mercy. Amen!

Farewell in the Lord Jesus Christ, and pray for me, and for those who are engaged, or intend to be engaged, on missionary pilgrimages; for by God's help such pilgrimages are very profitable, and bring in a harvest of many souls. Do not worry then about seeing me again, unless it is in these regions, or in that paradise where is our rest and comfort and refreshment and heritage, even the Lord Jesus Christ.

And for that he has said that when the Gospel will have been preached throughout the whole world, then will the end come, it is for me to preach among diverse nations, to show sinners their guilt, and to declare the way of salvation, but it is for God almighty to pour into their souls the grace of conversion.

Dated at Alimali, on the feast of Saint Lawrence [10 August], AD 1338, in the empire of the Medes.

Questions: What did Pascal think about the Muslim religion and other Christian groups? How did he attempt to convert Muslims to his belief? What preparation was necessary before he could carry out his missionary work? According to Pascal, how was his message received? Was Pascal seeking martyrdom, that is, to be killed for his beliefs? Was he more interested in travel to the afterlife or travel on earth?

21. *THE BOOK OF MARGERY KEMPE*

Margery Kempe (c. 1393–after 1439) was an English mystic whose piety often involved heightened displays such as bursting into tears, which contemporaries sometimes criticized as exhibitionism. Unusually, Kempe came to a life dedicated to religion not as a nun, but after having been married and borne fourteen children. Her public preaching sometimes raised suspicions of heresy. Among Kempe's religious exercises were pilgrimages to many of the popular sites of her day, including Canterbury, Santiago de Compostela, Rome, and Jerusalem. We know about Kempe's activities from her autobiography, which was dictated in English to a priest and preserved in a single manuscript. Throughout she refers to herself in the third person.

Source: ed. and trans. John Shinners, Margery Kempe, "The Book of Margery Kempe," in *Medieval Popular Religion, 1000–1500: A Reader*, 2nd ed. (Peterborough, ON; Orchard Park, NY: Broadview, 2007), pp. 204–10. Middle English.

28. Also this company [of pilgrims], which had forbidden the aforesaid creature [Margery] to eat at the same table with them, hired a ship for them to sail in [to Jerusalem]. They bought containers for their wine and ordered bedding for themselves but nothing for her. Seeing their unkindness, she went to the same man they did and purchased bedding as they had done. She went to where they were and showed them what she had done, proposing that she sail with them in the ship they had hired. Then, while this creature was in contemplation, our Lord warned her mentally that she should not sail in that ship; he assigned her another ship, a galley, to sail in. She told this to some of the company and they told it to the rest of the band, who then dared not sail in the ship they had hired. So they sold the vessels they had bought for their wine and wanted to travel in the galley where she was. Though it was against her will, she departed accompanied by them, for they dared not do otherwise.

When it was time to make her bed, they had locked up her bed linens and a priest in their company took a sheet from the creature, saying it was his. She took God as her witness that it was her sheet. Then the priest swore a great oath by the book in his hand that she was as false as she could be, and scorned her, and thoroughly rebuked her. So she suffered very much tribulation until she came to Jerusalem. Before she arrived there, she said to them that she supposed they were annoyed with her: "I pray you, sirs, be in charity with me, for I am in charity with you, and forgive me that I have annoyed you along the way. And if any of you has trespassed against me in any way, may God forgive you as I do." And so they went forth into the Holy Land until they could see Jerusalem [in the summer of 1414].

And when, riding on an ass, this creature saw Jerusalem, she thanked God with all her heart, praying to him for his mercy that, as he had brought her to see this earthly Jerusalem, he would grant her the grace to see the blissful city of Jerusalem above, the city of heaven. Our Lord Jesus Christ, answering her thought, granted her desire. Then, out of the joy she had and the sweetness she felt from her conversation with our Lord, she was on the point of falling off her ass, for she could not bear the sweetness and the grace God wrought in her soul. Then two German pilgrims, one of them a priest, went up to her and kept her from falling off. The priests put spices in her mouth to comfort her, thinking that she was sick. And so they helped her on the way to Jerusalem.

When she arrived there she said, "Sirs, I ask you not to be displeased if I weep terribly in this holy place where our Lord Jesus Christ lived and died." Then they went to the Temple [the Church of the Holy Sepulcher] in Jerusalem and were let in late in the day at evensong and stayed there until the next day at evensong. Then the [custodian Franciscan] friars lifted up a cross and led the pilgrims around from one place to another where our Lord had suffered his pains and his passion, all the men and women carrying candles in their hands. As they went about, the friars always told them what our Lord had suffered in each place. The aforesaid creature wept and sobbed copiously as though she was seeing our Lord with her own eyes suffering his passion right there. Through contemplation, in her soul she truly saw him, which caused her to suffer with him.

When they came to Mount Calvary, she fell down unable to stand or kneel, but she wallowed and writhed with her body, spreading her arms wide and crying with a loud voice as though her heart would burst asunder—for in the city of her soul she saw truly and freshly how our Lord was crucified. Before her face she heard and saw with her spiritual vision the mourning of our Lady [Mary], Saint John, Mary Magdalene, and many others who loved our Lord. She had such great compassion and such great pain to see our Lord's pain that she could not keep herself from crying and howling even if it killed her.

This was the first time that she ever cried during contemplation, and this kind of crying lasted many years afterward no matter what anyone might do. Thus, she suffered much scorn and reproof. Her crying was so loud and so awful that it astonished people unless they had heard it before or else knew its cause. She had [these crying spells] so often that they left her quite weak physically, especially if she heard [stories] of our Lord's passion. Sometimes, when she saw the crucifix, or if she saw a wounded man or beast, or if a man beat a child in front of her or hit a horse or other animal with a whip—whether in the field or in town, alone or among people—when she saw or heard it, she thought she saw our Lord being beaten or wounded like the man or the animal. When she first had her crying spells in Jerusalem she had them often, and in Rome too. After she came home to England, when she first arrived they seldom happened—once a month as it were; then, once a week; later, daily; and once she had fourteen in one day, and another day she had seven. And so God would visit her, sometimes in the church, sometimes in the street, sometimes in her room, sometimes in the field God would send them. For she never knew the time or hour when they would come. . . .

She had such intense contemplation in her mind's eye [on Mount Calvary], it was as if Christ were hanging before her eyes in his manhood. When, through the dispensation of the high mercy of our sovereign savior Christ Jesus, it was granted this creature to behold so realistically his precious, tender body altogether rent and torn with scourges, more full of wounds than ever was a dovecote full of holes, hanging upon the cross with the crown of thorns upon his head, his blessed hands, his tender feet nailed to the hard tree, the rivers of blood flowing copiously out of every member, the grisly and grievous wound in his precious side shedding out blood and water for her love and salvation, then she fell down and cried with loud voice, wondrously turning and twisting her body on every side, spreading her arms wide as if she would have died, and could not keep from crying—these physical movements done for the fire of love that burned so fervently in her soul with pure pity and compassion.

It is no marvel if this creature cried and showed an astonishing demeanor and expression when we may see each day men and women—some through friendships, through too much study or earthly affection, and most of all through inordinate love and physical affection—if their friends are parted from them, they will cry and howl and wring their hands as if they had lost their wits and minds, yet they know well enough that they displease God. And if someone counsels them to cease and desist their weeping or crying, they will say that they cannot: they loved their friend so much, and he was so gentle and kind to them that they cannot forget him. How much more would they weep, cry, and howl if their most beloved friends were taken with violence before their eyes, and with all kinds of reproof brought before a judge, wrongfully condemned to death—namely, so vicious a death as our merciful Lord suffered for our sake? How would they endure it? No doubt they would both cry and howl and avenge him if they could, or else men would say they were no friends. Alas, alas, how sad that the death of a creature which has often sinned and trespassed against its Maker should be so disproportionately mourned and grieved over. It is an offense to God and a hindrance to the souls on either side [of this and the next world]. The piteous death of our savior, by which we are all restored to life, is not kept in the mind of us unworthy and unkind wretches, nor will we support our Lord's own confidants whom he has endowed with love. Instead, we detract them and hinder them as much as we can.

29. When this creature with her companions came to the grave where our Lord was buried, as soon as she entered that holy place she fell down with her candle in her hand as though she would die from grief. Afterward she got up again with great weeping and sobbing, as though she had seen our Lord buried right before her. Then she thought she saw our Lady in her soul—how she mourned and wept over her son's death—and our Lady's sorrow became *her* sorrow.

So, overall, wherever the friars led them to in that holy place, she always wept and sobbed wondrously, especially when she came to where our Lord was nailed to the cross. There she cried and wept without measure so that she could not restrain herself. Also, when they came to the marble stone on which our Lord was lain when he was taken down from the cross, she wept there with great compassion, mindful of our Lord's passion. Afterward, she received communion on Mount Calvary, and then she wept, she sobbed, she cried so loudly that it was a wonder to hear it. She was so full of holy thoughts, meditations, and holy contemplations on the passion of our Lord Jesus Christ and the holy words that our Lord Jesus Christ spoke to her soul that she could never afterward express them, so exalted and holy were they. Our Lord showed this creature much grace during the three weeks she was in Jerusalem.

Another day, early in the morning, they went to the great hills [around Jerusalem], and the guides described where our Lord bore the cross on his back, and where his mother met with him and how she swooned, how she fell down and he fell down too. So they went around all morning before noon until they came to Mount Zion. All the while this creature wept abundantly everywhere she went out of compassion for our Lord's passion.

At Mount Zion is the place where our Lord washed his disciples' feet a little before he gave his commandment to his disciples [John 13:5, 34]. Therefore, this creature had a great desire to receive communion in that holy place where our merciful Lord Jesus Christ first sacrificed his precious body in the form of bread and gave it to his disciples. And she did, with great devotion, with copious tears, and with noisy sobbing, for in this place plenary remission [of sins] is granted, as it is in four other places in the Temple. One is Mount Calvary; another, the grave where our Lord was buried; the third is the marble stone on which his precious body was laid when it was taken off the cross; the fourth is where the holy cross was buried—and in many other places in Jerusalem.

When this creature went inside the place where the apostle received the Holy Spirit [Acts 2], our Lord gave her great devotion. Afterward she went to the place where our Lord was buried. As she kneeled on her knees while hearing two Masses, our Lord Jesus Christ said to her: "You do not come here, daughter, out of need but for merit and reward; for your sins were forgiven you before you came here, and therefore you come here to increase your reward and your merit. I am well pleased with you, daughter, for you stand in obedience to holy Church and you obey your confessor and follow his counsel, which, through the authority of holy Church, has cleansed you of your sins and dispensed you from going to Rome or to Saint James [at Compostela] unless you yourself wish it. Nevertheless, I command you in the name of Jesus, daughter, to go visit these holy places and do as I ask you, for I am above holy Church and I will go with you and keep you well."

Then our Lady spoke to her soul in this manner, saying: "Daughter, you are well blessed, for my son Jesus will pour so much grace into you that the whole world will be in wonder of you. Do not be ashamed, my dear, worthy daughter, to receive the gifts that my son will give you, for I tell you truthfully that they will be great gifts that he will give you. Therefore, dear, worthy daughter, do not be ashamed of him who is your God, your Lord, and your love and any more than I was when I saw him hanging on the cross, my sweet son Jesus, to cry and weep for the pain of my son Jesus Christ. Nor was Mary Magdalene ashamed to cry and weep for my son's love. Therefore, daughter, if you partake in our joy you must partake in our sorrow." This creature heard these sweet words and conversations at our Lady's grave, and much more than she could ever recount.

Afterward she rode on an ass to Bethlehem, and when she came to the church and to the crib where our Lord was born, she had much devotion and many words and conversations in her soul, and lofty spiritual comfort with much weeping and sobbing so that her companions would not let her eat with them and she ate her meal alone by herself. But then the Gray Friars [Franciscans] who led her from place to place took her in and had her sit with them at dinner so that she would not eat alone. One of the friars asked one of her companions if she was the Englishwoman who, they had heard it said, spoke with God. When she found out about this, she knew well that what our Lord had said to her before she left England was true: "Daughter, I will make all the world wonder at you, and many men and many women will speak of me out of love of you and honor me in you."

30. Another time this creature's companions wanted to go to the River Jordan and would not let her go with them. Then this creature prayed to our Lord Jesus Christ that she could go with them, and he ordered that she go with them whether they wanted her to or not. And then she set out by the grace of God and did not ask their permission. When she came to the River Jordan, the weather was so hot that she thought she would burn her feet due to the heat she felt. Later she went with her companions to Mount Quarantine [the Mount of Temptation, near Jericho], where our Lord fasted for forty days. There she asked her companions to help her up the mount, but they said no, for they could barely help themselves. Then she was very sad since she couldn't go up the hill. Soon a Saracen [Muslim], a handsome man, happened to come by, and she put a groat [a silver coin] in his hands, making a sign to him to help her up the mount. The Saracen quickly took her under his arm and led her up onto the high mountain where our Lord fasted for forty days. Then she was very thirsty but got no comfort from her companions. But God, through his infinite goodness, moved the Gray Friars to compassion and they comforted her when her countrymen would not acknowledge her. . . .

Later, when this creature came down the mount, as God willed, she went to the place where Saint John the Baptist was born. Afterward she went to Bethany where Mary and Martha lived and to the grave where Lazarus was buried and raised to life. She also went to the chapel where our blessed Lord appeared to his blessed mother before anyone else on Easter day at morning. She stood in the same place where Mary Magdalene stood when Christ said to her, "Mary, why do you weep?" [John 20:15]. She was in many more places than are written here because she was in Jerusalem and the country thereabout for three weeks; and she had great devotion for as long as she was in that country.

The friars of the Temple gave her great cheer and gave her many great relics, desiring her to stay among them longer, if she wished, due to the faith they had in her. The Saracens, also, made much of her, and conveyed her and led her around the country wherever she wanted to go. She found all the people good and gracious to her, except her own countrymen.

After she left Jerusalem and went to Ramla, she wished she had turned back to Jerusalem because of the great spiritual comfort she felt when she was there and in order to acquire more pardon for herself. Then our Lord commanded her to go to Rome and then home to England. He said to her: "Daughter, as often as you say or think 'Worshipped be all the holy places in Jerusalem that Christ suffered bitter pain and passion in,' you will have the same pardon as if you were there physically, both for yourself and for all those you wish to give it to."

Questions: How does Margery depict herself? Why does she refer to herself as "creature"? How did the other pilgrims who accompanied her treat Margery, and why do you think that they reacted to her in this way? What kinds of visions did Margery receive, and why were they important for her religious experience? How did Margery react to seeing the holy sites in Jerusalem? Which biblical figures or events were important for her to commemorate?

CHAPTER THREE

BUSINESS JOURNEYS

Of the categories of travel presented in this book, perhaps none is more familiar to modern readers than the business trip. But even if the ultimate point of these journeys is the same in the medieval and modern worlds, the experience of planning and executing the journeys was entirely different. This starts with the remote, uncharted, and dangerous areas that the travelers had to traverse in order to sell their wares. Readers should also pay attention to the items often characterized as luxury goods that long-distance traders peddled in the Middle Ages. Which practical arrangements did travelers have to make in order to be successful? For instance, how did they approach questions regarding money and weights and measures? Travel was never solely a matter of doing business, and the travelers comment at length on the cultures they observed, whether or not their observations were strictly necessary to increase their profit margins. Readers should contemplate what the travelers notice about the people they meet. Business travel could alter human relationships, whether it be to strengthen them or break them apart. In some cases it even inspires religious crises. Commercial and personal interests cannot be easily separated on these journeys.

22. IBN KHURRADDADHBIH, *BOOK OF ROUTES AND REALMS*

Ibn Khurraddadhbih (c. 820–912) was a subject of the mighty Abbasid caliphate and a polymath. He served the caliph as postmaster general, a position that required him not only to direct mail but also to maintain considerable information about geography inside and outside of the empire to keep trade running smoothly, to collect taxes, and to spy on neighbors. He used what he had learned in this position to compose the work excerpted here, one of the first Muslim geographical treatises, which was to become a popular genre. Today we have only a portion of the original work.

Source: trans. John F. Romano, "Le livre des routes et des provinces, par Ibn Khordadbeh," ed. and trans. Charles Barbier de Meynard, in *Journal Asiatique*, sixth series, vol. 5 (1865): 227–30, 291–96, 463–64. Arabic.

Oh my God, bless Muhammad and his family!

In the name of God, merciful and forgiving. Lord, facilitate good enterprises.

Let us praise God. Thanks for his blessing. I confess that there is no other God than God, in confessing his unity. I proclaim that God is great, in humiliating myself before his power. May he bless Muhammad his Prophet and the best of his creatures! Blessings and salvation for the posterity of the Prophet.

The present work, which handles the description of the earth and the beings that are created in it, the *qibla* [direction for prayer] of each country, the kingdoms and routes that extend to the ends of the globe, has as its author Abu 'l Qasim 'Ubayd Allah, son of 'Abd Allah, son of Khurraddadhbih.

Abu 'l Qasim says: The earth is round like a sphere, and placed in the middle of the celestial space, like the yolk in the interior of an egg. The air envelops it and pulls it, on all the points of its surface, toward the celestial space. All bodies are stable on the surface of the globe, because the air draws the light principles of which these bodies are composed, whereas the earth draws into its center their heavy parts, in the same fashion that a magnet acts on fire.

The earth is divided into two parts by the equator, which extends from the east into the west. This is the extent of the earth in length, and the most important line of the terrestrial globe, just as the zodiac line is the most important of the celestial sphere. The earth extends itself in width from the South Pole, above which revolves the constellation of the Pleiades, at the North Pole, below which revolves the constellation of Ursa Major.

The circumference of the globe at the equator is 360 degrees. The degree can be considered 25 parasangs; the parasang, 12,000 cubits; the cubit, 24 fingers; the finger, 6 grains of barley lined up one after another by order of their thickness. As a consequence, the circumference of the earth is 9,000 parasangs. Between the equator and each of its two poles, we count 90 degrees. Such is also the extent of the earth, in the sense of its latitude; but it is not inhabited until the twenty-fourth degree, starting from the equator.

The globe being almost entirely surrounded by the deep waters of the great sea, the northern quarter is the one in which we live, whereas the southern quarter is desert, because of the excessive heat that prevails in it. The other half of the earth, located below us, does not contain any inhabitants.

The two quarters of the earth, the one in the north and the one in the south, are both divided up into seven climates. Ptolemy says in his *Geography* that, in his time, the number of cities on earth was 7,200. . . .

Itinerary from China

In departing from Ma'it [?], the island of Pulau Tioman, which produces Indian aloeswood and camphor, is found on the left. From there one goes, in five days, to Khmer, a country that produces the Indian aloeswood and rice. From Komar to Champa, three days, following the coast. The aloeswood of Champa, named because of that Champan, is better than the one from Khmer, because it sinks in water; this proves its superior quality. On this island are found oxen and beaver. . . .

From Champa to Hanoi, which is the first port of China, is 100 farsakhs either by the land or sea route. In Hanoi excellent Chinese iron, porcelain, and rice are found. One can go from Hanoi, which is a great port, to Guangzhou, in 4 days by the sea, or in 20 days by land. Guangzhou produces every kind of fruits and vegetables, wheat, barley, rice, and sugarcane. From Guangzhou one arrives in eight days at Quanzhou, a city that offers the same products as Guangzhou. From there to Yangzhou, where the same products are also found, six days. In all of the ports of China there is a great navigable river which is subject to the influence of the tide. In the river of Yangzhou geese, duck, and other fowl are found. The great length of the Chinese coast, from Almaid until the other end, is a two month journey. China contains 300 cities, all prosperous and well known. This country is bounded by the sea, Tibet, and the country of the Turks. The foreigners coming from India are established in the eastern provinces.

The country of Waqwaq [Japan?] is so rich in gold mines that the inhabitants manufacture metal chains with this for their dogs and collars for their monkeys. They sell tunics embroidered with gold.

'Abd el-Ghaffar the sailor, a native of Syria, being asked about tides, gave for it the following explanation: this phenomenon manifests itself in the Persian Sea, at the rising of the moon; in the great sea, it is divided into two seasons: the one in the summer, in the direction east-north-east, during six months; in this era, the sea rises in the eastern regions, like China, and it falls in the western regions; the other in winter, in the direction of west–south–west, during the other six months; so the sea rises in the western countries.

What is beyond China is unknown. Across from Yangzhou high mountains rise up. This is the country of Sila [Korea?] where gold abounds. Muslims who go there settle permanently because of all of the advantages that it offers. One ignores what is located further on. The country of Sila supplies for exportation: ghorraib [ginseng?], kino resin [lacquer?], musk, aloeswood, camphor, sails, saddles, porcelain, satin, cinnamon, and galangal. From the country of Waqwaq are extracted gold and ebony; from India, aloeswood, camphor, nutmeg, clove, root of nymphaea [water lily], cubeb, coconut, fabric of cotton and velvet, elephants. From Ceylon [modern Sri Lanka] are exported all the varieties of rubies and other stones of this kind, the diamond, pearls, emery, which serves to test metals; from Malabar and Sendan [?], powder and rock crystal; from Kalah [?], the lead called *alkali*; from the regions of the south, wood from *bokam* [?] and *dary* [?], the costus, calamus, and bamboo. The length of this sea, between Suez and the country of Waqwaq, is 4,500 farsakhs. One principally exports from Yemen silks striped with diverse colors and several other fabrics, amber, saffron, and gum.

India is divided into seven castes: first, the Sabekferya [?], that is the caste of the nobles and the king. All the other castes prostrate themselves in front of them; but they do not do homage to anyone; second, the Brahmins, who neither drink wine nor fermented liquor; third, the Kshatriya; they only drink three small glasses of wine; they cannot contract an alliance with the families of the Brahmins, but they marry their daughters; fourth, the Sudra or the farmers; fifth, Vaishya, artisans and laborers; sixth, Chandala, service and escort people; seventh, Zenya [?], musicians and acrobats. There are 42 religious sects among the Indians; some people believe in God (may his holy name be glorified!) and in the mission of the prophets; others reject the prophets, others reject all these beliefs at the same time. In this country is found a class of magicians who carry out all that they want by their spells, and they heal all illnesses. Well-versed in the occult sciences and in the art of divination, they exercise an absolute authority, they do good and evil, summoning ghosts and phantoms that strike the spirit of terror, they command rain and hail. . . .

From the western Mediterranean are exported eunuchs taken from the country of the Slavs; young Christian slaves; Spanish girls; beaver pelts and other furs; perfumes, among others storax; and among the drugs, mastic. At the bottom of this sea, close to the country of the Franks, *bussadh*, a substance ordinarily known under the name of coral, is extracted.

The sea that extends beyond the country of the Slavs to the city of Boulyah [?] is not frequented by any vessel nor a commercial building, and no other product is extracted from it. Similarly, the western ocean, where the Fortunate

Isles are found, is not explored by sailors and it does not furnish any consumable item for the market.

Questions: Do the author's descriptions of the earth seem reliable? Why does he think that the earth is a sphere? Which products can one acquire from southeast Asia or east Asia? What difference is there between the items that one can acquire in the western Mediterranean and eastern lands? In what ways can you classify the different items offered for trade? Do they tend to be expensive, and if so, why might this be the case? Which aspects of India does the author find most striking?

23. THE REPORTS OF OHTHERE AND WULFSTAN

Nothing about the travelers Ohthere or Wulfstan is preserved aside from this one brief source. From it we learn that they visited England at some point during the reign of King Alfred of Wessex (r. 871–899), who is credited with having successfully resisted the Vikings in his lands and having supported a cultural flowering in his kingdom. The reports here were incorporated into an Old English translation of the early fifth-century Latin history of Orosius.

Source: trans. Janet Bately, *Ohthere's Voyages: A Late 9th-Century Account of Voyages along the Coasts of Norway and Denmark and its Cultural Context*, eds. Janet Bately and Anton Englert (Roskilde: Viking Ship Museum, 2007), pp. 44–50 [modern English pages only]. Old English. Revised.

Ohthere's Report

Ohthere said to his lord, King Alfred, that he lived furthest north of all Norwegians. He said that he lived in the northern part of the land, beside the West Sea [the Atlantic]. He said however that the land extends a very long way north from there, but it is all waste, except that in a few places here and there Sami [people of northern Europe] camp, engaged in hunting in winter and in summer in fishing by the sea. He said that on a certain occasion he wished to investigate how far the land extended in a northerly direction, or whether anyone lived north of the waste.

Then he went north along the coast; he kept the waste land on his starboard side and the open sea on his port side all the way for three days. Then he was as far north as the furthest the whale hunters go. Then he continued to travel north, as far as he could sail in the next three days.

Then the land there turned east, or the sea into the land, he did not know which of the two, but he knew that he waited there for a wind from the west and slightly north and then sailed east along the coast as far as he could sail in four days. Then he had to wait there for a wind from the north, since the land there turned in a southerly direction, or the sea into the land, he did not know which of the two. Then he sailed from there in a southerly direction along the coast as far as he could sail in five days.

Then a large river there stretched up into the land. Then they turned up into that river, because they dared not sail on past the river because of hostility, since the land was all settled on the other side of the river. He had not previously encountered any settled land since he traveled from his own home, but there was waste land all the way on his starboard side, except for fishermen and fowlers and hunters, and they were all Sami, and open sea was always on his port side.

The Biarmians had settled their land very well, but they dared not come in there. But the land of the Ter Sami [?] was all waste, except where hunters camped, or fishermen, or fowlers. The Biarmians told him many stories about their own land and about the lands that were around them, but he did not know what there was of truth in it, because he did not see it himself. The Sami and the Biarmians, it seemed to him, spoke practically one and the same language.

He chiefly went there, in addition to the surveying of the land, for the walruses, because they have very fine bone in their teeth—they brought some of the teeth to the king—and their hide is very good for ship's ropes. This whale [the walrus] is much smaller than other whales—it is not longer than seven ells long—but the best whale hunting is in his own land: they are forty-eight ells long and the biggest fifty ells long; he said that he and six others killed sixty of them in two days.

He was a very prosperous man in respect of those possessions that their wealth consists of, that is, of wild animals. When he sought the king, he still had six hundred domesticated animals unsold. These animals they call reindeer; six of them were decoy reindeer. They are very valuable among the Sami, since they catch the wild reindeer with them. He was among the foremost men in that land. However, he did not have more than twenty head of cattle and twenty sheep and twenty pigs, and the little that he plowed he plowed with horses. But their wealth consists mostly of the tribute that the Sami pay them. The tribute consists of animals' skins and of birds' feathers and whale's bone and of those ship's ropes that are made from whale's hide and from seal's. Each pays according to his rank: the highest in rank has to pay fifteen marten's skins and five reindeer's and one bear's skin and ten measures of feathers and a bear- or otter-skin tunic and two ship's ropes: each must be sixty ells long, one must be made from whale's hide, the other from sealskin.

He said that the land of the Norwegians was very long and very narrow. All of it that may be grazed or plowed, that lies along the sea, and that is nevertheless very rocky in some places, and wild moors lie to the east and above, running parallel to the inhabited land. On the moors dwell Sami. And the inhabited land is broadest toward the east [southern Norway], and ever the further north the narrower; to the east it may be sixty miles broad or somewhat broader and in the middle thirty or broader; and to the north, where it was narrowest, he said that it might be three miles broad to the moorland, and the moorland subsequently in some places as broad as may be crossed in two weeks and in some places as broad as may be crossed in six days. Then alongside the southern part of the land, on the other side of the moorland, is the land of the Swedes [?], up to the northern part of the land; and alongside the northern part of the land the land of the Finns [?]. The Finns sometimes make raids on the Norwegians over the moorland, sometimes the Norwegians on them. And there are very large fresh water lakes throughout the moors, and the Finns carry their boats over on to the lakes and from there make raids on the Norwegians; they have small and very light boats.

Ohthere said that the district in which he lived is called Halogaland. He said that no one lived to the north of it. Then there is a port in the southern part of the land which is called Skiringssal [Kaupang]. To this he said that it was not possible to sail in one month, if one camped at night and each day had a favorable wind; and all the time he must sail along the coast; and on his starboard side there will be first Ireland and then the islands [Orkneys and Shetlands] that are between Ireland and this land [England]. Then this land is in that position until he comes to Skiringssal, and all the way on the port side Norway.

To the south of this Skiringssal a very great sea penetrates up into the land; it is broader than any man may see over, and Jutland is on the other side opposite to it and afterward Sillende [central and southern Denmark]. The sea stretches many hundreds of miles up into the land. And from Skiringssal he said that he sailed in five days to the port which is called Hedeby, which stands between Wends and Saxons and Angles and is subject to the Danes.

When he sailed toward that place from Skiringssal, then Denmark was on his port side and the open sea on his starboard side for three days. And then, for two days before he came to Hedeby, Jutland, and Sillende and many islands were on his starboard side—in those lands the English lived, before they came to this country—and for two days the islands that are subject to Denmark were then on his port side.

Wulfstan's Report

Wulfstan said that he traveled from Hedeby, that he was in Truso [Janów Pomorski] in seven days and nights, that the boat was all the way running under sail. Wendland [Pomerania] was on his starboard side, and on his port side were Langeland and Lolland and Falster and Skåne, and these lands are all subject to Denmark.

And then Bornholm was on our port side and they have their own king. Then after Bornholm there were on our port side these lands that are called Blekinge and Möre and Øland and Gotland, and these lands are subject to the Swedes. And Wendland was on our starboard side all the way to the mouth of the Vistula. This Vistula is a very large river and it separates Witland [northeast Poland?] and Wendland, and the above-mentioned Witland belongs to the Ests [Estonians], and the Vistula extends out of Wendland and extends into Estlake [Zalew Wiślany; Frisches Haff], and this Estlake is at least fifteen miles broad; then the Elbing comes from the east into Estlake from the lake that Truso stands on the shore of, and they come out simultaneously into Estlake, the Elbing from the east from Estland and the Vistula from the south from Wendland; and then the Elbing makes off with the Vistula's name and extends from the lake west and north into the sea; therefore it is called Vistula mouth.

The above-mentioned Estland is very large, and there is very many a town, and in each town there is a king. And there is very much honey and fishing, and the king and the most powerful men drink mare's milk and the poor and the slaves drink mead. There is very much conflict between them. And there is not any ale brewed among the Ests, but there is mead enough.

And there is among the Ests a custom, when a man is dead there, that he lies indoors uncremated with his kinsmen and friends for a month and sometimes two, and the kings and the other high-ranking men as much longer as they have more wealth, [so it is] sometimes for half a year that they are uncremated and lie above ground in their houses. And all the time that the body is indoors, there has to be drinking and entertainment, until the day that they cremate him. Then the same day that they wish to carry him to the funeral pyre, they then divide up his property, what there is left over after the drinking and the entertainment, into five or six parts, sometimes into more, according to the amount of property there is. They then lay it down, the biggest portion in approximately one mile from the settlement, then the second, then the third, until it is all laid out in that one mile. And the smallest portion has to be nearest the settlement that the dead man is lying in. Then all the men who have the fastest horses in that land have to be assembled, approximately five or six miles from the property. Then they all gallop toward the property. Then the man who has the fastest horse comes to the first and the biggest portion; and so each after the other, until it is all taken; and he takes the smallest portion who gets by galloping to the property nearest the settlement. And then each rides on his way with the property and they may have it all, and for that reason the fast horses are excessively valuable there. And when his wealth is thus all spent, then he is carried out and cremated with his weapons and clothing, and especially they use up all his wealth with the long lying of the dead man indoors and with what they lay down by the highways, which the strangers gallop to and take. And that is a custom among the Ests that people of every tribe must be cremated there and if a single bone is found unburned there, they must atone for it greatly.

And there is among the Ests a people who are able to cause coldness, and that is why the dead men lie there so long and do not decompose, because they bring about the coldness on him. And although two vessels full of ale or water should be set down, they bring it about that one of them is frozen over, whether it is summer or winter.

Questions: How do Ohthere and Wulfstan describe the routes that they sailed? Would it be possible for a later traveler to reconstruct their journeys, given what they said? Which animals are available in these territories, and what can one do with them? Why do the travelers emphasize material things? Do they seem to be anthropologists or ethnographers in reporting about the different customs that they witnessed?

24. LETTERS FROM JEWISH MERCHANTS IN THE CAIRO GENIZA

While members of many religious communities traded in the Middle Ages, historians are best informed about the activities of Jewish traders. A unique archive of thousands of letters was preserved in Cairo by medieval Jews, who buried any letters that mentioned the divine name so that God's name would not be desecrated. In addition to religious texts, there are many secular ones that focus on business matters, as excerpted here. These letters are all from the eleventh to the thirteenth century; most of them center on the Mediterranean Sea, although some of the merchants also had dealings in India. Some of these letters are fragmentary, although the lost phrases can sometimes be reconstructed.

Source: ed. and trans. S.D. Goitein, *Letters of Medieval Jewish Traders* (Princeton, NJ: Princeton University Press, 1973), pp. 29–34, 46–49, 53–55, 63–65, 203–06, 209–12, 221–26, 312–15, 317–19, 324–27. Judeo-Arabic. The letters are given numbers here to facilitate discussion.

1. I am writing to you, my esteemed elder, master, and chief, may God prolong your life and make lasting [your honored position], well-being, and security, on Elul 23 [late August or early September]. I am safe and in good health, many [thanks be to God]. [I am yearning for] the sight of your blessed countenance; may God unite us in the best of circumstances and in perfect happiness. Your enjoyable letters have arrived and I have gathered from them that you are fine; may God ordain that it should always be so; may he ever increase his boons to you and shower on you his favors.

My elder and master, you say that I *took* the brazilwood [Indian red dye] and sent it to Spain. I did not take it for myself, nor have I made any profit from it. Rather, it caused me losses. I acted thus because I rely on you and because you are helpful to me with your high rank in matters of the goods sent by me to you on my account. I was sure that you would write me exactly the opposite of what you have written, which offended me so much and for which I do not know any reason. Your shipment was sent in Iyyar [April/May] and mine was sent to you in Av [July/August]; could your consignment possibly have come from Spain and made all this in two months? And even if this was possible, would you not have acted similarly?

You w[rite in your letters that] I should send you the 420 pounds of silk. But one-third of this is my brother's investment, besides which he is entitled to a third of the profit along with you. Moreover, the merchants are unanimously of the opinion that silk sells in Qayrawan standard weight. I wished I had immediately forwarded to you your share, as you instructed me, for most of the proceeds are still outstanding and I have debited myself with all that is due my brother and due you. I have received payment for 100 pounds from Salama of al-Mahdiyya only eight days before the writing of this letter. With Ibn al-Sabbagh ["Mr. Dyer"] there is also a debt outstanding, for I sold to him on credit. I also lost much money which was due us from the colorists, but I did not charge anything to the two of you, for my brother settled his accounts with me before his departure and took what was due him. And this is my reward from you after all this.

I sent you 100 less one-quarter 'Azizi dinars [gold pieces] in the caravan of the Sijilmasis with Abu 'l-Surur b. Barhun. This was taken from my own money, for at that time I had not received a penny from the price of the silk. I acted thus because of my esteem for you and because of your illustrious position, your noble character, and piety. All I ask from you is that you act with respect to my goods sent to you in the same manner as I acted with your goods sent to me.

Then you sent those pearls and I worked hard collecting their price. For how long will this go on?! Should I not have taken one quarter of the profit? Through me you have made a profit of close to 1 dinar per dinar, and all this was of no advantage to me. I expected only that you would exert yourself for me, at least that you would send me what you owe me. Had I owed you 2,000 dinars, would I withhold them from you? Would they not reach you [even] by sea to your satisfaction? If you had sent my money, I would have made good use of it—as you have made of yours. And what had happened if, God forbid, your goods had traveled a second time and entered my account? How would I then stand before you? But God, may he be praised and exalted, knows my good intentions, and he rewards every man according to his intention.

What disturbed me most was your failure to pay to Ibn Yazdad and Salama, the son-in-law of Jurayj, the sum that I asked you to pay them or to give them the equivalent in goods, although I had advised you expressly to do so. You have withheld payment from them, while this is a debt upon me. And this, at a time when your merchandise was in Spain! Their letters vituperating me have now come here to everyone and my honor has been disgraced. Had you only made promises to them and said: "He has given instructions for you," they would have been patient and I would have been spared those vituperations.

Our Maghrebi friends told me what they had heard in your name from Abu 'l-Khayr b. Barhun, that I had written to you asking you to replace Ibn Majjani by myself. I have not wanted this. I am not prepared to undertake it, nor have I any need for this. What I do need is to benefit from your high position and that you exert yourself for my goods as I do for yours. What I did say is that you should entrust me with your affairs just as I entrust you with mine. But after having taken care of someone else's affairs or having formed a partnership with him, God forbid that I and my honor should then be treated in this improper way. I never withhold a penny from anyone else, nor is any claim made against me at any time.

I had made an agreement with Farah ["Joy"] of Fez with regard to the remainder of the brazilwood, to the effect that I take it and send it to Spain [at a c]ommission, but on the condition that I will bear responsibility [for its loss]. Each qintar was appraised at 12 dinars in the presence of a number of our friends. You, not I, had to have the choice since all this was to be on your behalf. Finally, Farah did not do it.

Thank God that this did not materialize, for you would have treated me in this manner as you have done before. But, by God, my master, the profit with this would have been even greater than with the first shipment. For this year the brazilwood which I had bought in Qayrawan for 265 dirhems [silver coins] was sold on my behalf for 125 dinars. God knew my good intentions and spared me many troubles in a matter from which I would not have had any advantages. . . .

I do not dare to say to you: "Send me your things and I will handle them," fearing that you may tell stories about me that I have asked you to put me in Ibn al-Majjani's place. I do not need this. The little we have here in Maghreb is worth the abundance you have over there. But after all, I am your servant and prepared to deal, for your profit and without advantage for me, with anything you might send me. By God, my lord, this will give me only pleasure. God knows.

Kindest personal regards to my master, the elder, and his two sons Hillel and Benjamin, may God protect and keep them.

[In the margin:] I copied for you from my account book the account for the sale of the silk, and the expenses involved from beginning to end, including a description of each item and showing how it was sold without any loss for you. May God replace that which has gone . . . for what has remained with the "colorists" can never be recovered. Please examine the account and take notice of all its details. If you have any doubts, let me know and I will give you the necessary explanations, if God wills.

[Address:] To my master and chief, the [illustrious] elder, Abu 'l-Faraj, may God prolong his life and make permanent his honored position and prosperity, Yusuf [Joseph] b. Ya'qub [Jacob] Ibn 'Awkal—[may his] s[oul] r[est in peace]. May God be his friend, protector, helper, and shepherd.

From Samhun b. Da'ud Ibn al-Siquilli ["Generous," son of David, the son of the Sicilian]. In Misr [Fustat] i[f God wills].

2. I trust in God. Praised be the Lord who resurrects the dead. My master and lord, may God prolong your life, make your well-being and happiness permanent, and keep away from you all evil in his mercy. I am writing from Ramla on the eighth of Teveth [January], feeling well in body, but being worried in my mind.

I set sail for Jaffa, the port of Ramla. But a wind arose against us from the land. It became a storm, chasing and driving us out to the high sea, where we remained for four days, giving up all hope for life. We were without sails and oars, the steering rudder and the sail yards were broken, and the waves burst into the barge. We cried: "Allah, Allah," for our ship was a mere riverboat, small as a ferry. We threw part of the cargo overboard, and I gave up all hope for my life and my goods. I vowed 1 dinar from the proceeds of the silk. Finally, God in his glory and majesty granted us to reach Caesarea, but my clothes and goods were completely soaked. I did not find a place to stay and to spread out my things. So I took domicile in the synagogue, where I remained for five days.

When I arrived in Ramla, I had to pay customs to a degree I am unable to describe. The price in Ramla of the Cyprus silk, which I carry with me, is 2 dinars per little pound. Please inform me of its price and advise me whether I should sell it here or carry it with me to you in Misr, in case it is fetching a good price there. By God, answer me quickly, I have no other business here in Ramla except awaiting answers to my letters. About 3 dinars worth of goods of mine were jettisoned from the barge; may God, the exalted, restore the loss. If you want me to carry the silk with me, instruct Makhluf b. Muhsina (write him!) to pay me 2–3 dinars, or have Abu Barhun write to his brother Ya'qub [Jacob] to give me this sum so that I do not have to sell my clothing or the silk. A man like you does not need to be urged. I know that my money and yours are one. Moreover, you have a share in this. I need not stress the urgency of a reply concerning the price of silk from Sham [Syria-Lebanon] and from Cyprus, and whether I should sell it here or carry it with me.

I wrote you from Tripoli and informed you that I had sent four bundles of cotton and twenty-one pieces of figs to Alexandria. I wrote to M. Marduk, asking him to receive this shipment. With Yahya b. al-Zaffaat I sent two bags and one basket with wheat, red earth, and two baskets with raisins and figs. I instructed him to deliver these to Marduk. Your share in the basket [of wheat] and the figs is 8 dinars, and your share in the silk also 8 dinars. I hope you have written to Alexandria instructing Marduk to take care of the matter, and also to attend to the sacking. Also write him to send you either the proceeds, or the goods to be bought for them, or broken dinars. And by God, answer. I have no business other than waiting for your letter. By God, do not neglect this. By the bread [we have eaten together], as soon as this letter arrives, send the answer to the warehouse of the representative of the merchants, Abu 'l-Barakat Ibn al-Hulaybi. A man like you needs no urging.

Describe to me the prices in the city [Fustat], and especially with regard to wheat and bread—I need not urge you to write me about this—as well as concerning the state of my father and the family. Special regards to you, and also to those who ask about me. Please honor me with any concern you might have. Regards also to Joseph and his mother [the writer's wife and son]. How are they? Regards also to our friends. And peace.

[Address:] To my lord and master Abu Yahya Nahray, son of Nissim, [may he] r[est in] E[den], may God prolong his life and make permanent his honored position, strength, and happiness.

From Ya'qub [Jacob] b. Salman al-Hariri

3. In [Your] name, O Merci[ful].

To my master and lord, my succor and sup[ort], may God prolong your life and m[ake permanent your high rank] and lofty position. May he crush those who envy you and not withhold from you [success]. May he substitute me [as ransom for all evil that might befall you and may he] never leave me [alone, being without you. May he let you suc]ceed in obeying him and eliciting his favor. May he unite us in happiness, soothe my solitude by your appearance and relieve my grief through your presence. See, he listens to your prayers and answers quickly.

I arrived in Fez on Friday, the second of Marheshvan [late September, early October]. At our arrival we were met by the informers and they found out exactly the number of loads [belonging to us]. They went to the superintendent of the customs and told him. On Sunday morning he sent for me and for Ibrahim and said to him: "Are you prepared to give an oath that all that arrived with you is entirely your property and that this man has no share in it?" Then he said to me: "Are you prepared to swear that nothing at all was brought by you to this place?" There was much talk, but he clearly knew that five camel loads had arrived with me. After great troubles it was agreed that the governor would take 10 mithqals [Egyptian dinars]; the superintendent of the customs, 3; the informers, 2; and the employees, ½. I was sick for three days out of anger and sorrow. Had I possessed here the same courage as I usually have in Almeria, I would have escaped with less than this. But I consoled myself with the solace of one who has no choice. I also said to myself, perhaps God may grant us some compensation for the loss. On the day of my arrival it was 3 and 2; today it is 2 and 4.

By God, if you can avoid it, do not go abroad. If God wills, I will set out for Marrakesh with the first company traveling there, and, if necessary, inform you about the situation, whereupon you may make your decision. I have no other aim, by God, than saving you from trudging along the streets and traveling overland. May God turn everything to a good end!

I should also like to inform you that I spread out the *nisfiyya* clothes [fine cloth made of silk or linen], and the very first garment that fell into my hands was spoiled by water in all its folds. I went out of my mind, but God, the exalted, had willed that only this one was spoiled. This happened because we had much rain on the way, but God, the exalted, granted rescue. As of late today I sold ten pairs of them for a total of 80 dinars, inclusive of the ten bad ones and the one spoiled by water.

I bought first-class, excellent antimony [kohl], about twenty qintars, the qintar for 1 dinar. If you think that I should buy more, send me a note and let me know.

For the lac [secretion of insects used as a dye] I was offered 24 [dinars]. I am holding on to it, perhaps I will get 25.

The good elastic [?] copper is worth here 9 dinars a qintar.

Scammony [weed used as medicine] is worth 3 dinars a pound. Inquire, and if it reaches that price in Almeria, sell it. Otherwise send me one half [of what we have] and leave there the other half.

All our lac and *nisfiyyas* are in the house of Ibrahim, for I did not want to leave anything at all with me in the house. I may be able to sell all the *nisfiyyas* in Fez.

Please note that indigo is very much in demand here in Fez.

I should also like to inform you that everyone, Muslims and Jews, tell me that Ibn Talw will pay me all he owes us, as soon as I arrive, for he is very rich today.

Hatred [of Jews] is rampant in this country to a degree that, in comparison with it, Almeria is a place of salvation. May God the exalted grant rescue and a good end in his mercy.

[Address:] To my lord, succor, and support, my father,

Japeth ha-Levi b. 'Ullah [may he] r[est in] E[den].

4. In [Your] name, O Merci[ful]!

"Your hand will be lifted upon your adversaries, and all your enemies will be cut off" [Micah 5:9]. I am writing to you, my lord and master, my chief, the illustrious elder—may God prolong your life and make permanent your prominent position, may he be for you and with you and guard you in all your affairs. I am writing to you out of a strong longing; may God make us meet together presently in the best circumstances in his favor and bounty, if God wills, for it is up to him and it is in his power alone.

I wish to inform you, my lord, that I had previously written to you at Tana. Meanwhile the accompanying boat of the ship arrived, and its soldiers told us that the ship in which your excellency my lord traveled was taken by pirates, and I was very sad about this. But afterward I praised God and thanked him, when I heard that your life was saved. "O that men would praise the Lord for his goodness" [Psalm 107:31]. Everything can be replaced except life; I would indeed like to mention to you, my lord, that your servant had a large shipment in the boat of Fofali ["Betel-nut merchant"], then God ordained what happened; in the end, however, God compensated me—praise and thanks to him. Likewise, my lord, do not be sad. God will replace your loss to you soon; you will live, if God wills and God will compensate you many times.

Your servant thought that your honor my lord was in Tana, and I had previously sent letters to the *nakhoda* [ship-owning merchant] Tinbu, advising him to pay to my lord 21 mithqals or more. Afterward, however, my lord the Sheikh Abu 'l-Qaism Ibn Qattan ["Dealer in cotton"] came to Mangalore. I inquired about you and he told me that your excellency was in Broach. In all circumstances please come quickly to Mangalore and do not tarry, for I am waiting here in Mangalore and—if God wills—we will embark on our way home as soon as possible. It is better for you to travel from Mangalore with me than to travel in the ships of foreign people. Please remember that there is no difference between us, my money is yours, it is just the same. The boats start presently from your place, from Kanbayat, and from Tana; please set out immediately so that you reach Mangalore with the vessels which, God willing, will soon be arriving in Malibarat, Kayakannur, and Mangalore. If, my lord, you need any gold, please take it on my account from the *nakhoda* Tinbu, for he is staying in Tana, and between him and me there are bonds of inseparable friendship and brotherhood.

You would certainly like to know, my lord, that a sum in favor of your excellency remained with me on account of the silk. With it I bought twelve . . . and sixteen large peppers for you, and I dispatch this for you under God's protection from Mangalore with the "Blessed" ship—may God ordain her safety.

Attached to this letter, is another one in Arabic characters of the same content as this letter; please notice this. And again, my lord, do not take to heart what you have lost; you have, my lord, praise be to God, plenty to have recourse to and to be compensated with. When life is saved, nothing else matters. Nor do I need to urge you again to come to Mangalore.

Accept, my lord, copious regards for your noble self and convey copious regards to the elder Abu Sa'd. The writer of these lines, Abraham b. Yiju, conveys to your excellency copious regards, and those who attend the writing of this letter do the same. May the well-being of my lord grow indefinitely and never become reduced.

[Address:] To be delivered to my noble lord, the light of my eyes, his honor, [our] M[aster] and T[eacher] Judah ha-Kohen, the wise and understanding, the son of his honor, greatness, and hol[iness], [our] M[aster] and T[eacher] Joseph ha-Kohen, may his soul be satiated with pleasures in the Gardens of Eden until he will be quickened at the end of the days.

From his servant Mahruz, the son of Jacob, [may he] r[est in] E[den].

Given in trust [no fees for delivery].

5. My brother, I do not know what to write; so strong is my longing and so ardent my yearning. I ask God to unite us all presently in the best of circumstances.

This is to announce to you, my brother, that I have set out from India and arrived safely in Aden, may God protect it, with my belongings, life, and children well preserved. May God be thanked for this. "O that men would praise the Lord for his goodness and for his miraculous deeds with the children of men" [Psalm 107:31].

Now I wish to let you know that I have enough to live on for all of us. May God, the exalted, let this money be a living for me and my children and be sufficient for you as well.

I have to reproach you, my brother, that you got as far as Egypt and did not come to Aden. I sent you to Egypt, with a shipment of my master, the elder Madmun, civet perfume worth 40 dinars, about fifty ounces of weight, carried by the elder Abu Nasr b. Elisha—may he be remembered with blessings. Afterward, I learned from the elder Abu Zikri, the Kohen Sijilmasi, the brother-in-law of my master, the elder Madmun, that the civet arrived duly in Misr; however, as they did not find you there, my brother, they forwarded it to you to Sicily with a trustworthy Jew called Samuel, himself a Sicilian. I hope it has reached you.

I also met the elder Sulayman Ibn Gabbay . . . and he told me that you have been reduced to one single loaf of bread; therefore, I ask you, my brother, come to me under any circumstances and without delay; "come down to me and do not tarry," "and I will sustain you there." I have a son and a daughter, take them and take with them all the money and riches—may God fulfill my wishes and yours for the good. Come quickly and take possession of this money; this is better than strangers taking it.

Also, find out who is the best of the sons of my brother Joseph or the sons of your sister Berakha, so that I may marry him off to my daughter. After your coming here, we will live in Aden or Fustat or Alexandria, if it will not be possible for us to go to al-Mahidiyya or to Ifriqiya, namely, to Tunis or Qayrawan. Everything is, of course, in God's hand.

Please convey the best greetings to your brother Joseph and to his children in my name, and say to him: Your brother Abraham says to you: "By God, I will not grudge you a thing; this money, which I have here, is at your disposal." Likewise, greet my sister Berakha and her children and tell her the same.

I heard that Ma'mar, Yumn's husband, died, but was not sure about it. If it is true, may God comfort you all; however, by these lines, it is hard for me to write words of consolation on the death of anyone.

Convey to my brother-in-law Marwan, son of Zikri, [may he] r[est in] E[den], Ibn Bihar the best greetings in my name—may God keep him alive and preserve him for you—and likewise to Abu 'l-Barakat b. Qayyoma the best greetings.

By God, and again by God, do not delay your coming here, take this dirhem, which I have earned, and buy and sell with it, if God will—saying less about this would have been enough. Would I try to write all that is in my heart, no letter could contain it and no epistle could comprise it.

Written on the seventh of Tishri, may God let you partake in the blessings of the month, of the year 1461 of the Documents [11 September 1149].

Kindest regards to the cantor Moses, son of the cantor Abraham. . . .

[Margin:] And peace. And to my brother, his children, and his wife special greetings. Likewise, to my sister, her husband Marwan, her sons and her daughter, special greetings. And to the daughters of my paternal uncle, their sons, and their daughters greetings. To my maternal aunt and her ch[ildren] greetings. Peace be upon you and peace on your house.

I gave instructions that my letters should be in the hands of the elder Abraham b. Joseph, . . . Ibn al-Baqqal ["Grocer"]—may God ordain his safe arrival. And, by God, come as quickly as possible to Aden.

And kiss the soil before my lord, our teacher Labrat, the Dayyan [Judge], son of his honor, our master and teacher Moses, the Dayyan—may he rest in the Garden of Eden (and convey to him) the best greetings; and to all my friends of my age class, the best greetings. And peace.

I heard what happened to the coastland of Ifriqiya, Tripoli, Jerba, Qarqanna, Sfax, al-Mahdiyya, and Susa. No letter, however, from which I could learn who died and who remained alive, has arrived. By God, write exact details and send your letters with reliable people to soothe my mind. And peace.

[Address, right side:] This letter will reach my dear brothers—may God prolong [their lives]—Joseph and Mevasser, the sons of Perahya, . . . Ben Yiju. God may recompense him that will be concerned to make an effort to transmit it into their hands, and from the Lord he will receive good reward. Convey and get remuneration. This is a deposit entrusted.

[Left side:] Their brother, who is longing for them, may God unite him with them, Abraham, son of Perahya, . . . Ben Yiju. To al-Mahdiyya, if God will, or anywhere else in Ifriqiya.

6. To my beloved brother R. Mos[es, son of R.] Maimon, [may the] m[emory of the] r[ighteous be] b[lessed].

David, your brother who is longing for you—may God unite me with you under the most happy circumstances in his grace.

I am writing this letter from 'Aydhab. I am well, but my mind is very much troubled, so that I walk around in the bazaar and do not know—by our religion—where I [am . . .], nor how come that I did not imagine how much you must worry [about m]e.

This is my story: I reached Qus and after Passover I booked for 'Aydhab in a caravan. . . . So we traveled alone out of fear of him [?]. No one has ever dared to embark on such a disastrous undertaking. I did it only because of my complete ignorance. But God [saved] us after many frightful encounters, to describe which would lead me too far afield. When we were in the desert, we regretted what we had done, but the matter had gone out of our hands. Yet God had willed that we should be saved. We arrived in 'Aydhab safely with our entire baggage. We were unloading our things at the city gate, when the caravans arrived. Their passengers had been robbed and wounded, and some had died of thirst. Among them was Ibn al-Rashidi, but he was unharmed. . . . We preceded him only slightly and there was only a small distance between us and those who were robbed. We were saved only because we had taken on ourselves those frightful experiences. All day long I imagine how you must feel when you hear about 'Ata Allah ["God's gift"] Ibn al-Rashidi, how he was robbed, and you believe that I was in his company. Then God comes between me and my reason.

To make a long story short: I arrived in 'Aydhab and found that no imports had come here . . . at all. I found nothing to buy except indigo. So I thought about what I had endured in the [des]ert [and how I was saved;] then it appeared to me an easy matter to embark on a sea voyage. I took Mansur as my travel companion, but not Ma'ani, for all my troubles came [only from him; you know] the man and how he behaves. Once, if God will, I will tell you [all that happened between us] on our way from Fustat to 'Aydhab.

My company in the Mala[bar] sea will be . . . , . . . , Salim, the son of the [female] broker and his brother's son, Makarim ["Noble character"] al-Hariri ["Silk merchant"] and his b[rother], and the brother of Sitt Ghazal. But Ma'ani embarked, together with Ibn al-Kuwayyis ["Nice"] on another ship, and Bu 'l-'Ala remains in Dahlak, since the ship in which he traveled foundered, but he was saved and absolutely nothing of his baggage was lost. Ibn 'Atiyya ["Gift"], however, was in another boat, together with Ibn al-Maqdisi ["The Man from Jerusalem"]. Their boat foundered and only their din[ars] remained with them.

Now despite all of this, do not [worry]. He who saved me from the desert with its . . . will save me while on sea. . . . And, please, calm the heart of the little one and her sister; do not frighten them and let them not despair, for crying to God for what has passed is a vain prayer. . . . I am doing all this out of my continuous efforts for your [plural] material well-being, although you [singular] have never imposed on me anything of the kind. So be steadfast; God will replace your losses and bring me back to you. Anyhow, what has passed, is past, and I am sure, this letter will reach you at a time when I, God willing, will have already made most of the way. "But the counsel of God alone will stand." Our departure will probably be around the middle of Ramadan.

I will trav[el with. . . . Tell this] to his uncle, and also that he is fine. Abraham is fine. [Best regards to you, to] Bu 'Ali and his brother, to the elder Bu Mansur and his brothers, to my sisters and the boys, to all our friends, to the freedman, and Mahasin ["Favors"].

Written on the twenty-second of Iyyar, while the express caravan is on the point of leaving.

7. In [Your name!]
"Just is the Lord in all his ways . . ." [Psalm 145:17].
"The righteous man has gone . . ." [Isaiah 51:1].
"Comfort, comfort my people . . ." [Isaiah 40:1].

From their father who is yearning after them, Solomon, son of Japheth, [may he] r[est in] E[den].

I am able to express only a fraction of my grief over the passing away of my lord, the illustrious leader, [his] h[onor], g[reatness, and] h[oliness], our master and teacher Manasse, the wise and prudent judge, whose demise has hurt the hearts and caused pain to the souls. [May the] m[emory of the] r[ighteous] be b[lessed]. How deeply was I afflicted by his death and his being taken away from those who relied on him. May God assign him a place with the saints, may he grant consolation to his mourners and heal their wounds and comfort them in his great mercy.

Would I try to describe the extent of my feelings of longing and yearning for you all the time, my letter would become too long and the words too many. But he who knows the secrets of the heart has the might to bring about relief for each of us by uniting us in joy.

Your precious letters have arrived; I have read and scrutinized them, and was happy to learn from them that you are well and healthy and that you have escaped from those great terrors, the like of which have not been experienced for many generations. Praise be to God for your deliverance and for granting you respite until you might be recompensed in a measure commensurate with your sufferings.

In your letters you alternately rebuke and offend me or put me to shame and use harsh words all the time. I have not deserved any of this. I swear by God, I do not believe that the heart of anyone traveling away from his wife has remained like mine, all the time and during all the years—from the moment of our separation to the very hour of writing this letter—so constantly thinking of you and yearning after you and regretting to be unable to provide you with what I so much desire: your legal rights on every Sabbath and holiday, and to fulfill all your wishes, great and small, with regard to dresses or food or anything else. And you write about me as if I had forgotten you and would not remember you had it not been for your rebukes, and as if, had you not warned me that the public would reprove me, I would not have thought of you. Put this out of your mind and do not impute such things to me. And if what you think or say about my dedication to you is the product of your mind, believing that words of rebuke will increase my yearning—no, in such a way God will not let me reach the fulfillment of my hope, although in my heart there is twice as much as I am able to write. But he is able to have us both reach compensation for our sufferings and then, when we will be saved, we will remember in what situation we are now.

You rebuke me with regard to the ambergris. You poor ones!!! Had you known how much trouble and expenses I have incurred to get this ambergris for you, you would have said: there is nothing like it in the world. This is the story: After I was resurrected from the dead and had lost all that I carried with me I took a loan of . . . dinars and traveled to countries beyond al-Ma'bar. I checked my accounts and found . . . with "the decimals" [a counting machine]. I took them and paid to one of our coreligionists who traveled back from al-Ma'bar to Aden . . . and for it he bought for you. . . .

This was my way of life from the moment I left you until I arrived in Aden (and from there to India) and from India back to Aden: Day and night I was constantly drinking, not of my free will, but I conducted myself in an exemplary way and if any one poked fun in foul speech in my presence, I became furious with him, until he became silent, he and others. I constantly fulfilled what God knows, and cured my soul by fasting during the days and praying during the nights. The congregations in Aden and in India often asked me to lead them in prayer, and I am regarded by them and regard myself as a pious man. . . .

Now in one of your letters you adjure me to set you free, then letters arrived from the old man saying the same. Later Ma'ani ["Eloquent"] b. al-Dajaji ["Seller of Fowl"] met me and told me that you came to his house before he set out on his travel. You had given him nutmeg paste as a collateral on a loan of 100 dirhems, but he released 20 dirhems to you. Please let me know whether this is correct, in which case I will return this sum to him. He reported also that you had asked him to return to you letters which your late father—may God have mercy on him—had sent with him, but he had said to you: "I have already packed them away on the boat." Then you said that these letters were not written with your consent and you asked him not to deliver them to me. On this Ma'ani had replied: The judge might have meanwhile sent a message demanding something from the elder, in which case the delivery of these letters might be useful to him.

Now, if this is your wish, I cannot blame you. For the waiting has been long. And I do not know whether the Creator will grant relief immediately so that I can come home, or whether matters will take time, for I cannot come home with nothing. Therefore I resolved to issue a writ which sets you free. Now the matter is in your hand. If you wish separation from me, accept the bill of repudiation and you are free. But if this is not your decision and not your desire, do not lose these long years of waiting: perhaps relief is at hand and you will regret at a time when regret will be of no avail.

And please do not blame me, for I never neglected you from the time when those things happened and made an effort to save you and me from people talking and impairing my honor. The refusal was on your side, not mine. I do not know whether this is your decision or that of someone else: this is our reward from him and our recompense. All day long I have a lonely heart and am pained by our separation. I feel that pain while writing these lines. But the choice is with you; the decision is in your hand: if you wish to carry the matter through, do so; if you wish to leave things as they are, do so. But do not act after the first impulse. Ask the advice of good people and act as you think will be best for you. May God inspire you with the right decision. . . .

[Best regards to my sister] and her husband, the illustrious elder Abu 'l-Khayr ["Mr. Good"] agreed to pay him 10 mithqals, which the elder Abu 'l-Makarim ["Noble Character"] will deliver to him.

Convey my greetings to the elder Abu Isaq, the son of your paternal uncle, to his mother, to the elder Abu 'Imran and his children, to . . . , the daughter of your paternal uncle, and to all those whom you know, my sincere regards.

I sent you 7 ½ mann of nutmeg, which is better than anything found in the Karim and worth more than other sorts of it by 1 dinar; 11 mann of good galingale; two futa cloths for the children; 2 ½ of celandine and 25 of odoriferous wood; fourteen pieces in number. . . .

8. You know, my lord, from my preceding letters that not a single bale of ours has remained on land and that all the bales in the ships are in the best places. I ask God to guarantee their safe arrival for us.

We have heard pleasing news from the west; for, by God, my lord, there have been many hideous rumors about Qayrawan, and every man added his own version, so that we had been very much upset. I ask God to let us hear good news from them, but we will have no peace of mind, until their letters have been received, confirming that the city is safe. I ask God that it will be so.

The ships, my lord, are in the last stage of preparations. Not a single soldier charged with their protection has remained on land. They have already loaded their water and provisions and are waiting now for the completion of the warship; they will set it afloat and sail, and the boats [of the merchants] will sail with them [the soldiers]. The day after the writing of this letter the galleys will be set afloat, for today they have completed their repair.

I wrote to M. Abu Sa'id Khalaf b. Ya'qub ["The Fortunate, Substitute, son of Jacob"]—may God keep him—a letter in four copies, sending each copy with coreligionists on different boats: namely, one with Salama Ibn Abi Kahil on the boat of al-Ba'shushi; another, on the boat of al-Andalusi, with Sahlan, may God keep him; a third copy, on the boat of Ibn al-Qaddar ["Mr. Potter"]—may God keep him—I gave to the owner of the boat, for no Jewish person traveled on it; the fourth, I gave to Salar ["Chieftain, leader"], the "boy" [employee] of Ibn al-Sahila ["The woman who neighs like a horse"]. I instructed all our coreligionists, may God keep them, to watch carefully the seventy bales and one barqalu [small bale] until they will deliver them in safety into the hands of Khalaf b. Ya'qub, the Andalusian.

I also sent a letter in five copies to Qayrawan, to my mother's brother, may God support him. I copied the letters which I will send to you, my lord. The letters indicated by you, twelve in all, were given by me to Wad'a ("Cowrie shell"), may God keep him. I will wrap up the remaining letters and send them with our coreligionists on five different boats.

Likewise, I wrote five letters to M. Abu Zikri Yahya, may God keep him, and informed him about all I had sent to al-Mahdiyya this year, a total of 179 bales and two barqalus, specifying the boats, the advantages on the freight collected for them, and similar matters. I ask God to mercifully grant them a safe passage.

I have asked my uncle, may God preserve his honored position, to send his son M. Abu Zikri Yahya to al-Mahdiyya as soon as our bales would arrive, to receive them all, to sell them in al-Mahdiyya during the height of the business season and send all the proceeds to my uncle in Qayrawan. I have asked the latter to buy for my lord all the goods you have ordered, such as lead, wax, brocade, textiles, saffron, etc.

I have already informed my lord, may God preserve his honored position, that I owed 30 dinars on account of the advances on the freight and that I had taken a suftaja [bill of exchange] of this amount from Ibn 'Abd al-Qudra ("Slave of [God's] Majesty"). I also took the 10 dinars which were with Salama, may God keep him, and made payments with them.

All the ships are ready to sail—may God grant them a safe passage. I intended to send Salama, when I learned that the ruler of Qayrawan had been defeated. There was great confusion here in the city and I was afraid that . . . and there were many bad rumors. . . .

[Address, right side:] To his excellency, my lord, the illustrious elder, Abu 'l-Faraj Joseph, son of Ya'qub Ibn 'Awkal, [may his] s[oul] r[est in peace]. May God make permanent his honored position, eminence, happiness, and prosperity.

[Left side:] From his servant, Ephraim, son of Isma'il, [may his] s[oul] r[est in peace], al-Jawhari. [To be delivered] in his office in Fustat, God willing.

9. My elder and master, may God prolong your life and make your welfare and happiness permanent. May he augment his bounty and gifts granted to you.

I am writing you from Palermo on the sixth of Tishri; may God make this a blessed year for me and for you and for all Israel.

What you wish to know: I was shipwrecked in Zahlaq, between Surt [Syrta; Sirte] and Hawwara [Lebda], and came out of it without a dinar or even a dirhem and no garment to wear; I arrived naked in Tripoli. By God, had I not met there a Jew who owed me a qintar of wax [sent to him] from Zawila and with whom I agreed on a price of 5 dinars, which I received from him and with which I bought clothing and provisions, I would have been destroyed and forced to have recourse to philanthropy.

Arriving in Palermo, I found that a man from Barqa had pulled down my small house and built there another. I quarreled with him, but, by God, I had no dinar or even a dirhem to spend [on a lawsuit]. Then I did not find my brother here so that I could not get from him part of what he owes me.

I sent you ten pounds of silk with Hayyim b. Sa'ada and sent you also 6 dinars gold, numbering 6 ¼. With you I left 2 dinars and with them in the house 1 dinar and the olive oil I bought from you. As you know, 10 dinars are due the girl as her second installment [of her marriage portion]. I wrote her a bill of divorce fearing the vicissitudes of fate, nor do I know whether I will be able to return to them in the course of two or even three years, for this town is menaced by enemy attack, and, at present, I do not have a thing.

I left with you promissory notes of: the "Son of the Swollen Woman," 6 ½ dinars; Isaac Qabisi, 1 ½ dinars; Hayyim Ibn Jasus, three qintars of tragacanth gum; all this besides what is owed me by Muslims. Collect these debts and keep the proceeds for the alimony for the boy. If she accepts the divorce, I will send every year the alimony for the boy. But if she prefers not to accept the divorce, deal with this matter cautiously in a way deserving my thanks: ask her whether she is prepared to settle with me in Sicily. [In case she does], let her confirm this by oath and inform me accordingly. I will then sell my apartment and bring her here together with my boy. By God, I did not write her the bill of divorce because I do not love her, but because I was afraid of the punishment of the Creator.

And, O God, O God, my lord, the little boy! Concern yourself with him in accordance with your [religiosity], so well known to me. When he becomes stronger, let him pass his time with a teacher. I will write to you and i[nform you about my situation]. By God, at this moment I have nothing. . . . But as soon as. . . .

[Address]: To my elder and master Abi Ibrahim Isma'il b. Abraham, may God be his protector.

From Joseph b. Samuel, known as al-Dny. Many greetings!

To Damsis, if God will.

10. "And say to him: All your life—peace upon you, peace upon your house, etc." [1 Samuel 25:6].

"The Lord will guard you from all evil, he will guard your soul. The Lord will guard your going out and coming in, from this time forth and forever" [Psalm 121:7–8].

To the presence of my brother, the delight of my eyes, my lord and leader, most esteemed by me, the crown of my head, and the one on whom I rely. May God prolong his life in happiness, guard and keep him and never deprive him of his good guidance. Dear brother, may God protect and never forsake you, may he be your help and sustainer, your support and trust from this time forth and forever.

I entered Sicily with my family coming from Tunis because of the privations suffered there and the horrors witnessed in Ifriqiya and also because of my longing for you. I intended to travel to Egypt via Sicily, for it is no longer possible to travel to Egypt directly from Ifriqiya. I planned to arrive in Egypt this very year, but God had willed otherwise. The obstacle to my travel and coming to you was illness in the family, which lasted four months. By Israel's religion, my misfortune forced me to spend 50 Murabiti dinars, for the wife fell ill and also the two little ones, and God willed that one of them died, the baby, he was one and a half years old—may your life be prolonged!

Then on the voyage to Sicily I was overcome by a disaster, the like of which I have never witnessed. A great storm seized us on the sea and we were forced to land on an island called Ghumur. We stayed there for twenty days with no food other than nettles. When we set out from there we did not have the look of human beings any more. The seas tormented us for thirty-five days and we were regarded as lost. For we set sail in four barges, but only ours survived. After arrival in Sicily we were so exhausted from our sufferings at sea that we were unable to eat our bread or to understand what was said to us for a full month.

This is the reason which prevented me from coming to Egypt this year. After all we have endured this year we are not prone to travel. You must see us with your own eyes; no description can do justice to our state.

Furthermore, it is now three years since I have seen a letter or an answer from you. I am very much upset, and this, too, makes me reluctant to come. Dear brother, by God, do not withhold your letters from me, for I am waiting for them. I am staying here in Sicily, by God, do not withhold your letters from me . . . for I am yearning after you and my mind is very much perturbed since the time your letters ceased to come. Write also about the poll tax.

If you intend to move, the best thing is to come to Sicily, for the spices of the east sell here well. Thus, it will be for both pleasure and business. We will help one another in enhancing the prestige of the family and will be happy with one another. . . .

This letter was written on the New Moon day of the month of Sivan. By God, I need not entreat you again to answer quickly, if God wills. Peace upon you and God's mercy and his blessings. And may your welfare increase forever and never decrease. Amen.

My son Abu 'l-Hasan sends greetings to you all, and so does the dweller of my house—to everyone, young and old.

[Address]: To my brother . . . Abu 'l-Barakat, son of . . . al-Abzari . . . Fustat. From his brother Abu Sa'id.

Questions: What were the merchants in these letters trading? Which annoyances, stresses, and dangers did they encounter in their work? How might some of these merchants' complaints be strategic, designed to mitigate obligations, or intended to achieve other goals? What do these letters tell us about relationships with friends and family? Why might long-distance trade end a marriage? How did their Jewish faith play a part in their work and letters? Were Jewish traders close to their coreligionists? In what way did government and the military intervene in merchants' work?

25. MARCO POLO, *TRAVELS*

Marco Polo (1254–1324) has become the most famous of all medieval travelers. Polo came from a family of Venetian merchants, although it is unclear to what degree he himself worked as one. During the late thirteenth century, Polo spent twenty-four years in the Mongol Empire, and he became a servant of the emperor. Polo was renowned for his encyclopedic knowledge of the people and wonders of this vast kingdom. Although it has widely been suspected that Polo exaggerated some of his accounts, most scholars today agree that his travels to China were genuine. Polo did not write his own account; instead, while he was in a prison in Genoa, he collaborated with a writer of romances, Rustichello of Pisa, who was more interested in entertaining the western European public with exotic rather than practical details.

Source: ed. and trans. Hugh Murray, Marco Polo, *The Travels of Marco Polo* (Edinburgh: Oliver & Boyd, 1845), pp. 95–119, 124–33, 137–43. Franco-Italian. Revised.

Introductory Narrative of the Journey: Prologue

Emperors, kings, dukes, marquises, counts, knights, and all persons wishing to know the various generations of men in the world, also the kingdoms, provinces, and all the regions of the east, read this book: in it you will find very great and wonderful things of the nations, chiefly of Armenia, Persia, and Mongolia, India, and various other provinces. In the present work Messer Marco Polo, a prudent and learned citizen of Venice, relates in order the various things which he himself saw, or heard from men of honor and truth. And those who read this book may be assured that all things in it are true.

For I would have you know that, from the creation of Adam to the present day, no pagan, or Saracen [Muslim], or Christian, or any other person of whatever race or generation, explored so many parts of the world, or saw such great wonders, as this Messer Marco Polo. He being in the year of our Lord 1295 shut up as a captive in the prisons of Genoa, thought within himself what a great evil it would be, if the wonders seen and heard by him should not be known to those who could not view them with their own eyes.

He therefore caused the accounts here contained to be written by Messer S. Rustichello of Pisa, who was confined with him in the same prison, in the year of our Lord 1298.

In the year of our Lord 1250, [with] the emperor Baldwin [II, r. 1228–1261] reigning at Constantinople, Niccolò Polo, father of the said Marco, and Maffio, brother of Niccolò, entered a ship, laden with diverse costly goods; and, spreading their sails, committed themselves to the deep. They arrived in safety at Constantinople, where they disposed of their cargo with advantage. They then determined to proceed together, in search of farther profit, to the Greater Sea [Black Sea]; and, having purchased many precious jewels, departed from Constantinople, and, entering a ship, sailed to Sudaq.

After remaining there some days, they resolved to proceed farther, and, mounting on horseback, came by continued journeys to Sara, the residence of Barka Khan, king and lord of the Tartars [Mongols], who then inhabited Bulgaria. That prince, who was much rejoiced at their arrival, received them very honorably and kindly. They gave him all the jewels brought from Constantinople, which he gladly accepted, and bestowed in return double their value.

After they had dwelt in this city a year, a most furious war arose between Barka and Alau, the ruler of eastern Mongolia. Their forces were led against each other; and, after a very sharp contest and much slaughter on both sides, Alau was victorious. This war rendered it impossible for the Venetians to return with safety by the same road, and they thought it advisable to proceed eastward, and endeavor by another route to find their way back to Venice. Departing from Barka they happily reached a certain city named Oukaka, subject to the dominion of a western chief. From there they passed a river named Tigris, and wandered through a desert during 17 successive days, finding no inhabitants, except Tartars dwelling in tents and subsisting by their cattle.

They then came to a city in the province of Persia, named Bokhara, the noblest in that country, governed by a king called Barak. Here, being unable to proceed, they remained three full years. While the brothers sojourned in Bokhara, it happened that Alau, lord of the east, dispatched ambassadors to the sovereign of all the Tartars, who in their language is called the great khan, meaning the king of kings, and whose name was Kublai [r. 1260–1294]. They [the ambassadors], on meeting the brothers, felt a little wonder, having never seen any men from the Latin countries. Addressing them courteously, they besought that they would accompany the embassy to the khan, promising much honor and wealth, since, though wonderfully desirous, he had never seen one of their nation.

The Venetians made a suitable answer, and frankly agreed to comply with the request. They set out and continued a whole year traveling in a northeastern direction; and though much delayed by heavy snows and the swelling of rivers, at length reached the residence of that mighty monarch, having beheld on their way many wonderful objects, which will be described hereafter in this book.

Kublai, illustrious for his benignity, received the brothers kindly and joyfully, being very desirous to see Latins. He urgently inquired what sort of emperor they had, how he lived and administered justice; asking questions also respecting the supreme pontiff, and all the acts and manners of the

Christians—to which they made judicious replies in the Tartar [Mongol] language, which they had learned.

This great king and master of all the Tartars in the world, and of all those regions, being informed respecting the actions of the Latins, was greatly pleased. Calling a council of his barons, he informed them, that he wished to send messengers to the pope, the lord of the Christians; which they unanimously approved. He then asked the brothers in friendly terms to be the bearers of his message; and this they prudently declared themselves ready and willing to undertake. He next ordered letters to be written, to be conveyed by them in company with a certain baron named Kogotal, whom he assigned as a companion. He instructed them, after the necessary salutations, to request of his holiness to send a hundred wise men, learned in all the seven arts, who might show to the idolaters, and others subject to his dominion, the diabolical nature of their law, and how that of the Christians was superior. Farther, he piously enjoined them to bring a portion of the oil of the lamp burning in Jerusalem before the sepulcher of our savior.

Moreover, he gave to them a golden tablet marked with his seal, containing an express order, that wherever they went they should have their necessities supplied. Having received this, and taken leave of the king, barons, and the whole court, they mounted their horses and commenced their journey. After some days, Kogotal, the baron, at a city named Alau, fell sick and could not proceed; but the brothers went on until they came safely to Laias, in Armenia. In this journey, however, owing to the bad roads, and the large rivers which they could not cross on horseback, three years were consumed. Wherever they went, on showing the golden tablet, they were received with the greatest honors, and supplied with whatever they wanted.

Departing from Laias in April 1269, the brothers arrived at Acre, where they learned with much grief that his holiness Clement IV [r. 1265–1268] was dead. They therefore went to Theobald, viscount of Piacenza, who resided there as a legate of the apostolical see, and was a man of high authority and virtue. They related to him the cause why they wished to visit the supreme pontiff. He was struck with admiration, and revolving in his mind, that the holy Roman Church and the Christian faith might hence derive the greatest benefit, advised them to wait until another pope should be named, to whom they might deliver their embassy. They therefore determined to spend the interval in visiting their families at Venice. Departing from Acre, they proceeded to Negroponte, and from there to their native city. Here Messer Niccolò found that his wife, whom he left pregnant, had died, leaving a son named Marco, the same who wrote this book.

Waiting the appointment of another pope, the travelers spent two full years at Venice. At last seeing that no pontiff was elected, and unwilling to delay their return to the great khan, they departed, taking with them Marco, son of Niccolò. They repaired to Acre, and told the legate, that having tarried too long, and there being no appearance of an election, they must beg permission, in conformity with that monarch's injunctions, to take the portion of oil from the lamp burning before the sepulcher.

Having obtained his consent, they went to Jerusalem, took what they desired, and returned, when he gave them letters, with permission to depart. They proceeded from Acre to Laias; but during their stay there, were informed that the legate himself had been appointed pope, under the name of Gregory X of Piacenza [r. 1271–1276], being the same who afterward held a council at Lyons, on the Rhône. The new pontiff sent a messenger after them, desiring their immediate return; and they joyfully obeyed, making the voyage in a galley prepared for them by the king of Armenia.

They paid their homage to his holiness, who received them graciously, loaded them [with] many honors, and gave them two very learned friars, of the Order of Preachers, the wisest that could be found in those parts, named Niccolò of Bicenza and William of Tripoli, to accompany them to the great khan. He bestowed on them letters and privileges, instructed them in the message which he wished to be conveyed to that monarch, and gave his benediction to Niccolò, Maffio, Marco, and the two friars. They then proceeded together to Laias; but while there, the sultan of Babylon [Baghdad], named Bonduchdaree, came with a mighty army to attack the city. In these circumstances, the preachers, struck with the fear of war, and with the dangers already encountered, gave to Niccolò and Maffio certain letters, and resolved to proceed no farther.

Then the brothers commenced their journey, and by constant marches arrived safely at a very rich and powerful city named Clemenfu, where the great khan resided. The observations made by them on this expedition will be narrated afterward in the proper place; but on account of the severe weather, as well as the difficulty and danger of passing the rivers, they completed it in three years and a half. When their return became known to the khan, he rejoiced exceedingly, and ordered forty of his messengers to go to meet them, by whom they were supplied with every necessity, and loaded with honors.

Having reached this great city, where the monarch had his abode, they went to his palace, presenting themselves most humbly on bended knees. He desired them to rise, and asked how they did; they replied, that, by the grace of God, they were well, especially since they had found him healthy and cheerful. He then inquired about their transactions with the supreme pontiff, when they explained to him all that they had done, delivering the letters confided to them by Pope Gregory. He received them graciously, commending them for their fidelity and attention. They next presented the oil from the sepulcher, which he reverently accepted. He inquired who was that young man with them, to which Niccolò replied: "My lord, he is your servant, my son." "Then," said the great khan, "he is welcome, I am much pleased with him." He celebrated their return by a joyful feast; and while they remained in his court, they were honored before all his barons.

During this stay, Messer Marco acquired the Tartar and four other languages, so as to speak and write them well; he learned also their manners, and became in all things exceedingly sensible and sagacious. When the great khan saw him display so much worth and prudence, he sent him as a messenger to a very distant land, which it required six months to reach. He returned and reported his embassy very sensibly, relating many new things respecting the countries through which he had traveled; while other ambassadors, being able to say nothing, except about the special message entrusted to them, were accounted foolish and ignorant by the khan, who was greatly delighted to become acquainted with the varieties of nations. Messer Marco, aware of this, studied all these strange objects, and thus pleased beyond measure his majesty and the barons, who predicted that, if he lived, he would become an eminent man. In short, he remained in the court of the khan 17 years, and never ceased to be employed as an ambassador. The other chiefs began to envy the honors paid to him, and his knowledge of the country, which exceeded that of any other person who ever visited it.

After Messer Niccolò, Messer Maffio, and Messer Marco had remained long at the court of the great khan, they felt a strong desire to revisit their native country. Niccolò therefore took an opportunity one day, when the monarch seemed in particularly good humor, to throw himself at his feet, and solicit for them all permission to depart; but the sovereign was so much attached to his visitors that he would by no means listen to this proposal.

It happened, however, that the Queen Bolgana, the spouse of Arghun [r. 1284–1291], lord of the east, died, and in her last will enjoined that he should receive no wife unless of her family. He therefore sent as ambassadors to the khan three barons, Uladai, Alpusca, and Coia, with a great train, requesting a lady of the same lineage with the deceased queen. The monarch received the embassy with joy, and selected a young princess of that house. Everything being arranged, and a numerous train of attendants appointed, they were graciously dismissed, and began their return; but after traveling eight months, their advance was rendered impossible by fresh wars that had arisen among the Tartar princes. They were therefore very reluctantly obliged to retrace their steps, and state the cause that had arrested their progress.

It happened that at that time Marco arrived from a voyage to India, and, by relating the novelties he had observed, pleased those envoys very much, proving himself well fitted to guide them by this route, which he recommended as shorter and easier than that by land. They therefore besought as a favor of the khan, that the Latins might accompany them and the queen. The khan granted this favor, yet unwillingly, on account of his love for them.

When that great monarch saw that they were about to depart, he called them before him, and delivering golden tablets signed with the royal seal, ordered that they should have free passage through his land, and that their expenses, with those of all their family, should be everywhere defrayed. He entrusted them with messages for the pope, the king of France, the king of Spain, and other kings of Christendom. He caused to be prepared 14 ships, each with 4 masts, and many with 12 sails; upon which the barons, the lady, and the three brothers took leave, and, with numerous attendants, went on board. The khan gave them their expenses for two years; and after sailing three months, they came to a certain island named Java, where there are many wonderful things, which I will relate in this book. They then departed from it; and I must tell you that they sailed through the Indian Sea 18 months, and saw many strange objects, which will also be hereafter described.

At length they came to the court of King Arghun, but found that he was already dead, when it was determined to give the princess in marriage to Ghazan [r. 1295–1304], his son. I must tell you, that though in that vessel there embarked full 600 persons, exclusive of mariners, all died except 18; and they found the dominion of the land of Arghun held by Kaikhatu [Arghun's brother], to whom they very tenderly recommended the lady on the part of the great khan. Ghazan was then at a place on the borders of Persia, which has its name from the *arbor secco* [dry tree], where an army of 60,000 men was assembled to guard certain positions against hostile irruption. They accordingly went there, fulfilled their mission, and then returned to the residence of Kaikhatu, where they reposed during the space of nine months. They then took leave and went on their way, when Kaikhatu presented four golden tablets, with instructions that they should be honored, and all the expenses defrayed. This was fully executed, so that they frequently went accompanied by 200 horsemen.

I have also to tell you about the honor of those three Latins, in whom the great khan had placed such confidence, appointing them to conduct Queen Kukachi, with a daughter of the king of Manji, to Arghun, the lord of the east—that those two young and beautiful ladies were guarded by them as if they had been their daughters, and bestowed on them the veneration due to fathers. Indeed, Kukachi and her husband Ghazan, now reigning, treated the messengers with such kindness, that there was nothing they would not have done for them; and when they were about to depart, the queen grieved very much, and even shed tears.

Thus, after much time and many labors, by the grace of God they came to Trebizond, then to Constantinople, Negropont, and finally to Venice. They arrived in the year 1295, bringing with them great riches, and giving thanks to God who had delivered them from many labors and dangers.

Description of China, and of the Court of the Emperor Kublai

Now I am to give you a wonderful account of the greatest king of the Tartars, still reigning, named Kublai, or lord of lords. That name is assuredly well merited, since he is the most powerful in people, in lands, and in treasure, that is, or ever was, from the creation of Adam to the present day; and by the statements to be made in this book, every man will be satisfied that he really is so.

Whosoever descends in the direct line from Genghis Khan is entitled to be master of all the Tartars, and Kublai is the sixth great khan. He began to reign in the year of our Lord 1256, and maintained the dominion by his valor, address, and wisdom. His brothers sought to oppose his succession, but by bravery and right he triumphed over them. From the beginning of his reign, 42 years have elapsed to the present day, in the year 1298. He is now full 85 years old, and before his accession commanded many armies, when he proved himself good at weapons, and a brave captain. But since that time he has joined the army only once, which was in the year 1286, and I will tell you on what occasion.

You must understand that a certain cousin of his, named Nayan, who, like his ancestors, was his vassal [subordinate], yet had many lands and provinces of his own, and could raise 400,000 horsemen, being 30 years old, refused to remain longer in subjection, and assumed the whole sovereignty to himself. He sent to a certain great lord, named Qaidu, a nephew of that monarch, but in rebellion against him, and desirous of doing him the greatest injury. To him Nayan proposed to attack the monarch on one side, while he himself advanced on another, so that they might acquire the dominion over his whole territory. Qaidu declared himself well pleased, and promised to be ready at the time appointed. He could bring into the field 100,000 cavalry; and those two assembled a mighty army on horseback and foot, and marched against the great khan.

When Kublai learned these things, he was not at all alarmed, but declared that he wished he might never wear a crown, nor hold sway over a kingdom, if he did not take the traitors to an evil death. He therefore made his whole army be prepared in 22 days, and so secretly, that nothing was known beyond his own council. He raised full 360,000 mounted soldiers, and 100,000 infantry;

and the reason of their number not being greater was that they consisted only of his huntsmen, and those immediately round his person, the rest being employed in carrying on distant wars; for if he could have assembled his whole host, the multitude would have been such as no man could have numbered. He then called his astrologers, and asked of them if he would be victorious; they answered, that he would do to his enemies according to his pleasure.

The great khan having assembled these forces, took his departure, and in 20 days came to a vast plain, where Nayan had assembled all his troops, amounting to 400,000 warriors. The khan took much care to scour the roads, and intercept all who could have carried the intelligence; so that when he approached at dawn of day, the rebel was lying asleep in bed with a favorite wife, not having the least dread of his arrival, and, consequently, no guard on any side of the camp.

Kublai then advanced, having a tower fixed upon four elephants, on which were placed his ensigns, so that he could be seen by the whole army. His men, divided into bands of 30,000, surrounded in a moment the adverse force, each soldier having a footman on the crupper behind him, with a bow in his hand.

When Nayan and his men saw their camp thus encircled by the khan and his host, they were completely confounded; yet they ran to arms, formed themselves in order of battle, and were soon prepared to strike. Then began the beating on many instruments, and singing with loud voices; for it is the custom of the Tartars, that until the drums sound the troops do not engage. But when that drum of the great khan was sounded, all the other performers began playing, and raising their voices very loud, making a noise that was truly most wonderful. Then the two armies rushed against each other with sword, spear, and lance, while the footmen were prepared with bow and quiver. The battle was fierce and cruel; the arrows filled the air like rain; horses and horsemen were seen falling to the ground; and the tumult was such, that if God had thundered, he could not have been heard. Nayan was a baptized Christian, and therefore had the cross upon his standard.

Never, in our day, was there so hard and terrible combat, nor so many assembled on one field, especially of horsemen; and the number who fell on both sides was fearful to behold. The battle continued from nine in the morning until midday; but the great khan at last remained master of the field. When Nayan and his men saw that they could hold out no longer, they committed themselves to flight; but it availed them nothing; he was taken, and all his troops surrendered.

When the great khan heard that Nayan was taken, he ordered him to be put to death in the manner I am now to tell you. He was wrapped in a carpet, and violently tossed to and fro until he died. This mode was adopted, that, being of imperial lineage, his blood might not be shed on the ground, nor his cries ascend into the air. When that battle was gained, four of his provinces paid tribute and homage to the great khan. These were Cicorcia, Cauli [Korea], Bastol, and Suchintin.

When the monarch had achieved this triumph, the Saracens, pagans, Jews, and other generations of men who believe not in God, expressed wonder at the cross which the vanquished leader had carried on his standard, and said in derision of the Christians, "See how the cross of your God has aided Nayan and his people." They made such a noise on this subject that it came to the ears of the khan, who was much displeased, and sending for the Christians, said to them, "If your God did not assist Nayan, he acted with great justice, because he is a good and righteous God. Nayan was a traitor and rebel against his lord, and therefore God did well in not assisting him." Then the Christians replied, "O, great sire! You have spoken the truth, for the cross will aid nothing unjust, and he met only what he well deserved."

Having gained this victory, the great khan returned to his capital, Khan-baliq, with much festival and rejoicing. When the other king, named Qaidu, heard how his ally had been worsted, he was struck with fear and did not attempt to lead his army against the monarch. Now you have seen how the great khan went to battle, and for what cause, while on all other occasions he sent his sons and barons; but this war was of such magnitude that it seemed to deserve his own immediate presence.

Now let us tell of the officers and barons of the great khan, and how he rewarded those who fought with him in the battle against Nayan. To those who commanded 100 men, he gave the command of 1,000, and to those of 1,000 that of 10,000; and he bestowed, according to their rank, tablets of gold or silver, on all of which was written, "By the might of the great God, and by the favor which he gave to our emperor: may that prince be blessed, and may all those who do not obey him die and be destroyed." Those who hold these documents enjoy certain privileges, with written instructions how they are to exercise their authority.

He who commands 100,000 men receives a golden one [tablet], weighing 300 *saggi*, under which is sculptured a lion on one side, and on the other the sun and moon. Those who bear these noble tablets have instructions that whenever they ride they should bear above their head an umbrella of gold, and as often as they are seated, it should be upon silver. There are also tablets on which is sculpted a gyrfalcon, which he gives to three great barons, who have then equal authority with himself. They can take whenever they please and lead from place to place the troops and horses of any prince or king; and whoever dares to disobey in anything their will and mandate must die as a rebel to the sovereign.

Now let us speak of the appearance and manners of this mighty prince.

The great khan, lord of lords, named Kublai, is of a fine middle size, neither too tall nor too short; he has a beautiful fresh complexion and well-proportioned limbs. His color is fair and vermilion like the rose, his eyes dark and fine, his nose well formed and placed.

He has four ladies, who always rank as his wives; and the eldest son, born to him by one of them, succeeds as the rightful heir of the empire. They are named empresses; each bears his name, and holds a court of her own; there is not one who has not 300 beautiful maidens, with eunuchs, and many other male and female attendants, so that some of the courts of these ladies contain 10,000 persons; and when he wishes to visit any one, he makes her come to his apartment, or sometimes goes to hers.

He maintains also a number of concubines. There is a race of Tartars who are called Migrat or Ungrat, and are a very handsome people. From them are selected 100 girls, the most beautiful in all their country, who are conducted to court. He makes them be guarded by the ladies of the palace; and they are examined if they have a sweet breath, if they are virgins, and are sound in all their limbs. Those that are approved in every respect wait upon their great lord in the following order: six of them attend every three days, then another six come in their place, and so on throughout the year.

Know too that the great khan has by his wives 22 sons; the elder was named Zhenjin Khan, and was to be lord of all the empire after his father; but he died, leaving a son named Temür [r. 1294–1307], who in time will succeed; he is a wise and good man, tried in many battles. The monarch has also 25 sons by his concubines; and each is a great baron; and of the 72 sons by his four wives, seven reign over large kingdoms, like wise and good men, because they resemble their father—and he is the best ruler of nations and conductor of wars in the world.

Now I have told you about himself, his wives, sons, and concubines; next I will relate how he holds his court.

He resides in the vast city of Khanbaliq, three months in the year, December, January, and February, and has here his great palace, which I will now describe.

It is a complete square, a mile long on every side, so that the whole is four miles in circuit; and in each angle is a very fine edifice, containing bows, arrows, cords, saddles, bridles, and all other implements of war. In the middle of the wall between these four edifices are others, making altogether eight, filled with stores, and each containing only a single article.

Toward the south are five gates, the middle one very large, never opened nor shut except when the great khan is to pass through; while on the other side is one by which all enter in common. Within that wall is another, containing eight edifices similarly constructed; in which is lodged the wardrobe of the sovereign.

These walls enclose the palace of that mighty lord, which is the greatest that ever was seen. The floor rises ten palms above the ground, and the roof is exceedingly lofty. The walls of the chambers and stairs are all covered with gold and silver, and adorned with pictures of dragons, horses, and other races of animals. The hall is so spacious that 6,000 can sit down to banquet; and the number of apartments is incredible. The roof is externally painted with red, blue, green, and other colors, and is so varnished that it shines like crystal, and is seen to a great distance around. It is also very strongly and durably built.

Between the walls are pleasant meadows filled with various living creatures, as white stags, the musk animal, deer, wild goats, squirrels, and other beautiful creatures. The whole enclosure is full of animals, except the path by which men pass. On the other side, toward the south, is a magnificent lake, to which many kinds of fish are brought and nourished. A river enters and flows out; but the fish are retained by iron gratings. Toward the north, about a bowshot from the palace, Kublai has constructed a mound, full a hundred paces high and a mile in circuit, all covered with evergreen trees which never shed their leaves. When he hears of a beautiful tree, he causes it to be dug up, with all the roots and the earth round it, and to be conveyed to him on the backs of elephants, from which the eminence has been made verdant all over, and is called the Green Mountain. On the top is a palace, also covered with verdure; it and the trees are so lovely that all who look upon them feel delight and joy. In the vicinity is another palace, where resides the grandson of the great khan, Temür, who is to reign after him, and who follows the same life and customs as his grandfather. He has already a golden bull and the imperial seal; but he has no authority while his grandfather lives.

Having described to you the palaces, I will tell you of the great city of Cathay [northern China], which contains them. Near it is another large and splendid one, also named Khanbaliq, which finds meaning in our language "city of the lord"; but the monarch, finding by astrology that this town would rebel, built another near it, divided only by a river, and bearing the same name, to which its inhabitants were compelled to remove.

It forms a regular square, six miles on each side, and thus 24 miles in circumference. It is surrounded by walls of earth, 10 paces thick and 20 in height; yet the upper part becomes gradually thinner, so that at the top the breadth is only three paces. There are 12 gates, each containing an edifice, making one in each square of that wall, and filled with men, who guard the palace.

The streets are so broad and so straight that from one gate another is visible. It contains many beautiful houses and palaces, and a very large one in the midst, containing a steeple with a large bell, which at night sounds three times; after which no man must leave the city without some urgent necessity, as of sickness or a woman about to bear a child. At each gate a thousand men keep guard, not from dread of any enemy, but in reverence of the monarch who dwells within it, and to prevent injury by robbers.

When the great khan holds a court, he is guarded, on account of his excellency and honor, by 12,000 horsemen, who are called *quesitan*, that is, "faithful servants of their lord"; and this he does not from fear, but regard to his high dignity. Over these 12,000 are four captains, so that each commands 3,000; and they keep guard in turn three days and three nights, eating and drinking at the expense of the prince. Then they go away, and another party comes; and so they proceed throughout the whole year.

When the khan wishes to celebrate a splendid festival, the tables are so arranged that his is much higher than the others, and he sits on the north with his face toward the south. His first wife is seated beside him on the left, while on the right are his sons and nephews, and all those of imperial lineage, who are so stationed that their head is on a level with the feet of the monarch. The barons sit still lower; while the ladies, daughters, and female relations of the khan are placed beneath the queen on the left side, and under them all the wives of the barons; every class knows the spot where they ought to sit. The tables are so arranged that the monarch can see all the company, who are very numerous; and outside of that hall there eat more than 50,000 persons, who have come with presents or remarkable objects from foreign parts, and attend on the days when he holds a court or celebrates a marriage.

In the midst of this hall is a very large vessel of fine gold, containing wine, and on each side two smaller ones, from which the liquor is poured out into flagons, each containing fully enough for eight men; and one of these is placed between every two guests, who have besides separate cups of gold to drink out of. This supply of plate is of very great value, and indeed the khan has so many vessels of gold and silver that none without seeing could possibly believe it. Those who serve the khan at table are great barons, who hold their mouths carefully wrapped in rich towels of silk and gold, that their breath may not blow upon the dishes.

When he begins to drink, all the instruments, which are very numerous, are sounded, and while the cup is in his hand, the barons and others present fall on their knees, and make signs of great humility; this is done every time he drinks, or when new food is brought in. These I will not attempt to recount, since anyone may believe that he will have the greatest variety of beasts and birds, wild and domestic, and of fishes in their season, and in the greatest abundance, prepared most delicately in various modes suitable to his magnificence and dignity. Every baron or knight brings his wife, and she sits at table along with the other ladies. When the great sire has eaten, and the tables are removed, a number of jesters, players, and other witty persons perform various pieces, exciting much mirth and pleasure among the company, who then all depart and go to their homes.

The Tartars celebrate a festival on the day of their nativity. The birthday of the khan is on 28 September, and is the greatest of all, except that at the beginning of the year. On this occasion he clothes himself in robes of beaten gold, and his 12 barons and 12,000 soldiers wear like him dresses of a uniform color and shape; not that they are so costly, but similarly made of silk, gilded, and bound by a cincture of gold. Many have these robes adorned with precious stones and pearls, so as to be worth 10,000 golden bezants [coins]. The great khan, 13 times in the year, presents to those barons and knights robes of the same color with his own; and this is what no lord in the world can do.

On the day of his nativity, all the Tartars from every province of the world, who hold lands under him, celebrate a festival, and bring presents suited to their station. The same is done by every individual who asks from him any favor or office. He has 12 barons who bestow commands on such persons as they think proper. On that day, the Christians, Saracens, and all the races of men who are subject to him, make prayers to their gods that they will preserve and grant him a long, healthy, and happy life. I will tell you no more of this festival, but of another which they celebrate at the beginning of the year, called the White Feast.

The Tartars begin their year in February, when the khan and all his people celebrate a feast, where all, both men and women, are clothed in white robes. They consider these as signifying joy and good fortune, and that hence all prosperity will happen to them throughout the year. On that day, all who hold land or any dominion under him, make the most magnificent presents in their power, consisting of gold, silver, pearls, precious stones, and rich white cloths; so that, during the whole year, he may have abundance of treasures, and the means of enjoying himself.

They present also more than 5,000 camels, with about 100,000 beautiful white horses. On that day, too, he is gratified with at least 5,000 elephants covered with cloths of silk and gold, finely wrought with figures of beasts and birds, and each having on his back a box filled with vessels of gold and silver, and other things necessary for the feast. They all pass before the great khan, and form the most brilliant spectacle ever seen in this world.

In the morning of that festal day, before the tables are spread, the kings, generals, counts, astrologers, physicians, falconers, and many other officers and rulers, repair to the hall of the sovereign, and those who are not admitted remain outside the palace in a place where the monarch can fully see them. They are in the following order: foremost, his sons, nephews, and others of his lineage, then kings, generals, and others according to their rank. As soon as each has taken his place, a great prelate rises and says, with a loud voice, "incline and adore," and presently all bend down, strike their foreheads on the earth, and make prayers to their master, adoring him as a god. This they do four times, and then go to an altar, on which is written the name of the great khan. Then, out of a beautiful box, they pour incense on that table in reverence of him, and return to their place; they next make those rich and valuable presents which I have described. When all these things have been done, and the prince has seen them all, the tables are placed, and they sit down, when the feast is ordered and celebrated in the manner already explained.

Now that I have described to you the joy of the White Feast, I will tell you of a most noble thing done by his monarch; for he has ordered vestments to be bestowed upon the barons there present.

He has 12 barons, who are called *quecitain*, or the faithful men of the supreme lord. He gives to each 13 vestments, differing in color, and adorned with precious stones, pearls, and other great and most valuable articles; also a golden girdle, and sandals worked with threads of silver, so that each, in these several dresses, appears like a king; and there is a regulation what dress ought to be worn at each of the feasts. The monarch has 13 robes of the same color with those of his barons, but more costly.

And now I will relate a most wonderful thing, namely, that a large lion is led into his presence, which, as soon as it sees him, drops down, and makes a deep sign of humility, owning him for its lord, and moving about without any chain. Now you will hear of the great huntings made by this powerful leader.

He resides in the city of Cathay three months, December, January, and February, and has commanded that, for 60 days' journey round, all the people should engage in hunting and falconry. The various lords of nations are ordered to bring to him large beasts, stags, boars, wild goats, and other animals. Those at the distance of 30 days' journey send the bodies preserved with the entrails taken out, while those at 60 send only the skins, which are employed as furniture for his army.

Now let us tell of the beasts which his majesty keeps for hunting. Among these are leopards and lynxes, or stag wolves, well fitted for that purpose. He has also many lions larger than those of Babylon, of a beautiful hair and color, striped lengthways, black, red, and white, and trained to catch stags, wild oxen, hogs, wild goats, and asses; and it is delightful to see one of these chases, where the hunters go out, carrying the lions in a cage, and with him a small dog. They have likewise an abundance of eagles, with which they capture hares, foxes, and even wolves; those which are trained to catch these last are very large, and of great weight, so that no wolf can escape them.

Now let us speak of the dogs kept by this monarch. He has two barons who are brothers, named Baian and Mingan; they are called *ciunci*, that is, the keepers of mastiff dogs, and each commands a party of 10,000 men, one clothed in vermilion, and the other in blue; whenever they go out with the monarch they are dressed in these vestments. In each party there are 2,000 of the men, who guide respectively one, two, or more large mastiffs, making altogether a vast multitude. When his majesty goes to hunt, these two brothers attend him on opposite sides, each with 10,000 men and 5,000 dogs; and they hunt thus a day's journey distant from each other, and never pursue any animal which is not captured. It is indeed beautiful to see the speed of these dogs and the hunters, for when the prince goes out with his barons, boars and other animals are running on every side, and dogs pursuing.

When the monarch has remained in Khanbaliq these three months, he departs and goes southward to the ocean two days' journey distant. He leads them with 10,000 falconers, conveying full 5,000 gyrfalcons, peregrine falcons in abundance, and also many vultures; but do not imagine that these are all kept in one place; there are 200 here, 300 there, and so on. The birds caught are mostly presented to the great sire, and when he goes to hunt with his gyrfalcons, vultures, and falcons, 10,000 men are ranged, two by two, so as to enclose much ground; these are called *toscaor*, meaning in our language "men who remain on the watch," and each has a call and a hood to invite the birds. And when any falconer, by order of his majesty, sends forth a falcon, he has no need to follow it, because wherever it may go, it is watched by the men ranged in double order, who can either catch it again, or if it is necessary offer it succor.

Each of the birds belonging to the sovereign and barons has a tablet of silver on its feet, with its name and that of the owner inscribed, so that wherever caught, it can be returned to him. If he is unknown, the animal must be carried to a chief named *bularguci*, or "guardian of things that are lost," who stands with his flag on an elevated spot, and all who have missed anything go to him to recover it. Whoever finds a horse, a bird, a sword, or anything else, and does not carry it to the owner or to this officer, is treated as a robber; thus scarcely anything is ever lost.

When the monarch goes upon these excursions, he has with him four elephants, and a chamber prepared, covered within with cloth of beaten gold, and outwardly with lions' skins, where he keeps 12 of his very best gyrfalcons, with 12 barons to amuse him by their society. As the falconers ride by, they call, "Sire, the birds are passing," when he throws open the chamber, and seeing the object, selects the gyrfalcons that please him, and sends them forth against the birds, few of which ever escape. Lying on his couch, he can view and enjoy the chase. Thus, I think, there is not, and never will be, any lord in the world who has or can have so much delight as the great khan. . . .

With regard to the money of Khanbaliq, the great khan may be called a perfect alchemist, for he makes it himself. He orders people to collect the bark of a certain tree, whose leaves are eaten by the worms that spin silk. The thin rind between the bark and the interior wood is taken, and from it cards are formed like those of paper, all black. He then causes them to be cut into pieces, and each is declared worth respectively half a silver pound, a whole one, a silver groat of Venice, and so on to the value of ten bezants [here silver coins]. All these cards are stamped with his seal, and so many are fabricated that they would buy all the treasuries in the world. He makes all his payments in them, and circulates them through the kingdoms and provinces over which he holds dominion; and none dares to refuse them under pain of death. All the nations under his sway receive and pay money for their merchandise, gold, silver, precious stones, and whatever they transport, buy or sell. The merchants often bring to him goods worth 400,000 bezants [silver coins], and he pays them all in these cards, which they willingly accept, because they can make purchases with them throughout the whole empire.

He frequently commands those who have gold, silver, cloths of silk and gold, or other precious commodities, to bring them to him. Then he calls 12 men skillful in these matters and commands them to look at the articles and fix their price. Whatever they name is paid in these cards, which the merchant cordially receives. In this manner the great sire possesses all the gold, silver, pearls, and precious stones in his dominions.

When any of the cards are torn or spoiled, the owner carries them to the place from where they were issued, and receives fresh ones, with a deduction of 3 per cent. If a man wishes gold or silver to make plate, girdles, or other ornaments, he goes to the office carrying a sufficient number of cards and gives them in payment for the quantity which he requires.

This is the reason why the khan has more treasure than any other lord in the world; no, all the princes in the world together have not an equal amount.

He has appointed 12 very great barons, who hold command over all things in the 34 provinces. They reside in a palace within the city of Khanbaliq, large and beautiful, containing many halls and apartments; and for every province there is an agent and a number of writers or notaries, having each a house to himself. They manage all the provincial affairs according to the will and pleasure of the 12 barons.

The latter have power to appoint lords of the provinces above mentioned; and having chosen the one whom they judge best qualified, they name him to the great khan, who confirms him, and bestows a golden tablet corresponding to his command. These 12 barons are called in the Tartar language *scieng*, that is, "the greater officers of state." They order the army to go where and in what numbers they please, but all according to the commands of the great sire; and they do every other thing necessary for the provinces. The palace in which they dwell is called *scien*, and is the largest in all the court; they have the power of doing much good to any one whom they favor.

I must now inform you that from the city of Khanbaliq many messengers are sent to diverse provinces, and on all the roads they find, at every 25 miles, a post called *ianb*, where the imperial envoys are received. At each is a large edifice, containing a bed covered with silk, and everything useful and convenient for a traveler; so that if a king were to come, he would be well accommodated. Here, too, they find full 400 horses that the prince has ordered to be always in waiting to convey them when sent to any quarter along the principal roads.

When they have to go through any district where there is no habitation, the monarch has caused such edifices to be reared at the distance of 35 or at most 40 miles; thus they go through all the provinces, finding everywhere inns and horses for their reception. This is the greatest establishment that was ever kept by any king or emperor in the world; for at those places there are maintained more than 200,000 horses. Also edifices, furnished and prepared in the manner now described, amount to more than 10,000.

Moreover, in the intervals between these stations, at every three miles, are erected villages of about 40 houses, inhabited by foot runners, also employed on these dispatches. They wear a large girdle, set round with bells, which are heard at a great distance. When one of them receives a letter or packet, he runs full speed to the next village, where his approach being announced by the bells, another is ready to start and proceed to the next, and so on. By these pedestrian messengers the khan receives news in one day and night from places distant ten days' journey; in two from those distant twenty; and in ten from those distant a hundred. From them he exacts no tribute, but gives them horses and many other things.

When his messengers go on horseback to carry intelligence into the provinces or bring tidings from distant parts, and more especially, regarding any district that has rebelled, they ride in one day and night 200, 250, or even 300 miles; and when there are two, they receive two good horses, bind themselves round the head and body, and gallop full speed from one station to the next at 25 miles' distance, where they find two others fresh and ready harnessed, on which they proceed with the same speed. They stop not for an instant day nor night, and are thus enabled to bring news in so short a period. Now, I will tell you the great bounty which the monarch bestows twice in the year.

He sends his messengers through all his kingdoms and provinces, to know if any of his subjects have had their crops injured through bad weather or any other disaster; and if such injury has happened, he does not exact from them any tribute for that season or year; no, he gives them grain out of his own stores to subsist upon, and to sow their fields.

This he does in summer; in winter he inquires if there has been a mortality among the cattle, and in that case grants similar exemption and aid. When there is a great abundance of grain, he causes magazines to be formed, to contain wheat, rice, millet, or barley, and care to be taken that it be not lost or spoiled; then when a scarcity occurs, this grain is drawn forth and sold for a third or fourth of the current price. Thus there cannot be any severe famine; for he does it through all his dominions; he bestows also great charity on many poor families in Khanbaliq; and when he hears of individuals who have not food to eat, he causes grain to be given to them. Bread is not refused at the court throughout the whole year to any who come to beg for it; and on this account he is adored as a god by his people.

His majesty provides them also with clothing out of his tithes of wool, silk, and hemp. These materials he causes to be woven into different sorts of cloth, in a house erected for that purpose, where every artisan is obliged to work one day in the week for his service. Garments made of the stuffs thus manufactured are given to destitute families for their winter and summer dresses. A dress is also prepared for his armies; and in every city a quantity of woolen cloth is woven, being defrayed from the tithes there levied.

He has also so arranged that in all the highways by which messengers, merchants, and other persons travel, trees are planted at short distances on both sides of the road, and are so tall that they can be seen from a great distance. They serve thus both to show the way and afford a grateful shade. This is done whenever the nature of the soil admits of plantation; but when the route lies through sandy deserts or over rocky mountains, he has ordered stones to be set up, or columns erected, to guide the traveler. Officers of rank are appointed, whose duty it is to take care that these matters be properly arranged, and the roads kept constantly in good order. Besides other motives, the great khan is influenced by the declaration of his soothsayers and astrologers, that those who plant trees receive long life as their reward.

You must know that the great part of the people of Cathay drink a wine made of rice and many good spices, and prepare it in such a way that it is more agreeable to drink than any other liquid. It is clear and beautiful, and it makes a man drunk sooner than any other wine, for it is extremely hot.

It may be observed, also, that throughout the whole province of Cathay, there is a kind of black stone [coal] cut from the mountain in veins, which burn like logs. They maintain the fire better than wood. If you put them on in the evening, they will preserve it the whole night, and will be found burning in the morning. Throughout the whole of Cathay this fuel is used. They have also wood indeed; but the stones are much less expensive.

Questions: What does one learn about the biography of Polo and his family from this source, and what kinds of facts are omitted? According to Polo, how did Kublai Khan react to the Polos? What request did he make of them? How did the emperor's support affect their travel? What was Kublai Khan like as a ruler and a man? How did he deal with his enemies? Which characteristics of Kublai Khan's court did Polo choose to describe? What might Polo have exaggerated, and why? What do you think his readers would have found most surprising?

26. FRANCESCO BALDUCCI PEGOLOTTI, *MERCHANT HANDBOOK*

Francesco Balducci Pegolotti (fl. 1310–1347) was a prominent merchant and diplomat from Florence. He worked for the Bardi Company, which provided banking services for some of the most important European rulers; it maintained commercial links throughout Europe, the Mediterranean, and farther east. Pegolotti undertook sensitive financial tasks for the company, which often entailed travel. The handbook that he composed toward the end of his career drew from the wisdom of many years of experience. In addition to informing the merchants of its own time, this source tells historians the extent and nature of European long-distance travel.

Source: trans. Henry Yule, Francesco Balducci Pegolotti, "Merchant Handbook," in *Cathay and the Way Thither*, vol. 3 (London: Hakluyt Society, 1914), pp. 146–71. Italian. Revised.

1. Information regarding the journey to Cathay [northern China], for such as will go by Tana [modern Azov] and will come back with goods.

In the first place, from Tana to Astrakhan may be twenty-five days with an ox wagon, and from ten to twelve days with a horse wagon. On the road you will find plenty of Mongols, that is to say, of armed men. And from Astrakhan to Sarai may be a day by river, and from Sarai to Sarachik, also by river, eight days. You can do this either by land or by water; but by water you will be at less charge for your merchandise.

From Sarachik to Urgench may be twenty days' journey in camel wagons. It will be for anyone traveling with merchandise to go to Urgench, for in that city there is a ready sale for goods. From Urgench to Otrar is thirty-five to forty days in camel wagons. But if when you leave Sarachik you go direct to Otrar, it is a journey of fifty days only, and if you have no merchandise it will be better to go this way than to go by Urgench.

From Otrar to Almaliq is forty-five days' journey with pack asses, and every day you find Mongols. And from Almaliq to Ganchau is seventy days with asses, and from Ganchau until you come to a river called . . . is forty-five days on horseback; and then you can go down the river to Qinsai, and there you can dispose of the *sommi* [ingots, masses of metal] of silver that you have with you, for that is a most active place of business. After getting to Qinsai you carry on with the money which you get for the *sommi* of silver which you sell there; and this money is made of paper, and is called *balishi*. And 4 pieces of this money are worth 1 *sommo* of silver in the province of Cathay. And from Qinsai to Cambalec [modern Beijing], which is the capital of the country of Cathay, is thirty days' journey.

2. Things needful for merchants who desire to make the journey to Cathay as described above.

In the first place, you must let your beard grow long and not shave. And at Tana you should furnish yourself with a dragoman [translator and guide]. And you must not try to save money in the matter of dragomen by taking a bad one instead of a good one. For the additional wages of the good one will not cost you so much as you will save by having him. And besides the dragoman it will be well to take at least two good men servants, who are acquainted with the Cuman tongue. And if the merchant likes to take a woman with him from Tana, he can do so; if he does not like to take one there is no obligation, only if he does take one he will be kept much more comfortably than if he does not take one. However, if he does take one, it will be well that she be acquainted with the Cuman tongue as well as the men.

And from Tana traveling to Astrakhan you should take with you twenty-five days' provisions, that is to say, flour and salt fish, for as to meat you will find enough of it at all the places along the road. And so also at all the chief stations noted in going from one country to another in the route, according to the number of days set down above, you should furnish yourself with flour and salt fish; other things you will find in sufficiency, and especially meat.

The road you travel from Tana to Cathay is perfectly safe, whether by day or by night, according to what the merchants say who have used it. Only if the merchant, in going or coming, should die upon the road, everything belonging to him will become the benefit of the lord of the country in which he dies, and the officers of the lord will take possession of all. And in like manner if he die in Cathay. But if his brother be with him, or an intimate friend and comrade calling himself his brother, then to such a one they will surrender the property of the deceased, and so it will be rescued.

And there is another danger: this is when the lord of the country dies, and before the new lord who is to have the lordship is proclaimed; during such intervals there have sometimes been irregularities practiced on the Franks, and other foreigners. (They call Franks all the Christians of these parts from Romania westward.) And neither will the roads be safe to travel until the other lord is proclaimed who is to reign in place of him who is deceased.

Cathay is a province which contained a multitude of cities and towns. Among others there is one in particular, that is to say the capital city, to which is a great resort of merchants, and in which there is a vast amount of trade; and this city is called Cambalec. And the said city has a circuit of one hundred miles, and is all full of people and houses and of dwellers in the said city.

You may calculate that a merchant with a dragoman, and with two men servants, and with goods to the value of 25,000 golden florins [coin of Florence], should spend on his way to Cathay from 60 to 80 *sommi* of silver, and not more if he manage well; and for all the road back again from Cathay to Tana, including the expenses of living and the pay of servants, and all other charges, the cost will be about 5 *sommi* per head of pack animals, or something less. And you may reckon the *sommo* to be worth 5 golden florins. You may reckon also that each ox wagon will require one ox, and will carry ten cantars Genoese weight; and the horse wagon will require one horse, and will commonly carry six and a half cantars of silk, at 250 Genoese pounds [silver coins or their weight] to the cantar. And a bale of silk may be reckoned at between 110 and 115 Genoese pounds.

You may reckon also that from Tana to Sarai the road is less safe than on any other part of the journey; and yet even when this part of the road is at its worst, if you are some sixty men in the company, you will go as safely as if you were in your own house.

Anyone from Genoa or from Venice, wishing to go to the places above-named, and to make the journey to Cathay, should carry linens with him, and if he visit Urgench he will dispose of these well. In Urgench he should purchase *sommi* of silver, and with these he should proceed without making any further investment, unless it is some bales of the very finest stuffs which go in small bulk, and cost no more for carriage than coarser stuffs would do.

Merchants who travel this road can ride on horseback or on asses, or mounted in any way that they like to be mounted.

Whatever silver the merchants may carry with them as far as Cathay the lord of Cathay will take from them and put into his treasury. And to merchants who thus bring silver they give that paper money of theirs in exchange. This is of yellow paper, stamped with the seal of the lord aforesaid. And this money is called *balishi*; and with this money you can readily buy silk and all other merchandise that you have a desire to buy. And all the people of the country are bound to receive it. And yet you will not pay a higher price for your goods because your money is of paper. And of the said paper money there are three kinds, one being worth more than another, according to the value which has been established for each by that lord.

And you may reckon that you can buy for 1 *sommo* of silver nineteen or twenty pounds of Cathay silk, when reduced to Genoese weight, and that the *sommo* should weigh eight and a half ounces of Genoa, and should be of the alloy of eleven ounces and seventeen deniers [silver coins] to the pound.

You may reckon also that in Cathay you should get three or three and a half pieces of damask [reversible figured] silk for a *sommo*; and from three and a half to five pieces of *nacchetti* [fine cloths] of silk and gold, likewise for a *sommo* of silver.

3. Comparison of the weights and measures of Cathay and of Tana.

The Maund in Genoa Weight

Sarai = 6 lb., 2 oz.
Urgench = 3 lb., 9 oz.
Otrar = 3 lb., 9 oz.
Almaliq = 2 lb., 8 oz.
Ganchau = 2 lb., 0 oz.

Tana on the Black Sea

At Tana, as will be next shown, they use a variety of weights and measures, that is:

The cantar, which is that of Genoa.
The great pound = 20 lb. Genoese.
The *ruotolo*, of which 20 = 1 great pound.
The little pound, which is the Genoese pound.
The *tocchetto*, of which 12 = 1 great pound.
The *saggio*, of which 45 = 1 *sommo*.
The *picco*.

Wax, ladanum [a gum resin], iron, tin, copper, pepper, ginger, all coarser spices, cotton, madder, and suet, flax, and oil, honey, and the like, sell by the great pound.

Silk, saffron, amber wrought in rosaries and the like, and all small spices sell by the little pound.

Vair skins by the 1,000; and 1,020 go to the 1,000.

Ermines by the 1,000; 1,000 to the 1,000.

Foxes, sables, fitches and martens, wolfskins, deerskins, and all cloths of silk or gold, by the piece.

Common stuffs, and canvasses of every kind sell by the *picco*.

Tails are sold by the bundle at 20 to the bundle.

Oxhides are sold by the hundred in total, giving a hundred and no more. Horses and pony hides by the piece.

Gold and pearls are sold by the *saggio*. Grain and all other wheat and pulse [a legume] is sold at Tana by a measure which they call *cascito* [?]. Greek wine and all Latin wines are sold by the casks as they come. Malmsey [wine] and wines of Triglia and Candia are sold by the measure.

Caviar is sold by the *fusco*, and a *fusco* is the tail-half of the fish's skin, full of fish's roe.

4. Charges on merchandise which are paid at Tana on things entering the city, nothing being paid on going forth from there.

Gold, silver, and pearls at Tana pay neither *comerchio* [duties of Greeks], nor *tamunga* [duties of Mongols], nor any other duties.

On wine, and ox hides, and tails, and horse hides, the Genoese and Venetians pay 4 per cent, and all other people 5 per cent.

What is paid for the transit of merchandise at Tana.

Silk, 15 aspers [silver coin] per pound.

All other things, at . . . aspers for 3 cantars.

At Tana the money current is of *sommi* and aspers of silver. The *sommo* weighs 45 *saggi* of Tana, and is of the alloy of 11 oz. 17 dwt. [pennyweight] of fine silver to the pound. And if silver is sent to the Tana mint, they coin 202 aspers from the *sommo*, but they pay you only 190, retaining the rest for the work of the mint and its profit. So a *sommo* at Tana is reckoned to be 190 aspers. And the *sommi* are ingots of silver of the alloy before mentioned, which are paid away by weight. But they do not all weigh the same, so the ingots are weighed at the time of payment, and if the weight is less than it ought to be the balance is paid in aspers, to make up every *sommo* to the value of 45 *saggi* of Tana weight.

And there are also current at Tana copper coins called *folleri*, of which 16 go to the asper. But the *folleri* are not used in mercantile transactions, but only in the purchase of vegetables and such small matters for town use. . . .

6. On the expenses which usually attend the transport of merchandise from Yumurtalik of Armenia to Tabriz, by land.

In the first place from Yumurtalik as far as Gobidar [?], that is, as far as the king of Armenia's territory extends, you pay altogether 41 *taccolini* and 3 ½ deniers (at the rate of 10 deniers to the *taccolino* [silver coin]) on every load, whether of camels or of other beasts. Now taking the *taccolino* to be about an asper, the amount will be about 41 aspers of Tabriz per load. And 6 aspers of Tabriz are equal to 1 Tabriz bezant [gold coin].

At Gandon [?], where you enter upon the lands of Abu Sa'id Bahadur Khan, that is, of the lord of the Tartars [Mongols], on every load	20 aspers
At the same place, for watching, ditto	3 aspers
At Casena [?]	7 aspers
At the Emir's Caravanserai [roadside inn]	2 aspers
At Gadue [?]	3 aspers
At the Caravanserai of Casa Jacomi [?]	3 aspers
At the entrance to Sivas from Yamurtalik	1 asper
Inside the city	7 aspers
Leaving the city on the road to Tabriz	1 asper
At Divriği	3 aspers
At Greboco [?]	4 aspers
At Mughisar [?]	2 ½ aspers
At ditto, as Tanauls [guards, patrols] for the watch	0½ asper
At Erzingan, at entrance to the town	5 aspers
Ditto, inside the city	9 aspers
Ditto, for the watchmen, on leaving	3 aspers
At the Caravanserai on the Hill	3 aspers
At Ligurti [?]	2 aspers
At ditto, at the bridge, for Tanauls	0½ asper
At the Caravanserai outside Erzerum	2 aspers
At Erzerum, at the Baths	1 asper
Ditto, inside the city	9 aspers
Ditto, as a present to the lord	2 aspers
Ditto, at the Baths toward Tabriz	1 asper
At Polorbecch	3 aspers
At ditto	0½ asper
At Sermessacalo [?] for Tanauls	0½ asper
At Aggia [?], for the whole journey	0½ asper
At the middle of the plain of Aggia [?], for duty	3 aspers
At ditto for Tanuals	0½ asper
At Karakilisa, ditto	0½ asper
At Uch Kilise [Three Churches], for Tanauls	0½ asper
Under Noah's Ark [?], for duty	3 aspers
Ditto ditto for Tanauls	0½ asper
At Scaracanti [?], ditto	0½ asper
At Locche [?] ditto	0½ asper
At the plain of the Falconers [?], ditto (twice together)	1 asper
At the said plain, for a ticket or permit from the lord	0½ asper
At the Camuzoni, for Tanauls	0½ asper
At the Plains of the Red River [?] for Tanauls	0½ asper
At Condro [?], for Tanauls	0½ asper
At Sandoddi [?], ditto	0½ asper
At Tabriz, ditto	0½ asper

And you may reckon that the exactions of the Mongols or Tartar troopers along the road, will amount to something like 50 aspers a load. So that the cost for a load of merchandise going by land from Yumurtalik of Armenia to Tabriz in central Asia will be, as appears by the above details, 209 aspers a load, and the same back again. . . .

8. Detail showing how all goods are sold and bought at Constantinople and in Pera [modern Beyoğlu], and of the expenses incurred by traders; but especially as regards Pera, because most of the business is done there, where the merchants are more constantly to be found. For the rest of Constantinople belongs to the Greeks, but Pera to the Franks, that is, to the Genoese. And from Constantinople to Pera, it is five miles by land, but half a mile by water.

Goods are sold at Constantinople in various ways.

The indigo called *baccaddeo* is [sold in packages] of a certain weight, and the weight you must know should be the cantar. And if the buyer chooses to take it from the seller without weighing it, it must be more or less than a cantar, it is to the profit or loss of the buyer. But they do almost always weigh it, and then payment is made according to the exact weight, be it more or less than a cantar. And the skin and wrapper are given with it but no tare [weight of wrapping] is deducted; nor is sifting allowed; nor do they allow the indigo to be examined except by a little hole, from which a small sample may be extracted. For such is the use and custom in those parts.

The following are sold by the cantar (of 150 Genoese lb.).

Wormwood; madder, and the bag goes as madder without any allowance for tare. Alum of every kind, and even if it is Roche alum, the sack and cord go as alum.

The following are sold by the cantar at Constantinople and in Pera.

Ox hides; buffalo hides; horse hides: in purchasing these they are shown to the quality testers up the hill, that is, in Pera; and if the hides smell damp or wet, then a fit allowance is made, and this is the system in Pera and in Constantinople, and they are not put in the sun unless they are exceedingly wet indeed.

Suet in jars; iron of every kind; tin of every kind; lead of every kind. Muscat [grape] of Alexandria or raisins of every kind, and the mats go as raisins, with no allowance for tare unless they are raisins of Syria. In that case the baskets or hampers are allowed for as tare, and remain with the buyer into the bargain.

Soap of Venice, soap of Ancona, and soap of Apulia in wooden cases. They make tare of the cases, and then these go to the buyer for nothing. But the soap of Cyprus and of Rhodes is in sacks, and the sacks go as soap with no tare allowance.

Broken almonds in bags; the bag goes as almonds; only if there be more than one sack and cord it must be removed, or deducted, so that the buyer will not have to take more than one sack and cord as almonds, but for any beyond that there will be tare allowed; and the cord will go to the buyer free of charge.

Honey in kegs or skins; tare is allowed for the keg or skin, but it remains with the buyer gratis.

Cotton wool; and the sack goes as cotton without tare. Cotton yarn; and the sack is allowed as tare, and remains with the buyer for nothing.

Rice; and the bag goes as rice, but if it be tied the cord is allowed as tare and remains with the seller. Turkey galls of every kind; and if they are in bags you weigh bag and all, and do not make tare of the bag. Dried figs of Majorca and Spain in hampers. Orpiment [arsenic sulfide mineral], and the bag goes as orpiment. Safflower [thistly plant], and you make tare of bag and cord, and after that they remain with the buyer free of charge.

Henna; and the bag goes as henna, only a tare of 4 per cent is allowed by custom of trade. Cumin; and the bag goes as cumin, and if tied with rope the rope is allowed as tare but remains with the buyer free of charge.

Pistachios; and the bag goes with them with no allowance for tare, unless there be more bags than one, and if there be, then the excess is weighed and allowed as tare, and the buyer has the one bag free of charge.

Sulfur; and the bag or barrel in which it is, is allowed as tare, and goes to the buyer free of charge. Senna [plant]; and the bag is tare and goes to the buyer. Pitch, and the mat is allowed for as tare, and goes to the buyer. Litharge [a form of lead]; the bag goes with it and no tare allowed.

The following are sold in the same way . . . saltmeat; cheese; flax of Alexandria and of Romania; camlet wool; washed wool of Romania; unwashed [wool]; washed or unwashed wool of Turkey; chestnuts.

The following are sold by the hundredweight of 100 Genoese pounds. . . .

Round pepper; ginger; barked brazilwood; lac; zedoary [a plant]; incense; sugar, and powdered sugar of all kinds; aloes of all kinds; quicksilver; *cassia fistula* [golden rain tree]; *sal ammoniac* or *lisciadro* [a mineral]; cinnabar [a mineral]; cinnamon; galbanum [a gum resin]; ladanum of Cyprus [sticky brown resin]; mastic; copper; amber, big, middling, and small, not wrought; stripped coral; clean and fine coral, middling and small.

The following are sold by the pound.

Raw silk; saffron; clove stalks and cloves; cubebs [a plant]; aloeswood; rhubarb; mace; long pepper; galangal [a plant]; broken camphor [waxy, transparent solid]; nutmegs; spike [a plant]; cardamoms [a plant]; scammony [weed used as medicine]; pounded pearls; manna; borax; gum Arabic; dragon's blood [resin from certain plants]; camel's hay [a plant]; turbit [domesticated pigeon]; silk-gauze; sweetmeats; gold wire; dressed silk; wrought amber in beads. . . .

Sold in half scores of pieces.
Buckrams [fine cotton cloth] of Erzingan and Cyprus.

By the piece.
Silk velvets; damasks; *maramati* [?]; gold cloth of every kind; *nacchetti* and *nacchi* [fine cloths] of every kind; and all cloths of silk and gold except gauzes.

Sold by the hundred piks of Gazaria.
Common stuffs and canvasses of all kinds, except those of Champagne; also French and north-country broadcloths.
Then follow details of the different kinds of cloths, with the length of the pieces. And then a detail of special modes of selling certain wares, such as:
Undressed vairs, and vair bellies and backs; Slavonian squirrels; martins and fitches; goat skins and ram skins; dates, filberts [nuts], walnuts; salted sturgeon tails; salt; oil of Venice; oil of the March; oil of Apulia, of Gaeta . . . wheat and barley; wine of Greece, of Turpia in Calabria, of Patti in Sicily, of Patti in Apulia, of Cutrone in Calabria, of the March, of Crete, of Romania; country wine. . . .
And don't forget that if you treat the customhouse officers with respect, and make them something of a present in goods or money, as well as their clerks and dragomen, they will behave with great civility, and always be ready to appraise your wares below their real value.

Questions: What tips does the author have for someone who is intending to do trade? What should someone take along to travel long distances? Why does the author spend so much time on weights, measures, and duties? What kinds of goods were being sold by merchants, and can we get an idea of their relative value? Why did this author think that traveling over long distances was safe?

27. AFANASY NIKITIN, *VOYAGE BEYOND THREE SEAS*

Afanasy Nikitin was a Russian merchant who between 1468 and 1474 traveled to India and spent around three years there. He died after having returned to Russia, but before he reached his hometown. During the course of his travels he kept a diary, unique among old Russian literature in that the author neither was a clergyman nor had any other mission aside from commerce. In addition to giving a realistic account of his journey, Nikitin's writings have provided historians with valuable information about contemporary India.

Source: ed. and trans. Mikhail Wielhorski, Afanasy Nikitin, "Voyage beyond Three Seas," in *India in the Fifteenth Century* (London: Hakluyt Society, 1857), pp. 3–32 [third set of pagination in the volume]. Russian. Revised.

By the prayer of our holy fathers, O Lord Jesus Christ, son of God, have mercy on me, your sinful servant, Afanasy, son of Nikita.

This is, as I wrote it, my sinful wandering beyond the three seas: the first, the sea of Derbend, or the Caspian Sea; the second, the India Sea, or Sea of Hindustan; the third, the Black Sea, or Sea of Stambul.

I started from the golden-domed cathedral of our holy savior, with the kind permission of the grand duke, Mikhail Borisovich [r. 1461–1485], and his grace [the bishop] Gennady of Tver; went down the Volga, came to the monastery of the holy life-giving Trinity, and the holy shrines of Boris and Gleb, the martyrs; and received the blessing of the hegumen [head of a monastery] Macarius and the brethren. From Kalyazin I went to Uglich; from there to Kostroma, to Prince Alexander, with a pass. And the grand duke of all Russia [Ivan III, r. 1462–1505] allowed me to leave the country unhindered, and I went on by Plesso to Nizhny Novgorod, to the governor Mikhail Kiselev, and to Ivan Sarayev, the collector of duties, both of whom let me pass freely.

Vasily Papin merely passed through that town; but I stopped a fortnight to wait for the Tartar [Mongol] ambassador of Shirvanshah—Hasan Beg, who was coming with falcons from the grand duke, Ivan, 90 in number.

With him I descended the Volga. We passed unmolested through Kazan, the Horde, Uslan, Sarai, and Berekezan, and we entered the river Buzan. Here we fell in with three godless Tartars, who told us false tidings: "Khan Kasim watches foreign merchants in the Buzan, and three thousand Tartars are with him."

Hasan Beg, the ambassador of Shirvanshah, gave to each of them a coat and a piece of linen, that they might guide him around Astrakhan, avoiding the town. They took the coats, but informed the tsar of Astrakhan.

I abandoned my boat and crept into the ambassador's with my companions, and we sailed by Astrakhan at moonlight. The tsar perceived us, and at once the Tartars cried: "Do not flee," and the tsar ordered the whole camp to chase us. For our sins we were overtaken at Bugun. One of our men was shot; but we shot two of theirs.

The smaller of our boats ran foul of some fishing stakes, was seized, and instantly plundered with all my things in her. In the larger we reached the sea, but having grounded at the mouth of the Volga we were taken, and the boat was hauled up again to the fishing stakes. There they took her and four

Russians, dismissing us bare and naked beyond the sea, and forbidding us to return home because of the news.

And so we went on to Derbent in two boats: in one, the ambassador Hasan Beg, some Iranians, and ten Russians; in the other, six Muscovites and six men from Tver. A storm having arisen at sea, the smaller boat was wrecked on shore. Then came the Kaitaks and made the whole party prisoners, and we came to Derbent, where Vasily Papin had arrived safe and well, but we had been robbed. I begged him and also Hasan Beg, the ambassador of Shirvanshah, as we had traveled together, to take pity on the men that had been plundered by the Kaitaks near Tarki. And this he did, and went up the hill to Bulat Beg; and Bulat Beg sent immediately to Shirvanshah Beg, to say that a Russian craft had been wrecked near Sarai, and that the Kaitaks coming up had taken the people and plundered their goods. Shirvanshah Beg at once dispatched a messenger to Khalil Beg, prince of Kaitaks, his brother-in-law, saying, "A ship of mine was wrecked near Tarki, and your people arriving seized my people and plundered their goods. Now, for the sake of me, you should send them to me and recover their goods, for these people are sent in my name. And if you should ever want anything of me, name it, and I will not refuse it to my brother; but for the sake of me let them go in liberty." Khalil Beg complied willingly, and immediately sent the prisoners to Derbent, from where they were directed to Shirvanshah's camp, his own camp. We all proceeded there, and prayed that he would give us the means to return to Russia; but he gave us nothing, as we were too many. So we wept and dispersed to wherever it was; whoever had anything in Russia returned home; whoever was in debt went where his eyes looked; some stayed at Shemakha; others sought work at Baku.

As for me, I went to Derbent and then to Baku, where the fire burns unextinguished, and from there across the sea to Chapakur. Here I lived six months, and one month I lived at Sari, in the land of Mazanderan, and one month at Amul. Then I went to Demavend, and from Demavend to Rai (here were killed the children of Shah Hussain, the grandchildren of Muhammad, and he cursed the Assassins, and 70 cities fell to ruins), and from Rai to Kashan, where I remained one month. I also spent a month at Nain, and another at Yezd. From Yezd I proceeded to Sirjan and to Tarum, where the cattle are fed with dates at four *altins* [a Russian copper coin] a *batman* [unit of weight]; and from Tareu to Lar, and from Lar to Old Hormuz; and here there is a seaport, Hormuz, and the Indian Sea, called in the Persian tongue the Sea of Hindustan.

Hormuz is four miles across the water and stands on an island. Twice a day the sea flows around it, and here I celebrated the first Easter, having reached

Hormuz four weeks before the feast. I have not named the many and large cities through which I passed.

At Hormuz the sun is scorching and burns one. I stopped there a month. On the first week after Easter, I shipped my horses in a *dabba* [a ship], and sailed across the Indian Sea in ten days to Muscat. From there in four days to Dega [?]; and farther to Gujarat and Cambay, where the indigo grows; and lastly to Chaul. We sailed six weeks in the *dabba* until we reached Chaul, and left Chaul on the seventh week after Easter.

This is an Indian country. People go about naked, with their heads uncovered and bare breasts; the hair tressed into one tail, and thick bellies. They bring forth children every year and the children are many; and men and women are black. When I go out many people follow me, and stare at the white man.

Their prince wears a dhoti [rectangular piece of unstitched cloth] on the head; and another on the loins; the boyars [nobles] wear it on the shoulders and on the loins; the princesses wear it also round the shoulders and the loins. The servants of the prince and of the boyars attach the dhoti round the loins, carrying in the hand a shield and a sword, or a scimitar, or knives, or a saber, or a bow and arrows—but all naked and barefoot. Women walk about with their heads uncovered and their breasts bare. Boys and girls go naked until seven years, and do not hide their private parts.

We left Chaul, and went by land in eight days to Pali, to the Indian mountains; from there in ten days to Umra, and from that Indian town to Junnar in six days.

Here resides the Indian Asad Khan, a servant of Malik-at-Tujjar. I hear he has 70,000 men from Malik-at-Tujjar, while Malik-at-Tujjar himself presides over 200,000. He has been fighting the *kafirs* [non-Muslims] for twenty years, being sometimes beaten, but mostly beating them.

The khan rides on men, although he has many good elephants and horses. Among his attendants are many Khorassanians, some of whom come from the countries of Khorassan or Arabia, the Turkoman land, and central Asia. They all are brought over by sea in *dabbas* or Indian ships.

And I, poor sinner, brought a stallion to the land of India; with God's help I reached Junnar all well, but it cost me a hundred rubles [unit of weight for silver coins].

The winter began from Trinity Sunday, and we wintered at Junnar and lived there two months; but day and night for four months there is nothing but rain and dirt. At this time of the year the people till the ground, sow wheat, rice, pulse, and all the other crops. Wine is made in big coconuts, and beer is brewed from *tatna* [a plant].

Horses are fed on pulse; also on *kichri* [salty porridge], boiled with sugar and oil; early in the morning they get rice cakes. Horses are not born in that country, but oxen and buffaloes are; and these are used for riding, conveying goods, and every other purpose.

Junnar stands on a stony island; no human hand built it—God made the town. A narrow road, which it takes a day to ascend, admitting of only one man at a time, leads up the hill to it.

In the land of India it is the custom for foreign traders to stop at inns; there is food cooked for the guests by the landlady, who also makes the bed and sleeps with the stranger. Women that know you willingly concede their favors, for they like white men. In the winter, the people put on the dhoti and wear it round the waist, on the shoulders, and on the head; but the princes and nobles put trousers on, a shirt and a caftan [a long coat], wearing a dhoti on the shoulders, another as a belt round the waist, and a third round the head.

O God, true God, merciful God, gracious God.

At Junnar the khan took away my horse, and having heard that I was not a Muslim, but a Russian, he said: "I will give you the horse and a 1,000 pieces of gold, if you will embrace our faith, the Muslim faith; and if you will not embrace our Muslim faith, I will keep the horse and take a ransom of a 1,000 pieces of gold." He gave me four days to consider, and all this occurred during the fast of the Assumption of our Lady [1–14 August], on the eve of our savior's day.

And the Lord took pity upon me because of his holy festival, and did not withdraw his mercy from me, his sinful servant, and allowed me not to perish at Junnar among the infidels. On the eve of our savior's day there came a man from Khorassan, Khoja Muhammad, and I implored him to pity me. He rode to the khan into the town, and begging him delivered me from being converted, and took from him my horse. Such was the Lord's wonderful mercy on the savior's day.

Now, Christian brothers of Russia, whoever of you wishes to go to the Indian country may leave his faith in Russia, confess Muhammad, and then proceed to the land of Hindustan [India]. Those Muslim dogs have lied to me, saying I should find here plenty of our goods; but there is nothing for our country. All goods are for the land of Muslims, as pepper and dyes, and these are cheap.

Merchandise conveyed by sea is free from duty, and people that would bring it to us will have no duty; but the duties are many. The sea is infested with pirates, all of whom are pagans, neither Christians nor Muslims; they pray to stone idols and do not know Christ.

We left Junnar on the eve of the Assumption of the very holy Mother of God [14 August] for Bidar, a large city, and we were a month on the road.

From there we went in five days to Kulungir, and in five days from the latter to Gulbarga. Between these large towns there are many small ones: three for each day, and occasionally four; so many *kos,* so many towns. From Chaul to Junnar it is 20 *kos;* from Junnar to Bidar, 40; from Bidar to Kulungir, 9 *kos;* and from Bidar to Gulbarga, 9.

In Bidar there is a trade in horses, goods, brocade, silks, and all sorts of other merchandise, and also in black people; but no other article is sold but Indian goods, and every kind of eatables; no goods, however, that will do for Russia. And all are black and wicked, and the women all prostitutes, or witches, or thieves and cheats; and they destroy their masters with poison.

The rulers and the nobles in the land of India are all from Khorassan. The Indians all walk on foot and walk fast. They are all naked and barefoot, and carry a shield in one hand and a sword in the other. Some of the servants are armed with straight bows and arrows.

Elephants are greatly used in battle. The men on foot are sent first, the Khorassanis being mounted in full armor, man as well as horse. Large scythes are attached to the trunks and tusks of the elephants, and the animals are clad in ornamental plates of steel. They carry a citadel, and in the citadel 12 men in armor with guns and arrows.

There is a place—the tomb of Sheik Ala-uddin at Alland—where there is a fair once a year, where people from all parts of India assemble and trade for ten days. As many as 20,000 horses are brought there for sale from Bidar, which is 20 *kos* distant, and besides every description of goods; and that fair is the best throughout the land of Hindustan. Everything is sold or bought in memory of Sheik Ala-uddin, whose feast falls on the Russian feast of the Intercession of the Holy Virgin [1 October].

In that Alland there is a bird, *ghuggu,* that flies at night and cries "ghuggu," and any roof it lands upon, there the man will die; and whoever attempts to kill it, will see fire flashing from its beak. Wild cats rove at night and catch fowls; they live in the hills and among stones. As to monkeys they live in the woods and have their monkey prince, who is attended by a host of armed followers. When any of them is caught they complain to their prince, and an army is sent after the missing; and when they come to a town they pull down the houses and beat the people; and their armies, it is said, are many. They speak their own tongues and bring forth a great many children; and, when a child is unlike its father or its mother, it is thrown out on the high road. Thus they are often caught by the Indians, who teach them every sort of handicraft, or sell them at night, that they may not find their way home, or teach them dancing.

Spring begins from the feast of the Intercession of the Holy Virgin. A fortnight after this festival they celebrate the memory of Sheik Ala-uddin for eight days. They make the spring three months, the summer three months, the winter three months, and the autumn three months. Bidar is the chief town of the whole of Muslim Hindustan; the city is large, and contains a great many people.

The sultan is a little man, 20 years old, in the power of the nobles. Khorassanians rule the country and serve in war. There is a Khorassanian boyar, Malik-at-Tujjar, who keeps an army of 200,000 men; Melik Khan keeps 100,000; Farkhad Khan, 20,000, and many are the khans that keep 10,000 armed men.

The sultan goes out with 300,000 men of his own troops.

The land is overstocked with people; but those in the country are very miserable, while the boyars are extremely opulent and delight in luxury. They are accustomed to be carried on their silver beds, preceded by some 20 chargers caparisoned in gold, and followed by 300 men on horseback and 500 on foot, and by horn men, ten torchbearers, and ten musicians.

The sultan's palace has seven gates, and in each gate are seated 100 guards and 100 Muslim scribes, who enter the names of all persons going in and out. Foreigners are not admitted into the town. This palace is very wonderful; everything in it is carved or gilded, and, even to the smallest stone, is cut and ornamented with gold most wonderfully. Several courts of justice are within the building.

Throughout the night the town of Bidar is guarded by 1,000 men posted by the governor, mounted on horses in full armor, carrying each a torch.

I sold my stallion at Bidar, and spent on him 68 *fanams* [gold or silver Indian currency], having kept him a whole year.

Snakes crawl about in the streets of Bidar, in length 14 feet.

I came to Bidar from Kulungir on the day of Saint Philip; sold my horse about Christmas and stayed at Bidar until Lent; and made acquaintance with many Indians, told them what was my faith; that I was not a Muslim, but a Christian; that my name was Afanasy, and my Muslim name was Khoja Yusuf Khorassani. After that they no more endeavored to conceal anything from me, neither their meals, nor their commerce, nor their prayers, nor other things; nor did they try to hide their women. And I asked them all about their religion, and they said: "We believe in Adam," and they hold the Buddhas to be Adam and his kin. There are in all 84 creeds, and all believe in Buddha, and no man of one creed will drink, eat, or marry with those of another. Some of them feed on mutton, fowls, fish, and eggs, but none on beef.

Having spent four months at Bidar, I agreed with some Indians to go to Parvat, which is their Jerusalem, or Mecca its Muslim name, where Buddha's House is. We were a month on the route. A fair is held there during five days.

The Buddha's House is a very extensive building, about the half of Tver, built in stone, and exhibiting in carvings on the walls the deeds of Buddha. All around it are cut out 12 wreaths, in which are shown how Buddha achieved miracles; how he appeared in different forms; first in the shape of a man, then as a man with an elephant's nose, then as a man with a monkey's face, and again as a man with the appearance of a savage beast and a tail rising seven feet above him.

People from all parts of the land of India congregate at Buddha's House, to witness the wonders of Buddha. Old women and girls shave their hair at Buddha's House, and everyone coming there shaves his beard and head and whatever hair is on his body; and a tribute of two *skeshkanis* [small silver coins] is levied on each person for the sake of Buddha, and also of four *fanams* on each horse. Twenty thousand people assemble at Buddha's House, but sometimes 100,000. At Buddha's House, Buddha is sculpted in stone of an immense size, his tail rising over him. His right hand is lifted up high and extended like that of Justinian, emperor of Constantinople [r. 527–565]; his left holding a sword; he is quite uncovered, with only a small cloth round the loins, and has the appearance of a monkey. Some other Buddhas are naked, without anything on their hinder parts, and the wives of Buddha and their children are also sculpted naked. A huge bull, carved in black stone and gilded, stands before Buddha; people kiss his hoof and adorn him with flowers as well as Buddha.

The Indians eat no meat, no cow flesh, no mutton, no chicken. The banquets were all on pork; and pigs are in great abundance. They take their meals twice a day, but not at night, and drink no wine nor mead; but with Muslims they neither eat nor drink. Their fare is poor. They eat not with one another nor with their wives, and live on rice and *kichri* with ghee, and different herbs. Always eating with the right hand, they will never set the left hand to anything nor use a knife; the spoon is unknown. In traveling everyone has a stone pot to cook his broth in. They take care that Muslims do not look into their pot, nor see their food, and should this happen they will not eat it; some, therefore, hide themselves under a linen cloth lest they should be seen when eating.

They offer their prayers toward the east, in the Russian way, lifting both hands high and putting them on the top of the head; then they lie down with the face to the ground, stretching their body to its full length, and such is their law.

They sit down to eat, and wash their hands and feet, and rinse their mouths before they do so.

Their Buddha's Houses have no doors, and are situated toward the east; and the Buddhas also stand eastward.

The bodies of the dead are burnt, and the ashes scattered on the waters.

When a woman is confined, her husband acts the midwife. He gives the name to a son, but the mother gives it to a daughter. Still there is no good about them, and they know not what shame is.

On meeting together, they bow to each other like the monks, touching the ground with both hands, but say nothing.

During Lent they go to Parvat, their Jerusalem. In the Muslim language it is named Mecca, in Russian Jerusalem. They come there all naked, with only a small linen round their loins; and the women also naked, with a dhoti round the middle; but some are dressed in dhotis, wearing necklaces of sapphire, bracelets round the arms, and golden rings, in faith.

They drive into the Buddha's House on bulls, the horns of which are cased in brass. These animals, called oxen, have their feet shod, and carry round the neck 300 bells. The Indians call the bull "father," and the cow "mother"; with their excrement they bake bread and boil food, and with their ashes sign the images of these animals on their own faces, foreheads, and whole bodies.

On Sundays and Mondays they only eat once in the day. In India women are attained by contract, and they are cheap; you can have sex for two *shitels* [silver coins]. For four *fanams* you can get a pretty one; for five, a pretty black woman, all black with little and pretty nipples.

From Parvat we returned to Beder, a fortnight before the great Muslim festival, Ulu Bayram. But I do not know the great day of Christ's resurrection; however, I guess by different signs, that the great Christian day is by nine or ten days sooner than the Muslim Bayram. I have nothing with me; no books whatever; those that I had taken from Russia were lost when I was robbed. And I forgot the Christian faith and the Christian festivals, and know not Easter nor Christmas, nor can I tell Wednesday from Friday, and I am between the two faiths. But I pray to Allah, the merciful, the creator. You are the Lord, king of glory, and creator of heaven and earth.

And I am going back to Russia thinking that my faith is dead, for I have fasted with Muslims. The month of March passed, and I had not eaten any meat for one month, having begun to fast with the Muslims on a Sunday. Abstaining from all animal or Muslim food, I fed myself twice a day with bread and water, abstained from female society, and prayed to God almighty, who made heaven and earth; and no other god of any other name did I invoke. God is Allah. God is munificent, God is merciful, God is Lord, God is great, God, king of glory, Allah exists, Allah, you are the merciful. You! Oh, you, Allah.

It takes ten days to go by sea from Hormuz to Kalhat; from Kalhat to Dega six days; from Dega to Muscat, six days; from Muscat to Gujarat ten days; from Gujarat to Cambay, four days; from Cambay to Chaul, twelve days; and from Chaul to Dabhol, six days.

Dabhol is the last seaport in India belonging to the Muslims. From there to Calicut, you have to travel 25 days, and from Calicut to Ceylon [modern Sri Lanka], 15; from Ceylon to Shabait, one month; from Shabait to Pegu, 20 days; and from Pegu to [southern] China, one month: all this by sea. From

China to Cathay [northern China], you go by land six months, but by sea in four days. May God adorn my shelter.

Hormuz is a vast emporium of all the world; you find there people and goods of every description, and whatever thing is produced on earth you find it in Hormuz. But the duties are high, one tenth of everything.

Cambay is a port of the whole Indian Sea, and a manufacturing place for every sort of goods; as *alacha* [twisted silk and cotton], taffeta, coarse cloth, and indigo are made there, and also lac, cornelian, and clove.

Dabhol is also a very extensive seaport, where many horses are brought from Egypt, Arabia, Khorassan, Turkestan, and Old Hormuz. It takes a month to walk by land from this place to Bidar and to Gulbarga.

Calicut is a port for the whole Indian sea, which God forbids any craft to cross, and whoever saw it will not go over it healthy. The country produces pepper, ginger, nutmeg, cloves, cinnamon, aromatic roots, *adrak* [a variety of ginger], and every description of spices, and everything is cheap, and slaves are very good; they are black.

Ceylon is another not inconsiderable port of the Indian Sea. There, on a hill, is the tomb of Adam, and in the vicinity are found precious stones, rubies, rock crystal, agates, amber, beryls, and emery. Elephants and ostriches live there and are sold, the former by the size, the latter by the weight.

Shabait [?], on the Indian Sea, is a very large place; a tribute of one *tanga* [silver coin] a day is paid there to each Khorassani, big or small. And when he marries, then the sovereign of Shabait pays him 1,000 *tangas* for the sacrifice and as a tribute, and he eats for ten *tangas* a month. At Shabait the country produces silk, sandalwood, pearls, and everything is cheap.

Pegu is no inconsiderable port, principally inhabited by Indian dervishes. The products derived from there are maniks [precious stones], sapphires, and rubies, which are sold by the dervishes.

The seaports of [southern] China are also large. Porcelain is made there, and sold by the weight and at a low price. Women sleep with their husbands in the day, but at night they go to the foreign men and sleep with them and [the women] pay for it, besides waiting on them with sweetmeats and supplying them with food and drink, that the foreigners may love them, because they like strangers and white people, their own men being so very black. And when a woman conceives a child by a stranger, the husband pays him a salary. If the child is born white, the stranger receives a duty of 18 *tangas*; if it is born black he gets nothing, but is welcome to what he ate and drank.

Shabait is distant three months from Bidar; but by sea it takes two months to go from Dabhol to Shabait. [Southern] China, where porcelain is made and everything is cheap, is four months' distance by sea from Bidar, and Ceylon two months by sea.

At Shabait nature produces silk, pearls, and sandalwood; elephants are sold by the cubit. At Ceylon you find monkeys, rubies, and crystals; at Calicut, pepper, nutmeg, clove, areca nuts, and dyes; at Guzrat there are indigo and lac; at Cambay, cornelian; at Raichur, diamonds—old and new ones; one *pockha* [old Russian weight for diamonds, c. 10 carats] of diamond is sold at five *kanis* [copper coins], but the best at ten; one *pockha* of new diamond, however, is only valued at five *kanis*; one of blackish color, from four to six *kanis*, and a white diamond, one *tanga*. Diamonds are found on a rocky hill, and the rough diamond from that hill is sold for 2,000 pounds' weight of gold per cubit; the old diamond is sold at 10,000 pounds of gold per cubit. That district belongs to Melik Khan, a vassal to the sultan, and is 30 *kos* from Bidar.

The Jews call the people of Shabait Jews like themselves; but this is not true, for the people of Shabait are neither Jews, nor Muslims, nor Christians, but belong to a different Indian religion. They do not eat with Hebrews nor Muslims, and use no meat. Silk and sugar are cultivated at a low expense, and everything generally is cheap at Shabait.

Monkeys and wild cats infest the woods and attack the traveler on the high roads; nobody, therefore, attempts to travel at night, on account of the monkeys and wild cats.

From Shabait it is ten months by land and four by sea, on a big ship.

There is a kind of deer, which, when fattened, have their navels cut, and a liquid is generated within. When wild they drop these navels, which give a very strong smell on the fields and in the woods, and anyone attempting to taste the liquid would immediately die.

I kept Easter in May at Bidar, the Muslim residence in Hindustan, having begun to fast on the first day of April; but the Muslims kept Bayram in the middle of May.

O true believing Christians! He that travels through many countries will fall into many sins, and deprive himself of the Christian faith. And I, Afanasy, servant of the Lord, have been longing for my faith with all my heart; Lent and Easter have already passed four times, but I, sinful man, do not know which is the great day, or when is Lent, or Christmas, or any other holiday, or Wednesday or Friday. I have no books; they were taken by those that plundered us. Driven by this great misfortune I went to India, for I had nothing to return with to Russia, being robbed of all my goods.

The first Easter I kept at Kain [?]; the second at Chapakur, in the country of Mazanderan: the third at Hormuz; the fourth in Bidar, in India, together with the Muslims; and there I wept bitterly because of the Christian faith.

A Muslim called Melik, forcibly exhorted me to go over to the Muslim faith. But I said to him: "Master, you observe your prayers, and I observe mine; you say five prayers, and I say three; I am a stranger, but you are not."

But he replied: "Truly you seem not to be a Muslim; but you do not know the Christian faith." And I was then engrossed by many a thought, and said to myself: "Woe to me, obdurate sinner, who wandered from the path of truth, and who no more knows where to go. Oh Lord almighty, creator of heaven and earth, turn not away your face from your servant, for I am near to despair in my trouble. Lord, bestow your glance upon me and have mercy upon me, for I am your creature; do not lead me, O Lord, from the path of truth, but direct my steps to wander in righteousness; for in my trouble I did no good for your sake, O Lord, and have spent the whole of my days in evil. My Lord, Allah the protector, Allah the most high, Allah the merciful, Allah the benefi-cent. Praise be to Allah. I have already passed the fourth Easter in the Muslim country, and have not renounced Christianity. But what may come hereafter, that God alone knows: 'O gracious Lord, on you I rely, and to you I pray to save me from destruction.'"

In Muslim India, at great Bidar, I watched the heavens on the night of Easter; the Pleiades and Orion stood low at Easter, and the Great Bear was headed eastwards.

During the Muslim Bayram, the sultan went out in procession, and with him 20 high viziers, 300 elephants, clad in Damask steel armor, carrying citadels equally fitted in steel, and each holding six warriors with guns and harquebuses [portable guns supported on a tripod]. The big elephants are mounted by 12 men. Each animal has two large standards and a heavy sword, weighing a *kantar*, attached to its tusks, and large iron weights hanging from the trunk. A man in full armor sits between the ears, holding in his hand a large iron hook wherewith he guides the animal. But besides this there may be seen in the train of the sultan about 1,000 ordinary horses in gold trappings, 100 camels with torchbearers, 300 trumpeters, 300 dancers, and 300 slave girls.

The sultan, riding on a golden saddle, wears a habit embroidered with sap-phires, and on his pointed headdress a large diamond; he also carries a suit of gold armor inlaid with sapphires, and three swords mounted in gold. Before him runs a Muslim playing with an umbrella, and behind a great many atten-dants follow on foot; also a mighty elephant, decked with silk and holding in his mouth a large iron chain. It is his business to clear the way of people and horses, in order that none should come too near the sultan.

The brother of the sultan rides on a golden bed, the canopy of which is cov-ered with velvet and ornamented with precious stones. It is carried by 20 men.

The sovereign sits on a golden bed, with a silken canopy to it and a golden top, drawn by four horses in gilt harness. Around him are crowds of people, and before him many singers and dancers, and all of them armed with bare swords or sabers, shields, spears, lances, or large straight bows; and riders and horses are in full armor. Some are naked, but wear a small garment round the waist.

At Bidar the moon remains full three days. I found there no fresh vegetables. The heat in Hindustan is not great; it is great at Hormuz and in Bahrein, where pearls are found; at Judda; at Baku; at Egypt; at Arabia; at Lar. In the land of Khorassan the climate is warm, but not to excess; it is, however, exceedingly hot in Jagatai, and in the cities of Shiraz, Yezd, and Kashan; but the winds blow there sometimes. At Gilan the air is sultry and extremely warm; the same at Shemakha and at Babylon [Baghdad], at Homs, at Damascus. It is less warm at Aleppo. But in Sivas and in the land of Georgia there is abundance of everything, as well as in the lands of the Turks and Wallachia, where eatables are plentiful and cheap. The land of Podolia also abounds in every produce.

May God preserve the Russian land! There is no land in the world like it, although the boyars in the Russian land are unjust. May the Russian land be well ordered, and may there be justice there. O Lord, I rely on you; spare my life. I have lost my road and do not know where to go! I can well get from Hindustan to Hormuz, but there is no road from there to Khorassan; nor to Jagatai, nor to Bahrein, nor to Yezd; for all these places have experienced strife, and their kings expelled. Uzun Hasan Beg killed Mirza Jahan Shah; Sultan Abu Said was poisoned; Uzun Hasan Beg took Shiraz; but the country refused to submit, and Yadigar Muhammad did not appear to make his allegiance, but continued in a state of defense. So there is no practicable way whatever.

If you proceed to Mecca you must take the Muslim faith, and on account of this Christians do not like to go to Mecca, for there they would be converted to Islam. On the other hand, living in India is very expensive. I have spent the whole of my money, and being alone I spend daily for my food two and a half *altins*; nor do I drink wine or mead.

Malik-at-Tujjar took two Indian towns, whose ships pirated on the Indian Sea, captured seven princes with their treasures, a load of precious stones, a load of diamonds and rubies, and a hundred loads of valuable goods; while the army took an immense quantity of various merchandise. The town had been besieged for two years by an army of 200,000 men, 100 elephants, and 300 camels. Malik-at-Tujjar came with his army to Bidar on the day of Kurban Bayram, in the Russian calendar Saint Peter's day [29 June]; and the sultan sent ten viziers to encounter him at a distance of ten *kos* (a *kos* is equal to ten versts), each at the head of 10,000 warriors, and of ten elephants in full equipment.

At the court of Malik-at-Tujjar 500 people sit down to dinner every day; but three viziers only are admitted to his table, and with each vizier 50 people, and besides 100 of his household nobles.

Two thousand horses stand in the stables of Malik-at-Tujjar, of which 1,000 are always saddled and kept in readiness day and night; and also 100 elephants.

His residence is guarded every night by 100 armed men, 20 trumpeters, and ten torchmen; while ten large kettledrums, each attended by two men, are alternately struck throughout the watch.

Nizam-ul-Mulk, Melik Khan, and Farkhad Khan took three large cities, with an army of 100,000 men and 50 elephants of their own, and captured an immense quantity of precious stones, sapphires, and diamonds, the whole of which was bought by Malik-at-Tujjar, who gave order that none of them should be sold to foreign traders. They came to Bidar on the day of the Assumption [15 August].

The sultan goes out hunting on Tuesdays and Thursdays and is accompanied by three viziers.

His brother, when in a campaign, is followed by his mother and sister, and 2,000 women on horseback or on golden beds; at the head of the train are 300 ordinary horses in gold equipment, and a great many troops on foot, 12 viziers, 50 elephants in cloth coverings, carrying each four naked natives with a small garment round the waist. The women that follow on foot are equally uncovered; they carry supplies of water for drinking and washing. No man will drink with another from the same vessel.

Malik-at-Tujjar moved from Bidar with his army, 50,000 strong, against the Indians, on the anniversary of Sheikh Ala-uddin, after the Russian calendar, on the feast of the Intercession of the Holy Mother of God. The sultan sent with him 50,000 of his own army and three viziers with 30,000 men, 100 elephants fully equipped, and carrying each a citadel and four men, the latter armed with harquebuses. With this force Malik-at-Tujjar went to fight against the great Indian dominion of Vijayanagar. But the king of Vijayanagar possessed 300 elephants, 100,000 men of his own troops, and 50,000 horses.

The sultan left Bidar on the eighth month after Easter, and with him 26 viziers, of whom 20 were Muslims and six Indians.

There went out of the household troops of the sultan, 100,000 horsemen, 200,000 foot soldiers, 300 elephants with citadels and clad in armor, and 100 savage beasts led in double chains. The brother of the sultan took the field with 100,000 horsemen and 100,000 foot soldiers, and 100 equipped elephants. And from the court of Mal Khan there went 20,000 horsemen and 60,000 foot soldiers, and 20 elephants in fighting array. And with Beder Khan and his brother there went 30,000 horsemen and 100,000 foot soldiers, and 25 elephants in fighting array, with citadels. And from the court of Sul Khan there went 10,000 horsemen and 20,000 foot soldiers, and 10 elephants, with citadels. And with Wazir Khan there went 15,000 horsemen and 30,000 foot soldiers, and 15 elephants in fighting array. And from the court of Kutar Khan there went 15,000 horsemen and 40,000 foot soldiers, and 10 elephants. And with each vizier there went 10,000, and with some 15,000 horsemen and 20,000 foot soldiers. And with the Autonomos [the ruler of Vijayanagar] went out 40,000 horsemen, 100,000 foot soldiers, 40 elephants in full armor, each carrying four men with arquebuses. The sultan mustered 26 viziers, each at the head of 10,000 horsemen and 20,000 foot soldiers. There are four great Indian viziers, having each an army of 40,000 horsemen and 100,000 foot soldiers. The sultan, being indignant that the Indians had turned out so few, added to them 20,000 foot soldiers, 2,000 horsemen, and 20 elephants. And this is the force of the Muslim sultan of India.

The Muslim faith is good. God alone knows the true faith, and the true faith bids us to know only one God and to invoke his name in every place. On the fifth Easter I thought of returning to Russia, and I set out from Bidar a month before the Muslim Ulu Bayram, according to the faith of Muhammad, the messenger of God. Knowing no more the great Christian day, the day of Christ's resurrection, I fasted with the Muslims and broke fasting with them. I kept Easter at Gulbarga, a city 20 *kos* from Bidar.

The sultan moved out with his army on the fifteenth day after the Ulu Bayram to join Malik-at-Tujjar at Gulbarga. But their campaign was not successful, for they only took one Indian town, and that at the loss of many people and treasures.

The Indian governor is a very powerful prince. He possesses a numerous army, and resides on a mountain at Vijayanagar. This vast city is surrounded by three moats, and intersected by a river, bordering on one side on a dreadful jungle, on the other on a valley; a wonderful place, and to any purpose convenient. On one side it is quite inaccessible; a road goes right through the town, and as the mountain rises high with a ravine below, the town is impregnable.

The enemy besieged it for a month and lost many people, owing to the want of water and food. Plenty of water was in sight, but could not be got at.

This Indian stronghold was ultimately taken by Khoja Malik-at-Tujjar, who stormed it, having fought day and night to reduce it. The army that made the siege with heavy guns, had neither eaten nor drunk for 20 days. He lost 5,000 of his best soldiers. On the capture of the town 20,000 inhabitants, men and women, had their heads cut off; 20,000, young and old, were made prisoners, and sold afterward at ten *tangas* and some at five *tangas* a head; the children at two *tangas* each. The treasure, however, having been found empty, the town was abandoned.

From Gulbarga I went to Kulur, where the cornelian is produced and worked, and from where it is exported to all parts of the world. Three hundred workers in diamonds reside in this place; they adorn weapons. I stopped there five months and then proceeded to Golconda, which is a large bazaar; from there I went to Gulbarga, and from Gulbarga to Sheikh Ala-uddin, and from Sheikh Ala-uddin to Kamendria, and from Kamendria to Kynarias, and from Kynarias to Suri, and from Suri to Dabhol, a port of the vast Indian Sea. It is a very large town, the great meeting place for all nations living along the coast of India and of Ethiopia.

And there it was that I, Afanasy, the sinful servant of God the creator of heaven and earth, pondered over the Christian religion, of the baptism of Christ, of the fasts ordained by the holy fathers, and of the commands of the apostles, and I made up my mind to go to Russia. So I embarked in a *dabba*, and settled to pay for my passage to Hormuz two pieces of gold.

We sailed from Dabhol three months before Easter—the Muslim fast, and were at sea a whole month, during which I saw nothing. On the following month we descried the mountains of Ethiopia, and then those on board exclaimed: "God our Lord, O God, O God, king of heavens, righteously you have doomed us to destruction."

I remained five days in that country, and, by the mercy of God, met with no evil, but distributed among the natives a quantity of rice, pepper, and bread, in order that they might not plunder our ship.

From there I reached Muscat in 12 days; and there I held the sixth Easter. Nine days journey brought me to Hormuz, where I stayed 20 days.

From Hormuz I proceeded thus: First to Lar, where I stopped three days; then in twelve days from Lar to Shiraz, stopped there seven days; in fifteen days from Shiraz to Aberkuh, stopped there ten days; in nine days from Aberkuh to Yezd, stopped there eight days; in five days from Yezd to Isfahan, stopped there six days; from Isfahan to Kashan, where I stopped five days; from Kashan I went to Kum, Savah, Sultaniya, Tabriz, and came to the camp of Hasan Beg. There I spent ten days, as there was no road further on.

The khan sent against the Turks an army of 40,000 men, who conquered the cities of Sivas, burnt down Tokat, took Amasya, and plundered many smaller places, carrying the war to the land of Karaman.

Leaving the camp I went to Erzincan, and from there to Trebizond, where I arrived on the festival of the Intercession of our Lady the holy Virgin Mary. After staying there five days I went on board a ship and agreed to be conveyed to Kaffa [modern Feodosia] for one coin of gold, the food to be paid at the end of the voyage.

I was very much annoyed at Trebizond by the *subasi* [a military leader in Ottoman Turkey] and Pasha [a governor in Ottoman Turkey]. They ordered the whole of my lumber to be brought up to his residence on the hill; it was searched, especially for writings, as I was coming from the camp of Hasan Beg.

However, by the mercy of heaven, I here came to the third sea, the Black Sea, called in the Persian tongue the Sea of Stambul. The wind was fair during the first five days, but having reached Vonada we encountered a heavy northern gale, which drove us back to Trebizond. We lay at anchor for 15 days at Platana, the weather continuing very bad, and then we twice attempted to sail and again met with a foul wind, that did not permit us to keep the sea. O God! Having crossed the sea, we were carried first to Balaklava, and from there to Gurzuf, where we lay at anchor for five days. At last, with God's blessing, I reached Kaffa, nine days before the fast of Advent [5 November]. Allah! True God, Allah the protector. Aside from him, we know no other God.

Through the mercy of God, I have crossed three seas. The rest the Lord alone knows, Allah the protector alone knows. Amen. In the name of Allah, the merciful and beneficent. God is great. There is no God but Allah, the creator. He is God and there is no God greater than he. Allah is king, the light, the world, the savior, the guardian, the glorious, the mighty, the great, the creator, the founder, the maker. He permits sins and punishes them, giving, feeding, ending all difficulties; knowing, accepting our souls; he, who lays out the heavens and the earth, preserver of all, almighty; who lifts up and casts down; hearing all, seeing all. Allah is the true judge, the good.

Questions: Where did Afanasy's travels bring him, and what difficulties did he encounter along the way? What kinds of items are traded in the areas that Afanasy visits? Was Afanasy a successful merchant? What can Afanasy's account tell historians about life in India at the time? How do women fit into the portrait he painted? How did war affect his journey? What kind of religious crisis did Afanasy experience? What was his religion by the end?

CHAPTER FOUR

DIPLOMATIC JOURNEYS

International diplomacy is no invention of the modern age, and in the Middle Ages, some of the travelers who had the most difficult and sensitive missions were ambassadors. Diplomats had a central role in regulating relationships between kingdoms, including critical negotiations to avoid war or forge new alliances. Especially in this period, diplomacy hinged on personal interactions, which is why the relationship between an ambassador and a foreign ruler was significant. The ultimate success of a mission might be out of the ambassador's hands, but a tactless representative could disrupt foreign relations. Everyone involved was sensitive to the ceremonial aspects of the interaction, which extended to the benefits and gifts that were exchanged. The honor shown to the ambassador was a reflection of the honor due to the ruler he was representing. Just as any other travelers, however, ambassadors did not confine their observations to the mission at hand, and being well educated, they were able to commit their thoughts to paper.

In reading through these sources, readers should focus on the missions of the various ambassadors and to what degree they were able to accomplish them. How were diplomats treated in the places where they were visiting? At the same time, the reader should notice the wide range of the ambassadors' observations. About what did the travelers have positive or negative reactions? Do they ever think the host country is lesser or undeveloped? How do ambassadors use religion to condemn or praise others? In these sources, we see two separate embassies that issued forth from the same ruler, allowing the reader to compare and contrast the responses of Timurid diplomats to both China and Calicut, India.

28. IBN FADLAN, *MISSION TO THE VOLGA*

In this source, the author, Ibn Fadlan, describes his participation in an embassy from Baghdad to the Volga Bulgars or Bulgarians in 921. Aside from what he relates here, we are ill informed about the rest of his life or even his exact job title. Baghdad was at the time the heart of the Muslim world and the Abbasid Caliphate, and the caliph al-Muqtadir (r. 908–932) had sent out the envoys to King Almish ibn Yiltawar (r. late ninth and early tenth century), a recent convert to Islam, likely to strengthen his newfound faith and foster an alliance. Ibn Fadlan was not the leader of the embassy, but he was the only one to leave a record of it.

Source: ed. and trans. James E. Montgomery, Ibn Fadlan, *Mission to the Volga*, in *Two Arabic Travel Books: Accounts of China and India* (New York: New York University Press, 2014), pp. 190–241 [English pages only]. Arabic. Revised.

This is the written account of Ahmad ibn Fadlan ibn al-'Abbas ibn Rashid ibn Hammad, the envoy of al-Muqtadir to the king of the Saqalibah [Slavs]. His patron was Muhammad ibn Sulayman. It records his observations in the realm of the Turks, the Khazars, the Rus, the Saqalibah, the Bashghird, and other peoples. It also includes reports of their various customs and ways of living, their kings, and many other related matters, too.

Ahmad ibn Fadlan said: In the letter of al-Hasan, son of Yiltawar, the king of the Saqalibah, which al-Muqtadir the commander of the faithful received, the king petitioned al-Muqtadir to send people to instruct him in law and acquaint him with the rules of Islam according to the sharia [Muslim law], and to construct a mosque and build a pulpit from which he could proclaim al-Muqtadir's name throughout his kingdom. He also beseeched him to build a fort to protect him against the kings who opposed him. His requests were granted.

The representative of the king of the Saqalibah at court was Nadhir al-Harami. I, Ahmad ibn Fadlan, was delegated to read al-Muqtadir's letter to him, to present him with the official gifts designated, and to supervise the jurists and instructors. Nadhir identified a fixed sum of money to be brought to him, to cover the construction costs and to pay the jurists and instructors. These expenses were to be covered by Arthakhushmithan, one of the estates of Ibn al-Furat in Khwarazm. The envoy from the king of the Saqalibah to the caliph was a man named 'Abdallah ibn Bashtu al-Khazari. The caliph's envoy was Sawsan al-Rassi. Sawsan's patron was Nadhir al-Harami. Takin al-Turki, Bars al-Saqlabi, and I accompanied him. As I said, I was charged with the following responsibilities: I presented him with the official gifts for him, his wife, children, brothers, and commanders. I also handed over the medication that the king had requested, in writing, from Nadhir.

We traveled from Baghdad, City of Peace, on Thursday, the twelfth of Safar, 309 [21 June 921]. We stayed one day in Nahrawan, then rode hard until we reached al-Daskarah, where we stayed three days. Then we traveled without delay or diversion and came to Hulwan, where we stayed two days.

From there we traveled to Qirmisin, where we stayed another two days, and next arrived at Hamadhan, where we stayed three days. We traveled to Sawah and, after two days, on to Rayy, where we stayed eleven days, until Ahmad ibn 'Ali, the brother of Su'luk, had left Khuwar al-Rayy. Then we traveled to Khuwar al-Rayy itself and three days later to Simnan, then on to al-Damghan, where our caravan happened to encounter Ibn Qarin, who was preaching on behalf of the *dai* [Ismaili mission]. We concealed our identity and hurried to Nishapur, where we met Hammawayh Kusa, the field marshal of Khurasan. Lili ibn Nu'man had just been killed. Then we proceeded to Sarakhs, Marw, and Qushmahan, at the edge of the Amul desert. We stayed three days there and changed camels for the desert journey. We crossed the desert to Amul and then reached Afribr [?], the outpost of Tahir ibn 'Ali, on the other side of the Jayhun [Oxus; Amu Darya].

We traveled via Baykand to Bukhara, where we went straight to al-Jayhani, the chancellor of the emir [commander or ruler] of Khurasan, known there as the chief *shaykh* [honorific title]. He had ordered a residence for us and had appointed someone to attend to all our needs and concerns and make sure that we experienced no difficulty in getting what we wanted. After a few days, he arranged an audience with Nasr ibn Ahmad [914–943]. We discovered that he was still a boy and did not even have a beard. We greeted him as befits an emir. He commanded us to be seated. His very first words were: "How was my patron, the commander of the faithful, when you left him? May God give him long life and cherish him, his retinue, and his spiritual companions." "He was well," we replied. He said, "May God increase his well-being!" The letter was then read out to him. It gave the following instructions: the estate of Arthakhushmithan was to be handed over by al-Fadl ibn Musa the Christian, Ibn al-Furat's agent, to Ahmad ibn Musa al-Khwarazmi; we were to be provided with funds, with a letter to his governor in Khwarazm ordering him not to hinder us, and with a letter to the garrison at the Gate of the Turks, who were to provide us with an escort and not detain us. "Where is Ahmad ibn Musa?" he asked. "We left the City of Peace without him, and he set off four days later," we replied and he said, "I hear and obey the commands of my patron, the commander of the faithful, may God give him long life!"

Ibn Fadlan said: al-Fadl ibn Musa the Christian, Ibn al-Furat's agent, got wind of this and came up with a plan to deal with Ahmad ibn Musa. He wrote to the deputies of the superintendent of the Khurasan highway, in the military district of Sarakhs-Baykand, as follows: "Tell your spies to keep a lookout for

Ahmad ibn Musa in the caravanserais and the lookout posts. Enclosed is his description. The man who catches him is to detain him until we specify the punishment in writing." Ahmad ibn Musa was later arrested in Marw and put in chains. We stayed twenty-eight days in Bukhara. 'Abdallah ibn Bashtu and other members of our party kept saying, "If we tarry, the winter onslaught will mean we will miss the crossing. Ahmad ibn Musa will catch up with us and will join us." Al-Fadl ibn Musa encouraged this.

Ibn Fadlan said: I noticed in Bukhara that the dirhams were made of different colored metals. One of them, the *ghitrifi* dirham, is made of red and yellow brass. It is accepted according to numerical value rather than weight: one hundred *ghitrifi* dirhams equals one silver dirham. In the dowries for their womenfolk they make the following stipulations: so-and-so, the son of so-and-so, marries so-and-so, the daughter of so-and-so, for so many thousand *ghitrifi* dirhams. This also applies to the purchase of property and the purchase of slaves—they specifically mention *ghitrifi* dirhams. They have other dirhams, made only of yellow brass, forty of which equal one *danaq*, and a further type of yellow-brass dirham called the *samarqandi*, six of which equal one *danaq*.

I listened to the warnings of 'Abdallah ibn Bashtu and the others about the onslaught of winter. We left Bukhara and returned to the river, where we hired a boat for Khwarazm, more than two hundred *farsakhs* from where we hired the boat. We were able to travel only part of the day. A whole day's travel was impossible because of the cold. When we got to Khwarazm, we were given an audience with the emir, Muhammad ibn 'Iraq Khwarazm-Shah, who gave us a warm and hospitable reception and a place to stay.

Three days later, he summoned us, quizzing us about wanting to enter the realm of the Turks. "I cannot let you do that," he said. "I am not permitted to let you risk your lives. I think all this is a ploy devised by this soldier." (He meant Takin.) "He used to live here as a blacksmith, when he ran the iron trade in the land of the infidels. He is the one who beguiled Nadhir and got him to speak to the commander of the faithful and to bring the letter of the king of the Saqalibah to him. The exalted emir," (he meant the emir of Khurasan) "has more right to have the name of the commander of the faithful proclaimed out there, if only he could find a safe way to do it. And then there are a thousand infidel tribes in your path. This is clearly an imposture foisted upon the caliph. Such is my counsel. I now have no recourse but to write to the exalted emir, so that he can write to the caliph (God give him strength!) and consult with him. You will remain here until the answer comes." We left things at that but came back later and pressured him. "We have the orders and the letter of the commander of the faithful, so why do you need to consult?" we said. In the end, he granted us permission and we sailed downriver from Khwarazm to al-Jurjaniyyah. The distance by water is fifty *farsakhs*.

I noticed that the dirhams in Khwarazm are adulterated and should not be accepted, because they are made of lead and brass. They call their dirham a *tazijah*. It weighs four and a half *danaqs*. The money changers trade in sheep bones, spinning tops, and dirhams.

They are the strangest of people in the way they talk and behave. When they talk they sound just like starlings calling. There is a village one day away called Ardkwa, whose inhabitants are called al-Kardaliyyah. When they talk they sound just like frogs croaking. At the end of the prayer they disavow the commander of the faithful, 'Ali ibn Abi Talib [r. 656–661], God be pleased with him.

We stayed several days in al-Jurjaniyyah. The River Jayhun froze over completely, from beginning to end. The ice was seventeen spans thick. Horses, mules, donkeys, and carts used it like a road and it did not move—it did not even creak. It stayed like this for three months. We thought the country we were visiting was an infernally cold portal to the depths of hell. When snow fell, it was accompanied by a wild, howling blizzard.

When people here want to honor each other and be generous they say, "Come to my house so we can talk, for I have a good fire burning." This is their custom for expressing genuine generosity and affability. God the exalted has been kind to them by making firewood plentiful and very cheap: a cart load of tamarisk wood costs only two local dirhams, and their carts can hold about three thousand *ratls* [?]. Normally, their beggars do not stand outside at the door but go into the house, sit for a while, and get warm by the fire. Then they say *bakand*, meaning bread.

We were in al-Jurjaniyyah for a long time: several days of Rajab and all of Sha'ban, Ramadan, and Shawwal. We stayed there so long because the cold was so severe. Indeed, I was told that two men had driven twelve camels to transport a load of firewood from a particular forest but had forgotten to take their flint and tinderbox and passed the night without a fire. In the morning it was so cold that they had frozen to death, as had their camels. The weather was so cold that you could wander round the markets and through the streets and not meet anyone. I would leave the baths, and, by the time I got home, I would look at my beard and see a block of ice. I would have to thaw it at the fire. I would sleep inside a chamber, inside another chamber, with a Turkish yurt of animal skins inside it, and would be smothered in cloaks and pelts, and even then my cheek would sometimes freeze and stick to the pillow. I noticed containers wrapped in sheepskins, to stop them shattering and breaking, but this did them no good at all. I even saw the ground open up into great rifts and mighty, ancient trees split in two because of the cold.

Halfway into Shawwal of 309 [February 922], the season began to change and the Jayhun melted. We set about acquiring the items we needed for our journey. We purchased Turkish camels, constructed the camel-skin rafts for crossing all the rivers we had to cross in the realm of the Turks, and packed provisions of bread, millet, and cured meat to last three months. The locals who knew us told us in no uncertain terms to wear proper clothing outdoors and to wear a lot of it. They gave us a terrifying description of the cold and impressed upon us the need to take the matter very, very seriously. But when we experienced it ourselves, it was so much worse than what they had described, even though we each wore a tunic, a caftan, a sheepskin, a horse blanket, and a burnoose with only our eyes showing, a pair of trousers, another pair of lined trousers, leggings, and a pair of animal skin boots with yet another pair on top of them. Mounted on our camels, we wore so many heavy clothes we couldn't move. The jurist, the instructor, and the retainers who had left the City of Peace with us stayed behind, too scared to enter the realm of the Turks. I pushed on with the envoy, his brother-in-law, and the two soldiers, Takin and Bars.

On the day we planned to set off, I said to them, "The king's man accompanies you. He knows everything. And you carry the letters of the caliph. They must surely mention the four thousand *musayyabi* dinars [gold coins] intended for the king. You will be at the court of a non-Arab king, and he will demand that you pay this sum." "Don't worry about it," they replied, "he will not ask us for them." "He will demand that you produce them. I know it," I warned. But they paid no heed. The caravan was ready to depart, so we hired a guide called Falus, an inhabitant of al-Jurjaniyyah. We trusted in almighty God, putting our fate in his hands.

We left al-Jurjaniyyah on Monday, the second of Dhu l-Qadah, 309 [4 March 922], and stopped at an outpost called Zamjan, the gate of the Turks. The following morning we traveled as far as a stopping post called Jit. The snow had fallen so heavily that it came up to the camels' knees. We had to stay there two days. Then we kept a straight course and plunged deep into the realm of the Turks through a barren, mountainless desert. We met no one. We crossed for ten days. Our bodies suffered terrible injuries. We were exhausted. The cold was biting, the snowstorms never-ending. It made the cold of Khwarazm seem like summertime. We forgot all about our previous sufferings and were ready to give up the ghost.

One day, the cold was unusually biting. Takin was traveling beside me, talking in Turkish to a Turk at his side. He laughed and said, "This Turk wants to know, 'What does our Lord want from us? He is killing us with this cold. If we knew what he wanted, then we could just give it to him.'" "Tell him," I replied, "that he wants you to declare 'There is no god but Allah.'" "Well, if we knew him, we'd do it," he said with a laugh.

We came to a place where there was a huge quantity of tamarisk wood and stopped. The members of the caravan lit fires and got them going. They took their clothes off and dried them by the fires. Then we departed, traveling as quickly and with as much energy as we could manage, from midnight until the midday or afternoon prayer, when we would stop for a rest. After fifteen nights of this, we came to a huge rocky mountain. Springs of water ran down it and gathered to form a lake at its foot.

We crossed the mountain and reached a Turkish tribe known as the Ghuzzi-yyah [Oguz]. Much to our surprise, we discovered that they are nomads who live in animal-hair tents that they pitch and strike regularly. Their tents were pitched with some in one place and the same number in another place, as is the practice of transhumant nomads. They lead wretched lives. They are like roaming asses. They practice no recognizable form of monotheism, they do not base their beliefs on reason, and they worship nothing—indeed they call their own chiefs "lord." When one of them consults his chief on a matter, he says to him, "My lord, what shall I do about such and such?" They decide matters by consultation, though it is quite possible for the lowliest and most worthless individual in their community to turn up and overturn the consensus they have reached. To be sure, I have heard them declare, "There is no god but Allah! Muhammad is Allah's emissary." But this was a way of ingratiating themselves with the Muslims passing through their lands and not out of conviction. When one of them is wronged or something unpleasant happens to him, he raises his head to the heavens and shouts, "*Bir tankri*," which in Turkish means "By God, by the one!" *Bir* means "one" and *tankri* is "God" in the language of the Turks. They do not clean themselves when they defecate or urinate, and they do not wash themselves when intercourse puts them in a state of ritual impurity. They avoid contact with water, especially in the winter.

Their womenfolk do not cover themselves in the presence of a man, whether he be one of their menfolk or not. A woman will not cover any part of her body in front of anyone, no matter who. One day we stopped at a tent and sat down. The man's wife sat with us. During conversation, she suddenly uncovered her vulva and scratched it, right in front of us. We covered our faces and exclaimed, "God forgive us!" but her husband simply laughed and said to the interpreter, "Tell them: we might uncover it in your presence and you might see it, but she keeps it safe so no one can get to it. This is better than her covering it up and letting others have access to it." Illicit intercourse is unheard of. If they catch anyone attempting it in any way, they tear him in half, in the following manner: they join the branches of two trees, tie the culprit to the branches and then let the trees loose. The man tied to the trees is torn in two.

One of them heard me reciting the Qur'an and found it beautiful. He approached the interpreter and said, "Tell him not to stop." One day, this man said to me via the interpreter, "Ask this Arab, 'Does our great and glorious Lord have a wife?'" I was shocked by his words, praised God and asked his forgiveness. He copied my actions. Such is the custom of the Turk: whenever he hears a Muslim declare God's glory and attest his uniqueness, he copies him.

Their marriage customs are as follows. One man asks another for one of his womenfolk, be it his daughter, sister, or any other woman he possesses, in exchange for such and such a number of Khwarazmi garments. When he is paid in full, he hands her over. Sometimes the dowry is in camels, horses, or the like. The man is not granted access to his future wife until he has paid the full dowry that he has agreed with her guardian. Once paid, he shows up unabashedly, enters her dwelling, and takes possession of her right there and then, in the presence of her father, mother, and brothers. No one stops him. When one of them dies and leaves a wife and sons behind, the eldest son marries his dead father's wife, provided she is not his birth mother. No one, merchant or anyone else for that matter, can perform a ritual wash in their presence, except at night when he will not be seen, because they get very angry. They exact payment from him and exclaim, "This man has planted something in the water and wants to put a spell on us!"

No Muslim can pass through their territory without first befriending one of them. He lodges with him and brings gifts from the Muslim lands: a roll of cloth, a headscarf for his wife, pepper, millet, raisins, and nuts. When he arrives, his friend pitches a yurt for him and provides him with sheep, in accordance with his status. In this way, the Muslim can perform the ritual slaughter, as the Turks do not do this but instead beat the sheep on the head until it dies. If someone has decided to travel and uses some of the camels and horses belonging to his friend the Turk, or if he borrows some money, his debt with his friend remains unpaid. He takes the camels, horses, and money he needs from his friend. On his return, he pays the Turk his money and returns his camels and horses. So too, if someone a Turk doesn't know passes through and says, "I am your guest. I want some of your camels, horses, and dirhams," he gives him what he asks for. If the merchant dies on the trip and the caravan returns, the Turk comes to meet the caravan and says, "Where is my guest?" If they say, "He is dead," he brings the caravan to a halt, goes up to the most eminent merchant he sees, unties his goods as the merchant looks on, and takes the exact number of dirhams he had advanced to the first merchant, not a penny more. He also takes back the exact number of camels and horses, saying, "He was your cousin, so you are under the greatest obligation to pay his debt." If the guest runs away, he behaves in the same way, only this time he says, "He was a Muslim like you. You get it back from him." If he does not meet his Muslim guest on the road, he asks three men about him, saying, "Where is he?" When told where he is, he travels, even for days, until he finds him and reclaims his property, along with the gifts he gave him. The Turk also behaves like this when he travels to al-Jurjaniyyah. He asks for his guest and stays with him until he leaves. If the Turk dies while staying with his Muslim friend and the Muslim later passes through this territory as a member of a caravan, they put him to death, with the words, "You imprisoned him and killed him. Had you not imprisoned him, he would not have died." Likewise, they kill the Muslim if he gives the Turk alcohol and he falls and dies. If he does not travel as a member of the caravan, they seize the most important member of the caravan and kill him.

They abhor pederasty. A man from Khwarazm lodged with the tribe of the *kudharkin* (the deputy of the king of the Turks) and lived for a while with one of his hosts. He was there to trade in sheep. The Turk had a beardless son, whom the Khwarazmi blandished and tried to seduce until he gave in. The Turk turned up, found the two of them in the act, and brought the matter to the *kudharkin*, who said to him, "Muster the Turks," which he did, as was the practice. The *kudharkin* said to the Turk, "Do you wish me to rule according to what is true or what is false?" "According to what is true." "Then fetch your son!" The son was fetched. "Both must be put to death together." The Turk was angered and said, "I shall not surrender my son." "Then let the merchant pay a ransom," he said. The Turk paid a number of sheep for what had been done to his son, and four hundred ewes to the *kudharkin*, for the punishment that had been averted. Then he left the realm of the Turks.

The first king and chief we met was Yinal the younger. He had converted to Islam but had been told that, "If you convert to Islam, you will never lead us," so he recanted. When we arrived at his camp, he said, "I cannot allow you to pass. This is unheard of. It will never happen." We gave him some gifts. He was satisfied with a Jurjani caftan worth ten dirhams, a cut of woven cloth, some flat breads, a handful of raisins, and a hundred nuts. When we handed them over, he prostrated himself before us. This is their custom: when a person is generous to another, the other prostrates himself before him. He said, "Were our tents not far from the road, we would bring you sheep and grain." He left us and we carried on.

The next morning we encountered a solitary Turk—a despicable figure, unkempt and really quite repulsive—a man of no worth at all. It had started to rain heavily. "Halt!" the man said. The entire caravan ground to a halt: it numbered about three thousand mounts and five thousand men. "Not one of you will pass," he said. We obeyed and said, "We are friends of the *kudharkin*." He approached and said with a laugh, "*Kudharkin* who? Do I not shit on the beard of the *kudharkin*?" Then he shouted, "*Bakand*"—"bread" in the language of Khwarazm—and I gave him some flat breads, which he took, saying, "Proceed. I have spared you out of pity."

Ibn Fadlan said: The members of a household do not approach someone who is ill. His slaves, male and female, wait on him. He is put in a tent, away from the other tents, where he remains until he dies or recovers. A slave or a pauper is simply thrown out onto the open plain and left. The Turks dig a large ditch, in the shape of a chamber for their dead. They fetch the deceased, clothe him in his tunic and girdle, and give him his bow. They put a wooden cup filled with alcohol in his hand and place a wooden vessel of alcohol in front of him. They bring all his wealth and lay it beside him, in the chamber. They put him in a sitting position and then build the roof. On top they construct what looks like a yurt made of clay. Horses are fetched, depending on how many he owned. They can slaughter any number of horses, from a single horse up to a hundred or two. They eat the horse meat, except for the head, legs, hide, and tail, which they nail to pieces of wood, saying, "His horses which he rides to the garden [heaven]." If he has shown great bravery and killed someone, they carve wooden images, as many as the men he has killed, place them on top of his grave and say, "His retainers who serve him in the garden." Sometimes they do not kill the horses for a day or two. Then an elder will exhort them: "I have seen so-and-so," (i.e., the deceased) "in a dream and he said to me, 'You see me here in front of you. My companions have gone before me. My feet are cracked from following them. I cannot catch up with them. I am left here, all alone.'" Then they bring his horses, slaughter them, and gibbet them at his graveside. A day or two later, the elder arrives and says, "I have seen so-and-so. He said, 'Inform my household and companions that I have caught up with those who went before me and have recovered from my exhaustion.'"

Ibn Fadlan said: Each and every one of the Turks plucks his beard but does not touch his mustache. I would often see one of their aged elders, clad in a sheepskin, his beard plucked but with a little left under his chin. If you caught sight of him from a distance, you would be convinced he was a billy goat.

The king of the Ghuzziyyah Turks is called *yabghu*. This is the title given to the ruler of the tribe and is their name for their emir. His deputy is called *kudharkin*. Anyone who deputizes for a chief is called *kudharkin*.

Upon leaving the region where this group of Turks was camped, we stopped with their field marshal, Atrak, son of al-Qataghan. Turkish yurts were pitched, and we were lodged in them. He had a large retinue with many dependents, and his tents were big. He gave us sheep and horses: sheep for slaughter and horses for riding. He summoned his paternal cousins and members of his household, held a banquet, and killed many sheep. We had presented him with a gift of clothing, along with raisins, nuts, pepper, and millet. I watched his wife, who had previously been the wife of his father, take some meat, milk, and a few of the gifts we had presented and go out into the open, where she dug a hole and buried everything, uttering some words. "What is she saying?" I asked the interpreter, and he replied, "She says, 'This is a gift for al-Qataghan, the father of Atrak. The Arabs gave it to him.'"

That night the interpreter and I were granted an audience in Atrak's yurt. We delivered the letter from Nadhir al-Harami, instructing him to embrace Islam. The letter specifically mentioned that he was to receive fifty dinars (some of them *musayyabis*), three measures of musk, some tanned hides, and two rolls of Marw cloth. Out of this we had cut for him two tunics, a pair of leather boots, a garment of silk brocade, and five silk garments. We presented his gift and gave his wife a headscarf and a signet ring. I read out the letter and he told the interpreter, "I will not respond until you have returned. Then I shall inform the caliph of my decision in writing." He removed the silk shirt he was wearing and put on the robe of honor we have just mentioned. I noticed that the tunic underneath was so filthy that it had fallen to pieces. It is their custom not to remove the garment next to their body until it falls off in tatters.

He had plucked all of his beard and mustache, so he looked like a eunuch. Even so, I heard the Turks state that he was their most accomplished horseman. In fact, I was with him one day, on horseback. A goose flew past. I saw him string his bow, move his horse into position under the bird, and fire. He shot the goose dead.

One day he summoned the four commanders of the adjacent territory: Tarkhan, Yinal, the nephew of Tarkhan and Yinal, and Yilghiz. Tarkhan was blind and lame and had a withered arm, but he was by far the most eminent and important. Atrak said, "These are the envoys from the king of the Arabs to my son-in-law, Almish, son of Shilki. I cannot rightfully allow them to go any further without consulting you." Tarkhan said, "Never before have we seen or heard of a thing like this. Never before has an envoy from the caliph passed through our realm, even when our fathers were alive. I suspect that it is the caliph's design to send these men to the Khazars and mobilize them against us. Our only option is to dismember these envoys and take what they have." Someone else said, "No. We should take what they have and let them go back naked where they came from." Another said, "No. We should use them as ransom for our fellow tribesmen taken prisoner by the king of the Khazars." They debated like this for seven long days. We were in the jaws of death. Then, as is their wont, they came to a unanimous decision: they would allow us to continue on our way. We presented Tarkhan with a robe of honor: a Marw caftan and two cuts of woven cloth. We gave a tunic to his companions, including Yinal. We also gave them pepper, millet, and flat breads as gifts. Then they left.

We pushed on as far as the Bghndi River, where the people got their camel-hide rafts out, spread them flat, put the round saddle frames from their Turkish camels inside the hides, and stretched them tight. They loaded them with clothes and goods. When the rafts were full, groups of people, four, five, and six strong, sat on top of them, took hold of pieces of birch tree and used them as oars. The rafts floated on the water, spinning round and round, while the people paddled furiously. We crossed the river in this manner. The horses and the camels were urged on with shouts, and they swam across. We needed to send a group of fully armed soldiers across the river first, before the rest of the caravan. They were the advance guard, protection for the people against the Bashghird. There was a fear they might carry out an ambush during the crossing. This is how we crossed the Bghndi River. Then we crossed a river called the Jam, also on rafts, then the Jakhsh, the Adhl, the Ardn, the Warsh, the Akhti, and the Wbna. These are all mighty rivers.

Then we reached the Bajanak. They were encamped beside a still lake as big as a sea. They are a vivid brown color, shave their beards, and live in miserable poverty, unlike the Ghuzziyyah. I saw some Ghuzziyyah who owned ten thousand horses and a hundred thousand head of sheep. The sheep graze mostly on what lies underneath the snow, digging for the grass with their hooves. If they do not find grass, they eat the snow instead and grow inordinately fat. During the summer, when they can eat grass, they become very thin.

We spent a day with the Bajanak, continued on our way, and stopped beside the Jaykh River. This was the biggest and mightiest river we had seen and had the strongest current. I saw a raft capsize in the river and all the passengers on board drown. A great many died, and several camels and horses drowned, too. It took the greatest effort to get across. Several days' march later, we crossed the Jakha, the Azkhn, the Baja, the Smwr, the Knal, the Suh, and the Kijlu.

We stopped in the territory of a tribe of Turks called the Bashghird. We were on high alert, for they are the wickedest, filthiest, and most ferocious of the Turks. When they attack, they take no prisoners. In single combat they slice open your head and make off with it. They shave their beards. They eat lice by carefully picking over the hems of their tunics and cracking the lice with their teeth. Our group was joined by a Bashghird who had converted to Islam. He used to wait on us. I saw him take a louse he found in his clothing, crack it with his fingernail, and then lick it. "Yum!" he said, when he saw me watching him.

Each carves a piece of wood into an object the size and shape of a phallus and hangs it round his neck. When they want to travel or take the field against the enemy, they kiss it and bow down before it, saying, "My lord, do such and such with me." I said to the interpreter, "Ask one of them to explain this. Why does he worship it as his lord?" "Because I came from something like it and I acknowledge no other creator," he replied. Some of them claim that they have twelve lords: a lord for winter, a lord for summer, a lord for rain, a lord for wind, a lord for trees, a lord for people, a lord for horses, a lord for water, a lord for night, a lord for day, a lord for death, a lord for the earth. The lord in the sky is the greatest, but he acts consensually, and each lord approves of the actions of his partners. God is exalted above what the wrongdoers say! We noticed that one clan worships snakes, another fish, and another cranes. They told me that they had once been routed in battle. Then the cranes cried out behind them, and the enemy took fright, turned tail, and fled, even though they had routed the Bashghird. They said, "These are his actions: he has routed our enemies." This is why they worship cranes. We left their territory and crossed the following rivers: the Jrmsan, the Urn, the Urm, the Baynaj, the Wti, the Bnasnh, and the Jawshin. It is about two, three, or four days' travel from one river to the next.

We were a day and night's march away from our goal. The king of the Saqalibah dispatched his brothers, his sons, and the four kings under his control to welcome us with bread, meat, and millet. They formed our escort. When we were two *farsakhs* away, he came to meet us in person. On seeing us, he got down from his horse and prostrated himself abjectly, expressing thanks to the great and glorious God! He had some dirhams in his sleeve and showered them over us. He had yurts pitched for us, and we were lodged in them. We arrived on Sunday the twelfth of Muharram 310 [12 May 922]. We had been on the road for seventy days since leaving al-Jurjaniyyah. From Sunday to Wednesday we remained in our yurts, while he mustered his kings, commanders, and subjects to listen to the reading of the letter.

When they had gathered on the Thursday, we unfurled the two standards we had brought with us, saddled the horse with the saddle meant for the king, dressed him in black, and placed a turban on his head. I brought out the letter of the caliph and said, "We are not permitted to remain seated during the reading of the letter." He stood up, as did the chiefs in attendance. He was big and corpulent. I read the beginning of the letter, and, when I reached the phrase, "Peace be upon you! On your behalf, I praise God—there is no god but him!" I said, "Return the greetings of the commander of the faithful." They did so, without exception. The interpreter translated everything, word by word. When we had finished the letter, they shouted "God Almighty!" at the top of their voices. The ground under our feet shook.

I next read the letter of the vizier Hamid ibn al-'Abbas. The king continued to stand. I told him to be seated, so he sat down for the reading of the letter of Nadhir al-Harami. When I had finished, his companions showered him with many dirhams. Then I produced the gifts meant for him and his wife: unguents, clothes, and pearls. I presented one gift after another until I had handed over everything. Then, in front of his people, I presented a robe of honor to his wife, who was seated by his side. This is their customary practice. The womenfolk showered dirhams on her after I had presented the robe. Then we left.

An hour later, he sent for us, and we were shown into his tent. The kings were on his right. He ordered us to sit on his left. His sons were seated in front of him. He sat alone, on a throne draped in Byzantine silk. He called for the table. It was carried in, laden with roasted meat and nothing else. He picked up a knife, cut off a piece of meat, and ate it, then a second piece and a third, before anyone else. Then he cut off a piece and handed it to Sawsan, the envoy, who had a small table placed in front of him in order to receive it. Such is their custom. No one reaches for the food before the king hands him a portion and a table is provided for him to receive it—the moment he receives it, he gets a table. He handed me a piece next, and I was given a table. He handed a piece to the fourth king, and he was given a table. Then he handed some meat to his sons, and they were given tables. Each of us ate from the table intended for his sole use. No one took anything from any other table. When the king was done with the food, everyone took what remained on his own table back to his lodging.

After the meat, he called for the honey drink *suju*, which he drinks night and day, and drank a cupful. Then he stood up and said, "Such is my joy in my patron the commander of the faithful, may God prolong his life!" The four kings and his sons stood up when he did. So did we. When he had done this three times, we were shown out. Before I turned up, the phrase "Lord God, keep in piety the king Yiltawar, king of the Bulgars!" was proclaimed from the pulpit during the Friday oration. I told the king, "God is the king, and he alone is to be accorded this title from the pulpit. Great and glorious is he! Take your patron, the commander of the faithful. He is satisfied with the phrase, 'Lord God, keep in piety the *imam* [leader of worship] Ja'far al-Muqtadir bi-llah, your humble servant, caliph, and commander of the faithful!' This is proclaimed from his pulpits east and west. His forefathers, the caliphs before him, did the same. The Prophet (God bless and cherish him!) said, 'Do not exaggerate my importance the way the Christians exaggerate the importance of Jesus, the son of Mary, for I am simply 'Abdallah: God's bondsman and his emissary.'" He asked me, "What proclamation can I rightly use for the Friday oration?" and I said, "Your name and that of your father." "But my father was an unbeliever," he said, "and I do not wish to have his name mentioned from the pulpits. Indeed, I do not wish to have even my own name mentioned, because it was given me by an unbeliever. What is the name of my patron, the commander of the faithful?" "Ja'far," I replied. "Am I permitted to take his name?" "Yes." "Then I take Ja'far as my name, and 'Abdallah as the name of my father. Convey this to the preacher." I did so. The proclamation during the Friday oration became, "Lord God, keep in piety your bondsman Ja'far ibn 'Abdallah, the emir of the Bulgars, whose patron is the commander of the faithful!"

Three days after I had read out the epistle and presented the gifts, he summoned me. He had learned of the four thousand dinars and of the subterfuge
employed by the Christian in order to delay their payment. The dinars had
been mentioned in the letter. When I was shown in, he commanded me to be
seated. I sat down. He threw the letter from the commander of the faithful at
me. "Who brought this letter?" "I did." Then he threw the vizier's letter at me.
"And this one?" "I did," I replied. "What has been done," he asked, "with the
money they refer to?" "It could not be collected. Time was short, and we were
afraid of missing the crossing. We left the money behind, to follow later." "You
have all arrived," he said. "My patron has given you this sum to be brought to
me, so I can use it to build a fort to protect myself against the Jews who have
reduced me to slavery. My man could have brought me the gifts." "Indeed
he could have. We did our best." Then he said to the interpreter, "Tell him
that I do not acknowledge any of the others. I acknowledge only you. They
are not Arabs. If my master (God give him support!) thought that they could
have read the official letter as eloquently as you, he would not have sent you
to keep it safe for me, read it, and hear my response. I do not expect to receive
one single dirham from anyone but you. Produce the money. This would be
the best thing for you to do." I left the audience, dazed and in a state of terror.
I was overawed by his demeanor. He was a big, corpulent man, and his voice
seemed to come from inside a barrel. I left the audience, gathered my companions, and told them about our conversation. "I warned you about this," I said.

At the start of the prayer, his muezzin [the caller to prayer] would repeat the
phrases announcing the start of prayer twice. I said to him, "These phrases are
announced only once in the realm of your patron the commander of the faithful." So he told the muezzin, "Accept what he tells you and do not contravene
him." The muezzin performed the call to prayer as I had suggested for several
days. During this time the king would interrogate me and argue about the
money. I would try to persuade him to give up his hopes and explained our
reasons. When he despaired of receiving the money, he instructed the muezzin
to revert to a repeated announcement. The muezzin did so. The king meant
it as a pretext for debate. When I heard the muezzin announce the start of
prayer twice, I shouted to him to stop. The muezzin informed the king. The
king summoned me and my companions.

He said to the interpreter, "Ask him (he meant me), what is his opinion on
two muezzins, one of whom announces the call once, the other twice, both
of whom lead the people in prayer? Is the prayer permissible or not?" "The
prayer is permissible," I said. "Is there any disagreement on this, or is there
consensus?" "There is consensus," I said. "Ask him, what is his opinion about
someone who has given to one group of people a sum of money intended for
another group of people, weak people, sorely beset and reduced to slavery,

betrayed by the first group?" "This is impermissible," I replied, "and they are wicked people." "Is there any disagreement, or is there consensus?" "There is consensus," I said. Then he said to the interpreter, "Ask him, do you think that if the caliph—God give him long life!—were to send an army against me he would be able to overpower me?" "No," I answered. "What about the emir of Khurasan, then?" "No." "Is it not because we are separated by vast distance and many infidel tribes?" he asked. "Of course," I answered. "Tell him, by God—here I am, in this far-off land where we are now, you and I both, yet still I fear my patron the commander of the faithful. I fear his curse, should he learn anything displeasing about me. I would die on the spot, though his kingdom is a great distance away. Yet you who eat his bread, wear his clothes, and look on him constantly have betrayed him in the matter of a letter he commanded you to bring to me, to my weak people. You have betrayed the Muslims. I shall accept no instruction from you on how to practice my religion until a sincere counselor arrives. I will accept instruction from such a man." He had dumbfounded us—we had no answer. We left. Ibn Fadlan said: From then on, he would show me favor and be affable toward me, addressing me as Abu Bakr the Veracious [a companion of Muhammad]. But he was aloof from my companions.

I lost count of the number of marvels I witnessed in his realm. For example, on our first night in his territory, at what I reckoned was about an hour before sunset, I saw the horizon turn a bright red. The air was filled with a mighty uproar, and I heard the din of many voices. I looked up and was surprised to see fiery-red clouds close by. Loud voices came from the clouds, where there were shapes that looked like soldiers and horses. These shapes brandished swords and spears. I could form a clear image of them in my mind. Then another group, similar to the first, appeared. I could make out men, animals, and weapons. This second group charged the first, one squadron attacking the other. We were scared and began to pray to God and entreat him. The locals were astonished at our reaction and laughed at us. Ibn Fadlan said: We watched as one unit charged the other, engaged in combat for an hour and then separated. After an hour they disappeared. We asked the king about this, and he told us that his forebears used to say, "These are two groups of *jinn* [spirits], believers and unbelievers, who do battle every evening." He added that this spectacle had occurred every night for as long as they could remember.

Ibn Fadlan said: I went into my yurt with the king's tailor, a man from Baghdad who had ended up there. We were chatting but did not chat for long—less time than it takes you to read halfway through one seventh of the Qur'an. It was beginning to grow dark, and we were waiting for the call to prayer at nightfall. When we heard it we went outside the yurt and noticed that the morning sun had already arisen. So I said to the muezzin, "Which prayer did you call?" "The daybreak prayer." "And what about the last call, the night call?" "We perform that along with the sunset prayer." So I said, "And what of the night?" "The nights are as short as you observed. They have been even shorter but now they have started to grow long." He said that he had not slept for a month, afraid he would miss the morning prayer. You can put a cooking-pot on the fire at the time of the sunset prayer, and by the time you have performed the morning prayer, the pot will not have started to boil. Daylight was very long. I observed that, for part of the year, the days were long and the nights short. Later on I observed the nights grow long and the days short.

On our second night, I sat down outside the yurt and watched the sky. I could make out only a few constellations, I think about fifteen. I noticed that the red glow that precedes sunset did not disappear—night was hardly dark at all. In fact you could identify another person at more than a bowshot away. The moon did not reach the middle of the sky. It would rise in one part of the sky for an hour, then dawn would break, and the moon would set. The king told me that a tribe called the Wisu lived three months from his territory, where night lasted less than an hour. Ibn Fadlan said: I noticed that, at sunrise, the whole country, the ground, the mountains, anything you cared to look at, grew red. The sun rose like a giant cloud. The red persisted until the sun was at its zenith. The inhabitants of Bulgar territory informed me, "In winter, night is as long as day is now and day is as short as night. If we set out at sunrise for a place called Itil less than a *farsakh* away, we will not get there before nightfall, when all the constellations have risen and cover the sky." When we left Bulgar territory, night had grown long and day short.

They consider the howling of dogs to be very auspicious, I observed. They rejoice and say, "A year of fertility, auspiciousness, and peace." Snakes, I noticed, are so numerous that ten, maybe even more, could be coiled around just one branch of a tree. The Bulgars do not kill them, and the snakes do not harm them. There was one place where I saw a felled tree more than one hundred cubits in length. I noticed that it had a very thick trunk, so I stopped to examine it. All of a sudden it moved. I was terrified. When I looked closely, I noticed a snake of almost the same length and bulk lying on top of it. When it saw me, it slid off the trunk and disappeared among the trees. I left in a state of alarm and told the king and his companions, but they were unimpressed. The king said, "Have no fear. It will do you no harm."

When we were traveling in the company of the king, we halted at a place where my comrades Takin, Sawsan, Bars, one of the king's companions, and I entered a copse. We saw a small piece of dark wood, slender as the staff of a spindle, though a bit longer, with a dark shoot. A broad leaf from the top of the shoot spread on the ground. What looked like berry-bearing calyxes were scattered on it. You could easily mistake the taste of these berries for sweet seedless pomegranates. We ate them, and they were delicious. We spent the rest of our time there looking for them and eating them.

The apples, I noticed, are dark. In fact, they are extremely dark and more acidic than wine vinegar. The female slaves eat them, and they get their name from them. Hazel trees grow in abundance. I saw hazel woods everywhere. One wood can measure forty by forty *farsakhs*. There is another tree that grows there, but I don't know what it is. It is extremely tall, has a leafless trunk, and tops like the tops of palm trees, with slender fronds, but bunched together. The locals know where to make a hole in the trunk. They place a container underneath it. Sap, sweeter than honey, flows from the hole. If someone drinks too much sap, he gets as intoxicated as he would from drinking wine.

Their diet consists chiefly of millet and horse meat, though wheat and barley are plentiful. Crop-growers keep what they grow for themselves. The king has no right to the crops, but every year they pay him one sable skin per household. When he orders a raid on a given territory, he takes a share of the booty they bring back. For every wedding feast or banquet the king is given a jug of honey wine, some wheat (of very poor quality, because the soil is black and so foul smelling), and a gift of food. The amount of food depends on the size of the banquet.

They have nowhere to store their food, so they dig holes in the ground as deep as wells to store it. It only takes a few days for it to rot and give off such an odor that it becomes inedible. They do not use olive oil, sesame oil, or any other vegetable oil. They use fish oil instead. Everything they prepare in it is unwholesome and greasy. They make a broth from barley and give it to slaves of both sexes. Sometimes they cook the barley with some meat. The owners eat the meat, and feed the female slaves the barley, unless the broth is made with the head of a goat, in which case the female slaves are given the meat.

They wear peaked caps. The king rides out alone, unaccompanied by his men or anyone else. If he passes through the market, everyone stands, removes his cap from his head, and places it under his arm. When the king has passed, they put their caps back on. The same is true of those who are given an audience with the king, the great and the lowly—even his sons and his brothers. The moment they are in his presence, they remove their caps and place them under their arms. Then they bow their heads, sit down, and stand up again, until he commands them to be seated. Those who sit in his presence, do so in a kneeling position. They keep their hats under their arms until they have left. Then they put them back on again.

They live in yurts. The king's yurt is enormous and can hold more than a thousand people. It is carpeted with Armenian rugs. In the middle the king has a throne bedecked with Byzantine silk.

One of their customs is for the grandfather, rather than the father, to pick up a newborn boy and declare, "It is my right to care for him and raise him to manhood. It is not the father's right to do so." The brother, not the son, inherits the estate of a deceased man. I told the king that this was impermissible, and I taught him clearly how the inheritance laws work [according to Muslim law]. He understood them.

I observed more lightning there than anywhere else. They do not approach a household struck by lightning but let it be, with all of its contents, people, and possessions—everything, in fact—until time destroys it. They say, "This household has incurred divine wrath."

They impose capital punishment upon anyone who kills on purpose. For manslaughter, they make a box out of birch wood, put the perpetrator inside and nail it fast. They give him three loaves of bread and a jug of water, erect three pieces of wood in the shape of the frame of a camel saddle and suspend him inside, saying, "We set him between heaven and earth, exposed to the rain and the sun. Perhaps God will have pity on him." He remains there until his body rots over time and is scattered to the winds.

If they notice that someone is clever and able, they say, "This man is fit for the service of our lord." They take hold of him, place a rope around his neck and hang him from a tree until he decomposes. The king's interpreter told me that a man from Sind turned up once and served him for a while. This man was clever and able. A group of Bulgars decided to go on one of their journeys. The man from Sind asked the king's permission to accompany them, but he refused. The man persisted until the king relented and gave his permission. So the man set sail with them. They noticed that he was quick-witted and clever and conspired as follows: "This man is fit for the service of our lord. Let us send him to him." Their route took them past a forest, so they took hold of the man, placed a rope around his neck, tied it to the top of a big tree, and left him there. Then they went on their way.

If one of them urinates on a march while still in full armor, everything he has with him, weapons and clothes, is removed as plunder. This is one of their customs. But they leave him alone if he undoes his weapons and puts them aside while urinating.

Men and women wash naked together in the river without covering themselves, and yet under no circumstance do they commit adultery. When they catch an adulterer, they set four rods in the ground and tie his hands and his feet to them, no matter who he may be. Then they take an axe, and cut him up, from neck to thigh. They treat the woman in the same manner. They hang the pieces from a tree. I spared no effort to exhort the women to cover themselves in the presence of the men, but that proved impossible. They kill a thief in the same way as they kill an adulterer.

There are bees in the woods, and honey is abundant. They know where the bees are to be found and gather the honey. Sometimes they are surprised by an enemy tribe who kills them.

Many merchants live there. They travel to the territory of the Turks and bring back sheep and travel to another land, called Wisu, and bring back sable and black fox.

There was one household of five thousand individuals, men and women. They had all converted to Islam and are known as the Baranjar. They had built a wooden mosque to pray in but did not know how to read the Qur'an. I taught one group how to conduct their prayers. A man named Saul converted to Islam under my supervision, and I gave him the name 'Abdallah, but he said, "I want you to give me your name—Muhammad." I did so. His wife, mother, and children also converted. They all took the name Muhammad. I taught him the *suras* [chapters of the Qur'an] "Praise be to God" and "Say, he is God, one." He took greater delight in these *suras* than if he had been made king of the Saqalibah.

We first encountered the king in an encampment at Khljh, a group of three unfathomable lakes, two large, one small. It was about a *farsakh* away from a large river called the Itil, which they used and which flowed to the realm of the Khazars. On the bank of this river there is a market, open from time to time, where many valuable goods are sold.

Takin had told me that a giant lived in the king's territory. When I arrived, I asked the king about this, and he replied, "Yes, he used to live among us, but he died. He was not one of the local inhabitants—in fact, he was not really human. This is his story. A group of merchants went to the Itil, one day away, as is their custom. Now, this river was in spate and had burst its banks. Barely a day later a group of merchants came back and said, 'Your Majesty, there is a man who has followed the course of the river. If he is from a community close by, then we cannot remain in our homes. We will have to migrate.' So I rode to the river with them. I was surprised by what I found when I got there—a man twelve cubits tall, using my forearm as a measure, with a head the size of a huge cooking-pot, a nose more than a span in length, two great eyes, and fingers longer than a span. He unnerved me, and I was gripped by the very terror that had gripped the others. We tried to speak to him, but he did not answer. He just looked at us. So I had him brought to my residence and wrote to the inhabitants of Wisu, three months distant, asking them for information. They wrote back: 'He is one of the Gog and Magog, who live three months away from us in a state of absolute nakedness. The sea separates us. They live on the far side of the sea, on its shore. They mate with one another, like the beasts of the field. Every day the great and glorious God provides them with a fish from the sea. They come one by one with their knives and cut as much as they need to feed them and their dependents. If they take more than they need, they develop a pain in their stomach. Their dependents also develop a pain in their stomachs. Should he die, then they all die too. When they have what they need from the fish, it flips over and is taken back into the sea. This is how they live day by day. On one side we are separated from them by the sea. They are hemmed in by mountains on all other sides. A wall separates them from the gate from which they will swarm forth. When almighty God intends them to swarm forth into the inhabited lands, he will cause the wall to be breached, the sea will dry up, and the fish will no longer be provided.'"

I asked the king about the man. He said, "He stayed with me for a while, but any boys who looked at him died, and pregnant women miscarried. His hands would crush to death anyone he took hold of. When I saw this happening, I hanged him from a tall tree and killed him. If you want to see his bones and skull, I will take you." "By God, I would like that very much," I said. So we rode out to a great wood, and he led me to a tree where the man's bones and skull had fallen. His head was like a bees' nest, and the bones of his ribs, legs, and forearms were larger than the boughs of a palm tree. I departed, filled with wonder.

Ibn Fadlan said: The king traveled from Khljh to a river called Jawshir, where he stayed for two months. When he was ready to leave, he sent a message to a people called Suwaz and commanded them to travel with him. They refused and split into two groups. One sided with his son-in-law Wiragh, who had become their king. The king sent them a message: "Almighty God has given me the gift of Islam and granted me membership in the kingdom of the commander of the faithful. I am his bondsman. He has made me his emir. I will wage war on those who oppose me." The other group aligned themselves with the king of the Askil tribe, who was under the king's sovereignty, though he had not accepted Islam. When the king of the Bulgars sent the Suwaz this epistle, they were afraid he might attack, so they joined him in his journey to the Jawshir river. This is not a very wide river—it is no more than five cubits wide, but the water reaches a man's navel, and comes up to his collarbone in some places. At its deepest point, it reaches the height of a man. It is surrounded by many trees, including birch trees.

There is a wide plain near the river, where they say an animal smaller than a camel but larger than a bull lives. It has the head of a camel, the tail and hooves of a bull, and the body of a mule. It has a single, round, thick horn in the middle of its head. As the horn grows it becomes narrow and resembles a spearhead. Some of these animals are five cubits tall, some three, with a degree of variation. It eats succulent and tasty leaves from the trees. It charges any horseman it sees. A fleet mare will just about escape, with some effort. But if the animal overtakes the horseman, it unseats him from his horse and tosses him in the air with its horn. Then it rushes him with its horn again and again and kills him, though it pays no heed whatsoever to the horse. They hunt it to death on the plain and in the woods. They climb the tall trees in the wood where the animal lives, and a group of archers with poisoned arrows work together. When the animal is in their midst they shoot it, exhaust it, and kill it. In the king's tent I saw three large bowls that looked as if they were made of Yemeni onyx. The king informed me that they were made out of the base of this animal's horn. Some of the locals claim that this animal is the rhinoceros.

Ibn Fadlan said: I saw no one in ruddy health. Most of them are sickly, and the majority regularly die from the colic. Even the child at the breast suffers from it. When a Muslim dies and a woman from Khwarazm is present, they wash the body as the Muslims do and then bear him on a cart, preceded by a standard, until they come to his grave. Then they take him from the cart and place him on the ground, draw a line around him, and remove him. They dig his grave, build his tomb, and bury him inside the line they have drawn. This is their burial custom. The women do not weep for the deceased, the men do. They arrive on the day of his death, stand at the entrance to his yurt, and howl and weep in the ugliest and wildest way. And these are freeborn men! When they have finished weeping, the slaves of the deceased bring leather thongs. The men continue to mourn and beat their flanks and exposed parts of their bodies with the leather thongs, leaving weals like those left by the lashes of a whip. At the entrance to his yurt they are required to erect a standard, bring his weapons, and place them around his grave. They weep for two years and then take the standard down and cut off their hair. The deceased's relatives hold a banquet to indicate that they have emerged from mourning. The deceased's wife, if he had one, then takes a husband. Such is their custom for their chieftains. Ordinary folk do not do as much as this for their dead.

The king of the Saqalibah is obliged to pay to the king of the Khazars a tribute of one sable skin for every tent in his kingdom. When the boat from Khazar territory reaches Saqalibah territory, the king goes on board and counts its contents, taking a tenth of its cargo. When the Rus or any other people come with slaves, the king of the Saqalibah has the right to choose one in every ten. The king of the Khazars holds the son of the king of the Saqalibah as a hostage. The king of the Khazars heard that the daughter of the king of the Saqalibah was beautiful, so he asked for her hand in marriage but was refused. He sent some troops and took her by force, though he is a Jew and she a Muslim. She died at his court, so he demanded a second daughter. As soon as the king of the Saqalibah heard this, he was afraid that the king of the Khazars might take her by force, as he had her sister, so he married her to the king of the Askil, who recognizes his authority. It was fear of the king of the Khazars that forced the king of the Saqalibah to write to the caliph and petition him to build him a fortress.

Ibn Fadlan said: I asked him the following question one day and said, "You have an extensive kingdom, many belongings, and considerable wealth from taxes. Why did you petition the caliph for an unspecified sum of money to build a fortress?" He replied, "I could see that the realm of Islam was flourishing and that the wealth of the Muslims was acquired lawfully. That is why I asked for it. If I had wanted to build a fort using my own silver and gold, I could have. I wanted the money of the commander of the faithful to bring me blessings, so I sent him my petition."

Questions: What obstacles did the author encounter on the trip to the Volga River? Did the embassy fulfill the mission for which it was sent? Why was the king the diplomats met primarily interested in the religious reasons for their visit? What did Ibn Fadlan think of the northern peoples he observed, in both positive and negative senses? What did he think of their practice of Islam? What things in nature and in the people's customs stood out to him, and why?

29. LIUDPRAND OF CREMONA, *RETRIBUTION* AND *EMBASSY*

Liudprand of Cremona (c. 920–972) was a clergyman, first a deacon and then a bishop. In the course of his studies, he acquired an excellent classical literary education, which he was never afraid to show off. Due to his knowledge of Greek, the king of Italy Berengar II (r. 950–961) chose him to serve as a diplomat to Constantinople (modern Istanbul), the capital of the Byzantine Empire, in 949. He would later have a falling out with Berengar, and he wrote the first source excerpted here against him. Later Liudprand would join the service of the German emperor Otto I (r. 962–973), whose power base was Saxony in northern Germany, and again served as a diplomat to Constantinople, this time in 968. Liudprand composed several works over the course of his career, although his observations on the Byzantines are some of the best known.

Source: trans. Paolo Squatrini, Liudprand of Cremona, *The Complete Works of Liudprand of Cremona* (Washington, DC: Catholic University of America Press, 2007), pp. 197–202, 245–53. Latin.

First Embassy (949)

Book 6

4. In fact, leaving Pavia on the day of the calends of August [2 August], after three days of following the course of the Po, I reached Venice, and there I also found Salemon, the envoy of the Greeks [Byzantines], a palace butler and a eunuch, who had returned from Spain and Saxony and intended to depart for

Constantinople, bearing great gifts and taking with him the messenger of our lord, then king, now emperor, the most wealthy prelate of Mainz, Liutefred. Leaving Venice at last on the eighth day before the kalends of September, we arrived at Constantinople on the fifteenth before the kalends of October [7 September]; it will not be a nuisance to write about the unheard-of and wondrous way in which we were received there.

5. For at Constantinople there is a palace next to the Great Palace, of wondrous beauty and size, that is called Magnaura by the Greeks, having inserted a "u" in the place of the digamma, as if it were *magna aura* [ceremonial hall]. And so Constantine [VII, r. 908–959] ordered this mansion to be prepared in due fashion both because of the messengers of the Spaniards, who then were coming there for the first time, and because of Liutefred and me. In front of the emperor's throne stood a certain tree of gilt bronze, whose branches, similarly gilt bronze, were filled with birds of different sizes, which emitted the songs of the different birds corresponding to their species. The throne of the emperor was built with skill in such a way that at one instant it was low, then higher, and quickly it appeared most lofty; and lions of immense size (though it was unclear if they were of wood or brass, they certainly were coated with gold) seemed to guard him, and striking the ground with their tails, they emitted a roar with mouths open and tongues flickering. Leaning on the shoulders of two eunuchs, I was led into this space, before the emperor's presence [Constantine VII]. And when, upon my entry, the lions emitted their roar and the birds called out, each according to its species, I was not filled with special fear or admiration, since I had been told about all these things by one of those who knew them well. Thus, prostrated for a third time in adoration before the emperor, I lifted my head, and the person whom earlier I had seen sitting elevated to a modest degree above the ground, I suddenly spied wearing different clothes and sitting almost level with the ceiling of the mansion. I could not understand how he did this, unless perchance he was lifted up there by a pulley of the kind by which tree trunks are lifted. Then, however, he did not speak at all for himself, since, even if he wished to, the great space between us would render it unseemly, so he asked about the life of Berengar and his safety through a minister. When I had answered him reasonably, and when his interpreter gave a sign, I left and was soon received in the hostel assigned to me.

6. But let it not be a nuisance to recollect what I did then for Berengar, in such a way that it might be acknowledged with what great kindness I loved him, and what manner of recompense I received from him for my good deeds. The messengers of the Spaniards and Liutefred, whom I mentioned above, the messenger of our lord Otto, then still king, had brought the emperor Constantine large gifts on behalf of their lords. Instead I had brought nothing more than a letter on behalf of Berengar, a letter full of lies. My spirit was therefore

not a little agitated because of the shame of it, and carefully pondered what it should do about this situation. In my agitation and great hesitation my mind suggested that the gifts for the emperor I had brought on my own behalf I should present as coming from Berengar, and that I should adorn the slight value of the gifts with words as best I could. I offered, therefore, nine excellent breastplates, seven excellent shields with gilt bosses, two gilt silver cups, swords, spears, skewers, and four *carizimasia* slaves, to this emperor the most precious of all these things. For the Greeks call a child-eunuch, with testicles and penis cut off, a *carazimasium*. The merchants of Verdun do this on account of the immense profit they can make, and they are accustomed to bring them to Spain.

7. Once these things had been accomplished in this way, after three days the emperor ordered me to be called to the palace. And having spoken to me with his own mouth, he invited me to a meal, and after the meal he gave my retainers and me a great gift. Truly, as the opportunity for telling about it presents itself, I consider it good not to be silent but to write down what his table is like, especially on feast days, and what games are performed at the table.

8. There is a residence near the hippodrome, toward the north, of wondrous height and beauty, which is called Decanneacubita. The name did not emerge from the structure itself but for quite obvious reasons; for in Greek the Latin "ten" is *deca* and "nine" is *enna*, while we may say *cubita* derives from incubating, or lying, on a slope, or something slightly curved. All the more so since on the birthday, according to the flesh, of our Lord Jesus Christ, ten and nine tables are placed inside the residence, at which the emperor, and equally his guests, do not eat sitting up, as on other days, but reclining on curved couches; and on those occasions they are served not with silver but only from gold dishes. After the food, apples are brought in three gold dishes that, because of their immense weight, are not carried on the arms of men but are brought on purple-veiled carts. Only two of these, however, are placed at table. Through three holes in the roof there are [three] ropes wrapped with gilt leather, and they have been positioned with gold rings. Placed through the handles that project from the vessels, these rings allow such bowls to be lifted onto the table and lowered in the same way by means of a jointed device above the ceiling, with four or more men helping below. Finally, I omit the shows I saw there, since it is a very long thing to write about; but one alone, on account of its astonishing quality, it will not be unpleasant to insert here.

9. There enters some fellow sustaining on his forehead without the help of his hands a wooden pole that is twenty-four and more feet long, which had, a cubit below its tip, a crosspiece two cubits long. Then two naked boys were led in, but girt with short knickers, that is, wearing brief costumes, who climbed up the wooden pole and played around there, and then, clambering

back down it with their heads turned upside-down, they maintained the pole so motionless that it appeared rooted to the earth. Finally, after the descent of one, the other, who remained there alone, cavorted up there and left me stunned with even greater admiration. For in some way it seemed possible as long as both played, since, although that was marvelous, too, actually by their not unequal weight they steadied the pole they had climbed up. But the one who, by balancing his weight, stayed on the top of the pole, where he even played, and then came down unscathed, left me so agape that my admiration did not escape the emperor himself. Wherefore, having invited an interpreter, he asked which seemed to me more wonderful: the boy who moved so circumspectly that the pole remained steady, or the fellow who held it with his forehead so resourcefully that neither the boys' weight not their playing tipped the pole even a little. And when I replied that I did not know which seemed *thaumastoteron* [more marvelous] to me, he swelled with loud laughter and said that he did not know, either.

10. But I reckon that this ought not to be passed over in silence, namely, what else I saw there that was novel and marvelous. During that week that comes before the *vaiphoron*—which we call "palm branches"—the emperor makes a payment of gold coins both to the soldiers and to those appointed to the various offices, according to what their rank deserves. Since he wanted me to be present at this pay day, he ordered me to come. It happened in this way. A table ten cubits in length and four in width had been set down, which supported the coins, bound in bags according to what each was owed, with numbers written on the outside of each bag. Thereupon, they entered before the emperor not in a jumble, but in an order, accepting to the summons of the herald who recited the written names of the men according to the dignity of their rank. The first of them to be called in is the rector of the palaces, on whose shoulders, and not into whose hands, the coins are placed in four military cloaks. After him are called *o domesticos tis ascalonas* and *o delongaris tis ploos*, of whom the former commands the army and the latter the navy. These two, taking an equal number of coins and cloaks, as their dignity is equal, because of the volume could not carry them away on their shoulders but dragged them off with an effort, aided by others. After them twenty-four generals are admitted, to whom are issued pounds of gold coins, twenty-four to each, according to his number, with two military cloaks. Lastly, right after them the order of the patricians follows and is given twelve pounds of coins and one military cloak. And since I do not know the number of the patricians [high nobles], I do not know the number of pounds either, except that given to each. After that is summoned the immense horde of first swordsmen, swordsmen, swordsmen-in-training, chamberlains, treasurers, first headsmen, of whom the first received seven, and the others according to their dignity received six, five, four, three,

two, and one. Nor do I want you to think that it was all accomplished in a single day. Having begun on the fifth day of the week at the first hour of the day, it was finished by the emperor at the fourth hour of the sixth and seventh days; for to those who receive less than a pound, the chief of the imperial bedchamber, not the emperor, makes payment throughout the whole week before Easter. Thus with me standing by and considering the procedure with admiration, the emperor asked through the minister what had pleased me about the whole matter. To this I answered: "Of course it would please me, if it profited me, just as the repose given to Lazarus would have benefited the rich man as he suffered the heat, if it had come his way; since it did not happen to him, how, I ask, could it please him?" [Cf. Luke 16:23–25] Chuckling and a little embarrassed, the emperor signaled with a nod of his head that I should come to him, and I gladly accepted a large cloak with a pound of gold that he gladly offered.

Second Embassy (968)

11. That same day he [Emperor Nikephoros II Phokas, r. 963–969] ordered me to be his dinner guest. He did not, however, consider me worthy to be placed before any of his nobles, so I sat fifteenth from him, and where there was no tablecloth. Of my party, not only did no one sit at table but none even saw the house in which I was a dinner guest. At this dinner, quite foul and repulsive in the manner of all drunkards' gatherings, impregnated with oil and sprinkled with a really awful fish sauce, he asked me a lot of questions about your power, and a lot about your realms and soldiers. When I would answer appropriately and truthfully, "You lie!" he said; "the soldiers of your lord are ignorant of horseriding and do not know about infantry combat! The size of shields, the weight of breastplates, the length of swords, and the heft of helmets does not allow them to fight in either way!" Then, chuckling, he said, "Also their gullets' voracity prevents them, that is, the gluttony of their stomachs; their gut is their god, their courage is debauchery, their steadfastness is drunkenness, going without rations is their undoing, and fear is their sobriety. Nor is there a large number of fleets afloat on the sea serving your lord; to me alone belongs the steadfastness of sailors, to me who will attack him with fleets and demolish his maritime cities in war and reduce to ashes those that are close to rivers. Who, I ask, can resist me even on land, with scanty forces? Otto's son was not absent, his wife was not missing, the Saxons, Swabians, Bavarians, and Italians were all with him; yet when they both did not know how and were not able to take one tiny city that resisted them, how will they resist me when I arrive, followed by armies numerous 'as are the crops of Gargarus, as are the grape bunches on Methymna, as are the stars in the sky, as are the waves in the sea' [Ovid, *The Art of Love*]?"

12. He did not permit it when I wanted to respond to this and throw out a counterargument worthy of his inflation; instead he added, as if to insult us: "You are not Romans, but Lombards!" Though he wanted to say something beyond this and waved his hand so that I would be quiet, I spoke out, upset: "The annals recognize that fratricidal Romulus, from whose name they are called Romans, was born to a whore, that is, he was generated in defilement; and he made a refuge for himself where he welcomed defaulted debtors from foreign climes, runaway slaves, murderers, and people who deserved death for their crimes, and he attracted such a throng of such people that he called them Romans; from this aristocracy there arose those whom you call *cosmocrators*, or emperors. We, that means the Lombards, Saxons, Franks, Lotharingians, Bavarians, Swabians, Burgundians, so disdain them that we utter no other insult than 'You Roman!' to our enemies when aroused, and we understand that single term, the name of the Romans, to include every baseness, every cowardice, every kind of greed, every promiscuity, every mendacity, indeed every vice.

"Since you say we are unwarlike and ignorant of riding skills, if the sins of Christians merit that you persist in this harshness, the coming wars will demonstrate what type of men you are and how pugnacious we are."

13. Nikephoros, angered by such words, called for silence with his hand and ordered the long, narrow table removed and myself returned to the hated house or, if I were to speak more truthfully, prison. There, after two days I was afflicted by such a deep prostration, first through my indignation and then the heat and thirst, that there was no one among my retainers who did not fear his last day approached after having drunk from my same cup. Why, I ask, did they, too, not fall ill, whose drink was brine in lieu of fine wine, whose bedding, in lieu of hay, straw, or even earth, was hard marble, who had stone in lieu of a pillow, whose wide-open house did not protect from heat, rain, or cold? Even health itself, poured over them, could not save them if it wanted to! Therefore, debilitated by my own suffering as well as that of my men, having summoned the guardian, or rather my persecutor, I arranged, not just by pleas but by paying a price, that he would deliver to the brother of Nikephoros my letter, saying things like this:

14. "Bishop Liudprand to Leo, chief of staff and minister 'logothete of the drome' [official responsible for public postal system]: The sufferings which I am undergoing here will not wear me out if the most serene emperor is thinking of granting the request [arranging a marriage alliance] on account of which I came; only that through a letter from me and a messenger my lord Otto should be told that I am not delaying the matter here. But if the emperor considers the matter differently, there is here a freight ship of the Venetians, which hastens to depart; let him permit me, sick as I am, to board it so that,

if the time of my collapse were to arrive, at least my corpse may be welcomed by the land of my birth."

15. When he read this, he ordered me to come to him after four days. There sat with him to debate your matter men very learned according to their tradition, strong in their Greek language: Basil, the head of the imperial bedchamber; the first secretary; the chief of the imperial wardrobe; and two teachers. This was the beginning of their narration:

"Explain, brother, what the cause might be that you wore yourself out to announce." When I spelled out to them the recompense of kinship which would be the opportunity for endless peace, they said: "It is unheard-of for the *porphyrogenita* of a *porphyrogenitus*, that is, the daughter born in the purple to one who was himself born in the purple, to be mixed up with the peoples. Truly, since you seek such a rarefied thing, you will receive what pleases you only if you give what is appropriate, that is, Ravenna and Rome with all the lands, uninterrupted, which extend from there to us here. If you in fact desire friendship without kinship, let your lord allow Rome to be free, and also let him hand over into their original slavery the Capuan and the Beneventan princes, formerly slaves of our holy empire and now rebels against it."

16. To them I said: "Even you are not unaware that my lord has mightier Slavic peoples under him than the king of the Bulgarians, Peter, who led off in marriage the daughter of the emperor Christopher!" "But Christopher," they said, "was not born in the purple."

17. "In truth," I said, "whom does Rome serve, that you clamor for it to wish to be freed? To whom does she pay tribute? Was she not serving whores before, and, with you snoozing and certainly not showing any valor, did not my master, the august emperor, free her from so base a form of servitude? As he was *cosmocrator*, the august emperor Constantine [r. 306–324], who built this city on his own name, contributed many gifts to the holy apostolic Roman church, and not just gifts in Italy, but in almost all the western kingdoms and in the eastern and southern ones, too, namely in Greece, Judea, Persia, Meso-potamia, Babylonia [southern Mesopotamia?], Egypt, and Libya, as testify his charters that are in our possession. Rightly my lord handed over to the vicar of the most holy apostles whatever belonged to the Church of the Most Holy Apostles in Italy, and Saxony, Bavaria, and all the kingdoms of my lord; and if it happened that my lord kept back anything from all of these, whether cit-ies, manors, soldiers, or a single family, then I have denied God. Why does not your emperor do the same thing, so that he returns to the Church of the Apostles its properties that are in his realms and thus renders richer and freer that church which, through the toil and generosity of my lord, is already rich and free?"

18. "But he will do that," said Basil, the head of the imperial bedchamber, "when he makes Rome and Roman church obedient to his nod." Then I said, "A certain fellow, having suffered much harm from another, approaches God with these words: 'Lord, avenge me of my enemy!' God answered him: 'I will do it,' he said, 'on the day when I will give to each according to his deeds.' But the fellow replied, 'How late!'"

19. Then all except the emperor's brother left the disputation shaking with laughter, and ordered me to be led back to the hated house and to be guarded with great care until the feast day of the holy apostles, celebrated by all clerics. On that feast day I was quite sick, but nevertheless he ordered me and the messengers of the Bulgarians, who had arrived the day before, to meet him at the Church of the Holy Apostles. When, after the wordiness of the chants and the celebration of the Masses, we were invited to table, he placed the messenger of the Bulgarians, shorn in the Hungarian style, girt with a bronze chain, and—as my mind suggested to me—not yet baptized, at the furthest end of the table (which was long and narrow) but closer than me to himself, obviously as an insult to you my august lords. For you I underwent contempt, for you I was disdained, for you I was scorned; but I give thanks to the Lord Jesus Christ, whom you serve with your whole spirit that I was considered worthy to suffer insults in your name. Truly, my lords, I left that table considering the insult not to me, but to you. As I sought to leave, indignant, Leo, the chief of staff and brother of the emperor, and the first secretary, Simon, followed behind me, howling: "When Peter the emperor of the Bulgarians led off Christopher's daughter as a spouse, symphonies, that is, accords, were written and sealed with oaths, so that we would give precedence to, give honor and favor to the Bulgarians' apostles, that is, the messengers, above the apostles of all the other nations. That apostle of the Bulgarians, though he is, as you say (and it is true), shorn, unwashed, and girt with a bronze chain, nevertheless is a noble, and we judge it unpropitious to give precedence over him to a bishop, especially one of the Franks. And since we perceive you bear this without dignity, we will not allow you to return to your hostel now as you think, but force you to savor the food with the slaves of the emperor in a certain cheap inn."

20. To them I answered nothing because of a boundless pain within my heart; but I did what they had ordered, considering dishonorable a table where precedence is given to a Bulgarian messenger over not me, that is, Bishop Liudprand, but over one of your messengers. But the holy emperor alleviated my pain with a great gift, sending me from his most refined foods a fat goat, one of which he himself had eaten, totally overloaded with garlic, onion, leeks, drowned in fish sauce, which I wish could appear on your own table, so that, whatever delectable you did not believe fitting for a holy emperor, at least, after having seen these ones, you might believe it.

21. When eight days had passed, once the Bulgarians had gone, thinking I would esteem his table highly, he invited me, still quite sick, to eat with him in the same place. The patriarch was there, along with many bishops, in whose presence he proposed to me many issues concerning the holy scriptures, which I elegantly explained with the Holy Spirit inspiring me. And suddenly, so as to make a joke of you, he asked what councils we accept. When I answered the Nicaean, Chalcedonian, Ephesian, Antiochene, Carthaginian, Ankaran, and Constantinopolitan, he said, "Ha! Ha! He! You forgot to say the Saxon one! If you ask why that one is not in our books, I answer because it is primitive and it could not yet make it through to us."

22. To that I answered: "In whatever limb illness prevails, there it must be driven out by cauterization. All the heresies originated from you, and they flourished among you; they were stifled, they were killed by us, that is, the westerners. Roman and Pavian councils, although held often, we will not count here. But it was a Roman cleric, later the universal pope Gregory [I, r. 590–604], who is called Dialogus [author of the book *Dialogues*] by you, who freed Eutychius, heretical patriarch of Constantinople, of his heresy. The same Eutychius not only said, but even taught, proclaimed, and wrote, that at our resurrection we would assume that flesh is not real, as we have here on earth, but somehow imaginary; his book of error was incinerated by Gregory in an orthodox way. But Ennodius, the Pavian bishop, was sent here, to Constantinople, by the Roman patriarch, on account of a certain other heresy, which, once he had suppressed it, he reshaped into an orthodox and catholic form. After it accepted news of holy baptism and of God, the Saxon nation was never stained with heresy so that a council was held there to correct error, since there was none. As you call the faith of the Saxons primitive, I confirm the very same thing. For among them the faith of Christ is always primitive and not old, where good works follow upon belief; here the faith is certainly not primitive, but old, where belief does not unite with good works but instead is disdained on account of its age, like some old garment. But I know for sure that a council was held in Saxony wherein it was discussed and established that it is more honorable to fight with spears than with pens, and to accept death before turning one's back on the enemy; and your army is now learning all about it." In my heart I said, "And how pugnacious the Saxons are, may the outcome itself show!"

23. He ordered me to rush to him in the palace in the afternoon of that same day, though I was weak and beside myself to the point that women I met in the street who earlier with wondering minds called out, "Mana! Mana!" [an obscure compliment about his physical appearance] now, pitying my pitiful condition, beating their breasts with their fists, would say, "Miserable and unhappy man!" May what I prayed for, with my hands outstretched to the

heavens, both for Nikephoros as he approached, and for you, who were absent, come true! Still I want you to believe me that he induced me to no small laughter, sitting as he was, quite tiny on a quite big, impatient, and unbridled horse. My mind pictured to itself that kind of doll your Slavs tie onto the young horse they send out unbridled to follow the lead of its mother.

24. Once these things had been done, I was led to the aforementioned hated house, to my fellow citizens and roommates, by now five lions, where I was granted conversation with no one except my people for over three weeks. Because of this, the notion that Nikephoros wanted never to send me home formed in my mind, and measureless sadness piled illness on illness in me, so that I would have died if the Mother of God had not obtained reprieve through her prayers from her Creator and Son, which was revealed to me by a vision, not an imaginary one but a real one.

Questions: What kind of ceremonial, banquets, and entertainments were prepared for Liudprand on his first embassy? What impression did they make on him? How had Berengar supposedly inadequately supplied Liudprand, and how did Liudprand compensate? How did the Byzantines treat Liudprand on his second embassy? How did Liudprand make the situation worse? What did the handling of Liudprand on the second embassy say about the Byzantines' attitude toward the ruler who sent him?

30. RABBAN SAUMA, *TRAVELOGUE*

The author of this travelogue, Rabban Sauma (c. 1220–1294), was a monk and priest of a branch of Christianity known as the Church of the East. The "Rabban" of his name is an honorific title meaning something like "Master." Sauma originated from central Asia, and he had traveled from there to Baghdad with his friend Yaballaha. Upon arriving in Baghdad, both he and his friend would be pressed into service by the Mongols, who were politically dominant throughout the Middle East. Sauma was dispatched to western Europe in 1287–1288 to propose a joint military expedition between the Mongols and western Europeans against Muslims, which would never be launched. However, Sauma would become celebrated as a kind of "reverse Marco Polo," a traveler from the east who observed cultural differences in the west.

Source: trans. E. A. Wallis Budge, Rabban Sauma, "Travelogue," in *The Monks of Kublai Khan* (London: Religious Tract Society, 1928), pp. 165–96. Syriac. Revised.

Now lord Yaballaha, the catholicus [bishop], increased in power, and his honor before the king and queens grew greater daily. He pulled down the church of lord Willita which was in Maragheh, and he rebuilt it at very great expense. And instead of using [the old] beams [and making a single roof] he made [the new church] with two naves; and by the side of it he built a [monastic] cell in which to live. For his affection for the house of King Arghun [r. 1284–1291] was very warm, because Arghun loved the Christians with his whole heart. And Arghun intended to go into the countries of Palestine and Syria and to subjugate them and take possession of them, but he said to himself, "If the western kings, who are Christians, will not help me I will not be able to fulfill my desire." As a result he asked the catholicus to give him a wise man, "one who is suitable and is capable of undertaking an embassy, that we may send him to those kings." And when the catholicus saw that there was no man who knew the language except Rabban Sauma, and knowing that he was fully capable of this, he commanded him to go [on the embassy].

Then Rabban Sauma said, "I desire this embassy greatly, and I long to go." Then immediately King Arghun wrote for him recommendations to the king of the Greeks, and the king of the Franks, that is to say Romans, and ordinances, and letters, and gave him gifts for each of the kings. And to Rabban Sauma he gave two thousand pounds of gold, and thirty good riding animals, and a tablet. And Rabban Sauma came to the palace of the catholicus to obtain a letter from lord Yaballaha, and to say farewell to him. The catholicus gave him permission to depart, but when the time for his departure arrived, it did not please the catholicus to permit him to go. For he said, "How can this possibly take place? You have been the manager of the monastery, and you know that through your departure my affairs will fall into a state of utter confusion." And having said such words as these they said farewell to each other, weeping as they did so. And the catholicus sent with him letters, and gifts which were suitable for presentation to the lord pope, and gifts according to his ability.

And Rabban Sauma set out on his journey, and there went with him a number of excellent men from among the priests and deacons of the monastery of the catholicus. And he arrived at the land of the Romans [Byzantines] on the borders of the Black Sea, and he saw the church that was there, and embarked in a ship and his companions were with him. Now there were more than three hundred souls in the ship, and each day he consoled them with a discourse on the faith. Now the greater number of those who were in the ship were Romans, and because of the savor of his speech they paid him honor in no small degree.

And after some days he arrived at the great city of Constantinople [modern Istanbul], and before they went into it he sent two young men to the Royal Gate to make known there that an ambassador of King Arghun had come. Then the king commanded certain people to go forth to meet them, and to bring them in with pomp and honor. And when Rabban Sauma went into the city, the king allotted to him a house, that is to say, a mansion in which to dwell. And after Rabban Sauma had rested himself, he went to visit the King

Basilios [Andronikos II Palaiologos, r. 1282–1328] and after he had greeted him, the king asked him, "How are you after the workings of the sea and the fatigue of the road?" And Rabban Sauma replied, "With the sight of the Christian king, fatigue has vanished and exhaustion has departed, for I was exceedingly anxious to see your kingdom, which may our Lord establish!"

And after they had enjoyed food and drink Rabban Sauma asked the king to be allowed to see the churches and the shrines of the fathers, and the relics of the saints that were there. And the king handed Rabban Sauma over to the nobles of his kingdom and they showed him everything that was there.

First of all he went to the great Church of Hagia Sophia, which has three hundred and sixty pillars, all made of marble. As for the dome of the altar it is impossible for a man to describe it to one who has not seen it, and to say how high and how spacious it is. There is in this church a picture of Saint Mary which Luke the Evangelist painted. He saw there also the hand of lord John the Baptist, and relics of Lazarus, and Mary Magdalene, and that stone which was laid on the grave of our Lord, when Joseph the Counselor brought him down from the cross. Now Mary wept on that stone, and the place where her tears fell is wet even at the present time; and however often this moisture is wiped away the place becomes wet again. And he saw also the stone bowl in which our Lord changed the water into wine at Cana of Galilee; and the casket of one of the holy women which is exposed to the public view every year, and every sick person who is laid under it is made whole; and the sarcophagus of lord John Chrysostom. And he saw also the stone on which Simon Peter was sitting when the cock crowed; and the tomb of King Constantine [r. 306–324], the Conqueror, which was made of porphyry; and also the tomb of Justinian [r. 527–565], which is of a green color; and also the stations of the Three Hundred and Eighteen Bishops [of the Council of Nicaea] who were all laid in one great church; and their bodies have not suffered corruption because they had confirmed the faith. And he saw also many shrines of the holy fathers, and many amulets of a magical character and icons made of bronze and stone.

And when Rabban Sauma went to King Basilios he said, "May the king live forever! I give thanks to our Lord that I have been held worthy to see these things. And now, if the king will permit me, I will go and fulfill the command of King Arghun, for the command to me was to enter the territory of the Franks." Then the king treated him with great kindness, and gave him gifts of gold and silver.

And he departed from Constantinople and went down to the sea. And he saw on the seashore a palace of the Romans, and there were laid up in its treasure house two caskets of silver; in the one was the head of lord John Chrysostom, and in the other that of the lord pope who baptized Constantine. And he embarked on a ship and came to the broad sea, where he saw a mountain from which smoke ascended all the day long, and in the nighttime fire showed itself on it. And no man is able to approach the neighborhood of it because of the stench of sulfur. Some people say that there is a great serpent there. This sea is called the "Sea of Italy." Now it is a terrible sea and very many thousands of people have perished there. And after two months of toil, and weariness, and exhaustion, Rabban Sauma arrived at the seashore, and he landed at the city by the name of Naples; now the name of its king was Charles II [r. 1285–1309]. And he went to the king and showed him the reason why they had come; and the king welcomed him and paid him honor. Now it happened that there was war between him and another king whose name was James II [r. 1285–1327]. And the troops of the one had come in many ships, and the troops of the other were ready, and they began to fight each other, and James II conquered King Charles II, and slew twelve thousand of his men, and sunk their ships in the sea. Meanwhile Rabban Sauma and his companions sat upon the roof of the mansion, and they admired the way in which the Franks waged war, for they attacked none of the people except those who were actually combatants.

And from that place they traveled inland on horses, and they passed through towns and villages and marveled because they found no land that was destitute of buildings. On the road they heard that the lord pope was dead.

After some days they arrived in Great Rome. And Rabban Sauma went into the Church of Peter and Paul, for the palace of the see of the lord pope was situated there. Now after the death of the lord pope, twelve men who were called cardinals administered the see. And while they were taking counsel together in order to appoint a new pope, Rabban Sauma sent a message to them saying, "We are ambassadors of King Arghun and of the catholicus of the east." And the cardinals ordered them to come in. And the Frank who accompanied Rabban Sauma informed them that when they were going into the palace of the lord pope, there was an altar at which they must worship, and then they must go in and greet the cardinals. And thus they did, and it was pleasing to those cardinals. And when Rabban Sauma went into their presence no man stood up before him, for by reason of the honorable nature of the see, the twelve cardinals were not in the habit of doing this. And they made Rabban Sauma sit down with them, and one of them asked him, "How are you after all the fatigue of the road?" And he made answer to him, "Through your prayers I am well and rested." And the cardinal said to him, "For what purpose have you come here?" And Rabban Sauma said to him, "The Mongols and the catholicus of the east have sent me to the lord pope concerning the matter of Jerusalem; and they have sent letters with me." And the cardinals said to him, "For the present rest, and we will discuss the matter together later." And they assigned him to a mansion and lodged him there.

Three days later the cardinals sent and summoned Rabban Sauma to their presence. And when he went to them they began to ask him questions, saying, "What is your region of the world, and why have you come?" And he replied with the same words he had already spoken to them. And they said to him, "Where does the catholicus live? And which of the apostles taught the Gospel in your region of the world?" And he answered them, saying, "Lord Thomas, and lord Addai, and lord Mari taught the Gospel in our region of the world, and we hold at the present time the statutes that they delivered to us." The cardinals said to him, "Where is the see of the catholicus?" He said to them, "In Baghdad." They answered, "What position do you have there?" And he replied, "I am a deacon in the monastery of the catholicus, and the master of the students, and the visitator-general [clergyman who corrects belief and discipline]." The cardinals said, "It is a marvelous thing that you are a Christian, and a deacon of the see of the patriarch of the east has come on an embassy from the king of the Mongols." And Rabban Sauma said to them, "Know, my fathers, that many of our fathers went into the countries of the Mongols, and Turks, and Chinese and have taught them the Gospel, and at the present time there are many Mongols who are Christians. For many of the sons of the Mongol kings and queens have been baptized and confess Christ. And they have established churches in their military camps, and they pay honor to the Christians, and there are among them many who are believers. Now the king, who is joined in the bond of friendship with the catholicus, has the desire to take Palestine, and the countries of Syria, and he desires from you to help in order to take Jerusalem. He has chosen me and has sent me to you because, being a Christian, my word will be believed by you." And the cardinals said to him, "What is your confession of faith? To which line of doctrine are you attached? Is it that which the lord pope holds today or some other one?" Rabban Sauma replied, "No man has come to us easterners from the pope. The holy apostles whose names I have mentioned taught us the Gospel, and to what they delivered to us we have clung to the present day."

The cardinals said to him, "What do you believe? Recite your belief, article by article."

[Rabban Sauma recited a statement of his beliefs, and afterward the cardinals interrogated him on certain disputed points about the Trinity.]

Then Rabban Sauma said to them, "I have come from remote countries neither to discuss, nor to instruct in matters of the faith, but I came that I might receive a blessing from the lord pope, and from the shrines of the saints, and to make known the words of the king and the catholicus. If it be pleasing to your eyes, let us set aside discussion, and give attention and direct someone to show us the churches here and the shrines of the saints; you will confer a very great favor on your servant and disciple."

Then the cardinals summoned the governor of the city and certain monks and commanded them to show him the churches and the holy places that were there; and they went forth straight away and saw the places which we will now mention. First of all they went into the Church of Peter and Paul. Beneath the throne is a chapel, and in this is laid the body of Saint Peter, and above the throne is an altar. The altar which is in the middle of that great temple has four doorways, and in each of these two folding doors worked with designs in iron. The lord pope celebrates the Mass at this altar, and no person besides himself may stand on the bench of that altar. Afterward they saw the throne of lord Peter on which they make the lord pope to sit when they consecrate him. And they also saw the strip of fine linen on which our lord impressed his image and sent to King Abgar [V., d. c. 40] of Edessa. Now the extent of that temple and its splendor cannot be described; it stands on one hundred eight pillars. In it is another altar at which the king of their kings receives the consecration, and is proclaimed "Emperor, king of kings" by the pope. And they say that after the prayers the lord pope takes up the crown with his feet and clothes the emperor with it. But he [the emperor] places it on the head [of the pope] to show, as they say, that priesthood reigns over kingship.

And when they had seen all the churches and monasteries that were in great Rome, they went outside the city to the Church of Lord Paul the Apostle, where under the altar is his tomb. And there, too, is the chain with which Paul was bound when he was dragged to that place. And in that altar there are also a reliquary of gold in which is the head of lord Stephen the Martyr, and the hand of lord Ananias who baptized Paul. And the staff of Paul the apostle is also there. And from that place they went to the spot where Paul the apostle was crowned [with martyrdom]. They say that when his head was cut off it leapt up three times into the air, and at each time cried out "Christ! Christ!" And that from each of the three places on which his head fell there came forth waters which were useful for healing purposes, and for giving help to all those who were afflicted. And in that place also there is a great shrine in which are the bones of martyrs and famous fathers, and they were blessed by them.

And they went also to the Church of the Lady Mary, and of lord John the Baptist, and they saw there the seamless tunic of our Lord. And there is also in that church the table on which our Lord consecrated the Eucharist and gave it to his disciples. And each year the lord pope consecrates on that table the Paschal mysteries. There are in that church four pillars of brass, each of which is six cubits in thickness; these, they say, the kings brought from Jerusalem. They saw also there the vessel in which Constantine, the victorious king, was baptized; it is made of dark polished stone. Now that church is very large and broad, and there are in the nave one hundred forty white marble pillars. They saw also the place where Simon Cephas disputed with Simon [Magus], and where the latter fell down and his bones were broken.

From that place they went into the Church of the Lady Mary, and they brought out for them reliquaries made of crystal, in which was the apparel of Lady Mary, and a piece of wood on which our Lord slept when a child. They saw also the head of Matthew, the apostle, in a reliquary of silver. And they saw the foot of Philip, the apostle, and the arm of James, the son of Zebedee, in the Church of the Apostles, which was there. And after this they saw buildings which it is impossible to describe in words, and as the histories of those buildings would make any description of them very long, I abandon [the attempt].

After this Rabban Sauma and his companions returned to the cardinals, and thanked them for having held him to be worthy to see these shrines and to receive blessings from them. And Rabban Sauma asked from them permission to go to the king who dwells in Rome; and they permitted him to go, and said, "We cannot give you an answer until a pope is elected."

And they went from that place to the country of Tuscany, and were honorably treated, and from there they went to Genoa. Now the latter country has no king, but the people there set up to rule over it some great man with whom they are pleased.

And when the people of Genoa heard that an ambassador of King Arghun had arrived, their chief went forth with a great crowd of people, and they brought him into the city.

And there was there a great church with the name of San Lorenzo, in which was the holy body of lord John the Baptist, in a casket of pure silver. And Rabban Sauma and his companions saw also a six-sided paten, made of emerald, and the people there told them that it was off this paten from which our Lord ate the Passover with his disciples, and that it was brought there when Jerusalem was captured. And from that place they went to the country of Lombardy and they saw that the people there did not fast during the first Saturday of Lent. And when they asked them, "Why do you do so, and separate yourselves from all Christians?" they replied, "This is our custom. When we were first taught the Gospel our fathers in the faith were weak and were unable to fast. Those who taught them the Gospel commanded them to fast forty days."

Afterward they went to the country of Paris to King Philip IV [r. 1285–1314]. And the king sent out a large company of men to meet them, and they brought them into the city with great honor and ceremony. Now the territories of the French king were in extent more than a month's journey. And the king of France assigned to Rabban Sauma a place in which to dwell, and three days later sent one of his emirs [commanders] to him and summoned him to his presence. And when he had come, the king stood up before him and paid him honor, and said to him, "Why have you come? And who sent you?"

And Rabban Sauma said to him, "King Arghun and the catholicus of the east have sent me concerning the matter of Jerusalem." And he showed him all the matters which he knew, and he gave him the letters which he had with him, and the gifts, that is to say, presents which he had brought. And the king of France answered him, saying, "If it indeed be so that the Mongols, though they are not Christians, are going to fight against the Arabs for the capture of Jerusalem, it is fitting especially for us that we should fight [with them], and if our Lord wills, go forth in full strength."

And Rabban Sauma said to him, "Now that we have seen the glory of your kingdom, and have looked on the splendor of your strength with the eye of flesh, we ask you to command the men of the city to show us the churches, and the shrines, and the relics of the saints, and everything else which is found with you, and is not to be seen in any other country, so that when we return we may make known in the countries what we have seen with you." Then the king commanded his emirs, saying, "Go forth and show them all the wonderful things which we have here, and afterward I myself will show them what I have." And the emirs went out with them.

And Rabban Sauma and his companions remained for a month of days in this great city of Paris, and they saw everything that was in it. There were in it thirty thousand students who were engaged in the study of ecclesiastical books of instruction, that is to say of commentaries and exegesis of all the holy scripture, and also of profane learning; and they studied wisdom, that is to say philosophy, and rhetoric, and medicine, geometry, arithmetic, and the science of the planets and the stars; and they engaged constantly in writing, and all these pupils received money for subsistence from the king. And they also saw one great church in which the coffins of dead kings lie, and statues of them in gold and silver were on their tombs. And five hundred monks were engaged in performing commemoration services in the tombs of the kings, and they all ate and drank at the expense of the king. And they fasted and prayed continually in the tombs of those kings. And the crowns of those kings, and their armor, and their apparel were laid upon their tombs. In short Rabban Sauma and his companions saw everything which was splendid and renowned.

And after this the king sent and summoned them, and they went to him in the church, and they saw him standing by the side of the altar, and they greeted him. And he asked Rabban Sauma, saying, "Have you seen what we have? And does there not remain anything else for you to see?" Then Rabban Sauma thanked him. Immediately he went up with the king into an upper chamber of gold, which the king opened, and he brought forth from it a casket of crystal in which was laid the crown of thorns which the Jews placed upon the head of our Lord when they crucified him. Now the crown was visible in the casket, which, thanks to the transparency of the crystal, remained unopened. And there was also in the casket a piece of the wood of the cross. And the king said to Rabban Sauma and his companions, "When our fathers took Constantinople, and sacked Jerusalem, they brought these blessed objects from it." And we blessed the king and persuaded him to give us the order to leave. And he said to us, "I will send you with one of the great emirs whom I have here with me to give an answer to King Arghun." And the king gave Rabban Sauma gifts and apparel of great price.

And they went forth from that place, that is to say, from Paris, to go to the king of England [Edward I, r. 1272–1307], to Gascony. And having arrived in twenty days at their city, the inhabitants of the city went forth to meet them, and they asked them, "Who are you?" And Rabban Sauma and his companions replied, "We are ambassadors, and we have come from beyond the eastern seas, and we are envoys of the king, and of the patriarch, and the kings of the Mongols." And the people made haste and went to the king and informed him, and the king welcomed them gladly, and the people introduced them into his presence. And those who were with Rabban Sauma immediately gave to the king the dispatches of King Arghun, and the gifts which he had sent to him, and the letter of the lord catholicus. And he rejoiced greatly, and he was especially glad when Rabban Sauma talked about the matter of Jerusalem. And he said, "We the kings of these cities bear on our bodies the sign of the cross, and we have no subject of thought except this matter. And my mind is relieved on the subject about which I have been thinking, when I hear that King Arghun thinks as I think." And the king commanded Rabban Sauma to celebrate the Eucharist, and he celebrated the glorious mysteries; and the king and his courtiers attended, and the king partook of the sacrament, and made a great feast that day.

Then Rabban Sauma said to the king, "We desire, O king, to give the order to show us whatever churches and shrines there are in this country, so that when we go back to the easterners we may give them descriptions of them." And the king replied, "So you will say to the King Arghun and to all the easterners: We have seen a thing than which there is nothing more wonderful, that is to say, that in the countries of the Franks there are not two confessions of faith, but only one confession of faith, namely, that which confesses Jesus Christ; and all the Christians confess it." And King Edward gave us many gifts and money for the expenses of the road.

And from that place we came to the city of Genoa, in order to pass the winter there. And when we arrived there we saw a garden which resembled paradise; its winter is not cold, and its summer is not hot. Green foliage is found there all the year round, and trees, the leaves of which do not fall, and which are not stripped of their fruit. There is in the city a kind of vine which yields grapes seven times a year, but the people do not press out wine from them.

At the end of winter there came from the country of Germany a man of high degree, who was the visitor of the lord pope, and who was on his way to Rome. And when he heard that Rabban Sauma was there, he went to visit him and greet him. And when he entered, they gave each other peace and they kissed each other in the love of Christ. And he said to Rabban Sauma, "I have come to see you. For I have heard about you, that you are a good and a wise man, and also that you have the desire to go to Rome." And Rabban Sauma said to him, "What can I say to you, O beloved and noble man? I have come on an embassy from King Arghun, and the catholicus of the east to the lord pope on the subject of Jerusalem. Behold I have been here a year, and a pope is not seated. When I go back, what will I say and what answer can I make to the Mongols? Those, whose hearts are harder than flint, wish to take the holy city, and those to whom it belongs never allow the matter to occupy their minds, and moreover, they do not consider this thing to be of any importance whatsoever! We do not know what we will go and say." Then the visitor said to him, "Your words are true. I myself will go and tell literally to the cardinals all the words which you have spoken, and will urge them to elect a pope."

And that visitor departed from him and went to Rome, and he explained the matter to the king, that is to say the lord pope, and that same day the pope sent a messenger that Rabban Sauma and his companions should go to him. And as soon as ever the messenger had arrived, they set out for Rome with the greatest readiness and they arrived there in fifteen days. And they asked, "Who is the pope whom they have appointed?" And they answered, "It is the bishop who conversed with you when you came here the first time, and his name is Nicholas IV [r. 1288–1292]." And Rabban Sauma and his companions rejoiced greatly.

And when they arrived the lord pope sent out a metropolitan bishop and a large company of men to meet them. And immediately Rabban Sauma went into the presence of the lord pope, who was seated on his throne. And he drew close to the pope, bowing down to the ground as he did so, and kissed his feet and his hands, and he withdrew walking backwards, with his hands clasped. And he said to the lord pope, "May your throne stand for ever, O our father! And may it be blessed above all kings and nations! And may it make peace to reign in your days throughout the Church to the ends of the earth! Now that I have seen your face my eyes are illumined, and I will not go away brokenhearted to the countries. I give thanks to the goodness of God who has held me to be worthy to see your face. Then Rabban Sauma presented to him the gift of King Arghun and his letters, and the gift of lord Yaballaha the catholicus, that is to say a blessing and his letter. And the lord pope rejoiced and was glad, and he paid more honor to Rabban Sauma than was customary, and he said to him, "It will be good if you observe the season with us, for you will see our liturgical rite." Now that day [marked] the middle of Lent. And Rabban Sauma replied, "Your command is high and exalted." And the lord pope assigned him to a mansion in which to dwell, and he appointed servants to give him everything that he might require.

Some days later Rabban Sauma said to the lord pope, "I wish to celebrate the Eucharist so that you may see our liturgical rite." And the pope commanded him to do as he had asked. And on that day a very large number of people were gathered together in order to see how the ambassador of the Mongols celebrated the Eucharist. And when they had seen they rejoiced and said, "The language is different, but the liturgical rite is the same." Now the day on which he celebrated was the sixth Sunday of Lent. And having celebrated the mysteries, he went to the lord pope and greeted him. And the pope said to Rabban Sauma, "May God receive your offering, and bless you, and pardon your transgressions and sins." Then Rabban Sauma said, "Besides the pardon of my transgressions and sins which I have received from you, O our father, I desire of your fatherliness, O our holy father, to let me receive the Eucharist from your hands, so that the remission of my sins may be complete." And the pope said, "So let it be!"

And on the following first day of the week, which was Palm Sunday [21 March 1288], from the morning onward, countless thousands and tens of thousands of people gathered together before the papal throne, and brought branches of olives, which the pope blessed and gave to the cardinals, and then to the metropolitans and then to the bishops, and then to the emirs, and then to the nobles, and then he threw them among all the people. And he rose up from the throne, and they brought him into the church with great ceremony. And he went into the apse of the altar and changed his apparel, and he put on a red vestment embroidered with gold, and ornamented with precious stones, and jacinths, and pearls, down to the soles of his feet, that is to say, sandals. And he went to the altar, and then went forth to the pulpit, and addressed the people and admonished them. And he consecrated the mysteries and gave the Eucharist to Rabban Sauma first of all—he having confessed his sins—and the pope pardoned his transgressions and his sins and those of his fathers. And Rabban Sauma rejoiced greatly in receiving the Eucharist from the hand of the lord pope. And he received it with tears and sobs, giving thanks to God and meditating upon the mercies which had been poured out on him.

Afterward, on the day of Maundy Thursday [25 March 1288], the lord pope went to the Church of lord John the Baptist, when a large number of people had gathered together. He went up into a great furnished and decorated platform which was there—and in front of this platform there was a large open space—and the cardinals, and the metropolitans, and the bishops went with him; and they began to recite a prayer. And when the prayer was ended, the lord pope addressed and admonished the congregation, according to custom. And from the multitude of people not one sound could be heard except "Amen." And when "Amen" was uttered, the ground shook through the outcries of the people. Then the lord pope came down from that place to the front of the altar, and he consecrated the chrism oil, that is to say, the oil of anointing. And afterward he consecrated the mysteries that grant pardon, and gave the Eucharist to the people. And he went forth from that place and entered the great nave and gave to each of the holy fathers two gold coins and thirty silver coins, and then went out. And the lord pope gathered together the clergy of his palace, and he washed their feet, and he wiped them with a cloth that he had wrapped round his loins, to the end. And when he had finished all the service of Maundy Thursday, at noon he made a great feast, and the servants placed before every man his portion of food. Now those who sat there were two thousand, more or less. And when they removed the bread from the table only three hours of the day were left.

And on the following day, which was Good Friday [26 March 1288], the lord pope put on a black chasuble, and all the reverend fathers did likewise. And they went forth barefoot and walked to the Church of my Lord, the Adorable Cross; and the lord pope did homage to it [the cross], and kissed it, and gave it to each one of the holy fathers. And when the crowds of people saw it they uncovered their heads, and they knelt down on their knees and adored it. Then the lord pope addressed and admonished the people. And he made the sign of the cross in the four directions, and when the prayer was concluded, he brought some of the Eucharist from Maundy Thursday and deposited it into the wine, and the lord pope partook by himself of that Eucharist, for it is not customary for Christians to celebrate the Eucharist on Good Friday. And he went back to his palace.

And on the day of Holy Saturday [27 March 1288] the lord pope went to the church, and they read the Books of the Prophets, and the prophecies concerning the messiah. And they placed a baptismal font, and arranged branches of myrtle round about it, and the lord pope consecrated the baptismal water and baptized three children, and signed them with the sign of the cross. Then he went to the apse and put on the vestments of the passion, and he put on his ceremonial vestments, the price of which is beyond the power of words, and he celebrated the holy mysteries.

And on Easter Sunday [28 March 1288] the lord pope went to the holy Church of my Lady Mary. And he and the cardinals, and the metropolitans, and the bishops, and the members of the congregation greeted each other, and they kissed each other on the mouth, and he celebrated the mysteries, and they received the Eucharist, and then he returned to his palace. And he made a great feast, and there was infinite gladness. And on the following Sunday [4 April

1288] the lord pope performed an ordination, and he consecrated three bishops. And Rabban Sauma and his companions saw the liturgical rite followed, and they celebrated the blessed feasts with them.

And when these things had taken place, Rabban Sauma asked the lord pope for permission to return. And the lord pope said to him, "We wish you to remain with us, and to abide with us, and we will keep you like the apple of our eye." But Rabban Sauma replied, "O our father, I came on an embassy to do you service. If my coming had been the result of my personal wish, I would willingly bring to an end the days of this my useless life in your service at the outer door of your palace. But when I go back and show the kings who are there the benefits which you have conferred on my poor person, the Christians will gain great satisfaction thereby. Now I desire for your holiness to bestow on me some of the relics that you have with you."

And the lord pope said, "If we had been in the habit of giving away these relics to everyone, even though the relics were as large as the mountains, they would have come to an end long ago. But since you have come from a far country, we will give you a few." And he gave to Rabban Sauma a small piece of the apparel of our Lord Christ, and a piece of the cape, that is to say, kerchief of my Lady Mary, and some small fragments of the bodies of the saints that were there. And he sent to lord Yaballaha a crown for his head which was of fine gold, and was inlaid with precious stones; and sacred vestments made of red cloth through which ran threads of gold; and socks and sandals on which real pearls were sewn; and the ring from his finger; and letters patent that authorized him to exercise patriarchal dominion over all the easterners. And he gave to Rabban Sauma letters patent that authorized him to act as visitator-general over all Christians. And the lord pope blessed him, and he caused to be assigned to him for expenses on the road one thousand, five hundred pounds of red gold. And to King Arghun he sent certain gifts. And he embraced Rabban Sauma and kissed him and dismissed him. And Rabban Sauma thanked our Lord who had held him to be worthy of such blessings as these.

And Rabban Sauma returned. He crossed the seas that he crossed when he came, and he arrived in peace at the place where King Arghun was, sound in body, and with soul safely preserved. And he gave to him the documents of blessing, and the gifts which he had brought from the lord pope and from all the kings of the Franks. And he showed him how they had welcomed him with love, and how they had listened gladly to the dispatches which he had carried, and he related the wonderful things which he had seen, and the power of the kingdom. And King Arghun rejoiced, and was glad, and thanked him, and said to him, "We have made you suffer great fatigue, for you are an old man. In future we will not permit you to leave us; no, we will set up a church at our royal court, and you will serve there and recite prayers." And Rabban Sauma said, "If my lord the king would command lord Yaballaha, the catholicus, to come and receive the gifts which have been sent to him by the lord pope, and the sacred vestments which he donated to him, he could set up the church which the king is going to set up in the royal court, and consecrate it." And these things came to pass in this way.

Questions: How was Rabban Sauma received by the rulers he visited? What hindrances did Sauma run into? What impressed Sauma the most about what he saw in the west? How, for instance, was the treatment of civilians in war different from what he knew? What did Sauma think of seeing so many Christians? To what degree did his journey become more of a religious than a diplomatic one? Which religious objects and experiences were most important to Sauma?

31. GHIYYATH AL-DIN NAQQASH, *A PERSIAN EMBASSY TO CHINA*

Ghiyyath al-Din Naqqash (fl. 1419–1422) was a painter, but he was also chosen as the official diarist of the embassy described here, which was from 1419 to 1422. It was issued by Shah Rukh (r. 1405–1447), the ruler of the Timurid Empire that encompassed Iran, Afghanistan, and central Asia. He sent a large diplomatic corps that included his sons, who were governors in the empire. They left from their capital, Herat, with their destination as the capital of China, Beijing, and its current ruler, the Yongle Emperor (Ming Dynasty, r. 1402–1424). Previously the two empires had come to the brink of war, and only slowly did their relations become normalized. Ghiyyath's work does not survive independently, but it was incorporated into compilations such as that of the court historian and geographer Hafiz-i Abru. Outside of its interest for international relations, this source provides descriptions of early Ming China. The excerpt starts as the ambassadors approach the imperial court.

Source: trans. K.M. Maitra, Hafiz Abru, *A Persian Embassy to China* (Lahore: Behari Lal,Verma, 1934; rpt. Paragon Book Reprint Corp., 1970), pp. 42–123. Persian. Revised.

They passed out of these post-houses and as soon as they arrived at any of the towns, banquets were given to the envoys and their attendants so that the nearer they approached Beijing, the greater became the formalities. The baggages and the animals of the envoys and their attendants that had been deposited at Qam-chou were made over to them quite intact on their return and whatever they had brought with them as presents for the emperor were taken away from the envoys and looked after by themselves.

Thus every day they arrived at a halting-place and every week at a new city, until on the fourteenth of Shawwal A.H. 823 [22 October 1420] they reached the river Qaramoran [Huang He, Yellow River]. It was a big river somewhat like the Oxus. There was a bridge over it composed of twenty-three boats, of great excellence and strength attached together by a long chain of iron as thick as a man's thigh, and this was moored on each side to an iron post as thick as a man's waist extending to a distance of ten cubits on the land and planted firmly in the ground, the boats being fastened to this chain by means of big hooks. There were placed big wooden planks over the boats so firmly and evenly that all the animals were made to pass over it without any difficulty. On the other side of the river Qaramoran there stood a large town. The envoys were treated to a feast which was bigger than all the previous feasts that had been hitherto given. In this city there was an exceedingly magnificent and splendid idol temple so that they had seen no building like it since their crossing the frontiers until now. There were also three big taverns within this town in which there were many beautiful girls. All kinds of artisans that were highly skilled were to be found in that town. Although the people of China were mostly handsome yet this town was known as the City of Beauty [?].

From that place they passed by several other towns until they reached on the twelfth of Dhu l-Qa'dah [18 November] a river that was twice the size of the Oxus and of which the waves rose high. The boats were provided and the whole party crossed over that river safely. After passing across several other rivers, some by boats and some by bridges, they reached on the twenty-seventh of Dhu l-Qa'dah [3 December] the town of Tingzhou fu. It was a magnificent city with a large population and fine buildings. Among others there was a big idol-temple of such character that in the midst of it there was erected an idol cast in bronze and so gilded over as to look like one made of solid gold, measuring fifty cubits in height. Its limbs were all made symmetrical in form. All over the limbs of this idol there were figures of hands set up and over the palm of every hand there was the image of an eye. It is called the thousand-handed image and is celebrated throughout the whole of China. First of all a big solid platform which was constructed out of finely cut stones is set up on which this idol and the whole building rests, around the idol rise a large number of alcoves, verandas, and galleries, several flights of stairs running along the same in such a manner that the first stairway passes a little beyond the ankle of the idol, the second stairway does not come as high as its knee, and the third stairway passes above the knee, while the fourth one reaches its breast and so on up to the head, the whole structure being executed with masterly elaboration. Thereafter the top of the building was surmounted by a conical dome and so covered up as to excite the wonder of men. The total number of stories being eight, around every one of which one could walk outside as well as inside the building. This idol is made in a standing position, its feet, of which the length is about ten cubits, each rest on a pedestal of cast metal. It has been estimated that at least one hundred donkey-loads of brass must have been used in that work. Besides all round that big idol there were smaller idols of plaster which were colored and painted in gold. There were the paintings of hills, peaks, caves with the figures of Buddhist monks, priests, and ascetics sitting in their cells doing religious penance. There were also pictures of rams, mountain goats, lions, leopards, dragons, and trees all painted on plaster. The rest of the walls were so painted with frescoes as to call forth the wonder of even skilled artists at their sight. Similar was the case with the surrounding buildings. Within this building there was also a moving tower like one seen at Ganzhou but more elaborately made and bigger in size.

Thus they continued their march riding four to five farsangs daily until they made an early start on the eighth of Dhu al-Hijjah [14 December] arriving at the gates of Beijing while it was still dark. It was a very magnificent city, so that every one of its walls was a farsang long, the total circumference being four farsangs. All around the city wall, owing to the fact that it was still under construction, there were set up one hundred thousand bamboo poles, each one of which being fifty cubits long, in the form of scaffoldings. Since it was still early dawn and the gates had not yet opened, the envoys were admitted to the city through the tower which was being constructed and made to dismount at the gate of the emperor's palace. At the entrance to the citadel there had been constructed pavement of cut stones of the size of seven hundred paces in length. As soon as the envoys reached the edge of the pavement they were asked to dismount. They crossed over to the other end of the pavement on foot and reached the gate of the citadel. There stood ten elephants on the further end of the gate, five on one side and five on the other with their trunks drawn over the path. The envoys passed between the trunks of elephants and entered the palace.

There were at that time when it was not yet daylight, about one hundred thousand men at the gate of the emperor's palace. As soon as they stepped in through the first gate they found themselves in a courtyard three hundred cubits long and two hundred fifty cubits wide. In front of that courtyard there was a basement of three cubits in height, and over this basement had been set up columns fifty cubits high supporting a building in which there was an open arcade sixty cubits long and forty cubits wide. There were after this three doors of which the central one was the bigger and those on the left and right being smaller. The central door served as a passage for the emperor and not everyone is allowed to pass through it. On the left and right passages there had been placed a large drum and a conch-shell hanging from the wall. Two persons were waiting for the emperor to appear and take his seat on the throne. There were about three hundred thousand people both men and women gathered in that open space, while nearly two thousand musicians stood singing in concert and chanting the praises of the emperor in the Chinese language and in accordance with their intonations. There were besides about two thousand men who held in their hands some sort of arms. Some of them had halberds [short spears], clubs, some javelins, while others had hunting spears, swords, and battle axes. There were some who held Chinese fans and umbrellas. All round the place there were apartments with roofed corridors in front of them and having magnificent columns at the edges of those corridors. The walls of the apartments were wholly made of latticed woodwork and the floors were of fine cut stones, such as all master craftsmen of every art would be astonished to look at them.

In short when it was broad daylight those people who were in the galleries waiting for the emperor to come and take his seat on the throne began to strike the big and small drums and play upon trumpets, cymbals, flutes, and conch shells. The three doors were flung open and the people rushed inside. Their custom is such that the people go running in order to see the emperor. After passing from the first courtyard they reached the second courtyard which was about three hundred paces long. At the other end of it there was a gallery much bigger and more open than the first one. A throne measuring four cubits [on each side] was placed in it. This throne was provided all round with a railing like the bars of a Christian tabernacle and covered with yellow Chinese satin wholly wrought in gold with figures of dragons, griffins, and other Chinese devices. A golden chair was placed on the throne to the left and right of which the Chinese officials were made to stand in rows. First came commanders of ten thousands, next commanders of thousands, and last commanders of hundreds, all numbering about one hundred thousand men. Every one of them held in his hand a tablet of a statute cubit in length and a quarter as much in breadth. None of them had the courage to look at any other place except these tablets. Behind them stood troops in close ranks two hundred thousand strong, some wearing cuirasses, others holding spears while some held drawn swords in their hands. The whole body of those infidels stood so silent, that it seemed as if there was not a breathing soul there.

As the emperor came out of the women's apartments they set against the throne a silver staircase of five steps, and placed a golden chair on the top of the throne. The emperor mounted and took his seat upon this chair. The emperor was of the middle height; his beard neither very large nor very small; nevertheless about two or three hundred hairs of his middle beard were long enough to form three or four curls on the chair he was seated. To the left and right of the throne stood two girls with faces like the moon, who had their hair drawn to a knot on the crown; their necks and faces were bare; they had fine large pearls in their ears; and they held paper and pen in their hands ready to take down what the emperor might say and order. They jot down whatever might fall from his lips on that particular day. When he returns to the private apartments they submit that document to him and take care that if any order should be changed a written instruction is sent out to that effect, so that the members of his council may act in accordance with it.

In short, when the emperor had taken his seat in the throne and the Chinese officials stood in lines on both sides, the party of ambassadors was brought forward in front of the emperor side by side with certain prisoners. First of all they asked for judgment concerning the prisoners, who were some seven hundred in number. Some of them had a wooden pillory on their necks, some were in chains, while some had one of their hands passed through a board; some five or six had their necks held together by one broad wooden plank, through holes in which their heads protruded, each one according to his status and degree of his crime. Each prisoner had a keeper by him who held him by the hair, waiting for the emperor's sentence. He condemned some to imprisonment and others to death. Throughout the whole of China no official or magistrate has the right to put any person whatsoever to death. When a man has committed a crime the details of his crime are written on a wooden board which is hung round his neck either by means of a chain or a pillory in accordance with the punishment of the crime as set down in their infidelish creed. The criminal is thus set off to Beijing. Should he have a year's journey to get there still he must never be allowed to halt until he reaches that place.

In short, when the prisoners had departed, the ambassadors were led forward, so that there intervened a distance of only fifteen cubits from the emperor's throne. One of those officers who held tablets in their hands came up and kneeling down read out of a written paper in the Chinese language the particulars concerning the ambassadors. Its gist was to the effect that the envoys had come from a distant country as representatives of his majesty the Persian king and his sons, bringing presents for the emperor and had come to the foot of the throne to offer their homage. When this statement had been completely read out, Mawlana Haji Yusuf, the judge who was one of the chiefs commanding ten thousand and one of the officers attached to the person of the emperor, and who knew Arabic, Persian, Turkish, Mongol, and Chinese languages and acted as an interpreter between the emperor and the envoys, as well as one of the twelve departmental heads came forward accompanied by several Muslims acquainted with Arabic and Persian, etc., who were among his followers and stood up around the Muslims, and said: "First prostrate yourselves then touch the ground three times with your heads." Accordingly the envoys bent their heads, but without letting their foreheads touch the ground. Thereafter raising both hands they presented the letter of his majesty the lord of sovereignty (may God perpetuate his dominion!) and that of his highness prince Bavsunqur Bahadur (may God perpetuate his dominion!), each of which was folded in a

227

piece of yellow satin. For their rule is that everything pertaining to the emperor must be wrapped up in a piece of some yellow stuff. Mawlana the qazi [judge] advanced, took the letters and handed them to an eunuch.

After this the emperor came down from the throne and took his seat on the chair. Three thousand suits of robes were brought in consisting of a cloak and a pair of tunics, and he invested his officers and their relations and sons with these. Thereafter seven individuals among the envoys were presented, first Shadi Khwaja and Kukja, after them Sultan Ahmad, Khwaja Ghiyasu'd-Din, Arghdaq, Ardwan, and Taju'd-Din of Badakhshan. They were told to kneel down and so they knelt down. The emperor questioned them concerning his majesty the lord of sovereignty (may almighty God perpetuate his dominion and power!). . . . Next he asked whether the grain was expensive or cheap in their country. They replied that grain was cheap and foodstuffs plentiful. He said in reply that indeed since their king's heart was rightly disposed toward God, the lord almighty had also bestowed on them good things in abundance. . . . Then he said that since they had come from a long journey they should get up and take their meal.

From this place the envoys were conducted to the first courtyard where they had been sitting. Every one of them was given a table and a chair and refreshments were served up on every table as has already been mentioned. When they had done with their meal they were conducted to the inn which had been appointed for them. Sultan Shah and Bakhshi Malik who were the retainers of his highness prince Ulugh Beg Gurgan (the refuge of truth and faith, may God almighty perpetuate his dominion!) were also made to stay at another inn quite close to it. In this inn every apartment was furnished with a fine bedstead with bedding and pillows of satin and brocade, as well as slippers of brocade sewn up with extreme delicacy, mosquito curtains, chairs, fire grates, and a settee of sofas to the left and right of which were coverlets and cushions of satin and brocade, carpets, and straw mats that could be rolled up both lengthwise and breadthwise without being crushed up. To every person was allotted an apartment done up in this manner, as well as a cooking vessel, cups, spoons, and trays. A group of ten men daily received a sheep, a goose and two fowls, while each person was given two standard maunds of flour, a big bowl of rice, two large loaves stuffed with sweets, a pot of honey, garlic, onions, vinegar, salt, and such variety of vegetables as are to be had in China, as well as two jugs of beer, a plate of desserts, together with several active and alert servants endowed with great beauty and ever on their feet from morning to evening and from evening to morning without absenting themselves for even a moment.

The next day being the ninth of Dhu al-Hijjah [15 December], [there] came the *shiqawul* [officer in charge of ambassadors] and awakened them saying:

"Get up, for the emperor is going to give a banquet." He had brought saddled horses for everyone. The ambassadors were made to mount the horses and led to the royal headquarters. They were made to dismount at the first gateway. The envoys were conducted to the foot of throne which was the hall of justice. They made prostration to the emperor five times and the emperor came down from the throne. The envoys were again taken out and were asked to go out of the royal palace as the banquet was going to take place. They were advised to relieve themselves, that they should not unexpectedly feel the necessity to rise in the middle of the banquet for some need when it would not be possible to go out. Accordingly the party went out and dispersed for a while. They again assembled and went in.

Passing through the first gateway, they reached the second gateway which was the throne room. Passing out from there they entered the third gateway. It was a very extensive courtyard paved most beautifully and exquisitely with cut stones. In the front had been set up a grand hall of the size of sixty cubits each way. The palace and the parlors opened in the direction of the south. It is customary with the Chinese buildings that they are always constructed with their faces and gates looking toward the south. Inside this hall there had been placed a magnificent throne higher than the height of a man with silver staircases on its three sides, one in front, one on the left, and the third on the right. There stood two eunuchs, whose mouths were bandaged up to their ear lobes with something made of papier-mâché. There was still another throne, of smaller size put up on that throne, on which sits the emperor. It is somewhat like a chair but much bigger in size that is placed on the throne. It is many-sided and provided with bolsters and peculiar legs. To the left and right of which were placed something like high incense burners. That throne, as well as the incense burners and the chair, were all carved out of wood and gilded in such a manner that Mawlana the qazi remarked that it was eight years since the throne had been gilded yet during this period none of its goldwork had faded. Moreover the columns, stairs, and other woodworks that were within this structure were all painted yellow and varnished in such a manner that the expert workmen of Iraq and Khurasan can never paint and polish like that.

The trays served with food, desserts, and bouquets were placed before the emperor. To the left and right of the throne there stood stalwart Chinese officers armed with quivers and swords and their shields slung behind. In the rear stood soldiers with long halberds in their hands and behind them yet another body of men with drawn swords. On the left hand side which is held by them in greater honor than the right hand a place was assigned for the envoys. They place before noblemen and those to whom they show a great regard three trays, and before those of a lower rank two trays and those still lower one tray apiece. On that particular day they must have served up a thousand trays or even more before the people. Now just beside the emperor's throne right in front of the window of the hall had been placed a huge drum, while a man stood upon a high chair and by him was an orchestra of a varied character quite ready and waiting. In front of the throne were set up seven umbrellas, each one of which was colored most gorgeously.

Outside the hall to the left and right were stationed about two hundred thousand armored men. At the distance of a good arrow shot there had been set up a kind of big buffet ten cubits by ten cubits enclosed on one side with a wall of yellow satin, inside which were being dressed up refreshments and drinks for the emperor. Whenever food or drink is brought up for the emperor, the orchestra begins playing all of a sudden and those seven royal umbrellas at once begin to spin until the food reaches close to the throne. All these refreshments and drinks are deposited in a big box with legs and having a lid of the same material on its top. As these preparations were being made the envoys stood on the tiptoe of expectation. Just behind the throne room there was a door leading into the harem, over which hung a big curtain to each corner of which was tied a silken cord on both sides. Two eunuchs held in their hands the two ends of this cord of which the center passed over a pulley, so that when the cord was pulled the curtain folded itself up just like a mat that is rolled up. In this way the door opened to the extent of one foot and the emperor emerged out of it and the orchestra began to play. When the emperor had taken his seat on the throne all resumed silence.

Over the emperor's head at the height of ten cubits was set up a canopy of yellow satin measuring fourteen cubits on each side in the manner of an awning on which were painted four dragons in the act of attacking one another. When the emperor had taken his seat the ambassadors were conducted near the throne and ordered to prostrate themselves on the ground. They prostrated themselves five times. Then he beckoned them to be seated. Every one of them was seated at his appointed place before whom had been set up the trays. Besides what was already on the trays they began to bring from time to time food, meat of lambs, geese, fowls, and rice wine. The acrobats commenced to perform their tricks. First a company of boys as beautiful as the moon with their faces painted red and white like girls, with pearl earrings in their ears, dressed in gold-embroidered clothes of China, holding in their hands and sticking into their heads bouquets of roses and tulips of different kinds made out of colored papers and silk began to dance to the tune of Chinese music. After that two boys ten years old turned somersaults on two wooden boards and performed various kinds of feats. Thereafter a man stretching himself on his back on the ground lifted up both his feet, on the soles of which several long bamboos were placed, then another person took the whole lot in his hand and a boy of ten or twelve years of age mounted on the top of these, the length of each bamboo being seven cubits, and performed various kinds of tricks over them, throwing away in the end all bamboos one by one until he arrived at the last on the top of which he turned somersaults and showed many tricks. After this by a wonderful movement he all of a sudden missed the top of that bamboo, so that all thought that he was going to fall, but the man who was lying on the ground with bamboos on the soles of his feet sprang off and caught him in midair. Again there was a party of musicians and an orchestra side by side. One of them played upon the organ producing twelve notes of music quite out of tune and lacking the melody of Chinese music. Similarly another person did the same with the fife. The next one did so with the Pandean pipe. Now one of them put one of his hands on the Pandean pipe and the other on the fife, while the player of the fife had one hand on the fife and the fingers of his other hand on the holes of the flute that was in the mouth of another person, while the flutist had the flute in his mouth and the castanets in his hands, all of them thus played in unison without any one of them going out of tune.

This assembly was prolonged until the end of midday prayer. The emperor gave rewards to the performers in that very gathering. He sent for paper money which was given to them. The emperor rose and went into the harem. The envoys were dismissed. In the midst of that courtyard there were thousands of birds, such as crows, kites, ravens, doves, turtledoves, and wood pigeons which picked up fruits and crumbs of food that were lying on the ground and were not at all afraid of the people. When the night approaches they take rest upon the trees within the palace without anybody ever bothering them.

In short these ambassadors sojourned in this city from the eighth of Dhu al-Hijjah 823 A.H. [14 December 1420] until the beginning of Jumada I 823 [May 1421], which constitutes a period of five months. Every day they received the same allowance of provisions as had been fixed on the first day in its full and entire measure. Over and above this they were entertained at public dinners several times and shown much consideration. Every time when a dinner was given the performers displayed tricks that were quite different from those that were shown at the previous dinners. In short, next day which happened to be the Feast of Sacrifice (in this city of Beijing the emperor has built a mosque for the Muslims) the ambassadors and the party of Muslims who were in that city went to that mosque and said their prayers. Two days after this, the ambassadors were entertained at another feast. Every time they gave a banquet, they displayed their grandeur more than ever before to the envoys, always giving it a new turn, while the performers showed tricks of a different kind, indulging in wonderful feats of magic.

On the seventeenth of Dhu al-Hijjah [23 December 1420] a number of criminals were sent to the place of execution. The Chinese law is laid down in their codes as to the nature of punishment provided for every crime. Some are beheaded; some are hanged on the gallows; while some are hacked to pieces. They proceed with caution in the matter of criminals. There are twelve courts of justice under the emperor. If a person has been accused of a crime, he must be proved guilty before every one of the twelve tribunals and his plaintiffs have to fight out the case against him. But if, for instance he has been proved guilty before eleven of these tribunals but not proved so in the last one that person may still have hopes of being acquitted. Should he bring forward a plea by reason of which a person living at the distance of more or less six months' journey has to be presented in order that his case may be investigated he is not put to death, but only remanded into custody. A messenger is dispatched to fetch him and then they cross-examine him and after that bring the case to conclusion. Many a criminal dies in their prisons. Any person who happens to die is not given a burial until the emperor issues a mandate to that effect.

On the twenty-third of Muharram [27 January 1421], it was recorded that on that day of severe cold they happened to go to the emperor's palace. Most of the Chinese living there as well as the prisoners that had come from distant towns had all died of cold at the emperor's gateway. Their corpses lay at the crossings of roads and were trampled upon by horses' hooves while they passed on. A person related that only the interior of the city was under protection, but outside the city about ten thousand people had died of that cold since yesterday. They were lying about like dead dogs in Islamic lands in the streets in a more disgraceful condition under the feet of those infidels. The state prisoners lay dead on the ground with pillories and chains just tied as they were fixed to their hands and feet!

On the twenty-seventh of aforesaid Muharram [31 January 1421] his worship the qazi sent a messenger to the ambassadors saying; "Tomorrow is the New Year. The emperor is going to visit his New Palace, and there is an imperial order that none should wear a turban, dress, cap, or socks of white color," for among these people it is the custom to wear white clothes in state of mourning.

On the night of the twenty-eighth while it was yet midnight the officer-in-charge came and awakened them and having mounted them on horseback conducted them to the palace. It was a magnificent building which had only now been finished after nineteen years. That night in that huge city every person had so illuminated his house and shop with torches, candles, and lamps that you would have thought the sun had risen already. So much so that if a needle fell it would be visible. That night the cold was much abated. Everybody was admitted into the New Palace. There were to be found in that place one hundred thousand people who had come from all parts of Cathay [northern China], [southern] China, Machin, Qalmaq, Tibet, Qamul, Qara-Khoja [Gaochang], Churché [Manchu country], and the seacoasts as well as other countries the names of which are not known. The emperor gave an entertainment to his officers of state. He had caused the envoys to be seated just outside his throne room. Thus a concourse of two hundred thousand men stood with swords, maces, halberds, lances, staves, javelins, battle-axes, and other weapons of war in their hands. About one to two thousand men held in their hands the Chinese fans of variegated colors and designs, each being about the size of a shield and slung up across their shoulders. The acrobats and boys danced in ever new fashions, and they wore such dresses with robes and small crowns that it is not possible to give an adequate description of it. To give a just account of that edifice is also not within the power of language. In short from the gate of the hall of audience to the outer gate there was a distance of one thousand nine hundred and twenty-five paces. None had any access to the harem. To the right and left there was an unbroken succession of buildings, pavilions, and gardens. The whole of its floor was constructed of polished blocks made out of bricks of China clay, which in luster are quite like white marble. It was in area two or three hundred cubits in length and breadth. All joints in the blocks of the floor did not show any deflection or curve even to the extent of a hair's breadth, so much so that one would think that they had been ruled with a pen. The blocks of stones were inlaid with Chinese dragons and griffins and polished like pieces of jasper in a way as to excite the wonder of a man. In the arts of stonecutting, woodwork, ornamentation, painting, and tilework there is nobody in the whole of these lands who can compare with them. If the master craftsmen of these lands were only to see these things then they would believe and express their appreciation of the same. In short this banquet terminated toward midday and the people went back to their quarters.

On the ninth of Safar [12 February 1421] in the morning, horses were brought and the ambassadors were taken out. Since the last eight days the emperor had been out of his harem and had been living in a green house built outside. This house contained no image or idol. It was a custom with the emperor that every year on these few days he did not partake of animal food or go into his harem, or admit anyone into his presence. He said that he worshipped the god of heaven, and was occupied in performing his devotions. In short, that was the day of his return and he was entering his harem with great pomp and magnificence accompanied by his troops and personal staff. Elephants richly caparisoned were led out in procession, and bore on their backs a circular gilded litter. Then came standards of black, red, yellow, green, and russet colors emblazoned with the figures of sun, moon, stars, mountains, rivers, and other Chinese devices both in the rear and in the front. These were followed by lancers, carrying swords, halberds, spears, staves, javelins, maces, scimitars, battle-axes, long-tufted fly whisks, and Chinese fans and umbrellas, and then five more ornamented sedan chairs completely gilded carried by men on their shoulders. There were many musical bands of which it is impossible to give an idea, and there marched about five thousand men before and behind the emperor keeping perfect steps together without daring to fall out of the marching line. No one had the courage to make any noise so that it seemed that there was not a breathing soul there but the sound of Chinese musical bands that intoned prayers for the emperor. As soon as the emperor had entered the harem, everybody returned to his quarters.

Another thing in those days was their custom of celebrating the Festival of Lanterns for a period of seven nights and days. Inside the compound of the imperial palace they set up a hillock of wood and cover its whole surface with cypress branches so as to make it look like a hill of emeralds. A hundred thousand lamps are put up there as well as several thousands of effigies of men made out of papier-mâché with such complexion, faces, and garments that they resemble human beings from a distance. All those lamps are connected by means of cords through which are made to pass a rocket of naphtha [petroleum or kerosene oil] in such a manner that as soon as a lamp is kindled the rocket begins to run along those cords and light up every lamp they come in contact with, so that in a single moment all those lamps from the top of the mountain to the bottom are set ablaze. Within the city also the people light a considerable number of lamps over the doors of their houses and shops. During those seven days no one is punished for any crime that one might commit. The emperor bestows much charity and those people who owe revenue to the government as well as prisoners in jails are all let off.

In that year, however, the astrologers had predicted that a conflagration would break out causing damage to the imperial residence, on account of which no illumination of the lamps had taken place, nevertheless the Chinese officials had assembled on that occasion of the Festival of Lanterns, and the emperor gave them a banquet and made presents.

On Sunday the thirteenth of Safar [16 February] the officers-in-charge came and led the whole body of the envoys to the emperor. They were made to take their seats in the first enclosure, where more than one hundred thousand people from all countries had assembled. In the first hall a bejeweled throne was put up and the doors of the hall were thrown open and the emperor took his seat on the throne. About one hundred thousand men knelt down at the foot of the throne and prostrated themselves on the ground. Thereafter the envoys took their seats and watched the scene. They saw that another high throne was brought and placed opposite that of the emperor. Three men stepped on to this throne, two of them held up the order and proclamation that they had heard from the emperor, while one of them read it out in a loud voice in such a way that it was audible to the whole of the assembly. But being in the Chinese language our people could not understand it. The contents of that order were as follows:

"The tenth of this month was the beginning of the year and the celebration of the Festival of Lanterns. All prisoners and offenders, as well as those persons who were in arrears in revenue to the government have been pardoned, except those who have committed murder. No ambassadors are to proceed to any country for three years." The copies of this proclamation were sent to every province. After that order had been read out, by way of doing honor to the royal mandate an umbrella was brought up and held over it. Now that mandate was made to slide down a gilded wooden pole that had round it a ring to which was attached a cord of yellow silk, while the umbrella also slid down along with it. In the act of the mandate coming down the whole orchestra at the foot of the hall began to play together with kettle drums and large drums. There were two gilded litters ready in waiting, as soon as that mandate came down it was placed in one of the litters, while the other litter sped along in front of it accompanied by the whole orchestra and the people went out with it. Thus this mandate was brought down to the hostelry where the envoys were staying in order that the copies of the proclamation may be dispatched to every province. However, when the emperor came down from the hall he sent for all the envoys and entertained them at a feast which lasted until midday. When the feast was over, everyone departed into different directions.

On the first of Rabi' I [5 March] the ambassadors were summoned, when the emperor had ordered for ten gyrfalcons to be kept in readiness. He observed that he never gave gyrfalcons to anyone who had not brought him good horses. He went on saying these kinds of things both covertly and overtly. At last he gave out of these ten gyrfalcons, three to Sultan Shah, the ambassador of the prince of the denizens of the world, Ulugh Beg Gurgan; three to Sultan Ahmed who was the ambassador of Prince Baysunqur Bahadur (may his dominion last forever!); and three more to Shadi Khwaja who was the ambassador of his majesty (may God perpetuate his dominion and power!). But he entrusted the gyrfalcons to his own gamekeepers. The next day he sent for the ambassadors and asked them to mark down their respective gyrfalcons which they said that they had already done so. The emperor said that his army was marching off toward the frontier of the country, so they should also make their preparations and go along with the troops to their country. To this they replied that they were willing to act according to the emperor's command. Thereafter turning to Arghdaq who was the envoy of Prince Suyurghatmish (may God illumine his grave!) he said: "I have no gyrfalcon to give to you, and even if I had one I would not have given it to you, that they should not snatch it away from you just as they snatched it away that time from Shir Azad, the retainer of Prince Ibrahim Bahadur." He said in reply: "If the emperor were graciously to bestow a gyrfalcon upon him he would see that nobody could snatch it away from him." The emperor said: "You stay here until the gyrfalcons arrive and

I would give them to you. Two gyrfalcons are going to arrive shortly; I will give them to you."

On the eighth of Rabi' I [12 March] Sultan Shah and Bakhshi Malik were summoned by the monarch, who gave them what is called *shankshi*. The word *shankshi* means a present in the Chinese language. He gave Sultan Shah eight bags of silver, three suits of royal robes with lining, twenty-four undergarments, ninety-one hawks, two horses (one saddled and the other without a saddle), one hundred cane arrows, five three-pronged hunting spears of the Chinese type, and five thousand in paper money. To Bakhshi Malik he gave a similar present, only he had one bag of silver less. The wives of the ambassadors were given half of those stuffs without any silver bags. On that day the envoy of Uwais Khan [r. 1418–1421, 1425–1429] happened to arrive with two hundred and fifty men. He was called Abu Yatimur Atka. The emperor granted him audience and he paid his homage by prostrating himself on the ground. All his retainers were given embroidered robes of royalty and had their allowances fixed.

On Monday the thirteenth of Rabi' I [17 March] the envoys were summoned when the emperor said to them: "I am going out on a hunting expedition; therefore take charge of your gyrfalcons and look after them, for in case I am late in coming you may not have to wait." He also taunted them several times by saying that they were taking away good gyrfalcons but had brought him bad horses. The gyrfalcons were made over to the charge of the ambassadors and the emperor went away on his hunting expedition. In his absence a prince came from the province of Tamnai [?] and sat in the place of the emperor on the days of audience. The ambassadors went to see him on the eighteenth of this month and they found him sitting on the eastern side of the imperial palace in the manner of the emperor. To his left and right there was the same ceremonial observance. The envoys were invited to sit at the table as before and they partook of refreshments and dispersed.

On the first of Rabi' II [4 April] the officers-in-charge brought news that the emperor was on his way back from the hunting field, and that they must go to meet him. They started off and remained out until the noon prayer time. At last they ascertained that the emperor would come next day and so they returned to their quarters. When they reached the inn they found that the blue gyrfalcon belonging to Sultan Ahmad was dead. About the same time the officers-in-charge called again and said: "Get ready to mount and stay out tonight so that you may be presented to the emperor early in the morning." It was raining at that time. As they were going to mount, they found at the post-house gate his worship the judge and a number of people standing with him looking extremely sad by reason of grief. Being questioned he answered in a low tone: "The emperor, having been thrown out during the chase by the horse that had been sent to him by his majesty the lord of sovereignty (almighty God perpetuate his dominion and power!), has hurt his foot. By reason of this he is enraged and has ordered the ambassadors to be put in chains and sent off to the eastern provinces of China." His friends [the envoys] were exceedingly distressed at this news. At the time of this distressful news it was morning prayer time when they got on their horses. By the time midmorning has passed, they had ridden some twenty marrahs. But owing to the great crowd of the soldiers who were on their way to the city there was no passage on the road. In short they arrived at the camp where the emperor had halted during the night. This occupied an area of some five hundred feet square, round which they had constructed the same night they had come down a wall of ten cubits in height and four feet in thickness. They erect such walls, built of *terre pisé* [made by earth being rammed into wooden molds], with much speed in Cathay. There were two gates left in it, where armed military men stood at guard. There were also armed men all round this ditch until the daytime. Inside it there were two square pavilions of yellow satin, supported by four pillars of twenty-five cubits in height, all round which were tents and awnings wholly made of yellow satin embroidered with gold. As soon as they had come out of the environs of the city into the plain it was visible.

In short when they were within five hundred paces of this place his worship the qazi asked his friends to dismount and stop where they were until the emperor should arrive, while he himself went on. As soon as he reached the emperor's presence he found Wali Daji and Jan Daji standing there. The emperor was then discussing the question of arresting the ambassadors. Thereafter Wali Daji, Jan Daji, and his worship the qazi bowed their foreheads to the ground and made their submission saying: "In case your majesty be offended with the ambassadors they are in no way to blame, for if their sovereigns had sent good or bad horses as presents, these persons had no choice in the matter, since they could not order their monarchs to send good presents. Moreover even if your majesty has the envoys cut in pieces, it will make no difference to their sovereigns. On the other hand an evil report concerning the emperor would spread here. The whole world would say that the emperor of China has acted contrary to all convention by imprisoning the envoys after so many years of absence from home and punishing them." The emperor approved of these suggestions taking them in good part and pardoned them. After this his worship the qazi came in great glee to convey this good news saying: "The most high God has shown mercy to this body of Muslim exiles through his grace and bounty and has cast the light of clemency on the emperor's heart."

After that the trays that the emperor had sent in were brought, but as on that day pork had been all mixed up with mutton the Muslims did not partake of them. The emperor then rode off. As soon as he came out of the camp gate he mounted on a high black horse with white points on its forelegs and hind legs that had been sent by the greatest prince, refuge of truth and faith, Ulugh Beg Gurgan (may most high God perpetuate his dominion!) and which had housings of yellow brocaded with gold. The emperor had on a red mantle brocaded with gold, to which was stitched a pocket of black satin in which the imperial beard was cased. Seven small covered palanquins were borne after the emperor on men's shoulders; these contained the young ladies who had accompanied the emperor to the chase. There was also a large palanquin of square shape carried by seventy men in their rear. Two grooms ran alongside the emperor leading the horse, and these were also dressed in gold brocade of royal pomp. This horse proceeded with its feet one after the other at slow steps. Right and left of the emperor, at the interval of a bow shot, were columns of horsemen who kept exactly abreast of him. These lines extended as far as the eye could reach and there was a space of twenty paces between their ranks. They marched from the encampment in this way, keeping exact alignment, to the gates of the city. The emperor rode in the middle, accompanied by ten governors, Mawlana Qazi, Wali Daji, and Jan Daji. Thereafter the qazi, coming forward, said to the ambassadors: "Dismount and when the emperor arrives prostrate yourself on the ground!" They did so. When the emperor came near he asked them to mount again. The ambassadors mounted and proceeded along with him. The emperor began to make complaint, saying to Shadi Khwaja: "I mounted for chase one of the horses which you brought me, and it being extremely old and feeble fell down, throwing me off. Ever since that day my hand is giving me pain and has become black and blue. It is only by applying ointment a good deal that the pain has abated a little." After that he called for a gyrfalcon and flew off a crane and sent the gyrfalcon after it. It overtook it and struck it with its talons three times and seized it. After this the emperor dismounted. A footstool was brought and placed under his feet while another chair was placed for him to sit on. He took his seat in the chair and called for Sultan Shah, and presented that gyrfalcon to him. He asked for another gyrfalcon and gave it to Sultan Ahmed but he gave none to Shadi Khwaja. He mounted again, when a hare came in sight. He had a gyrfalcon in his hand and let it off against the hare as well as two hounds in its pursuit. They disappeared from view as far as one could see. In short he went out in safety. When he reached near the city, he was met by huge crowds of Chinese and other people who had come out to see him. Large groups of Chinese people were full of acclamations of prayer in behalf of the emperor in the Chinese language. So when he had entered the city with this pomp and show the ambassadors returned to their quarters. . . .

In the meanwhile one of the favorite wives of the emperor happened to die and on account of the mourning it was not possible to see the emperor again. This matter was not disclosed before the preparations of the mourning had been completed. A few days after this it was announced on the twentieth of Jumada I [22 May], that the queen who had died would be given her burial on the next day. On this night by chance a conflagration started through the decree of God from the sky in the wake of lightning striking the top of the palace that had been newly constructed by the emperor. The fire that started in that building enveloped it in such a manner that it seemed as if a hundred thousand torches provided with oil and wicks had been lit up in that place. This part of the building in which the fire started first was a hall eighty cubits long and thirty cubits wide supported on polished columns made of molten lapis lazuli, of such thickness that even three men could not grip them within their embrace. So much so that the whole city was set ablaze with the light of that conflagration and the fire spreading from that place to a parlor which was at the distance of twenty cubits from it burnt down also the ladies' apartments behind the hall of audience built in a style even more sumptuous than it. All round that building there stood parlors and chambers used as a treasury which also caught fire and as the result of that about two hundred and fifty quarters were consumed to ashes, burning a large number of men and women. It continued burning like that until it was day and in spite of all efforts the fire could not be brought under control before it was afternoon prayer time. The emperor, however, along with his courtiers had gone out that day and did not concern himself about that conflagration, because according to their infidelish creed that day was considered to be one of their holidays. But in his anguish he repaired to the temple and prayed with great impunity saying: "The god of heaven is angry with me, and therefore, has burned my palace; although I have done no evil act: I have neither offended my father, nor mother; nor have I acted tyrannically!" He fell ill owing to this anguish and on account of this it could not be ascertained as to in what manner the dead personage was buried and when she was taken to the burial place. Anyway there had been a good deal of elaborate ceremony.

Among other things they had prepared a large number of flags and staves of colored paper painted with devices. They had made a coffin of cardboard ten cubits long, embellished with figures of human beings and horses and camels of large size. These horses and camels were all of variegated colors wearing artificial hair and provided with saddles, bridles, etc. There were also one to two thousand trays full of all kinds of food and wines. The private horses of the deceased lady were let loose to graze freely at their will and without anybody catching them on the mountain where the sepulcher was situated. They had also posted about that sepulcher a number of maidens and eunuchs of her suite inside the grottos dug up by all of them, leaving for them provisions to last for five years so that after that period when their food got exhausted they might likewise die there. Notwithstanding all these preparations, on account of that conflagration it could not be known how she was carried there. The illness of the emperor having increased, his son used to come and sit in the audience hall. The ambassadors were dismissed, but their preparations for departure had not yet been ready. During the period that they remained in that city after being dismissed, they received no rations.

On the fifteenth of Jumada I [17 May 1421] they made their departure from Beijing, the Chinese officers being made to escort them. It was a very fine and orderly town, where it was customary to open the baggages of people with a view to examine their contents to see whatever was ordered not to be taken out of China, as for example the Chinese tea. But the envoys had obtained permits that their baggages should not be searched. Next day the envoys were given a magnificent feast using a good deal of formalities.

From this place onward they went on marching daily until they reached the river of Qaramoran on the fifth of Sha'bar [4 August]. From then on they arrived nearly every day at a new town and were given feasts, until they arrived at the city of Ganzhou on the twenty-third of Sha'bar [22 August], where they had left their animals and servants on their outward journey. They had found their men along with whatever they had left there quite safe. But there were tidings of rebellion in the neighborhood of Mongolia and the roads were given out to be unsafe. Owing to this they had to halt there for two months and a half. They departed from Ganzhou on the seventh of Dhu al-Qa'dah [3 November] and arrived at Sukju on the seventeenth of Dhu al-Qa'dah [13 November] in which place they got the news about the way. They halted there for a few days.

The envoys from Shiraz and Isfahan also reached there: Pahlwan Jamalu'd-Din, the envoy of Prince Rustam from Isfahan and Amir Hasan, the ambassador of the great Prince Ibrahim Sultan Bahadur from Shiraz. They described the unsafe character of the road as being exceedingly great, saying that they had reached by fleeing from the main road through bypaths and crossing over the mountains. Owing to this fact they halted again for some time at Sukju, until they departed from Sukju on the fifteenth of the sacred month of Muharram 825 A.H. [9 January 1422]. When they reached Qarawul the men in the fortress told them that the regulations of the Chinese people were such that just as at the time of their entry the names of their men had been taken down, so at the time of their going out also the same register would be brought for making the record, otherwise the emperor would be angry with them. They had passed out of the Chinese outpost on Friday the nineteenth of Sha'bar in the year 823 A.H. [19 August 1420] while going into that country and came out of the Chinese outpost on Friday the nineteenth of Muharram in the year 825 [13 January 1422].

By reason of their fear of rebellion of tribes they took the road of the desert. After passing out of the desert on the eighth of Rabi' I [2 March] by reason of being alarmed at conditions in Hotan they spent a few days in the deserts, reaching Hotan on the tenth of Jumada I of the abovementioned year [2 May 1422]. Setting out from there they arrived at Kashghar on the sixth of Rajab [26 June]. On the twenty-first of Rajab [11 July] they passed through the pass of Andijan. From this point some went by Samarqand route, while others proceeding by way of Frinkent and Badakhshan arrived at Hisar-i-Shadman on the twenty-first of Sha'bar [9 August]. They reached Balkh on the first of Blessed Ramadan [19 August]. Setting out from there they dismounted at the capital city of Herat (May Most High God protect it against calamities and mishaps!) on the tenth of the Blessed Ramadan in the year 825 [28 August] and attained to the threshold of his majesty the lord of sovereignty (with his grace and mercy).

Questions: How did the emperor of China present himself and his court to the ambassadors? What messages was he trying to convey to them? What can this source tell us about the customs of Ming China? What customs and features of Ming China does the author disapprove of? How does the author's profession as a painter surface in his descriptions? What incident almost led to a diplomatic crisis, and how was it resolved? What does the author report about local beliefs? Did the Chinese respect Muslim beliefs?

32. ABD-AL-RAZZAQ SAMARQANDI, *NARRATIVE OF THE JOURNEY*

Abd-al-Razzaq Samarqandi (1413–1482), like the author of the previous source, was a servant of the Timurid Empire and the ruler Shah Rukh. He too would undertake a diplomatic mission, this one to western India between 1442 and 1444—an area that was at least nominally under Shak Rukh's control—in response to an earlier embassy sent to the Timurids. His report is known for its vibrant contemporary description of Calicut, India. The author was well educated and composed several histories of his own time, among them an account of the relationship between the Timurid Empire and Ming China.

Source: ed. and trans. R. H. Major, Abd-al-Razzaq Samarqandi, "Narrative of the Journey," in *India in the Fifteenth Century* (London: Hakluyt Society, 1857), pp. 13–19 [First pagination in volume]. Persian. Revised.

Narrative of our arrival in Hindustan [India], and description of the customs and institutions of that country, and of the marvels and astonishing facts which it presents.

Calicut is a perfectly secure harbor, which, like that of Hormuz, brings together merchants from every city and from every country; in it are to be found an abundance of precious articles brought there from maritime countries, and especially from Abyssinia [Ethiopia], Sumatra and Java, and Zanzibar; from time to time ships arrive there from the shores of the House of God [Mecca] and other parts of the Hejaz, and abide at will, for a greater or longer space, in this harbor; the town is inhabited by infidels, and situated on a hostile shore. It contains a considerable number of Muslims, who are constant residents, and have built two mosques, in which they meet every Friday to offer up prayer. They have one *qadi* [judge], a priest, and for the most part they belong to the sect of Shafi'i. Security and justice are so firmly established in this city, that the most wealthy merchants bring there from maritime countries considerable cargoes, which they unload, and unhesitatingly send into the markets and the bazaars, without thinking in the meantime of any necessity of checking the account or of keeping watch over the goods. The officers of the customhouse take upon themselves the charge of looking after the merchandise, over which they keep watch day and night. When a sale is effected, they levy a duty on the goods of one-fortieth part; if they are not sold, they make no charge on them whatsoever.

In other ports a strange practice is adopted. When a vessel sets sail for a certain point, and suddenly is driven by a decree of divine providence into another roadstead, the inhabitants, under the pretext that the wind has driven it there, plunder the ship. But at Calicut, every ship, whatever place it may come from, or wherever it may be bound, when it puts into this port is treated like other vessels, and has no trouble of any kind to put up with.

His majesty, the happy Khaqan, had sent as a present for the prince of Calicut, some horses, some cloaks, some robes of cloth of gold, and some caps, similar to those distributed at the time of the Nowruz [New Year's day]; and the motive which had induced him to do so was as follows. Some ambassadors appointed by this monarch, returning from Bengal in company with the ambassadors of the latter country, having been obliged to put into Calicut, the description which they gave of the greatness and power of the Khaqan reached the ears of the sovereign of that city. He learned from authentic testimony, that the kings of all the habitable globe, of the east as well as of the west, of the land and of the sea, had sent rival ambassadors and messages, showing that they regarded the august court of that monarch as the *qibla* [direction for prayer], to which they should pay their homage, as the Kaaba, the object to which they should direct their aspirations.

A short time afterward, the king of Bengal, complaining of the invasion of Ibrahim [Shah, r. 1402–1440], Sultan of the Jaunpur sultanate, had laid his cause before the court, which is the asylum of kings, and asked for aid. The [Timurid] emperor dispatched to the country of the Jaunpur sultanate Shaykh al-Islam [chief judge] Khwajah Shihab al-Din Abu 'l-Makarim, bearer of peremptory orders addressed to the king. His message was to the effect that the king must refrain from interfering with the kingdom of Bengal, in default of which he might take the responsibility to himself of whatever the consequence should be. The prince of the Jaunpur sultanate, having received this summary ultimatum, gave up all idea of an attack upon the country of Bengal.

As soon as the sovereign of Calicut was informed of these occurrences, he prepared some presents, consisting of objects of value of different kinds, and sent an ambassador charged with a dispatch, in which he said: "In this port, on every Friday and every solemn feast day, the *khutbah* [sermon] is celebrated, according to the prescribed rule of Islam. With your majesty's permission, these prayers will be adorned and honored by the addition of your name and of your illustrious titles."

The sound of his *khutbah* has become so acceptable to the world, that all the infidels have shown themselves willing to adopt it.

These deputies, setting out in company with the ambassadors from Bengal, reached the noble court of the emperor, and the emirs [commanders] laid before that monarch the letter and the presents by which it was accompanied. The messenger was a Muslim, distinguished for his eloquence; in the course of his address he said to the prince, "If your majesty will be pleased to favor my master, by dispatching an ambassador sent especially to him, and who, in literal pursuance of the precept expressed in that verse, 'By your wisdom and by your good counsels engage men to enter on the ways of your lord,' will invite that prince to embrace the religion of Islam, and draw from his beclouded heart the bolt of darkness and error, and cause the flame of the light of faith, and the brightness of the sun of knowledge to shine into the window of his heart, it will be, beyond all doubt, a perfectly righteous and meritorious deed." The emperor acceded to this request, and gave instructions to the emirs that the ambassador should make his preparations for setting out on his journey. The choice fell upon the humble author of this work. Certain individuals, however, hazarded their denunciations against his success, imagining in their own minds that it was likely he would never return from so long a voyage. He arrived, nevertheless, in good health after three years of absence, and by that time his calumniators were no longer in the land of the living.

As soon as I landed at Calicut I saw beings such as my imagination had never depicted the like of. Extraordinary beings, who are neither men nor devils, at sight of whom the mind takes alarm; if I were to see such in my dreams, my heart would be in a tremble for many years. I have loved a beauty, whose face was like the moon; but I could never fall in love with a black woman.

The blacks of this country have the body nearly naked; they wear only bandages round the middle, called *lankoutah,* which descend from the navel to above the knee. In one hand they hold an Indian dagger, which has the brilliance of a drop of water, and in the other a shield of oxhide, which might be taken for a piece of mist. This costume is common to the king and to the beggar. As to the Muslims, they dress themselves in magnificent apparel after the manner of the Arabs, and manifest luxury in every particular. After I had had an opportunity of seeing a considerable number of Muslims and infidels, I had a comfortable lodging assigned to me, and after the lapse of three days was conducted to an audience with the king. I saw a man with his body naked, like the rest of the Indians. The sovereign of this city bears the title of Sameri [Zamorin]. When he dies it is his sister's son who succeeds him, and his inheritance does not belong to his son, or his brother, or any other of his relations. No one reaches the throne by means of the strong hand.

The infidels are divided into a great number of castes, such as the Brahmins, the yogis, and others. Although they are all agreed upon the fundamental principles of polytheism and idolatry, each sect has its peculiar customs. Among them there is a class of men, with whom it is the practice for one woman to have a great number of husbands, each of whom undertakes a special duty and fulfills it. The hours of the day and of the night are divided between them; each of them for a certain period takes up his abode in the house, and while he remains there no other is allowed to enter. The Sameri belongs to this sect.

When I obtained my audience of this prince, the hall was filled with two or three thousand Indians, who wore the costume above described; the principle personages among the Muslims were also present. After they had made me take a seat, the letter of his majesty, the happy Khaqan, was read, and they caused to pass in procession before the throne, the horse, the cloak, the garment of cloth of gold, and the cap to be worn at the ceremony of Nowruz. The Sameri showed me but little consideration. On leaving the audience I returned to my house. Several individuals, who brought with them a certain number of horses, and all sorts of things besides, had been shipped on board another vessel by order of the king of Hormuz; but being captured on the road by some cruel pirates, they were plundered of all their wealth, and narrowly escaped with their lives. Meeting them at Calicut, we had the honor to see some distinguished friends.

Thanks be to God we are not dead, and we have seen our very dear friends; we have also attained the object of our desires.

From the close of the month of Jumada II [beginning of November 1442], to the first days of Dhu al-Hijjah [beginning of April 1443], I remained in this disagreeable place, where everything became a source of trouble and weariness. During this period, on a certain night of profound darkness and unusual length, in which sleep, like an imperious tyrant, had imprisoned my senses and closed the door of my eyelids, after every sort of disquietude, I was at length asleep upon my bed of rest, and in a dream I saw his majesty, the happy Khaqan, who came toward me with all the pomp of sovereignty, and when he came up to me said: "Do not afflict yourself any longer." The following morning, at the hour of prayer, this dream recurred to my mind and filled me with joy.

Although, in general, dreams are but the simple wandering of the imagination, which are seldom realized in our waking hours, yet it does sometimes occur that the facts which are shown in sleep are afterward accomplished; and such dreams have been regarded by the most distinguished men as intimations from God. Everyone has heard of the dream of Joseph, and that of the minister of Egypt.

My reflections led me to the hope, that perhaps the morning beam of happiness was about to dawn upon me from the bosom of divine goodness, and that the night of chagrin and weariness had nearly reached its close. Having communicated my dream to some skillful men, I asked them its interpretation. Suddenly a man arrived, who brought me the intelligence that the king of Vijayanagara, who holds a powerful empire and a mighty dominion under his sway, had sent to the Sameri a delegate charged with a letter, in which he desired that he would send on to him the ambassador of his majesty, the happy Khaqan. Although the Sameri is not subject to the laws of the king of Vijayanagara, he nevertheless pays him respect, and stands in extreme fear of him; since, if what is said is true, this latter prince has in his dominions three hundred ports, each of which is equal to Calicut, and on dry land his territories comprise a space of three months' journey. The coast, which includes Calicut with some other neighboring ports, and which extends as far as Kayalpatnam, a place situated opposite the Island of Sri Lanka, otherwise called Ceylon, bears the general name of Malabar. From Calicut are vessels continually sailing for Mecca, which are for the most part laden with pepper. The inhabitants of Calicut are adventurous sailors: they are known by the name of "son of the Chinese," and pirates do not dare to attack the vessels of Calicut. In this harbor one may find everything that can be desired.

One thing alone is forbidden, namely, to kill a cow, or to eat its flesh: whosoever should be discovered slaughtering or eating one of these animals, would be immediately punished with death. So respected is the cow in these parts, that the inhabitants take its dung when dry and rub their foreheads with it—the curse of God on them!

Questions: How graciously was the diplomat received by the king of Calicut? Why did he enjoy his time there? What does the author think about the commercial life in

Calicut? What does he have to say about the religious and social customs of the local inhabitants? Is he prejudiced against black women or blackness? What evidence is there for the author's Muslim viewpoint on the world? How does the author interpret the meaning of the dream he had?

CHAPTER FIVE

JOURNEYS OF DISCOVERY AND ADVENTURE

The sources in this section have been broadly classified under the headings of discovery and adventure. The travelers discover territories that are new to them, whether it be the Americas, West Africa, or a single mountain; or they discover people, like fellow Jews. The narratives also contain adventure, such as participating in war or traveling through the dangers of the desert or sea. Some of these sources contain both of these qualities, if not others besides. While a few authors seem to love the road and the adventure inherent in travel as a modern traveler might, most stumble on adventure in pursuit of other goals. For example, two travelers start out on the pilgrimage to Mecca, but their journeys develop into something more extended and interesting. Jörg von Ehingen sets out to make a name for himself and is willing to do whatever necessary to secure that goal.

In working through these sources, readers should reflect on how the authors regard the discoveries they make along their path. To what degree do they consider the way of life of those they meet as positive or negative? How do they plan to interact with the newly discovered places and people? Readers may also contemplate what adventures the travelers experience, and how they resolve the difficult situations in which they sometimes find themselves. The reader may further think about how religion provides a rationale for adventure and a framework with which to explain the worlds into which the travelers entered.

33. *SAGA OF THE GREENLANDERS*

Vikings are most often known for their destructive raids on western Europe, but at the same time that some of their number were engaging in attacks, other Vikings were simultaneously conducting expeditions to areas new to them. Especially important among the Norse discoveries were Greenland and North America. Based on the indications in this and another source, it appears that they landed in Newfoundland, the Labrador coast, and Baffin Island, although they did not stay long. Archaeologists have found evidence of their settlement in Newfoundland. As with most saga literature, the Saga of the Greenlanders *was written long after the events it describes—it was not composed until the thirteenth century, more than two centuries after the late-tenth-century travel—but there is an historical core that had been passed down orally.*

Source: B.F. DeCosta, *A Pre-Columbian Discovery of America by the Northmen*, 2nd ed. (Albany, NY: J. Munsell's Sons, 1890), pp. 78–154. Old Norse. Revised.

There was a man named Thorvald, son of Asvald, the son of Ulf, the son of Oxen-Thorir, and he was the father of Eirik the Red. Thorvald and his son were obliged to leave Jaederen and go to Iceland, on account of manslaughter. At that time Iceland was generally colonized. They first lived in Drangar, where Thorvald died. Then Eirik married Thjodhild, daughter of Jorund and Thorbjorg Shipbreast, whom afterward Thorbjorn of Haukadale married. Eirik moved from the north, and fixed his abode in Erikstead opposite Vatnshorn. The son of Eirik and Thjodhild was named Leif.

But after Eyjolf Saur and Hrafn the Dueller's murder, Eirik was banished from Haukadale. Eirik went westward to Breidafjord and lived at Oxen Island in Eirikstead. He lent Thorgest his seat posts, and he could not get them again. He then demanded them. Then came disputes and hostility between him and Thorgest, which is told in the history of Eirik. Styr Thorgrim's son, Eyjolf of Svin Island, the sons of Thorbrand of Alptafjord, and Thorbjorn Vilfilsson pled the cause of Eirik; Thord Gellir and Thorgeir of Hitardale pled for Thorgest.

Eirik was declared outlawed by the Thing [assembly], and prepared his ship for sea in Eirik's Bay. Styr and the others went with him beyond the island. Then Eirik declared it to be his resolution to seek the land which Gunnibjorn, Ulf Crow's son, saw when driven into the western ocean, where he found Gunnbjarnar's Skerries, saying, that if he did not find the land he would return to his friends. Eirik set sail from Snaefells Glacier, and found land which from its height he called Mid Glacier, now called Blaserk. From there he sailed along the shore in a southerly direction, seeking for the nearest habitable land. The first winter he passed in Eiriks Island, near the middle of the east district. The following year he came into Eiriksfjord, where he fixed his dwelling place.

The same summer he explored the western desert, and gave names to many places. The following winter he passed on a holm [small island] opposite Hvarfs Peak, and the third year he came into Iceland and brought his ship into Breidafjord. The land which he found, he named Greenland, saying that men would be persuaded to go to a land with so good a name. Eirik stayed in Iceland that winter, and the summer after he went over to the land which he had found, and fixed his abode in Brattahlid in Eiriksfjord. Men acquainted with affairs say that this same summer in which Eirik went to settle in Greenland, thirty-five ships sailed from Breidafjord and Borgafjord, of which only fourteen arrived, and the rest were driven back or lost. This event took place fifteen winters before the Christian religion was established in Iceland. The same summer, Bishop Frederick and Thorvold Kodransson went from Iceland. Among those who emigrated with Eirik and established themselves, were Herjolf Bardarson who took Herjolfsfjord, and abode in Herjolfsness, Ketil took Ketilsfjord, Hrafn [took] Hrafnsfjord, Solvi [took] Solvadale, Helgi Thorbrandsson [took] Alptafjord, Thorbjorn Glora [took] Sigluffjord, Einar [took] Einarsfjord, Hafgrim [took] Hafgrimsfjord and Vatna District, Arnlaug [took] Arnlaugsfjord, and other men went to the west district.

Herjolf was the son of Bard, Herjolf's son, who was a relation of Ingolf the first settler of Iceland. Ingolf gave Herjolf land between Vog and Reykjaness. Herjolf dwelt first at Drepstokk. His wife was called Thorgerd, and their son was called Bjarni. He was a promising young man. In his earliest youth he had a desire to go abroad, and he soon gathered property and reputation; and was by turns a year abroad, and a year with his father. Bjarni was soon in possession of a merchant ship of his own. The last winter while he was in Norway, Herjolf prepared to go to Greenland with Eirik, and gave up his dwelling. There was a Christian man belonging to the Hebrides along with Herjolf, who composed the *Hafgerdinga Song*, in which is this refrain: "May he whose hand protects so well/The simple monk in lonely cell,/And over the world upholds the sky,/ His own blue hall, still stand me by."

Herjolf settled at Herjolfsness and became a very distinguished man. Eirik the Red took up his abode at Brattahlid, and was in great consideration, and honored by all. These were Eirik's children: Leif, Thorvald, and Thorstein; and his daughter was called Freydis. She was married to a man called Thorvard, and they dwelt at Gardar, which is now a bishop's seat. She was a haughty, proud woman; and he was but a mean man. She was much given to gathering wealth. The people of Greenland were heathen at this time.

Bjarni came over the same summer with his ship to the beach which his father had sailed abroad from in the spring. He was much struck with the news, and would not unload his vessel. When his crew asked him what he intended to do, he replied that he was resolved to follow his old custom by taking up his winter abode with his father. "So I will steer for Greenland if you will go with me." They one and all agreed to go with him. Bjarni said, "Our voyage will be thought foolish as none of us have been on the Greenland sea before." Nevertheless they set out to sea as soon as they were ready, and sailed for three days, until they lost sight of the land they left. But when the wind failed, a north wind with fog set in, and they knew not where they were sailing to; and this lasted many days. At last they saw the sun, and could distinguish the quarter of the sky; so they hoisted sail again, and sailed a whole day and night, when they made land. They spoke among themselves what this land could be, and Bjarni said that, in his opinion, it could not be Greenland. On the question, if he should sail nearer to it, he said, "It is my advice that we sail up close to the land." They did so; and they soon saw that the land was without mountains, was covered with woods, and that there were small hills inland. They left the land on the port side, and had their sheet on the land side.

Then they sailed two days and nights before they got sight of land again. They asked Bjarni if he thought this would be Greenland; but he gave his opinion that the land was no more Greenland than the land they had seen before. "For on Greenland, it is said, there are great snow mountains." They soon came near to the land, and saw that it was flat and covered with trees. Now, as the wind fell, the ship's people talked of its being advisable to make for the land; but Bjarni would not agree to it. They thought that they would need wood and water; but Bjarni said: "You are not in want of either." The men blamed him for this. He ordered them to hoist the sail, which was done. They now turned the ship's bow from the land, and sailed for three days and nights, with a fine breeze from southwest. Then they saw a third land, which was high and mountainous, and with snowy mountains. Then they asked Bjarni if he would land here; but he refused altogether: "For in my opinion this land is not what we want." Now they let the sails stand and kept along the land and saw it was an island. Then they turned from the land and stood out to sea with the same breeze; but the gale increased, and Bjarni ordered a reef to be taken in, and not to sail harder than the ship and her tackle could easily bear. After sailing three days and nights, they made, the fourth time, land; and when they asked Bjarni if he thought this was Greenland or not, Bjarni replied: "This is most like what has been told me of Greenland; and here we will take to the land." They did so, and came to the land in the evening, under a ness [promontory], where they found a boat. On this ness dwelt Bjarni's father, Herjolf; and from that it is called Herjolfness. Bjarni went to his father's, gave up seafaring, and after his father's death, continued to dwell there when at home.

It is next to be told that Bjarni Herjolfsson came over from Greenland to Norway, on a visit to Earl Eirik, who received him well. Bjarni tells of this expedition of his, in which he had discovered unknown land; and people thought he had not been very curious to get knowledge, as he could not give any account of these countries, and he was somewhat blamed on this account. Bjarni was made a courtier of the earl, and the summer after he went over to Greenland; and afterward there was much talk about discovering unknown lands. Leif, a son of Eirik the Red of Brattahild, went over to Bjarni Her-jolfsson, and bought the ship from him, and manned the vessel, so that in all, there were thirty-five men on board. Leif begged his father Eirik to go as commander of the expedition; but he excused himself, saying he was getting old, and not so able as formerly to undergo the hardship of a sea voyage. Leif insisted that he among all their relations was the most likely to have good luck on such an expedition; and Eirik consented, and rode from home with Leif, when they had got all ready for sea; but as they were getting near the ship, the horse on which Eirik was riding stumbled, and he fell from his horse and hurt his foot. "It is destined," said Eirik, "that I should never discover more lands than this of Greenland, on which we live; and now we must not run hastily into this adventure." Eirik accordingly returned home to Brattahild, but Leif, with his comrades, in all thirty-five men, rigged out their vessel.

There was a man from the south country [Germany] called Tyrkir, with the expedition. They put the ship in order, and went to sea when they were ready. They first came to the land which Bjarni had last discovered, sailed up to it, cast anchor, put out a boat, and went on shore; but there was no grass to be seen. There were large snowy mountains up the country; but all the way from the sea up to these snowy ridges, the land was one field of snow, and it appeared to them a country of no advantages. Leif said: "It will not be said of us, as it was of Bjarni, that we did not come upon the land; for I will give the country a name, and call it Helluland [Slab-land]. Then they went on board again and put to sea, and found another land. They sailed toward it, put out a boat and landed. The country was flat, and overgrown with wood; and the strand far around consisted of white sand, and low toward the sea. Then Leif said: "We will give this land a name according to its kind," and call it Mark-land [Forest-land].

Then they hastened on board, and put to sea again with the wind from the northeast, and were out for two days and made land. They sailed toward it, and came to an island which lay on the north side of the land, where they disembarked to wait for good weather. There was dew upon the grass; and, having accidentally gotten some of the dew upon their hands and put it in their mouths, they thought that they had never tasted anything so sweet as it was. Then they went on board and sailed into a sound that was between the island and a ness that went out northward from the land, and sailed westward past the ness. There was very shallow water in ebb tide, so that their ship lay dry; and there was a long way between their ship and the water. They were so desirous to get to the land that they would not wait until their ship floated, but ran to the land, to a place where a river comes out of a lake. As soon as their ship was afloat they took the boats, rowed to the ship, towed her up the river, and from there into the lake, where they cast anchor, carried their beds out of the ship, and set up their tents.

They resolved to put things in order for wintering there, and they erected a large house. They did not want for salmon, both in the river and in the lake; and they thought the salmon larger than any they had ever seen before. The country appeared to them of so good a kind, that it would not be necessary to gather fodder for the cattle for winter. There was no frost in winter, and the grass was not much withered. Day and night were more equal than in Greenland and Iceland; for on the shortest day the sun was in the sky between 9 a.m. and 3 p.m. Now when they were ready with their house building, Leif said to his fellow travelers: "Now I will divide the crew into two divisions and explore the country. Half will stay at home and do the work, and the other half will search the land; but so that they do not go farther than they can come back in the evening, and that they do not wander from each other." This they continued to do for some time. Leif changed about, sometimes with them and sometimes with those at home. Leif was a stout and strong man and of manly appearance, and was, besides, a prudent and sagacious man in all respects.

It happened one evening that a man of the party was missing, and it was the south countryman, Tyrkir. Leif was very sorry for this because Tyrkir had long been in his father's house, and he loved Tyrkir in his childhood. Leif blamed his comrades very much, and proposed to go with twelve men on an expedition to find him; but they had gone only a short way from the station when Tyrkir came to meet them, and he was joyfully received. Leif soon perceived that his foster father was quite merry. Tyrkir had a high forehead, sharp eyes, with a small face, and was little in size and ugly; but was very dexterous in all feats. Leif said to him, "Why are you so late, my foster father, and why did you leave your comrades?" He spoke at first long in German, rolled his eyes and knit his brows; but they could not make out what he was saying. After a while, and some delay, he said in Norse, "I did not go much further than they; and yet I have something altogether new to relate, for I found vines and grapes." "Is that true, my foster father?" said Leif. "Yes, true it is," answered he, "for I was born where there was no scarcity of grapes."

They slept all night, and the next morning Leif said to his men, "Now we will have two occupations to attend to, on alternate days; namely, to gather grapes or cut vines, and to fell wood in the forest to load our vessel." This advice was followed. It is related that their stern boat was filled with grapes, and then a cargo of wood was hewn for the vessel. Toward spring they made ready and sailed away, and Leif gave the country a name from its products, and called it Vinland [Wine-land].

They now sailed into the open sea and had a fair wind until they came in sight of Greenland and the lands below the ice mountains. Then a man put in a word and said to Leif, "Why do you steer so close on the wind?" Leif replied, "I mind my helm and tend to other things too; do you notice anything?" They said that they saw nothing remarkable. "I do not know," said Leif, "whether I see a ship or a rock." They looked and saw that it was a rock. But he saw so much better than they, that he discovered men upon the rock. "Now I want," said Leif, "for us to hold to the wind, that we may come up to them if they should need help; and if they should not be friendly inclined, it is in our power to do as we please and not theirs." Now they sailed under the rock, lowered their sails, cast anchor, and put out another small boat which they had with them. Then Tyrkir asked who their leader was. He said his name was Thorir, and said he was a Norwegian. "But what is your name?" said he. Leif told his name. "Are you the son of Eirik the Red of Brattahild?" he asked. Leif said that was so. "Now I will," said Leif, "take you and all on board my ship, and as much of the goods as the ship will store." They took up this offer, and sailed away to Eiriksfjord with the cargo, and from there to Brattahild, where they unloaded the ship. Leif offered Thorir and his wife, Gudrid, and three others, lodging with himself, and offering lodging elsewhere for the rest of the people, both of Thorir's crew and his own. Leif took fifteen men from the rock, and thereafter was called Leif the Lucky. After that time Leif advanced greatly in wealth and consideration. That winter, sickness came among Thorir's people, and he himself, and a great part of his crew, died. The same winter Eirik the Red died.

This expedition to Vinland was much talked of, and Leif's brother, Thorvald, thought that the country had not been explored enough in different places. Then Leif said to Thorvald, "You may go, brother, in my ship to Vinland if you like; but I will first send the ship for the timber which Thorir left upon the rock." So it was done.

Now Thorvald made ready for his voyage with thirty men, after consulting his brother Leif. They rigged their ship, and put to sea. Nothing is related of this expedition until they came to Vinland, to the booths put up by Leif, where they secured the ship and tackle, and remained quiet all winter and lived by fishing. In the spring Thorvald ordered the vessel to be rigged, and that some men should proceed in the long boat westward along the coast, and explore it during the summer. They thought the country was beautiful and well wooded, the distance small between the forest and the sea, and the beach full of white sand. There were also many islands and very shallow water. They found no abode for man or beast, but on an island far toward the west, they found a grain barn constructed of wood. They found no other traces of human work, and came back in the autumn to Leif's booths.

The following spring Thorvald, with his merchant ship, proceeded eastward, and toward the north along the land. Opposite to a cape they met bad weather, and drove upon the land and broke the keel, and remained there a long time to repair the vessel. Thorvald said to his companions: "We will stick up the keel here upon the ness, and call the place Kjalarness," which they did. Then they sailed away eastward along the country, entering the mouths of the bays, to a point of land which was everywhere covered with woods. They moored the vessel to the land, laid out gangways to the shore, and Thorvald, with all his ship's company, landed. He said, "Here it is so beautiful, and I would willingly set up my abode here."

They afterward went on board, and saw three humps upon the sand within the point, and went to them and found there were three skin boats with three men under each boat. They divided their men and took all of them prisoners, except one man, who escaped with his boat. They killed eight of them, and then went to the point and looked about them. Within this bay they saw several humps, which they took to be habitations. Then a great drowsiness came upon them and they could not keep themselves awake, but all of them fell asleep.

A sudden scream came to them, and they all awoke; and mixed with the scream they thought they heard the words: "Awake, Thorvald, with all your comrades, if you will save your lives. Go on board your ship as fast as you can, and leave this land without delay." In the same moment an innumerable multitude, from the interior of the bay, came in skin boats and laid themselves alongside. Then said Thorvald, "We will put up our war screens along the gunwales and defend ourselves as well as we can, but not use our weapons much against them." They did so accordingly. The Skraelings [Indigenous peoples] shot at them for a while, and then fled away as fast as they could. Then Thorvald asked if anyone was wounded, and they said nobody was hurt. He said: "I have a wound under the arm. An arrow flew between the gunwale and the shield under my arm: here is the arrow, and it will be my death wound. Now I advise you to make ready with all speed to return; but you will carry me to the point which I thought would be so convenient for a dwelling. It may be said that it was true what I said, that here would I dwell for a while. You will bury me there, and place a cross at my head and one at my feet, and call the place Krossaness." Christianity had been established in Greenland at this time; but Eirik the Red was dead before Christianity was introduced. Now Thorvald died, and they did everything as he had ordered. Then they went away in search of their fellow voyagers, and they related to each other all the news. They remained in their dwelling all winter, and gathered vines and grapes, and put them on board their ships. Toward spring, they prepared to return to Greenland, where they arrived with their vessel, and landed at Eiriksfjord, bringing heavy tidings to Leif.

In the meantime it had happened in Greenland that Thorstein of Eiriksfjord had married and taken as a wife Gudrid, the daughter of Thorir, who had been married, as before related, to Thorir, the Eastman. Thorstein Eiriksson was eager now to go to Vinland for his brother Thorvald's body. He rigged out the same vessel and chose an able and stout crew. He had with him twenty-five men and his wife Gudrid, and as soon as they were ready he put to sea. They quickly lost sight of the land. They drove about on the ocean the whole summer without knowing where they were, and in the first week of winter they landed at Lysufjord in Greenland, in the western settlement. Thorstein looked for lodgings for his men and got his whole ship's crew accommodated, but not himself and wife, so that for some nights they had to sleep on board. At that time Christianity was but recent in Greenland.

One day, early in the morning, some men came to their tent and the leader asked them what people were in the tent? Thorstein replies, "Two; who is it that asks?" "Thorstein," was the reply, "and I am called Thorstein the Black, and it is my errand here to offer you and your wife lodging beside me." Thorstein said that he would speak to his wife about it, and as she gave her consent he agreed to it. "Then I will come for you tomorrow with my horses, for I do not want means to entertain you; but few care to live in my house; I and my wife live lonely, and I am very gloomy. I have also a different religion from yours, although I think the one you have the best."

Now the following morning he came for them with horses, and they took up their abode with Thorstein the Black, who was very friendly toward them. Gudrid had a good outward appearance and was knowledgeable, and understood well how to behave with strangers. Early in the winter a sickness prevailed among Thorstein Eiriksson's people, and many of his shipmen died. He ordered that coffins should be made for the bodies of the dead and that they should be brought on board and stowed away carefully, for he said, "I will transport all the bodies to Eiriksfjord in the summer." It was not long before sickness broke out in Thorstein the Black's house, and his wife, who was called Grimhild, fell sick first. She was very stout and as strong as a man, but yet she could not bear up against the illness. Soon after Thorstein Eiriksson also fell sick and they both lay ill in bed at the same time; but Grimhild, Thorstein the Black's wife, died first.

When she was dead, Thorstein went out of the room for a skin to lay over the corpse. Then Gudrid said, "My dear Thorstein, be not long away," which he promised. Then said Thorstein Eiriksson, "Our housewife is wonderful, for she raises herself up with her elbows moves herself forward over the bedframe, and is feeling for her shoes." In the same moment, Thorstein the Black came back, and instantly, Grimhild laid herself down, so that it made every beam that was in the house crack. Thorstein now made a coffin for Grimhild's corpse, removed it outside, and buried it. He was a stout and strong man, but it required all his strength to remove the corpse from the house. Now Thorstein Eiriksson's illness increased on him, and he died, which Gudrid his wife took with great grief. They were all in the room, and Gudrid had set herself upon a stool before the bench on which her husband Thorstein's body lay. Now Thorstein the Black took Gudrid from the stool in his arms, and set himself with her on a bench just opposite to Thorstein's body, and spoke much with her. He consoled her, and promised to go with her in summer to Eiriksfjord, with her husband Thorstein's corpse, and those of his crew. "And," said he, "I will take with me many servants to console and assist." She thanked him for this.

Thorstein Eiriksson then raised himself up and said, "Where is Gudrid?" And three times he said this; but she was silent. Then she said to Thorstein the Black, "Will I give answer or not?" He told her not to answer. Then went Thorstein the Black across the room, and sat down in a chair, and Gudrid set herself on his knee; and Thorstein the Black said: "What will you make known?" After a while the corpse replied, "I wish to tell Gudrid her fate beforehand, that she may be the better able to bear my death; for I have come to a blessed resting place. This I have now to tell you, Gudrid, that you will be long married to an Icelandic man, and you will live long together and from you will descend many men, brave, gallant, and wise, and a well-pleasing race of posterity. You will go from Greenland to Norway, and from there to Iceland, where you will dwell. Long will you live together, but you will survive him; and then you will go abroad, and go southward, and will return to your home in Iceland. And there must a church be built, and you must remain there and be consecrated a nun, and there end your days."

And then Thorstein sank backward, and his corpse was put in order and carried to the ship. Thorstein the Black did all that he had promised. He sold in spring his land and cattle, and went with Gudrid and all her goods; made ready the ship, got men for it, and then went to Eiriksfjord. The body was buried at the church. Gudrid went to Leif's at Brattahild, and Thorstein the Black took his abode in Eiriksfjord, and dwelt there as long as he lived; and was reckoned an able man.

That same summer came a ship from Norway to Greenland. The man was called Thorfinn Karlsefni who steered the ship. He was a son of Thord Horsehead, a son of Snorri, the son of Thord of Hofdi. Thorfinn Karlsefni was a man of great wealth, and was in Brattahild with Leif Eiriksson. Soon he fell in love with Gudrid, and courted her, and she referred to Leif to answer for her. Afterward she was betrothed to him, and their wedding was held the same winter.

At this time, as before, much was spoken about a Vinland voyage; and both Gudrid and others persuaded Karlsefni much to [undertake] that expedition. Now this expedition was resolved upon, and they got ready a crew of sixty men and five women; and then they made the agreement, Karlsefni and his people, that each of them should have equal share in what they made of gain. They had with them all kinds of cattle, having the intention to settle the land, if they could. Karlsefni asked Leif for his houses in Vinland, but he said he would lend them, not give them. Then they put to sea with the ship, and came to Leif's houses safe, and carried up their goods. They soon had in hand a great and good prize, for a whale had been driven on shore, both large and excellent. They went to it and cut it up, and had no want of food. Their cattle went up into the land; but soon they were unruly, and gave trouble to them. They had one bull with them. Karlsefni let wood be felled and hewed for shipping it, and had it laid on a rock to dry. They had all the good of the products of the land, which were these: both grapes and wood, and other products.

After that first winter, and when summer came, they were aware of Skraelings being there; and a great troop of men came out of the woods. The cattle were near to them, and the bull began to bellow and roar very load. With that the Skraelings were frightened, and made off with their bundles, and these were of furs and sables and all sorts of skins. And they turned and wanted to go into the houses, but Karlsefni defended the doors. Neither party understood the language of the other. Then the Skraelings took their bundles and opened them, and wanted to have weapons in exchange for them, but Karlsefni forbade his men to sell weapons. Next he adopted this plan with them, that he told the women to carry out milk and dairy products to them. When they saw these things, they would buy them and nothing else. Now the trade for the Skraelings was such that they carried away their winnings in their stomachs; and Karlsefni and his comrades got both their bags and skin goods, and so they went away.

Next is to be told that Karlsefni let a good strong fence be made around the habitation, and strengthened it for defense. At this time Gudrid, Karlsefni's wife, gave birth to a male child, and the child was called Snorri. In the beginning of the next winter, came the Skraelings again to them, and in much greater numbers than before, and with the same kind of wares. Then said Karlsefni to the women, "Now you will carry out the same kind of food as was best liked the last time, and nothing else." Then they saw that they threw their bundles in over the fence, while Gudrid sat in the door within, by the cradle of Snorri, her son. Then came a shadow to the door, and a woman went in with a black skirt on, rather short, with a band around her head; clear, yellow hair; pale, with large eyes, so large that none ever saw such eyes in a human head. She went to where Gudrid was sitting, and said: "What are you called?" "I am called Gudrid; and what are you called?" "I am called Gudrid," said she. Then the goodwife, Gudrid, put out her hand to her, that she might sit down beside her. At the same time Gudrid heard a great noise, and the woman had vanished. At that same time one of the Skraelings was killed by one of Karlsefni's house men, because he was about to take one of their weapons; and they made off as soon as possible, leaving behind them goods and clothes. No one had seen this woman but Gudrid.

"Now," says Karlsefni, "we must be cautious, and take counsel; for I think they will come the third time with hostility and many people. We will now take the plan, that ten men go out to the ness and show themselves there, and the rest of our men will go into the woods and make a clearance for our cattle against the time the enemy comes out of the forest; and we will take the bull before us, and let him go in front." So it happened that at the place where they were to meet, there was a lake on the one side, and the forest on the other. The plan which Karlsefni had laid down was adopted. The Skraelings came to the place where Karlsefni proposed to fight; and there was a battle there, and many of the Skraelings fell. There was one stout, handsome man among the Skraeling people, and Karlsefni thought that he must be their chief. One of the Skraelings had taken up an ax and looked at it a while, and wielded it against one of his comrades and cut him down, so that he fell dead instantly. Then the stout man took the ax, and threw it into the sea as far as he could. They then fled to the woods as fast as possible, and so ended the fight.

Karlsefni stayed there with his men the whole winter; but toward the spring he made known that he would not stay there any longer and would return to Greenland. Now they prepared for their voyage and took many goods—vines, grapes, and skin wares. They put to sea, and their ship came to Eiriksfjord, and they there passed the winter.

Now the conversation began again to turn to a Vinland voyage, as the expedition was both gainful and honorable. The same summer that Karlsefni returned from Vinland, a ship arrived in Greenland from Norway. Two brothers commanded the ship, Helgi and Finnbogi; and they remained that winter in Greenland. The brothers were of Icelandic descent, from the Eastfjords. Freydis, Eirik's daughter, came home from Garda, and went to the abode of Finnbogi and Helgi, and proposed to them that they should go to Vinland with their vessel, and splitting with her all the goods they could get there. They agreed to this.

Then she went to the abode of her brother Leif, and asked him to give her the houses he had built in Vinland. He answered as before, that he would lend, but not give the houses. It was agreed upon between the brothers and Freydis, that each should have thirty fighting men, besides women. But Freydis broke this, and had five men more, and concealed them. The brothers knew nothing of it until they arrived in Vinland. They went to sea, and had agreed beforehand to sail in company, if they could do so. The difference was little, although the brothers came a little earlier, and had carried up their baggage to Leif's houses. When Freydis came to the land, her people cleared the ship, and carried her baggage up to the house. Then said Freydis: "Why are you carrying your things in here?" "Because we thought," said they, "that the whole of the agreement with us should be held." She said, "Leif lent the houses to me, not to you." Then said Helgi, "In evil, we brothers cannot strive with you," and bore out their luggage and made a shed, and built it farther from the sea, on the borders of a lake, and set all about it in order.

Freydis had trees cut down for her ship's cargo. Now winter set in, and the brothers proposed to have some games for amusement to pass the time. So it was done for a time, until discord came among them, and the games were given up, and none went from one house to the other; and things went on so during a great part of the winter. It happened one morning that Freydis got out of her berth, and put on her clothes, but not her shoes; and the weather was such that much dew had fallen. She took the cloak of her husband over her, and went out, and went to the house of the brothers, and to the door.

A man had gone out a little before and left the door behind him, half shut. She opened the door, and stood in the doorway a little, and was silent. He said: "What do you want here, Freydis?" She said, "I want you to get up and go out with me, for I would speak with you." He did so; they went to a tree that was lying under the eaves of the hut and sat down. "How do you like this place?" said she. He said, "The country, I think, is good, but I do not like this quarrel that has arisen among us for I think there is no cause for it." "You are right," says she, "and I think so too, and it is my errand to your dwelling that I want to buy the ship of your brothers as your ship is larger than mine and I would leave from here." "I will let it be so," he said, "if that will please you." Now they parted so and she went home, and Finnbogi to his bed.

She went up into her berth and with her cold feet awakened Thorvard, who asked why she was so cold and wet. She answered with great warmth, "I went to these brothers," said she, "to treat about their ship, for I want a larger ship, and they took it so ill that they struck and abused me. And you, useless man, will never avenge my affront or your own. Now must I feel that I am away from Greenland, but I will separate from you if you do not avenge this." Then he could not bear her reproaches and told his men to rise as fast as possible and take their weapons. They did so and went to the huts of the brothers and went in as they lay asleep and seized them all, bound them, and led them out bound, one after the other, and Freydis had each of them put to death as he came out. Now all the men were killed, but the women were left and nobody would kill them. Then said Freydis, "Give me an ax in my hand." This was done, and she turned on those five women and did not give over until they were all dead.

Now they returned to their own hut after this evil deed, and the people could only observe that Freydis thought she had done exceedingly well, and she said to her comrades, "If it be our lot to return to Greenland I will take the life of the man who speaks of this affair, and we will say that we left them here when we went away." Now they got ready the ship in early spring, which had belonged to the brothers, with all the goods they could get on that the ship would carry, sailed out to sea, and had a good voyage, and the ship came early in the summer to Eiriksfjord. Karlsefni was there still and had his ship ready for sea, but waited a wind; and it was a common saying that never a richer ship sailed from Greenland than that which he steered.

Questions: How did the Norse create the names that they gave to the places they found? What led one group of them to arrive in the Americas, and what did they think about this new land? Why was Bjarni criticized for his trip into this territory? What were relations between the Indigenous peoples and the Norse like? How does the supernatural intrude into mundane life in this saga? What kind of role did women play in the expeditions to the Americas?

34. NASIR-I KHUSRAW, *BOOK OF TRAVELS*

Nasir-i Khusraw (1003–1088) was born in what today is Tajikistan, and he received a well-rounded education in the Qur'an, literature, science, and philosophy. Before undertaking his travel, he was an economic minister to the Seljuk Turks, but, after receiving a vision, he decided to depart on pilgrimage to the Muslim holy cities of Mecca and Medina. Most of his travelogue, however, focused on Muslim countries of the Mediterranean, and in particular Palestine and Egypt. This source has proved useful in presenting the state of the Muslim world and its international, multicultural flavor on the eve of the Crusades, after which it was fundamentally changed. The author is also admired for the beauty of his poetry.

Source: trans. Wheeler M. Thackston, Nasir-i Khusraw, *Nasir-i Khusraw's Book of Travels: Safarnamah* (Costa Mesa, CA: Mazda Publishers, 2001), pp. 83–88, 106–27 [English pages only]. Persian.

To the south of this city [Aswan] is a mountain, and the river Nile comes out of a defile in the mountain. It is said that boats can proceed no farther up the river because the water flows through narrow defiles and large boulders. Four leagues from the city is the province of Nubia [modern Sudan], the population of which is all Christian. The king of this province continually sends gifts to the sultan of Egypt and makes treaties so that Egyptian soldiers will not enter his land and molest the populace. The city of Aswan is very strong lest anyone attack from the direction of Nubia. There is a permanent garrison stationed there to defend the city and province. Opposite the city in the middle of the Nile is an island, which is like a garden, with date groves, olives, and other trees and crops irrigated by waterwheels. There I remained for twenty-one days because there was a large desert before us to cross and two hundred leagues to the shore. It was the time for returning pilgrims to be arriving by camel. We waited until the camels were returned before hiring one, and then we set off.

While in Aswan, I came to know a man called Abu-Abdullah Muhammad ibn Falij. He was a pious and righteous man and knew something about logic. He helped me to hire a camel, to inspect our traveling companions, etc. I got a camel for one and a half dinars [gold coins] and set forth on the fifth of Rabi' I 442 [28 July 1050].

Having gone eight leagues southeast, we came to a station called Dayqa, which is in a valley in the desert and surrounded on two sides by wall-like mountains. Between the two is an open space one hundred cubits wide where a well had been dug; the water was plentiful but not very good. Past this place there are five days of desert with no water whatsoever, so each person had to draw a jar of water. Next we came to a station called Hawdish, which is a stone mountain with two holes from which water flows. The water stays in a pool and is fresh, but someone has to go inside one of the holes to bring out water for the camels. It had been seven days since the camels had been watered or fed, since there had been no water or pasturage. The camels stopped once every twenty-four hours, from the time the sun got hot in the day until the afternoon prayer, and they proceeded the rest of the day and night. The stopping places are all known, because you cannot stop just anywhere, since there might not be anything to make a fire with, and only in stopping places can camel dung be found to burn for cooking. It was almost as though the camels themselves knew that if they poked along they would die of thirst; they did not need to be driven and, setting their own direction, went of their own accord, although there was no trace whatsoever of a road. Always headed east, there were stretches of fifteen leagues with little water, only brackish, and stretches of thirty and forty leagues with no water at all.

On the twentieth of Rabi' I 442 [12 August 1050] we reached the town of Aydhab, having traveled from Aswan an estimated two hundred leagues in fifteen days.

The town of Aydhab is situated by the sea and has a Friday mosque and a population of some five hundred. It belongs to the sultan of Egypt and is a customs station for ships coming from Abyssinia [Ethiopia], Zanzibar, and the Yemen. From there goods are transported by camel across the desert, the same way we had come, to Aswan and from there by boat to Cairo.

To the right of this town, facing the *qibla* [direction for prayer], is a mountain beyond which is a large desert with many herbivorous animals and people called the Bajawis. This nation has no religion and has had no prophet or spiritual leader because they are so far from civilization. They inhabit a desert more than one thousand leagues long and three hundred wide. In all this expanse there are not more than two small hamlets, one called Bahr al-Na'am and the other Aydhab. The desert runs lengthwise from Egypt to Abyssinia, which is from north to south, and across from the province of Nubia to the Red Sea, from west to east. This nation, the Bajawis, who live in this desert, are not a bad people and do not steal or make raids but tend their flocks. Muslims and others, however, kidnap their children and take them to sell in the cities of Islam.

The Red Sea is a gulf that splits off from the ocean at Aden and goes northward to the hamlet of Qulzum. Everywhere on the coast of this gulf they call the sea by the name of that place. For example, at Qulzum they call it the Qulzum Sea, at Aydhab they call it the Aydhab Sea, and at Bahr al-Na'am they call it the Bahr al-Na'am Sea. More than three hundred islands are said to be in the Red Sea, and ships bring oil and dried curds from there. There are said to be many cows and sheep on those islands, and the inhabitants are said to be Muslims, some belonging to Egypt and others to the Yemen.

In the hamlet of Aydhab there is no water from wells or springs, only rainwater. When rain fails, the Bajawis bring water to sell. During the three months we were there, we bought water at the rate of one or two dirhems [silver coins or their weight] a jug. As the wind was northerly and we needed a southerly wind, the ship could not sail.

When the people saw me, they asked me to preach to them. I obliged and acted as a preacher until the winds changed and the boat could sail north and from there on to Jeddah. They said that nowhere were such good camels to be had as in that desert, and they are exported even to Egypt and the Hejaz.

In the town of Aydhab a man whose word I trust told me that once a ship set out from that town for the Hejaz carrying camels for the emir [commander or ruler] of Mecca. One of the camels died so it was thrown overboard. Immediately a fish swallowed it whole, except for one leg that stuck a bit out of the fish's mouth. Then another fish came and swallowed whole the fish that had swallowed the camel. "That fish is called *qarsh*," he said.

While in Aswan I had a friend, as I have said before, named Abu-Abdullah Muhammad ibn Falij. For my arrival in Aydhab he had written a letter to an agent friend he had there to the effect that he should give me whatever I required and write him to that effect so that he could settle the account. As I had been in Aydhab for three months, and everything I had was spent, of necessity I presented myself to that person with the letter. He acted very politely and said, "Oh yes, I am holding a great deal of his money. You may just sign for any amount you require." I was surprised at Muhammad Falij's generosity, that, with no prior dealing with me, he should be so kind. Had I been a rogue and of a mind to do such a thing, I could have taken a great sum of money from him by means of that letter. Anyhow, I took one hundred maunds of flour, which was extremely valuable there, and gave him a note in that amount. He then sent the paper I had signed to Aswan, and before I departed from Aydhab, a reply came from Muhammad Falij, saying, "That much was nothing. Give him as much as he wants from my funds there, and even if you should give him out of your own pocket, I will make it good, for the commander of the faithful Ali ibn Abi-Talib [r. 656–661] has said, 'The believer does not hold back or take advantage.'" I have included this little vignette so that my readers may know that people can rely on others, that generosity exists everywhere, and that there have been and still are noble men. . . .

Ta'if is situated on top of a mountain, and in the month of Khurdad [May–June] it was so cold that you had to sit in the sun, whereas in Mecca melons had been plentiful. The entire district of Ta'if consists of a wretched little town with a strong fortress. It has a small market and a pitiful little mosque. There is running water, and pomegranate and fig trees abound. The tomb of Abdullah ibn Abbas is there near the town. On this spot the Baghdad caliphs constructed a large mosque which incorporated the tomb into one corner, to the right of the mihrab and pulpit. Now, however, people have built houses and live there. We left Ta'if.

All along the way were mountains and rubble, and there were small fortresses and villages everywhere. In the midst of some rubble, they showed me a small ruined fortress, which the Arabs said had been Layla's house, although they tell many such strange tales. Further on, we came to a fortress called Mutar, which is twelve leagues from Ta'if. From there, we proceeded to a district called Thurayya, where there were many date palm groves in which agriculture was maintained by means of irrigation from wells with water-wheels. They told me there was no ruler or sultan in that area: each place has an independent chieftain or headman. They are a people who are robbers and murderers and constantly fight among themselves. This place is twenty-five leagues from Ta'if.

We continued on past that place and saw a fortress called Jaz'. Within half a league we passed four fortresses, the largest of which, where we stopped, was called the Bani Nusayr fortress, and it had a few date palms.

As the man from whom I had hired my camel was from Jaz', I stayed there for fifteen days, there being no *khafir* to take us on farther. The Arab tribes of that region each have a particular territory in which they graze their flocks and herds, and no stranger can enter one of these territories, since anyone who does not have a *khafir* will be captured and stripped. Therefore, there is a *khafir* from each tribe who can pass through a given territory. A *khafir* is an escort, also called *qalavuz*.

By chance, the leader of the Arabs who were ahead of us, the Bani Sawad, came to Jaz', and we took him as our *khafir*. His name was Abu-Ghanim Abs ibn al-Ba'ir, and we set out under his protection. A group of Arabs, thinking they had found "prey" (as they call all strangers), came headed toward us; but since their leader was with us, they passed without saying anything. Had he not been with us, they most certainly would have killed us.

In short, we had to remain among these people for a while because there was no *khafir* to take us further. Finally we found two men to act as *khafirs* and paid them ten dinars each to take us to the next tribe.

Among one tribe, some seventy-year-old men told me that in their whole lives they had drunk nothing but camels' milk, since there is nothing in the desert but bitter scrub eaten by the camels. They actually imagined the whole world was like this!

Thus I was taken and handed over from tribe to tribe, the entire time in constant mortal danger. God, however, willed that we get out of there alive.

In the midst of an expanse of rubble, we reached a place called Sarba, where there were mountains shaped like domes. I have never seen anything like them anywhere. They were not so high that an arrow could not have been shot to the top, and they were as bald and smooth as an egg, not the slightest crack or unevenness showing.

Along the way, whenever my companions saw a lizard they killed and ate it. The Arabs, wherever they are, milk their camels for drink. I could neither eat lizards nor drink camels' milk; therefore, wherever I saw a kind of bush that yielded small berries the size of lentils, I picked a few and subsisted on that.

After enduring much hardship and suffering great discomfort, on the twenty-third of Safar [17 July 1050] we came to Falaj, a distance of one-hundred eighty leagues from Mecca. Falaj lies in the middle of the desert and had once been an important region, but internal strife had destroyed it. The only part left inhabited when we arrived was a strip half a league long and a mile wide. Inside this area there were fourteen fortresses inhabited by a bunch of filthy, ignorant bandits. These fourteen fortresses had been divided up between two rival factions who were constantly engaged in hostilities. They claimed to be the lords of al-Raqim, mentioned in the Qur'an. They had four irrigation canals for their palm grove, and their fields were on high ground and watered from wells. They plow with camels, not oxen. As a matter of fact, I never saw a cow or ox there. They produce very little in the way of agriculture, and each man has to ration himself with ten seers of grain a day. This is baked as bread and suffices from the evening prayer until the next evening, as in the month of Ramadan, although they do eat dates during the day. I saw excellent dates there, much better than in Basra and other places. These people are extremely poverty stricken and destitute; nonetheless, they spend the whole day fighting and killing each other. They have a kind of date called *maydun* that weighs ten dirhems, the pit weighing not more than one and a half *dangs* [approximately 12 grains]. They claimed that this particular date could be kept for twenty years without spoilage. Their currency is Nishapuri gold.

I stayed in this Falaj for four months under the worst possible conditions. Nothing of this world remained in my possession except two satchels of books, and they were a hungry, naked, and ignorant people. Everyone who came to pray brought his sword and shield with him as a matter of course. They had no reason to buy books.

There was a mosque in which we stayed. I had a little red and blue paint with me, so I wrote a line of poetry on the wall and drew a branch with leaves up through the writing. When they saw it, they were amazed, and everybody in the compound gathered around to look at what I had done. They told me that if I would paint the *mihrab* [niche showing direction of prayer] they would give me a hundred maunds of dates. Now a hundred maunds of dates was a fortune for them. Once while I was there, a company of Arab soldiers came and demanded five hundred maunds of dates. They refused to give it and fought, which resulted in the death of ten people from the compound. A thousand palms were cut down, but they did not give up even ten maunds of dates. Therefore, when they offered me that much, I painted the *mihrab*, and that hundred maunds of dates was an answer to our prayers, since we had not been able to obtain any food.

We had almost given up hope of ever being able to get out of that desert, the nearest trace of civilization in any direction being two hundred leagues away through fearful, devastating desert. In all those four months, I never saw five maunds of wheat in one place. Finally, however, a caravan came from Yamama to take goat's leather to Lahsa. Goat's leather is brought from the Yemen via Falaj and sold to merchants. An Arab offered to take me to Basra, but I had no money to pay the fare. It is only two hundred leagues to Basra from there, and the hire for a camel was one dinar, whereas a good camel could be bought outright for two or three dinars. Since I had no cash with me, they took me on credit on condition that I pay thirty dinars in Basra. I was forced to agree to these terms, although I had never in my life so much as set foot in Basra!

The Arabs packed my books and seated my brother on a camel, and thus, with me on foot, we set out, headed toward the ascent of Ursa. The ground was flat, without so much as a mountain or hill, and wherever the earth was a bit harder, there was rainwater standing in pools. As these people travel night and day, without the slightest trace of a road visible, they must go by instinct.

What is amazing is that with no indication or warning, suddenly they come upon a well.

To make a long story short, in four days and night we came to Yamama, which has a large, old fortress, and outside the fortress is a town with a market containing all sorts of artisans and a fine mosque. The emirs there are Alids of old, and no one has ever been able to wrest the region from their control, since, in the first place there is not, nor has there been, a conquering ruler or king anywhere near, and, in the second, those Alids possess such might that they can mount three to four hundred horsemen. They are of the Zaydi sect, and when they stand in prayer they say, "Muhammad and Ali are the best of mankind," and, "Come to the best deed." The inhabitants of this town are Sharifis, and they have running water, subterranean irrigation canals, and many palm groves in the district. They told me that when dates are plentiful, a thousand maunds are only one dinar.

It is forty leagues from Yamama to Lahsa. During the winter it is possible to travel because potable rainwater collects in pools, but not in summer.

To reach the town of Lahsa from any direction, you have to cross vast expanses of desert. The nearest Muslim city to Lahsa that has a ruler is Basra, and that is one hundred and fifty leagues away. There has never been a ruler of Basra, however, who has attempted an attack on Lahsa.

All of the town's outlying villages and dependencies are enclosed by four strong, concentric walls made of reinforced mud brick. The distance between these walls is about a league, and there are enormous wells inside the town, each the size of five millstones around. All the water of the district is put to use so that none goes outside the walls. A really splendid town is situated inside the fortifications, with all the appurtenances of a large city, and there are more than twenty thousand soldiers.

They said that the ruler had been a *sharif* [Muslim religious leader] who prevented the people from practicing Islam and relieved them of the obligations of prayer and fasting by claiming that he was the ultimate authority on such matters. His name was Bu-Sa'id, and when you ask the townspeople what sect they belong to, they say they are Busa'idis. They neither pray nor fast, but they do believe in Muhammad and his prophecy. Bu-Sa'id told them that he would come among them again after his death, and his tomb, a fine shrine, is located inside the city. He directed that six of his [spiritual] sons should maintain his rule with justice and equity and without dispute among themselves until he should come again. Now they have a huge palace that is the seat of state and a throne that accommodates all six kings in one place, and they rule in complete accord and harmony. They have also six viziers, and when the kings are all seated on their throne, the six viziers are seated opposite on a bench. Thus all affairs are handled in mutual consultation. At the time I was there they had thirty thousand Zanzibari and Abyssinian slaves working in the fields and orchards.

They take no tax from the peasantry, and whenever anyone is stricken by poverty or contracts a debt, they take care of his needs until the debtor's affairs are cleared up. And if anyone is in debt to another, the creditor cannot claim more than the amount of the debt. Any stranger to the city who possesses a craft by which to earn his livelihood is given enough money to buy the tools of his trade and establish himself, when he repays however much he was given. If anyone's property or implements suffer loss and the owner is unable to undertake necessary repairs, they appoint their own slaves to make the repairs and charge the owner nothing. The rulers have several gristmills in Lahsa where the citizenry can have their grain ground into flour for free, and the maintenance of the buildings and the wages of the miller are paid by the rulers. The rulers are called simply "lord" and the viziers "counsel."

There was once no Friday mosque in Lahsa, and the sermon and congregational prayer were not held. A Persian man, however, named Ali ibn Ahmad, who was a Muslim, a pilgrim, and very wealthy, did build a mosque in order to provide for pilgrims who arrived in the city.

Their commercial transactions are carried out in lead tokens, which are kept in wrappers, each of which is equivalent to six thousand dirhem-weights. When paying for something, they do not even check the wrappers but take them as they are. No one takes this currency outside, however. They also weave fine scarves that are exported to Basra and other places.

They do not prevent anyone from performing prayers, although they themselves do not pray. The ruler answers most politely and humbly anyone who speaks to him, and wine is not indulged in.

A horse outfitted with collar and crown is kept always tied close by the tomb of Bu-Sa'id, and a watch is continually maintained day and night for such time as he should rise again and mount the horse. Bu-Sa'id said to his sons, "When I come again among you, you will not recognize me. The sign will be that you strike my neck with my sword. If it be me, I will immediately come back to life." He made this stipulation so that no one else could claim to be him.

In the time of the Baghdad caliphs one of the rulers attacked Mecca and killed a number of people who were circumambulating the Kaaba at the time. They removed the Black Stone from its corner and took it to Lahsa. They said that the stone was a "human magnet" that attracted people, not knowing that it was the nobility and magnificence of Muhammad that drew people there, for the stone had lain there for long ages without anyone paying any particular attention to it. In the end, the Black Stone was bought back and returned to its place.

In the city of Lahsa they sell all kinds of animals for meat, such as dog, cat, donkey, cow, sheep, and so on, and the head and skin of whatever animal it is are placed next to the meat so that the customer will know what he is buying. They fatten up dogs, just like grazed sheep, until they are too heavy to walk, and then they are slaughtered and eaten.

Seven leagues east of Lahsa is the sea. In this sea is the island of Bahrain, which is fifteen leagues long. There is a large city there and many palm groves. Pearls are found in the sea thereabouts, and half of the divers' take belongs to the sultan of Lahsa. South of Lahsa is Oman, which is on the Arabian peninsula, but three sides face desert that is impossible to cross. The region of Oman is eighty leagues square and tropical. Coconuts, which they call *nargel*, grow there. Directly east of Oman across the sea are Kish and Mukran. South of Oman is Aden, while in the other direction is the province of Fars.

There are so many dates in Lahsa that animals are fattened on them and at times more than one thousand maunds are sold for one dinar. Seven leagues north of Lahsa is a region called Qatif, where there is also a large town and many date palms.

An Arab emir from there once attacked Lahsa, where he maintained siege for a year. One of the fortification walls he captured and wrought much havoc, although he did not obtain much of anything. When he saw me, he asked whether or not it was in the stars for him to take Lahsa, as they were irreligious. I told him what was expedient for me to say, since, in my opinion, the Bedouins [nomadic Arabs] and people of Lahsa were as close as anyone could be to irreligion, there being people there who never performed ritual ablutions from one year to the next. What I record is told from my own experience and not from false rumors, since I was there among them for nine consecutive months, and not at intervals.

I was unable to drink their milk, and whenever I asked for water to drink they offered me milk instead. As I did not take the proffered milk and asked for water, they would say, "Wherever you see water, ask for it there!"; in all their lives they had never seen a bath or running water.

Now let me return to my story. Having set out for Basra from Yamama, we encountered some way stations with water and others with no water. On the twentieth of Sha'ban 443 [27 December 1051] we arrived in Basra.

The city has a large wall, except for the portion that faces the water, where there is no wall. The water here is all marsh, the Tigris and Euphrates coming together at the beginning of the Basra district, and when the water of the Hawiza joins the confluence, it is called Shatt al-Arab. From this Shatt al-Arab, two large channels have been cut, between the mouths of which is a distance of one league, running in the direction of the *qibla* for four leagues, after which they converge and run another one league to the south. From these channels numerous canals have been dug in all directions among palm groves and orchards. The higher of these two channels, the one that is northeast, is called the Ma'qil channel, whereas the southwestern one is called the Ubulla channel. These two channels form an enormous rectangular "island," on the shortest side of which Basra is situated. To the southwest of Basra is open plain that supports neither settlement nor agriculture. When I arrived, most of the city lay in ruins, the inhabited parts being greatly dispersed, with up to half a league from one quarter to another. Nonetheless, the walls were strong and well kept, the populace numerous, and the ruler with plenty of income. At that time, the emir of Basra was the son of Aba-Kalijar the Daylamite, king of Fars. His vizier was a Persian, Abu-Mansur Shahmardan by name.

Every day there are three markets in Basra. In the morning commerce is held at a place called the Khuza'a Market; in the middle of the day at Uthman's Market; and at the end of the day at the Flintmakers' Market. The procedure at the market is as follows: you turn over whatever you have to a moneychanger and get a draft in return; then you buy whatever you need, deducting the price from the moneychanger's draft. No matter how long you stayed in the city, you would never need anything more than a moneychanger's draft.

When we arrived we were as naked and destitute as madmen, for it had been three months since we had unloosed our hair. I wanted to enter a bath in order to get warm, the weather being chilly and our clothing scant. My brother and I were clad only in old lungis [garment wrapped around the waist] with a piece of coarse fabric on our back to keep out the cold. "In this state who would let us into a bath?" I asked. Therefore, I sold a small satchel in which I kept my books and wrapped the few rusty dirhems I had received in a piece of paper to give the bath attendant, thinking that he might give us a little while longer in the bath in order for us to remove the grime from our bodies. When I handed him the coins, he looked at us as though we were madmen and said, "Get away from here! People are coming out of the bath." As he would not allow us in, we came away humiliated and in haste. Even the children who were playing at the bathhouse door thought we were madmen and chased after us, throwing stones and yelling. We retired into a corner and reflected on the state of the world.

Now, as we were in debt to the camel driver for thirty dinars, we had no recourse save the vizier of the king of Ahwaz, Abu 'l-Fath Ali ibn Ahmad, a worthy man, learned in poetry and *belles-lettres,* and very generous, who had come to Basra with his sons and retinue and taken up residence but who, at present, had no administrative position. Therefore, I got in touch with a Persian, also a man of learning, with whom I had some acquaintance and who had entrée to the vizier but who was also in straightened circumstances and totally without means to be of assistance to me. He mentioned my situation to the vizier, and as soon as he heard, he sent a man with a horse for me to come to him just as I was. Too ashamed of my destitution and nakedness, I hardly thought it fitting to appear before him, so I wrote a note of regret, saying that I would come to him later. I had two reasons for doing this: one was my poverty, and the other was, as I said to myself, that he now imagines that I have some claim to being learned, but when he sees my note he will figure out just what my worth is so that when I go before him I need not be ashamed.

Immediately he sent me thirty dinars to have a suit of clothing made. With that amount I bought two fine suits and on the third day appeared at the vizier's assembly. I found him to be a worthy, polite, and scholarly man of pleasant appearance, humble, religious, and well spoken. He had four sons, the eldest of whom was an eloquent, polite, and reasonable youth called Ra'is Abu-Abdullah Ahmad ibn Ali ibn Ahmad. Not only a poet and administrator, he was wise and devout beyond his youthful age. We were taken in and stayed there from the first of Sha'ban until the middle of Ramadan. The thirty dinars due the Arab for our camel were paid by the vizier, and I was relieved of that burden. (May God thus deliver all his servants from the torment of debt!)

When I desired to depart he sent me off by sea with gifts and bounteous good things so that I reached Fars in ease and comfort, thanks to the generosity of that noble man. (May God delight in such noble men!)

In Basra there are thirteen shrines in the name of the commander of the faithful Ali ibn Abi-Talib, one of which is called the Bani Mazin shrine. The commander of the faithful Ali came to Basra during the Rabi' I in the year 36 [September 655], while Ayisha was waging war against him, and married Layla, the daughter of Mas'ud Nahshali. This shrine was the house of that lady, and the commander of the faithful stayed there for seventy-two days, after which he returned to Kufa. There is another shrine next to the Friday mosque called the Bab al-Tib shrine.

Inside the Friday mosque I saw a wooden post thirty cubits long and five spans, four fingers thick, although it is somewhat thicker at one end. This post is from India, and the commander of the faithful is said to have picked it up and brought it there. The other eleven shrines are in different places, and I visited them all.

After our worldly condition had taken a turn for the better and we each had on decent clothing, we went back one day to the bathhouse we had not been allowed to enter. As soon as we came through the door the attendant and everyone there stood up respectfully until we went inside, and the scrubber and servant came to attend to us. When we emerged from the bath all who were in the dressing room rose and remained standing until we had put on our clothes and departed. During that time the attendant said to a friend of his, "These are the very young men we refused admission one day." They imagined that we did not know their language, but I said in Arabic, "You are perfectly correct. We are the very ones who had old sacks tied to our backs." The man was ashamed and most apologetic.

Now these two events transpired within twenty days, and I have included the story so that everyone may know not to lament adversity brought on by fate and not to despair of the creator's mercy, for he is merciful indeed.

Every twenty-four hours the Sea of Oman flows twice, rising approximately ten ells. When high tide has been reached, it gradually ebbs, receding ten to twelve ells. The ten ells just mentioned can be seen either on a post erected at Basra or against the city walls. Where the ground is flat the tide covers an enormous area inland. The Tigris and Euphrates actually flow so calmly that in places it cannot be determined which direction the water is flowing, and when the tide floods, the river water rises for nearly forty leagues, and one would think the flow had reversed itself and the water was backing up. In other places along the coast, however, the shore it relatively steep. Where the land is flat the water covers a large area, but where it is steep less ground is taken by the tide. . . .

In short, the middle of Shawwal 443 [February 1052] we left Basra by boat. For four leagues out of Ubulla there was on both sides of the channel an uninterrupted series of gardens, orchards, kiosks, and belvederes. Tributaries of the channel, each the size of a river, opened up on each side. When we reached Shati Uthman we disembarked just opposite the city of Ubulla and stayed a while.

On the seventeenth we boarded a type of boat called *busi,* and great multitudes of people on either side called out, "O *busi,* may God speed you in safety!"

When we reached Abbadan everyone got out of the boat. Abbadan is a coastal town something like an island because the marsh splits in two there, and the only way to reach the town is by water. To the south is the sea itself, which, during high tide, comes right up to the city walls; at low tide, however, the sea recedes a little less than two leagues. Some of our party bought carpets in Abbadan and others something to eat. The next morning the ship set out again toward the north. For ten leagues the sea water was drinkable and good, since it was marsh water, the marsh flowing like a tongue out into the sea.

At dawn something like a small bird could be seen on the sea. The closer we approached the larger it appeared. When it was about one league to our left, an adverse wind came up so they dropped anchor and took down the sail. I asked what that thing was and was told that it was called a *khashab.* It consisted of four enormous wooden posts made of teak and was shaped something like a war machine, squarish, wide at the base and narrow at the top. It was about forty ells above the surface of the water and had tile and

271

stone on top held together by wood so as to form a kind of ceiling. On top of that were four arched openings where a sentinel could be stationed. Some said this *khashab* had been constructed by a rich merchant, others that a king had it made. It served two functions: first, that area was being silted in and the sea consequently becoming shallow so that if a large ship chanced to pass, it would strike bottom. At night lamps were encased in glass so that the wind would not blow them out were lit for people to see from afar and take precaution, since there was no possibility of rescue. Second, one could know the extent of the land and, if there were pirates, steer a ship away. When the *khashab* was no longer visible, another one of the same shape came into view; but this one did not have the watchtower on top, as though it had not been finished.

Next we came to Mahruban, a large coastal town with a market and fine mosque. Their only water is from rain, there being no freshwater wells or canals, although they have enough tanks and cisterns to ensure an adequate supply. Three large caravanserais [inns] have been built there, each one as strong and as tall as a fortress. I saw the name of Ya'qub ibn Layth written on the pulpit of the Friday mosque, and I asked how this had come to be. They told me that Ya'qub ibn Layth had conquered up to this town but that no other emir of Khurasan had ever had the might to do it. When I was there, the town was in the hands of the sons of Aba-Kalijar, the king of Fars. Foodstuffs and commodities all have to be brought in from outside since there is nothing but fish in the town, which serves as a customs station and port.

South along the coast are Tavva and Kazarun, but I remained in Mahruban because they said the way was not safe, since the sons of Aba-Kalijar had each rebelled against the other and had put the countryside into confusion. I was told that in Arrajan there was a great and learned man called Shaykh Sadid Muhammad ibn Abdul-Malik. When I heard this, since I was so weary of staying in that town, I wrote him a note explaining my situation and pleaded with him to get me out of there and into a safe place. Three days later thirty armed foot soldiers approached me and told me they had been sent by the *shaykh* [honorific title] to take me to Arrajan. Thus we were hospitably taken to Arrajan.

Arrajan is a large town with a population of twenty thousand, to the east of which is a river that comes from the mountains and flows to the north. Four large canals have been cut at great expense to bring water through the town and out the other side to where there are gardens and orchards of dates, oranges, citrons, and olives in abundance. The city is so constructed that for every house above ground there is also one below. Water flows through these basements and cellars so that during the summer they can be comfortable. The people there are of most every sect, and the Mu'tazilites have an imam called Abu-Sa'id of Basra, an eloquent man with some claim to knowledge of geometry and mathematics. We held discussions together on dialectic, theology, and mathematics.

We left on the first of Muharram [3 May 1052] and headed for Isfahan via the mountains. Along the way we came to a mountain with a narrow pass, said by the common people to have been cut by Bahram Gor with his sword. They call it Shamsherburid ("Sword-Cut"). There we saw a great stream that emerged on our right from a hole and then tumbled down a great height. The common people said that this water flows continuously during the summer but stops and freezes over during the winter months.

We reached Lurdaghan, which is forty leagues from Arrajan and which is the border of Fars. From there we continued on to Khan Lanjan, where I noticed the name of Toghril Beg inscribed over the gate. It was only seven leagues from there to Isfahan, and the people of Khan Lanjan were remarkably safe and secure, everyone occupied with his own business. We departed from there.

It was the eighth of Safar 444 [9 June 1052] when we reached Isfahan. It is one hundred and eight leagues from Basra to Isfahan, a city situated on a flat plain and with a delightful climate. Wherever one sinks a well ten ells into the ground, refreshing cold water comes out. The city has a high, strong wall with gates, embrasures, and battlements all around. Inside the city are courses for running water, fine tall buildings, and a beautiful and large Friday mosque. The city wall is said to be three and a half leagues long, and everything inside is in a flourishing state, as I saw nothing in ruins. There were many markets. One that I saw was only for moneychangers and contained two hundred stalls. Every market has doors and gates, as do all quarters and lanes. The caravanserais are exceptionally clean, and in one lane, called Ku-Taraz, there were fifty fine caravanserais, in each of which were retail merchants and shopkeepers. The caravan we entered with had one thousand three hundred *kharvars* of goods, yet there was no difficulty in finding space since there seemed to be no lack of room or fodder.

When Sultan Toghril Beg Abu-Talib Muhammad ibn Mikal ibn Saljuq took the city, he appointed as governor a young Nishapuri, a good administrator with a fine hand, composed, well met, a patron of learning, well spoken, and generous, called Khwaja Amid. The sultan ordered him not to levy taxes on the people for three years, and, as he followed this order, the peasantry that had fled returned home. He had been one of the bureaucrats serving under Suri.

Before our arrival there had been a great famine, but by the time we came they were harvesting barley, and one and a half maunds of wheat bread were selling for one dirhem, as were three maunds of barley bread. The people, however, were still complaining that never in this city had less than eight maunds of bread been more than one dirhem. Of all Persian-speaking cities, I never saw a finer, more commodious, or more flourishing city than Isfahan. They claimed that wheat, barley, and other grains could be left for twenty years without spoiling, although some said that before the walls had been built the air was even better than now and that it had changed with the construction of the wall so that some things would spoil. The villages, however, were said to be as good as ever.

As the caravan was not going to leave for some time, I remained in Isfahan for twenty days. On the twenty-eighth of Safar [29 June 1052] we departed and came to the village of Haythamabad. From there we reached Naïn via the desert and mountains of Mashginan, a distance of thirty leagues.

From Naïn we traveled forty-three leagues to the village of Garma in the Biaban district, which comprises some ten or twelve villages. It is warm there, and there are date trees. This region was formerly held by the Kufi-jan, but when we passed through, Prince Gilaki had seized the region from them and stationed a deputy in a small fortress in a village called Piyada in order to control the area and keep the roads safe. Whenever the Kufijan attempted banditry, Prince Gilaki's cavalry were sent to capture and kill them. It was due to the maintenance of that prince that the road was safe and the people secure. (May God keep just princes and have mercy on the souls of the departed!)

Every two leagues along this Biaban road, small towers with water tanks have been built to collect rainwater in places that are not brackish so that people will not lose their way and also so that travelers may stop off and rest for a while out of the heat and cold.

Questions: In what ways did Nasir-i Khusraw rely on the kindness of strangers in order to continue his journey? What did he admire or dislike about the people whom he met? What kinds of observations did he make about the areas he visited? What, for instance, can he tell historians about food, trade, politics, war, religion, nature, and buildings? Do you trust the accuracy of his report?

35. BENJAMIN OF TUDELA, *ITINERARY*

Benjamin of Tudela (d. 1173) is generally regarded as the greatest Jewish traveler in the Middle Ages. At some point between 1159 and 1168, he traveled extensively in the Medi-terranean world, leaving behind observations particularly focused on Jewish communities. The exact impetus for his journey is unknown: some scholars have suggested, based on his commercial interests, that Benjamin was a gem merchant; others have said that he wanted to find a community in which Jews would be freer to practice their religion than his native Spain; and yet others have thought this to be a pilgrimage. In addition to his comments on his coreligionists, Benjamin's interests in politics and economics have made him a valuable source to modern scholars.

Source: ed. and trans. Marcus N. Adler, Benjamin of Tudela, *The Itinerary of Benjamin of Tudela: Critical Text, Translation and Commentary* (London: Henry Frowde, 1907), pp. 2–8, 11–14, 20–25, 35–42. Hebrew. Revised.

I journeyed first from my native town to the city of Saragossa, and from there by way of the River Ebro to Tortosa. From there I went [on] a journey of two days to the ancient city of Tarragona with its Cyclopean and Greek buildings. The like thereof is not found among any of the buildings in the country of Sepharad [Spain]. It is situated by the sea, and two days' journey from the city of Barcelona, where there is a holy congregation, including sages, wise and illustrious men, such as R[abbi] Sesheth, R[abbi] Shealtiel, R[abbi] Solomon, and R[abbi] Abraham, son of Chisdai. This is a small city and beautiful, lying upon the seacoast. Merchants come there from all quarters with their wares, from Greece, from Pisa, Genoa, Sicily, Alexandria in Egypt, Palestine, Africa and all its coasts. From there it is a day and a half to Gerona, in which there is a small congregation of Jews. A three days' journey takes one to Narbonne, which is a city preeminent for learning; from there the Torah [Law] goes forth to all countries. Sages, and great and illustrious men, abide here. At their head is R[abbi] Kalonymos, the son of the great and illustrious R[abbi] Todros of the seed of David, whose pedigree is established. He possesses inherited property and lands given him by the ruler of the city, of which no man can forcibly dispossess him. Prominent in the community is R[abbi] Abraham, head of the academy: also R[abbi] Machir and R[abbi] Judah, and many other distinguished scholars. At the present day 300 Jews are there.

From there it is four parasangs to the city of Beziers, where there is a congregation of learned men. At their head is R[abbi] Solomon Chalafta, R[abbi] Joseph, and R[abbi] Nethanel. From there it is two days to Har Gaash, which is called Montpellier. This is a place well situated for commerce. It is about a parasang from the sea, and men come for business there from all quarters, from Edom [Christian lands], Ishmael [Muslim lands], Morocco, Lombardy, the dominion of Rome the great, from all the land of Egypt, Palestine, Greece, France, Asia, and England. People of all nations are found there doing business through the medium of the Genoese and Pisans. In the city there are scholars of great eminence, at their head being R[abbi] Reuben, son of Todros, R[abbi] Nathan, son of Zechariah, and R[abbi] Samuel, their chief rabbi, also R[abbi] Solomon and R[abbi] Mordecai. They have among them houses of learning devoted to the study of the Talmud. Among the community are men both rich and charitable, who lend a helping hand to all that come to them.

From Montpellier it is four parasangs to Lunel, in which there is a congregation of Israelites, who study the Law day and night. Here lived Rabbenu Meshullam the great rabbi, since deceased, and his five sons, who are wise, great, and wealthy, namely: R[abbi] Joseph, R[abbi] Isaac, R[abbi] Jacob, R[abbi] Aaron, and R[abbi] Asher, the recluse, who dwells apart from the world; he pores over his books day and night, fasts periodically, and abstains from all meat. He is a great scholar of the Talmud. At Lunel live also their brother-in-law R[abbi] Moses, the chief rabbi, R[abbi] Samuel the elder, R[abbi] Ulsarnu, R[abbi] Solomon Hacohen, and R[abbi] Judah the physician, the son of Tibbon, the Sephardi. The students that come from distant lands to learn the law are taught, boarded, lodged, and clothed by the congregation, so long as they attend the house of study. The community has wise, understanding, and saintly men of great benevolence, who lend a helping hand to all their brethren both far and near. The congregation consists of about 300 Jews—may the Lord preserve them.

From there it is two parasangs to Posquières [modern Vauvert], which is a large place containing about 40 Jews, with an academy under the auspices of the great Rabbi, R[abbi] Abraham, son of David, of blessed memory, an energetic and wise man, great as a talmudical authority. People come to him from a distance to learn the law at his lips, and they find rest in his house, and he teaches them. Of those who are without means he also pays the expenses, for he is very rich. The munificent R[abbi] Joseph, son of Menachem, also dwells here, and R[abbi] Beneviste, R[abbi] Benjamin, R[abbi] Abraham, and R[abbi] Isaac, son of R[abbi] Meir of blessed memory. From there it is four parasangs to the suburb Bourg de St-Gilles, in which place there are about a hundred Jews. Wise men abide there; at their head being R[abbi] Isaac, son of Jacob, R[abbi] Abraham, son of Judah, R[abbi] Eleazar, R[abbi] Jacob, R[abbi] Isaac, R[abbi] Moses, and R[abbi] Jacob, son of Rabbi Levi of blessed memory. This is a place of pilgrimage of the gentiles who come here from the ends of the earth. It is only three miles from the sea, and is situated upon the great River Rhône, which flows through the whole land of Provence. Here dwells the illustrious R[abbi] Abba Mari, son of the late R[abbi] Isaac; he is the bailiff of Count Raymond.

From there it is three parasangs to the city of Arles, which has about 200 Israelites, at their head being R[abbi] Moses, R[abbi] Tobias, R[abbi] Isaiah, R[abbi] Solomon, the chief rabbi R[abbi] Nathan, and R[abbi] Abba Mari, since deceased.

From there it is two days' journey to Marseilles, which is a city of princely and wise citizens, possessing two congregations with about 300 Jews. One congregation dwells below on the shore by the sea, the other is in the castle above. They form a great academy of learned men, among them being R[abbi]

Simeon, R[abbi] Solomon, R[abbi] Isaac, son of Abba Mari, R[abbi] Simeon, son of Antoli, and R[abbi] Jacob his brother; also R[abbi] Libero. These persons are at the head of the upper academy. At the head of the congregation below are R[abbi] Jacob Purpis, a wealthy man, and R[abbi] Abraham, son of R[abbi] Meir, his son-in-law, and R[abbi] Isaac, son of the late R[abbi] Meir. It is a very busy city upon the seacoast.

From Marseilles one can take ship and in four days reach Genoa, which is also upon the sea. Here live two Jews, R[abbi] Samuel, son of Salim, and his brother, from the city of Ceuta, both of them good men. The city is surrounded by a wall, and the inhabitants are not governed by any king, but by judges whom they appoint at their pleasure. Each householder has a tower to his house, and at times of strife they fight from the tops of the towers with each other. They have command of the sea. They build ships which they call galleys, and make predatory attacks on Edom and Ishmael and the land of Greece as far as Sicily, and they bring back to Genoa spoils from all these places. They are constantly at war with the men of Pisa. Between them and the Pisans there is a distance of two days' journey.

Pisa is a very great city, with about 10,000 turreted houses for battle at times of strife. All its inhabitants are mighty men. They possess neither king nor prince to govern them, but only the judges appointed by themselves. In this city are about 20 Jews, at their head being R[abbi] Moses, R[abbi] Chayim, and R[abbi] Joseph. The city is not surrounded by a wall. It is about six miles from the sea; the river which flows through the city provides it with ingress and egress for ships.

From Pisa it is four parasangs to the city of Lucca, which is the beginning of the frontier of Lombardy. In the city of Lucca are about 40 Jews. It is a large place, and at the head of the Jews are R[abbi] David, R[abbi] Samuel, and R[abbi] Jacob.

From there it is six days' journey to the great city of Rome. Rome is the head of the kingdoms of Christendom, and contains about 200 Jews, who occupy an honorable position and pay no tribute, and among them are officials of the pope, Alexander [III, r. 1159–1181], the spiritual head of all of Christendom. Great scholars reside here, at the head of them being R[abbi] Daniel, the chief rabbi, and R[abbi] Jechiel, an official of the pope. He is a handsome young man of intelligence and wisdom, and he has the entry of the pope's palace; for he is the steward of the house and of all that he has. He is a grandson of R[abbi] Nathan, who composed the Aruch and its commentaries. Other scholars are R[abbi] Joab, son of the chief rabbi R[abbi] Solomon, R[abbi] Menachem, head of the academy, R[abbi] Jechiel, who lives in Trastevere, and R[abbi] Benjamin, son of R[abbi] Shabbethai of blessed memory. Rome is divided into two parts by the Tiber River. In the one part is the great church which they call St-Peter of Rome. The great palace of Julius Caesar was also in Rome. There are many wonderful structures in the city, different from any others in the world. Including both its inhabited and ruined parts, Rome is about 24 miles in circumference. In the midst of it there are 80 palaces belonging to 80 kings who lived there, each called *imperator* [emperor], commencing from King Tarquin down to Nero [r. 54–68] and Tiberius [r. 14–37], who lived at the time of Jesus the Nazarene, ending with Pepin [r. 751–768], who freed the land of Sepharad from Islam, and was father of Charlemagne [r. 768–814].

There is a palace outside of Rome (said to be of Titus [r. 79–81]). The consul and his 300 senators treated him with disfavor, because he failed to take Jerusalem until after three years, though they had bidden him to capture it within two.

In Rome is also the palace of Vespasian [r. 69–79], a great and very strong building; also the Colosseum, in which edifice there are 365 sections, according to the days of the solar year; and the circumference of these palaces is three miles. There were battles fought here in olden times, and in the palace more than 100,000 men were slain, and there their bones remain piled up to the present day. The king caused to be engraved a representation of the battle and of the forces on either side facing one another, both warriors and horses, all in marble, to exhibit to the world the war of the days of old.

In Rome there is a cave which runs underground, and catacombs of King Tarmal Galsin and his royal consort who are to be found there, seated upon their thrones, and with them about a hundred royal personages. They are all embalmed and preserved to this day. In the Church of St-John in the Lateran there are two bronze columns taken from the Temple, the handiwork of King Solomon, each column being engraved "Solomon the son of David." The Jews of Rome told me that every year on the ninth of Av [commemoration of Jewish disasters] they found the columns exuding moisture like water. There also is the cave where Titus, the son of Vespasian, stored the Temple vessels which he brought from Jerusalem. There is also a cave in a hill on one bank of the River Tiber where are the graves of the ten martyrs. In front of St-John in the Lateran there are statues of Samson in marble, with a spear in his hand, and of Absalom the son of King David, and another of Constantine the Great [r. 306–324], who built Constantinople and after whom it was called. The last-named statue is of bronze, the horse being overlaid with gold. Many other edifices are there, and remarkable sights beyond enumeration.

From Rome it is four days to Capua, the large town which King Capys built. It is a fine city, but its water is bad, and the country is fever stricken. About 300 Jews live there, among them great scholars and esteemed persons, at their heads being R[abbi] Conso, his brother R[abbi] Israel, R[abbi] Zaken, and the chief rabbi R[abbi] David, since deceased. They call this district the principality.

From there one goes to Pozzuoli which is called Sorrento the Great, built by Zur, son of Hadadezer, when he fled in fear of David the king. The sea has risen and covered the city from its two sides, and at the present day one can still see the markets and towers which stood in the midst of the city. A spring issues forth from beneath the ground containing the oil which is called petroleum. People collect it from the surface of the water and use it medicinally. There are also hot-water springs to the number of about 20, which issue from the ground and are situated near the sea, and every man who has any disease can go and bathe in them and get cured. All the afflicted of Lombardy visit it in the summertime for that purpose. . . .

A three days' voyage brings one to Abydos, which is upon an arm of the sea which flows between the mountains, and after a five days' journey the great town of Constantinople is reached. It is the capital of the whole land of Javan, which is called Greece. Here is the residence of the King Emmanuel the Emperor [Manuel I Komnenos, r. 1143–1180]. Twelve ministers are under him, each of whom has a palace in Constantinople and possesses castles and cities; they rule all the land. At their head is King Hipparchus, the second in command is the *megas domesticus*, the third *dominus*, and the fourth is *megas ducas*, and the fifth is *oeconomus megalus*; the others bear names like these. The circumference of the city of Constantinople is 18 miles; half of it is surrounded by the sea, and half by land, and it is situated upon two arms of the sea, one coming from the sea of Russia, and one from the sea of Sepharad.

All sorts of merchants come here from the land of Babylon, from central Mesopotamia, from Persia, Media [northwest Iran], and all the sovereignty of the land of Egypt, from the land of Canaan, and the empire of Russia, from Hungary, Patzinakia [part of modern Romania], Khazaria [kingdom between the Caspian and Black Seas], and the land of Lombardy and Sepharad. It is a busy city, and merchants come to it from every country by sea or land, and there is none like it in the world except Baghdad, the great city of Islam. In Constantinople is the Church of Hagia Sophia, and the seat of the pope of the Greeks, since the Greeks do not obey the pope of Rome. There are also churches according to the number of the days of the year. A quantity of wealth beyond telling is brought here year by year as tribute from the two islands and the castles and villages which are there. And the like of this wealth is not to be found in any other church in the world. And in this church there are pillars of gold and silver, and lamps of silver and gold more than a man can count. Close to the walls of the palace is also a place of amusement belonging to the king, which is called the Hippodrome, and every year on the anniversary of the birth of Jesus the king gives a great entertainment there. And in that place

men from all the races of the world come before the king and queen with juggling and without juggling, and they introduce lions, leopards, bears, and wild
asses, and they engage them in combat with one another; and the same thing is
done with birds. No entertainment like this is to be found in any other land.

This king, Emmanuel, built a great palace for the rest of his government
upon the seacoast, in addition to the palaces which his fathers built, and he
called its name Blachernae. He overlaid its columns and walls with gold and
silver, and engraved on them representations of the battles before his day and
of his own combats. He also set up a throne of gold and of precious stones, and
a golden crown was suspended by a gold chain over the throne, so arranged
that he might sit underneath. It was inlaid with jewels of priceless value, and at
nighttime no lights were required, for every one could see by the light which
the stones gave forth. Countless other buildings are found in the city. From
every part of the empire of Greece tribute is brought here every year, and they
fill strongholds with garments of silk, purple, and gold. Like these storehouses
and this wealth, there is nothing in the whole world to be found. It is said that
the tribute of the city amounts every year to 20,000 gold pieces, derived both
from the rents of shops and markets, and from the tribute of merchants who
enter by sea or land.

The Greek inhabitants are very rich in gold and precious stones, and they
go clothed in garments of silk with gold embroidery and they ride horses, and
look like princes. Indeed, the land is very rich in all cloth stuffs, and in bread,
meat, and wine.

Wealth like that of Constantinople is not to be found in the whole world.
Here also are men learned in all the books of the Greeks, and they eat and
drink every man under his vine and his fig tree.

They hire from among all nations warriors called Loazim [Barbarians] to
fight with the sultan [Ghiyath al-Din] Mas'ud [r. 1134–1152], king of the Togarmim [Seljuks], who are called Turks; for the natives are not warlike, but are
as women who have no strength to fight.

No Jews live in the city, for they have been placed behind an inlet of the
sea. An arm of the Sea of Marmora shuts them in on the one side, and they are
unable to go out except by way of the sea, when they want to do business with
the inhabitants. In the Jewish quarter are about 2,000 Rabbanite [mainstream]
Jews and about 500 Karaites [Jews who only accept written, biblical traditions,
not oral ones], and a fence divides them. Among the scholars are several wise
men, at their head being the chief rabbi R[abbi] Abtalion, R[abbi] Obadiah,
R[abbi] Aaron Bechor Shoro, R[abbi] Joseph Shir-Guru, and R[abbi] Elia-
kim, the warden. And among them there are craftsmen in silk and many rich
merchants. No Jew there is allowed to ride on horseback. The one exception
is R[abbi] Solomon Hamitsri, who is the king's physician, and through whom

the Jews enjoy considerable alleviation of their oppression. For their condition is very low, and there is much hatred against them, which is fostered by the tanners, who throw out their dirty water in the streets before the doors of the Jewish houses and defile the Jews' quarter [the ghetto]. So the Greeks hate the Jews, good and bad alike, and subject them to great oppression, and beat them in the streets, and in every way treat them with rigor. Yet the Jews are rich and good, kindly and charitable, and bear their lot with cheerfulness. The district inhabited by the Jews is called Pera. . . .

Six parasangs from here is Caesarea, the Gath of the Philistines [Tell es-Safi?], and here there about 200 Jews and 200 Cuthim. These are the Jews of Shomron, who are called Samaritans. The city is fair and beautiful, and lies by the sea. It was built by Caesar, and called after him Caesarea. From there it is half a day's journey to Kako, the Keilah of scripture. There are no Jews here. From there it is half a day's journey to St-George, which is Ludd, where there lives one Jew, who is a dyer. From there it is a day's journey to Sebastiya, which is the city of Shomron [Samaria], and here the ruins of the palace of Ahab the son of Omri may be seen. It was formerly a well-fortified city by the mountainside, with streams of water. It is still a land of brooks of water, gardens, orchards, vineyards, and olive groves, but no Jews dwell here. From there it is two parasangs to Nablus, which is Sechem on Mount Ephraim, where there are no Jews; the place is situated in the valley between Mount Gerizim and Mount Ebal, and contains about 1,000 Cuthim, who observe the written law of Moses alone, and are called Samaritans. They have priests of the seed [of Aaron], and they call them Aaronim, who do not intermarry with Cuthim, but wed only among themselves. These priests offer sacrifices, and bring burnt offerings in their place of assembly on Mount Gerizim, as it is written in their law: "And you will set the blessing on Mount Gerizim" [Deuteronomy 11:29]. They say that this is the proper site of the Temple. On Passover and the other festivals they offer up burnt offerings on the altar which they have built on Mount Gerizim, as it is written in their law: "You will set up the stones on Mount Gerizim, of the stones which Joshua and the children of Israel set up at the Jordan" [Deuteronomy 27:4]. They say that they are descended from the tribe of Ephraim. And in the midst of them is the grave of Joseph, the son of Jacob our father, as it is written: "and the bones of Joseph buried they in Sechem" [Joshua 24:32]. Their alphabet lacks three [Hebrew] letters, namely He, Het, and Ayin. The letter He is taken from Abraham our father, because they have no dignity, the letter Het from Isaac, because they have no kindliness, and the letter Ayin from Jacob, because they have no humility. In place of these letters they make use of the Alef, by which we can tell that they are not of the seed of Israel, although they know the law of Moses with the exception of these three letters. They guard themselves from the defilement of the dead, of the bones of the slain, and of graves; and they remove the garments which they have worn before they go to the place of worship, and they bathe and put on fresh clothes. This is their constant practice. On Mount Gerizim are fountains and gardens and plantations, but Mount Ebal is rocky and barren; and between them in the valley lies the city of Sechem.

From the latter place it is a distance of four parasangs to Mount Gilboa, which the Christians call Mont Gilboa; it lies in a very parched district. And from there it is five [blank in source] a village where there are no Jews. From there it is two parasangs to the valley of Ajalon, which the Christians call Val-de-Luna. At a distance of one parasang is Mahomerie-le-Grand, which is Gibeon the Great; it contains no Jews.

From there it is three parasangs to Jerusalem, which is a small city, fortified by three walls. It is full of people whom the Muslims call Jacobites, Syrians, Greeks, Georgians, and Franks, and of people of all tongues. It contains a dyeing house, for which the Jews pay a small rent annually to the king, on condition that besides the Jews no other dyers be allowed in Jerusalem. There are about 200 Jews who dwell under the Tower of David in one corner of the city. The lower portion of the wall of the Tower of David, to the extent of about ten cubits, is part of the ancient foundation set up by our ancestors, the remaining portion having been built by the Muslims. There is no structure in the whole city stronger than the Tower of David. The city also contains two buildings, from one of which—the hospital—there issue forth 400 knights; and there all the sick who come there are lodged and cared for in life and in death. The other building is called the Temple of Solomon; it is the palace built by Solomon the king of Israel. Three hundred knights are quartered there, and issue from there every day for military exercise, besides those who come from the land of the Franks and the other parts of Christendom, having taken upon themselves to serve there a year or two until their vow is fulfilled. In Jerusalem is the great church called the Sepulcher, and here is the burial place of Jesus, to which the Christians make pilgrimages.

Jerusalem has four gates—the gate of Abraham, the gate of David, the gate of Zion, and the gate of Gushpat, which is the gate of Jehoshaphat, facing our ancient Temple, now called *templum domini*. Upon the site of the sanctuary Omar ben al Khataab erected an edifice with a very large and magnificent cupola, into which the gentiles [non-Jews] do not bring any image or effigy, but they merely come there to pray. In front of this place is the western wall, which is one of the walls of the Holy of Holies. This is called the Gate of Mercy, and there come all the Jews to pray before the wall of the court of the Temple. In Jerusalem, attached to the palace which belonged to Solomon, are the stables built by him, forming a very substantial structure, composed of large stones, and the like of it is not to be seen anywhere in the world. There is also visible up to this day the pool used by the priests before offering their sacrifices, and the Jews coming there write their names on the wall. The gate of Jehoshaphat leads to the valley of Jehoshaphat, which is the gathering place of the nations. Here is the pillar called Absalom's hand, and the sepulcher of King Uzziah.

In the neighborhood is also a great spring, called the waters of Siloam, connected with the brook of Kidron. Over the spring is a large structure dating from the time of our ancestors, but little water is found, and the people of Jerusalem for the most part drink the rainwater, which they collect in cisterns in their houses. From the valley of Jehoshaphat one ascends the Mount of Olives; it is the valley only which separates Jerusalem from the Mount of Olives. From the Mount of Olives one sees the Sea of Sodom, and at a distance of two parasangs from the Sea of Sodom is the pillar of salt into which Lot's wife was turned; the sheep lick it continually, but afterward it regains its original shape. The whole land of the plain and the valley of Shittim as far as Mount Nebo are visible from here.

In front of Jerusalem is Mount Zion, on which there is no building, except a place of worship belonging to the Christians. Facing Jerusalem for a distance of three miles are the cemeteries belonging to the Israelites, who in the days of old buried their dead in caves, and on each sepulcher is a dated inscription, but the Christians destroy the sepulchers, employing the stones from there in building their houses. These sepulchers reach as far as Zelzah in the territory of Benjamin. Around Jerusalem are high mountains.

On Mount Zion are sepulchers of the house of David, and the sepulchers of the kings that ruled after him. The exact place cannot be identified, inasmuch as 15 years ago a wall of the church of Mount Zion fell in. The patriarch commanded the overseer to take the stones of the old walls and restore the church with them. He did so, and hired workmen at fixed wages; and there were 20 men who brought the stones from the base of the wall of Zion. Among these men there were two who were sworn friends. On a certain day the one entertained the other; after their meal they returned to their work, when the overseer said to them, "Why have you tarried today?" They answered, "Why need you complain? When our fellow workmen go to their meal, we will do our work." When the dinnertime arrived, and the other workmen had gone to their meal, they examined the stones, and raised a certain stone which formed the entrance to a cave. Shortly afterward one said to the other, "Let us go in and see if any money is to be found there." They entered the cave, and reached a large chamber resting upon pillars of marble overlaid with silver and gold. In front was a table of gold and a scepter and a crown. This was the sepulcher of King David. On the left of it in similar fashion was the sepulcher of King Solomon; then followed the sepulchers of all the kings of Judah that were buried there. Closed coffers were also there, the contents of which no man knows. The two men tried to enter the chamber, when a fierce wind came forth from the entrance of the cave and hit them, and they fell to the ground like dead men, and there they lay until evening. And there came forth a wind like a man's voice, crying out: "Arise and go forth from this place!" So the men rushed forth in terror, and they came to the patriarch, and related these things to him. Thereupon the patriarch sent for Rabbi Abraham el Constantini, the pious recluse, who was one of the mourners of Jerusalem, and to him he related all these things according to the report of the two men who had come forth. Then Rabbi Abraham replied, "These are the sepulchers of the house of David; they belong to the kings of Judah, and tomorrow let us enter, I and you and these men, and find out what is there." And on the next day they sent for the two men, and found each one of them lying on his bed in terror, and the men said: "We will not enter there, for the Lord does not desire to show it to any man." Then the patriarch gave orders that the place should be closed up and hidden from the sight of man to this day. These things were told me by the said Rabbi Abraham. . . .

From there it is two days to Baghdad, the great city and the royal residence of the caliph, Emir al Muminin al Abbasi [al-Mustanjid, r. 1160–1170] of the family of Muhammad. He is at the head of the Muslim religion, and all the kings of Islam obey him; he occupies a similar position to that held by the pope over the Christians. He has a palace in Baghdad three miles in extent, in which is a great park with all the varieties of trees, fruit-bearing and otherwise, and all manner of animals. The whole is surrounded by a wall, and in the park there is a lake whose waters are fed by the river Tigris. Whenever the king desires to indulge in recreation and to rejoice and feast, his servants catch all manner of birds, game, and fish, and he goes to his palace with his counsellors and princes. There the great king, Al Abbasi the Caliph [Hafiz], holds his court, and he is kind to Israel, and many belonging to the people of Israel are his attendants; he knows all languages, and is well versed in the law of Israel. He reads and writes the holy language [Hebrew]. He will not partake of anything unless he has earned it by the work of his own hands. He makes bedspreads to which he attaches his seal; his courtiers sell them in the market, and the great ones of the land purchase them, and the proceeds thereof provide his sustenance. He is truthful and trusty, speaking peace to all men. The men of Islam see him but once in the year. The pilgrims that come from distant lands to go to Mecca, which is the land Yemen [?], are anxious to see his face, and they assemble before the palace exclaiming "Our lord, light of Islam and glory of our Law, show us the effulgence of your countenance," but he pays no regard to their words. Then the princes who minister to him say to him, "Our lord, spread forth your peace to the men that have come from distant lands, who crave to abide under the shadow of your graciousness," and shortly afterward he arises and lets down the hem of his robe from the window, and the pilgrims come and kiss it, and a prince says to them, "Go forth in peace, for our master the lord of Islam grants peace to you." He is regarded by them as Muhammad and they go to their houses rejoicing at the salutation that the prince has granted to them, and glad at heart that they have kissed his robe.

Each of his brothers and the members of the family has an abode in his palace, but they are all fettered in chains of iron, and guards are placed over each of their houses so that they may not rise against the great caliph. For once it happened to a predecessor that his brothers rose up against him and proclaimed one of themselves as caliph. Each one of them resides in his palace in great splendor, and they own villages and towns, and their stewards bring them the tribute from it, and they eat and drink and rejoice all the days of their life. Within the domains of the palace of the caliph there are great buildings of marble and columns of silver and gold, and carvings upon rare stones are fixed in the walls. In the caliph's palace are great riches and towers filled with gold, silken garments, and all precious stones. He does not issue forth from his palace save once in the year, at the feast which the Muslims call Eid al-Fitr, and they come from distant lands that day to see him. He rides on a mule and is attired in the royal robes of gold and silver and fine linen; on his head is a turban adorned with precious stones of priceless value, and over the turban is a black shawl as a sign of his modesty, implying that all this glory will be covered by darkness on the day of death. He is accompanied by all the nobles of Islam dressed in fine garments and riding on horses, the princes of Arabia, the princes of Togarma [Seljuks] and Daylam [Gilan] and the princes of Persia, Media, and Ghuzz [Transoxiana], and the princes of the land of Tibet, which is three months' journey distant, and westward of which lies the land of Samarkand. He proceeds from his palace to the great mosque of Islam which is by the Basra Gate. Along the road the walls are adorned with silk and purple, and the inhabitants receive him with all kinds of song and exultation, and they dance before the great king who is styled the caliph. They salute him with a loud voice and say, "Peace to you, our lord the king and light of Islam!" He kisses his robe, and stretching forth the hem of it he salutes them. Then he proceeds to the court of the mosque, mounts a wooden pulpit and expounds to them their Law. Then the learned ones of Islam arise and pray for him and extol his greatness and his graciousness, to which they all respond. Afterward he gives them his blessing, and they bring him a camel which he slays, and this is their Passover sacrifice. He gives of it to the princes and they distribute it to all, so that they may taste of the sacrifice brought by their sacred king; and they all rejoice. Afterward he leaves the mosque and returns alone to his palace by way of the river Tigris, and the grandees of Islam accompany him in ships on the river until he enters his palace. He does not return by the way he came; and the road which he takes along the riverside is watched all the year through, so that no man will tread in his footsteps. He does not leave the palace again for a whole year. He is a benevolent man.

He built, on the other side of the river, on the banks of an arm of the Euphrates which there borders the city, a hospital consisting of blocks of houses and hospices for the sick poor who come to be healed. Here there are about 60 physicians' stores which are provided from the caliph's house with drugs and whatever else may be required. Every sick man who comes is maintained at the caliph's expense and is medically treated. Here is a building which is called Dar-al-Maristan, where they keep charge of the demented people who have become insane in the towns through the great heat in the summer, and they chain each of them in iron chains until their reason becomes restored to them in the wintertime. While they abide there, they are provided with food from the house of the caliph, and when their reason is restored they are dismissed and each one of them goes to his house and his home. Money is given to those that have stayed in the hospices on their return to their homes. Every month the officers of the caliph inquire and investigate whether they have regained their reason, in which case they are discharged. All this the caliph does out of charity to those that come to the city of Baghdad, whether they be sick or insane. The caliph is a righteous man, and all his actions are for good.

In Baghdad there are about 40,000 Jews, and they all dwell in security, prosperity, and honor under the great caliph, and among them are great sages, the heads of academies engaged in the study of the Law. In this city there are ten academies. At the head of the great academy is the chief rabbi R[abbi] Samuel, the son of Eli. He is the head of the Academy Gaon Jacob. He is a Levite, and traces his pedigree back to Moses our teacher. The head of the second academy is R[abbi] Hanania his brother, warden of the Levites; R[abbi] Daniel is the head of the third academy; R[abbi] Elazar the scholar is the head of the fourth academy; and R[abbi] Elazar, the son of Zemach, is the head of the order, and his pedigree reaches to Samuel the prophet, the Korahite [singer]. He and his brethren know how to chant the melodies as did the singers at the time when the Temple was standing. He is the head of the fifth academy. R[abbi] Hisdai, the glory of the scholars, is head of the sixth academy. R[abbi] Haggai is head of the seventh academy. R[abbi] Ezra is the head of the eighth academy. R[abbi] Abraham, who is called Abu Tahir, is the head of the ninth academy. R[abbi] Zakkai, the son of Bostanai the Nasi, is the head of the Sium [the last or tenth academy]. These are the ten Batlanim [scholars who do communal work], and they do not engage in any other work than communal administration; and all the days of the week they judge the Jews their countrymen, except on the second day of the week, when they all appear before the chief rabbi Samuel, the head of the Yeshiba Gaon [Jacob], who in conjunction with the other Batlanim judges all those that appear before him. At the head of them all is Daniel the son of Hisdai, who is styled "Our lord the head of the captivity of all Israel." He possesses a book of pedigrees going back as far as David, king of Israel. The Jews call him "Our lord, head of the captivity," and the Muslims call him "Saidna ben Daoud," and he has been invested with authority over all the congregations of Israel at the hands of the Emir al Muminin, the lord of Islam. For thus Muhammad commanded concerning him and his descendants; and he granted him a seal of office over all the congregations that dwell under his rule, and ordered that every one, whether Muslim or Jew, or belonging to any other nation in his dominion, should rise up before him [the exilarch] and salute him, and that anyone who should refuse to rise up should receive 100 stripes.

And every fifth day when he goes to pay a visit to the great caliph, horsemen, gentiles as well as Jews, escort him, and heralds proclaim in advance, "Make way before our lord, the son of David, as is due to him," the Arabic words being "Amilu Tarik la saidna ben Daud." He is mounted on a horse, and is attired in robes of silk and embroidery with a large turban on his head, and from the turban is suspended a long white cloth adorned with a chain upon which the cipher of Muhammad is engraved. Then he appears before the caliph and kisses his hand, and the caliph rises and places him on a throne which Muhammad had ordered to be made for him, and all the Muslim princes who attend the court of the caliph rise up before him. And the head of the captivity is seated on his throne opposite to the caliph, in compliance with the command of Muhammad to give effect to what is written in the law: "The scepter will not depart from Judah nor a lawgiver from between his feet, until he come to Shiloh: and to him will the gathering of the people be" [Genesis 49:10]. The authority of the head of the captivity extends over all the communities of central Mesopotamia, Persia, Khurasan, and Sheba which is Yemen, and upper Mesopotamia, and over the dwellers in the mountains of Ararat and the land of the Alans [central Asia?], which is a land surrounded by mountains and has no outlet except by the iron gates which Alexander made, but which were afterward broken. Here are the people called Alani [Alans]. His authority extends also over the land of Siberia, and the communities in the land of the Togarmim [Seljuks] to the mountains of Asveh [?] and the land of Gorgan, the inhabitants of which are called Gurganim who dwell by the river Gihon [?], and these are the Girgashites who follow the Christian religion. Further it extends to the gates of Samarkand, the land of Tibet, and the land of India. In respect of all these countries the head of the captivity gives the communities power to appoint rabbis and ministers who come to him to be consecrated and to receive his authority. They bring him offerings and gifts from the ends of the earth. He owns hospices, gardens, and plantations in Babylon, and much land inherited from his fathers, and no one can take his possession from him by force. He has a fixed weekly revenue arising from the hospices of the Jews, the markets, and the merchants, apart from that which is brought to him from far-off lands. The man is very rich, and wise in the scriptures as well as in the Talmud, and many Israelites dine at his table every day.

At his installation, the head of the captivity gives much money to the caliph, to the princes, and the ministers. On the day that the caliph performs the ceremony of investing him with authority, he rides in the second of the royal equipages, and is escorted from the palace of the caliph to his own house with timbrels and fifes. The exilarch appoints the chiefs of the academies by placing his hand upon their heads, thus installing them in their office. The Jews of the city are learned men and very rich.

In Baghdad there are 28 Jewish synagogues, situated either in the city itself or in Al-Karkh on the other side of the Tigris; for the river divides the metropolis into two parts. The great synagogue of the head of the captivity has columns of marble of various colors overlaid with silver and gold, and on these columns are sentences of the Psalms in golden letters. And in front of the ark are about ten steps of marble; on the topmost step are the seats of the head of the captivity and of the princes of the house of David. The city of Baghdad is 20 miles in circumference, situated in a land of palms, gardens, and plantations, the like of which is not to be found in the whole land of central Mesopotamia. People come there with merchandise from all lands. Wise men live there, philosophers who know all manner of wisdom, and magicians expert in all manner of witchcraft.

Questions: What are the results of Benjamin's census of Jewish people in the lands to which he travels? Why is he so interested in the size of Jewish communities? Why does Benjamin identify the Jewish religious leaders, the rabbis? Compare and contrast Benjamin's depiction of the cities of Rome, Constantinople, Jerusalem, and Baghdad. How did Benjamin measure the quality of the rulers in these cities? Why does he point out the Jews who worked for non-Jewish rulers? Why was he not more critical of the adverse conditions under which many Jews lived?

36. IBN JUBAYR, *TRAVELS*

Ibn Jubayr (1145–1217) was a Muslim pilgrim and native of Spain who made three journeys in the Mediterranean in the late twelfth and early thirteenth centuries; the excerpt here records only the beginning of his first journey. Throughout the record of his travels, Ibn Jubayr showed himself to be a pious Muslim, and he distrusted Christians and intermixing between Muslims and Christians, which he feared might tempt Muslims to embrace Christianity. In spite of his religious stance, Ibn Jubayr's observations are held to be accurate and the form of the travelogue he created would be widely imitated by later Muslim authors.

Source: trans. John F. Romano, Ibn Gubayr, *Viaggio in Ispagna, Sicilia, Siria e Palestina, Mesopotamia, Arabia, Egitto compiuto nel secolo XII*, trans. Celestino Schiaparelli (Rome: Casa editrice italiana, 1906), pp. 3–8. Arabic.

May God by his grace grant us salvation.

Ahmad ibn Hassan and Muhammad ibn Jubayr left Granada—may God defend it—to make the holy pilgrimage [to the Hejaz]—may God make it prosperous and easy, and grant it his gracious favor—at the first hour of Thursday, the eighth of Shawwal 578, that is the third of February 1183 of the foreigners [non-Muslims]. We passed through Jaen to take care of some business and departed from there at the first hour of Monday the nineteenth of the same month, that is the fourteenth of February, extending our first stage up to the fortress of Alcaudete. From there we passed to the fortress of Cabra, to the city of Ecija, to the fortress of Osuna, to Willabar [Jeliver], to the fortress of Arcos, to the castle called Qashmah [Casma in Medina Sidonia], which is a castle subject to Madinat Ibn as-Salim, and then to the island of Tarifa, where we arrived on Monday the twenty-sixth of the month [of Shawwal, the twenty-first of February]. When it was noon on the [following] Tuesday, that is the [twenty-]second [of February], God granted to us a delightful crossing of the sea, and we made landfall at Ksar es-Seghir. Praise be to God! The morning of Wednesday the twenty-eighth of the month, we moved through Ceuta where we found a Rumi [Byzantine] Genoese ship ready to set sail to Alexandria, by the power of the strong and gracious God, and with his favor, we embarked on it without difficulty; and at noon on Thursday the twenty-ninth of the same month, that is the twenty-fourth of February, we set sail with the power and help of God almighty. There is no god but he.

We kept our course along the coast of Spain, and when it was Thursday the sixth of the following month of Dhu al-Qa'dah [the third of March] and we found ourselves opposite Denia, we departed from it [the coast of Spain]. The morning of Friday the seventh of the same month we were opposite the island of Ibiza, the following Saturday the island of Majorca, and the Sunday afterward the island of Minorca. From Ceuta to this island [Minorca] measures eight *majari*; the *majra* equals one hundred [miles].

Having left this island, we found ourselves all of a sudden at the beginning of the night on Tuesday the eleventh of the same month, that is the eighth of March, near the coast of Sardinia, at a distance of around a mile or a little less. The two islands of Sardinia and Minorca are separated by about four hundred miles, so it was a journey of extraordinary speed. In the night we were surprised by a terrible storm from the shore accompanied by wind that almighty God stirred up from the coast at that moment and that pushed us back to the high seas—from which God saved us. Praise be to God for that. On the morning of the same Tuesday a storm rose against us that made the sea agitated, which caused us to keep tacking near the coast of Sardinia until the following Wednesday. In this state of discouragement, both with the storm having blocked the horizon from every side and our inability to tell the east from the west, God revealed to us a Rumi ship that was steering toward us, and when it was close to us, we asked it where it was headed. It responded that it was on course for Sicily, and that it came from Cartagena in the province of Murcia. We who, without realizing it, had been going in front of it on its course, started to follow in its wake. God is the one who makes success easy; there is no other god than he.

Then in front of us appeared a promontory of the coast of Sardinia, where we started to retrace our path and turning around, we reached another promontory of the coast named Qusmarkah [Cape St-Mark at the north of the Gulf of Orisanto], which had an anchorage well known to those sailors. There we anchored at noon of the same Wednesday, and the same ship was with us. In that place there were the ruins of an ancient building, which we were told had in past times been a Jewish lodging. We left from that anchorage at noon on Sunday, the sixteenth of the month. During our stop in this port we refreshed the water, wood, and provisions. A Muslim who knew the language of the Rumi, together with a party of these [Byzantines], went to the closest inhabited place to us, and then informed us that he had seen a number of Muslim captives, about eighty between men and women, for sale at the market, and that this was the case because the enemy—may God destroy them—had just arrived with this merchandise from the seacoasts of Muslim countries. May God expend his mercy on them. On Friday, the third day that we had anchored there, the lord of the island arrived there accompanied by a number of knights. The foremost people on the Rumi ship came ashore to render him homage, and he received them in a long audience; they took their leave, while he returned to his residence.

When wind favorable to us rose up, we left the aforementioned ship where it had been anchored, because part of its crew had left for the town, and the night of Tuesday the eighteenth of Dhu al-Qa'dah, the fifteenth day of March, and precisely at the last quarter of the night, we left Sardinia. We sailed along the long coast of this island for around two hundred miles. Its circuit, according to what was told to us, surpassed five hundred [miles]. There thanks to God we escaped easily from the sea [of this island], which is the most dangerous of the journey, and emerging unscathed from it is something difficult in the majority of times. Praise be to God for that.

On the beginning of the night of Wednesday, the sea became turbulent because of the violent blowing of wind accompanied by rain, so that the storm drove [us] with such force that it seemed as if clouds of arrows poured down on us. The matter became serious and our anxiety grew; waves like walking mountains beset us on every side. We spent the whole night like this, while despair had reached its height, and nothing remained for us save for the hope that with the rising of the sun, some comfort would come to lift us from some of the trouble that afflicted us. The day broke, and it was Wednesday the nineteenth of Dhu al-Qaʻdah, accompanied by a stronger storm and greater worry. The sea had become rougher and the horizon darker; the wind and rain raged stronger than ever, such that no sail could resist its force. So we were forced to resort to the small sails; but the wind took one of them and ripped it and it broke the pole to which they were attached, which is called by sailors the *qariyah* [mast]. Then despair took over our spirits, and the hands of the Muslims were raised to heaven to implore the mighty and gracious God. We stayed like that for the entire day and when night fell, the condition improved somewhat, and we continued to drift until morning with wind at the stern, speeding along quickly. During the day we were opposite Sicily.

The night after, which was Thursday night, we spent tossed between hope and despair, but when dawn appeared God extended his mercy, the clouds disappeared, the good weather returned, the sun shone, and the sea became calm, so that people started to live and socialize again, and their despair disappeared. Praise be to God who showed us his gracious mercy and perfect goodness; praises equal to his favor and his grace. The same morning we caught sight of the coast of Sicily, most of which we had already traveled past, and little of it remained. Those who were present, Rumi and Muslim sea captains, [who were] accustomed to sea voyages and storms, agreed in saying that never had they seen a squall similar to this one. Telling the story cuts the reality of the episode down to size. Between the two aforementioned lands, that is Sardinia and Sicily, measure approximately four hundred miles. We had sailed along the coast of Sicily for two hundred miles when, the wind having stopped, we were tacking opposite to it.

When the evening of Friday the twenty-first of this month came, we spread the sails from the place where we had moored, and, having distanced ourselves from the land at dusk on Saturday morning, we were already separated from it by a great distance. It was then that we saw the mountain on which there is a volcano, an enormous mountain that rises into the air, all covered in snow. We heard that when the weather is calm, you can see it from the sea at a distance of more than one hundred miles. From that point we launched onto the high seas.

The closest land there we anticipated glimpsing was the island of Crete that belongs to the Rumi and is subject to the lord of Constantinople. Between that and Sicily measure seven hundred miles. God with his favor guarantees prosperous and easy success. That island of Crete measures in length around three hundred miles. The night of Tuesday the twenty-fifth of the month [of Dhu al-Qaʻdah], that is the twenty-second of March, according to our calculations we should have found ourselves opposite this island, but we could not catch sight of it. On the morning of the same day, we went away from it, pushing ahead to our destination. Between this island and Alexandria measure six hundred miles.

On Wednesday the twenty-sixth of the month, just before morning, the large dry land that extended up to Alexandria appeared to us, and it was called Barr al-Gharb [Land of the West]. There we sailed along the coast at the expanse called Jaza'ir al-Hamam [the Island of the Doves], between which and Alexandria it is said that around four hundred miles lay. Continuing on our course, we kept the coast on our right side. On the morning of the Saturday the twenty-ninth of the month, God gave us the good news that we were out of danger with the appearance of the lighthouse of Alexandria at a distance of around twenty miles. So praise be to God, praises suitable to the excess of his favor and his generous works. Around the end of the fifth hour of that day we cast anchor in the port of the city and we came ashore. We invoke God for help because of his grace for what remains [of the journey].

We had stayed at sea for thirty days and on the thirty-first we came ashore, since we had embarked on Thursday the twenty-ninth of Shawwal and disembarked on Saturday the twenty-ninth of Dhu al-Qaʻdah, that is the twenty-sixth of March. Praise be to God for having granted us a prosperous and easy voyage. We ask that he, may he be glorified, fulfill his favor to us, to have us reach the destination promised to us and to return soon to our homeland safe and sound, since he alone can do this favor for us; there is no god but he. We took a lodging in the city in the hostel called "of the copper workers" next to the soap factory.

Questions: Why is Ibn Jubayr setting out on a journey? What signs can you find in this source of Ibn Jubayr's religiosity? Did he think that God is guiding his journey? When does his writing sound like a prayer? Does Ibn Jubayr know the difference between different European groups, such as Italians and Byzantines?

37. IBN BATTUTA, *RIHLA*

Ibn Battuta (1304–1368) is best known for the extensive series of travels that he undertook, and the detailed account of them known as the Rihla (the Journey). He started out from Morocco in 1325 with the intention of going on pilgrimage to Mecca, but he did not return until 1349, after having seen nearly all of the territories in which Islam was

practiced, including north Africa, the Middle East, and India. Between 1353 and 1355
he also visited West Africa. The motives for Ibn Battuta's journey are likely mixed:
while in India, he served as a judge, but he was also motivated by his personal religiosity,
wanderlust, and a desire to experience the best in life.

Source: trans. H. A. R. Gibb, Ibn Battuta, *Travels in Asia and Africa, 1325–1354* (London: G. Routledge & Sons, 1929), pp. 43–62, 64–72, 73–77, 317–35. Arabic. Revised.

I left Tangier, my birthplace, on Thursday, the second of Rajab, 725 [14 June 1325], being at that time twenty-two [lunar] years of age, with the intention of making the pilgrimage to the Holy House [at Mecca] and the tomb of the Prophet [in Medina]. I set out alone, finding no companion to cheer the way with friendly intercourse, and no party of travelers with whom to associate myself. Swayed by an overmastering impulse within me, and a long-cherished desire to visit those glorious sanctuaries, I resolved to leave all my friends and tear myself away from my home. As my parents were still alive, it weighed grievously upon me to part from them, and both they and I were afflicted with sorrow.

On reaching the city of Tlemcen, whose sultan at that time was Abu Tashifin [r. 1318–1337], I found there two ambassadors of the sultan of Tunis, who left the city on the same day that I arrived. One of the brethren having advised me to accompany them, I consulted the will of God in this matter, and after a stay of three days in the city to procure all that I needed, I rode after them with all speed. I overtook them at the town of Miliana, where we stayed ten days, as both ambassadors fell sick on account of the summer heats. When we set out again, one of them grew worse, and died after we had stopped for three nights by a stream four miles from Miliana. I left their party there and pursued my journey, with a company of merchants from Tunis. On reaching Algiers we halted outside the town for a few days, until the former party rejoined us, when we went on together through the Mitija [a plain] to the Djurdjura [mountain range] and so reached Béjaïa. The commander of Béjaïa at this time was the chamberlain Ibn Sayyid an-Nas. Now one of the Tunisian merchants of our party had died leaving three thousand dinars of gold, which he had entrusted to a certain man of Algiers to deliver to his heirs at Tunis. Ibn Sayyid an-Nas came to hear of this and forcibly seized the money. This was the first instance I witnessed the tyranny of the agents of the Tunisian government. At Béjaïa I fell ill of a fever, and one of my friends advised me to stay there until I recovered. But I refused, saying, "If God decrees my death, it will be on the road with my face set toward Mecca." "If that be your resolve," he replied, "sell your ass and your heavy baggage, and I will lend to you what you require. In this way you will travel light, for we must make haste on our journey, for fear of meeting roving Arabs on the way." I followed his advice and he did as he had promised—may God reward him! On reaching Constantine we camped outside the town, but a heavy rain forced us to leave our tents during the night and take refuge in some houses there. Next day the governor of the city came to meet us. Seeing my clothes all soiled by the rain he gave orders that they should be washed at his house, and in place of my old worn headcloth sent me a headcloth of fine Syrian cloth, in one of the ends of which he had tied two gold dinars. This was the first alms I received on my journey. From Constantine we reached Bona [modern Annaba] where, after staying in the town for several days, we left the merchants of our party on account of the dangers of the road, while we pursued our journey with the utmost speed. I was again attacked by fever, so I tied myself in the saddle with a turban cloth in case I should fall by reason of my weakness. So great was my fear that I could not dismount until we arrived at Tunis. The population of the city came out to meet the members of our party, and on all sides greetings and questions were exchanged, but not a soul greeted me as no one there was known to me. I was so affected by my loneliness that I could not restrain my tears and wept bitterly, until one of the pilgrims realized the cause of my distress and coming up to me greeted me kindly and continued to entertain me with friendly talk until I entered the city.

The sultan of Tunis at that time was Abu Yahya, the son of Abi Zakariya II, and there were a number of notable scholars in the town. During my stay the festival of the breaking of the fast [Eid al-Fitr] fell due, and I joined the company at the praying ground. The inhabitants assembled in large numbers to celebrate the festival, making a brave show and wearing their richest apparel. The sultan, Abu Yahya, arrived on horseback, accompanied by all his relatives, courtiers, and officers of state walking on foot in a stately procession. After the recital of the prayer and the conclusion of the sermon the people returned to their homes.

Sometime later the pilgrim caravan for the Hejaz was formed, and they nominated me as their qadi [judge]. We left Tunis early in November, following the coast road through Susa, Sfax, and Gabès, where we stayed for ten days on account of incessant rains. From there we set out for Tripoli, accompanied for several stages by a hundred or more horsemen as well as a detachment of archers, out of respect for whom the Arabs kept their distance. I had made a contract of marriage at Sfax with the daughter of one of the syndics at Tunis, and at Tripoli she was escorted to me, but after leaving Tripoli I became involved in a dispute with her father, which necessitated my separation from her. I then married the daughter of a student from Fez, and when she was escorted to me I detained a caravan for a day by entertaining them all at a wedding party.

At length on 5 April [1326] we reached Alexandria. It is a beautiful city, well-built and fortified with four gates and a magnificent port. Among all the ports in the world I have seen none to equal it except Kollam and Calicut in India, the port of the infidels [Genoese] at Sudak in the land of the Turks, and the port of Quanzhou in China, all of which will be described later. I went to see the lighthouse on this occasion and found one of its faces in ruins. It is a very high square building, and its door is above the level of the earth. Opposite the door, and of the same height, is a building from which there is a plank bridge to the door; if this is removed there is no means of entrance. Inside the door is a place for the lighthouse keeper, and within the lighthouse there are many chambers. The breadth of the passage inside is nine spans and that of the wall ten spans; each of the four sides of the lighthouse is one hundred forty spans in breadth. It is situated on a high mound and lies three miles from the city on a long tongue of land which juts out into the sea from close by the city wall, so that the lighthouse cannot be reached by land except from the city. On my return to the west in the year 750 [1349] I visited the lighthouse again, and found that it was not possible to enter it or climb up to the door. Al-Malik an-Nasir had started to build a similar lighthouse alongside it but was prevented by death from completing the work. Another of the marvelous things in this city is the awe-inspiring marble column on its outskirts which they call the "Pillar of Columns." It is a single block, skillfully carved, erected on a base of square stones like enormous platforms, and no one knows how it was erected there nor for certain who erected it.

One of the learned men of Alexandria was the qadi, a master of eloquence, who used to wear a turban of extraordinary size. Never either in the eastern or the western lands have I seen a more voluminous headgear. Another of them was the pious ascetic Burhan ad-Din, whom I met during my stay and whose hospitality I enjoyed for three days. One day as I entered his room he said to me, "I see that you are fond of traveling through foreign lands." I replied, "Yes, I am" (though I had as yet no thought of going to such distant lands as India or China). Then he said, "You must certainly visit my brother Farid ad-Din in India, and my brother Rukn ad-Din in Sind, and my brother Burhan ad-Din in China, and when you find them give them greeting from me." I was amazed at his prediction, and the idea of going to these countries having been cast into my mind, my journeys never ceased until I had met these three that he named and conveyed his greeting to them.

During my stay at Alexandria I had heard of the pious Shaykh al-Murshidi, who bestowed gifts miraculously created at his desire. He lived in solitary retreat in a cell in the country where he was visited by princes and ministers. Parties of men in all ranks of life used to come to him every day and he would supply them all with food. Each one of them would desire to eat some flesh or fruit or sweetmeat at his cell, and to each he would give what he had suggested, though it was frequently out of season. His fame was carried from mouth to mouth far and wide, and the sultan too had visited him several times in his retreat. I set out from Alexandria to seek this *shaykh* [honorific title] and passing through Damanhur came to Fuwwah, a beautiful township, close by which, separated from it by a canal, lies the *shaykh*'s cell. I reached this cell about mid-afternoon, and on saluting the *shaykh* I found that he had with him one of the sultan's aides-de-camp, who had encamped with his troops just outside. The *shaykh* rose and embraced me, and calling for food invited me to eat. When the hour of the afternoon prayer arrived he set me in front as prayer leader, and did the same on every occasion when we were together at the times of prayer during my stay. When I wished to sleep he said to me, "Go up to the roof of the cell and sleep there" (this was during the summer heats). I said to the officer, "In the name of God," but he replied [quoting from the Qur'an], "There is none of us but has an appointed place." So I mounted the roof and found there a straw mattress and a leather mat, a water vessel for ritual ablutions, a jar of water and a drinking cup, and I lay down there to sleep.

That night, while I was sleeping on the roof of the cell, I dreamed that I was on the wing of a great bird which was flying with me toward Mecca, then to Yemen, then eastward, and after that going toward the south, then flying far eastward, and finally landing in a dark and green country, where it left me. I was astonished at this dream and said to myself, "If the *shaykh* can interpret my dream for me, he is all that they say he is." Next morning, after all the other visitors had gone, he called me and when I had related my dream interpreted it to me saying: "You will make the pilgrimage [to Mecca] and visit [the tomb of] the Prophet, and you will travel through Yemen, Iraq, the country of the Turks, and India. You will stay there for a long time and meet there my brother Dilshad the Indian, who will rescue you from a danger into which you will fall." Then he gave me a traveling provision of small cakes and money, and I bade him farewell and departed. Never since parting from him have I met on my journeys anything but good fortune, and his blessings have stood me in good stead.

We rode from here to Damietta through a number of towns, in each of which we visited the principal men of religion. Damietta lies on the bank of the Nile, and the people in the houses next to the river draw water from it in buckets. Many of the houses have steps leading down to the river. Their sheep and goats are allowed to pasture at liberty day and night; for this reason the saying goes of Damietta, "Its walls are sweetmeats and its dogs are sheep." Anyone who enters the city may not afterward leave it except by the governor's seal. Persons of repute have a seal stamped on a piece of paper so that they may show it to the gatekeepers; other persons have the seal stamped on their forearms. In this city there are many seabirds with extremely greasy flesh, and the milk of its buffaloes is unequalled for sweetness and pleasant taste. The fish called *buri* [flathead grey mullet] is exported from there to Syria, Anatolia, and Cairo. The present town is of recent construction; the old city was that destroyed by the Franks in the time of al-Malik as-Salih.

From Damietta I traveled to Fariskur, which is a town on the bank of the Nile, and halted outside of it. Here I was overtaken by a horseman who had been sent after me by the governor of Damietta. He handed me a number of coins, saying to me, "The governor asked for you, and on being informed about you, he sent you this gift"—may God reward him! From there I traveled to Ashmun Tanah [modern Ashmun al-Rumman], a large and ancient town on a canal derived from the Nile. It possesses a wooden bridge at which all vessels anchor, and in the afternoon the baulks are lifted and the vessels pass up and down. From here I went to Samannud, from where I journeyed upstream to Cairo, between a continuous succession of towns and villages. The traveler on the Nile need take no provision with him, because whenever he desires to descend on the bank he may do so, for ablutions, prayers, provisioning, or any other purpose. There is an uninterrupted chain of bazaars from Alexandria to Cairo, and from Cairo to Aswan in Upper Egypt.

I arrived at length at Cairo, mother of cities and seat of pharaoh the tyrant, mistress of broad regions and fruitful lands, boundless in multitude of buildings, peerless in beauty and splendor, the meeting place of feeble and mighty, whose throngs surge as the waves of the sea, and can scarce be contained in her for all her size and capacity. It is said that in Cairo there are twelve thousand water carriers who transport water on camels, and thirty thousand hirers of mules and donkeys, and that on the Nile there are thirty-six thousand boats belonging to the sultan and his subjects, which sail upstream to Upper Egypt and downstream to Alexandria and Damietta, laden with goods and profitable merchandise of all kinds. On the bank of the Nile opposite Old Cairo is the place known as the garden, which is a pleasure park and promenade, containing many beautiful gardens, for the people of Cairo are given to pleasure and amusements. I witnessed a feast once in Cairo for the sultan's recovery from a fractured hand; all the merchants decorated their bazaars and had rich stuffs, ornaments, and silken fabrics hanging in their shops for several days. The mosque of Amr is highly venerated and widely celebrated. The Friday service is held in it, and the road runs through it from east to west. The madrasas [college mosques] of Cairo cannot be counted for multitude. As for the maristan [hospital], which lies "between the two castles" near the mausoleum of Sultan Qala'un, no description is adequate to its beauties. It contains an innumerable quantity of appliances and medicines, and its daily revenue is put as high as a thousand dinars.

There are a large number of religious establishments, which they call *khanqahs*, and the nobles vie with one another in building them. Each of these is set apart for a separate school of dervishes, mostly Persians, who are men of good education and adepts in the mystical doctrines. Each has a superior and a doorkeeper and their affairs are admirably organized. They have many special customs, one of which has to do with their food. The steward of the house comes in the morning to the darvishes, each of whom indicates what food he desires, and when they assemble for meals, each person is given his bread and soup in a separate dish, none sharing with another. They eat twice a day. They are each given winter clothes and summer clothes, and a monthly allowance of from twenty to thirty dirhams [silver coins]. Every Thursday night they receive sugar cakes, soap to wash their clothes, the price of a bath, and oil for their lamps. These men are celibate; the married men have separate convents.

At Cairo too is the great cemetery of Qarafa, which is a place of peculiar sanctity, and contains the graves of innumerable scholars and pious believers. In the Qarafa the people build beautiful pavilions surrounded by walls, so that they look like houses. They also build chambers and hire Qur'an readers, who recite night and day in agreeable voices. Some of them build religious houses and madrasas beside the mausoleums and on Thursday nights they go out to spend the night there with their children and womenfolk, and make a circuit of the famous tombs. They go out to spend the night there also on the "Night of mid-Sha'ban," and the market people take out all kinds of eatables. Among the many celebrated sanctuaries [in the city] is the holy shrine where there reposes the head of al-Husayn. Beside it is a vast monastery of striking construction, on the doors of which there are silver rings and plates of the same metal.

The Egyptian Nile surpasses all rivers of the earth in sweetness of taste, length of course, and utility. No other river in the world can show such a continuous series of towns and villages along its banks, or a basin so intensely cultivated. Its course is from south to north, contrary to all the other [great] rivers. One extraordinary thing about it is that it begins to rise in the extreme hot weather, at the time when rivers generally diminish and dry up, and begins to subside just when rivers begin to increase and overflow. The river Indus resembles it in this feature. The Nile is one of the five great rivers of the world, which are the Nile, Euphrates, Tigris, Syr Darya, and Amu Darya; five other rivers resemble these, the Indus, which is called the Punjab, the river of India which is called Ganges—it is to it that the Hindus go on pilgrimage, and when they burn their dead they throw the ashes into it, and they say that it comes from paradise—the river Jun [Yamuna?] in India, the river Itil [Volga] in the Kipchak steppe, on the banks of which is the city of Sara, and the Yellow River in the land of Cathay [northern China]. All these will be mentioned in their proper places, if God so wills. Some distance below Cairo the Nile divides into three streams, none of which can be crossed except by boat, winter or summer.

The inhabitants of every township have canals led off the Nile; these are filled when the river is in flood and carry the water over the fields.

From Cairo I traveled into Upper Egypt, with the intention of crossing to the Hejaz. On the first night I stayed at the monastery of Dayr at-Tin, which was built to house certain illustrious relics—a fragment of the Prophet's wooden basin and the pencil which he used to apply kohl [black makeup], the awl he used for sewing his sandals, and the Qur'an belonging to Caliph Ali [and] written in his own hand. These were bought, it is said, for a hundred thousand dirhams by the builder of the monastery, who also established funds to supply food to all comers and to maintain the guardians of the sacred relics. From there my way lay through a number of towns and villages to Minya, a large town which is built on the bank of the Nile, and most emphatically excels all the other towns of Upper Egypt. I went on through Manfalut, Asyut, Akhim, where there is a *berba* [ancient Egyptian temple] with sculptures and inscriptions which no one can now read—another of these *berbas* there was pulled down and its stones used to build a madrasa—Qina, Qus, where the governor of Upper Egypt resides, Luxor, a pretty little town containing the tomb of the pious ascetic Abu 'l-Hajjaj, Esna, and from there a day and a night's journey through the desert country to Edfu. Here we crossed the Nile and, hiring camels, journeyed with a party of Arabs through a desert, totally devoid of settlements but quite safe for traveling. One of our halts was at Humaythira, a place infested with hyenas. All night long we kept driving them away, and indeed one got at my baggage, tore open one of the sacks, pulled out a bag of dates, and made off with it. We found the bag next morning, torn to pieces and with most of the contents eaten.

After fifteen days' traveling we reached the town of 'Aydhab, a large town, well supplied with milk and fish; dates and grain are imported from Upper Egypt. Its inhabitants are Bejas. These people are black skinned; they wrap themselves in yellow blankets and tie headbands about a fingerbreadth wide round their heads. They do not give their daughters any share in their inheritance. They live on camels' milk and they ride on dromedaries. One-third of the city belongs to the sultan of Egypt and two-thirds to the king of the Bejas, who is called al-Hudrubi. On reaching 'Aydhab we found that Al-Hudrubi was engaged in warfare with the Turks [troops of the sultan of Egypt], that he had sunk the ships and that the Turks had fled before him. It was impossible for us to attempt the sea crossing, so we sold the provisions that we had made ready for it, and returned to Qus with the Arabs from whom we had hired the camels. We sailed from there down the Nile (it was at the flood time) and after an eight days' journey reached Cairo, where I stayed only one night, and immediately set out for Syria. This was in the middle of July 1326.

My route lay through Bilbeis and as-Salihiya, after which we entered the sands and halted at a number of stations. At each of these there was a hostelry, which they call a *khan*, where travelers dismount with their beasts. Each *khan* has a water wheel supplying a fountain and a shop at which the traveler buys what he requires for himself and his beast. At the station of Qatya customs dues are collected from the merchants, and their goods and baggage are thoroughly examined and searched. There are offices here, with officers, clerks, and notaries, and the daily revenue is a thousand gold dinars. No one is allowed to pass into Syria without a passport from Egypt, nor into Egypt without a passport from Syria, for the protection of the property of the subjects and as a measure of precaution against spies from Iraq. The responsibility of guarding this road has been entrusted to the Bedouin. At nightfall they smooth down the sand so that no track is left on it, then in the morning the governor comes and looks at the sand. If he finds any track on it he commands the Arabs to bring the person who made it, and they set out in pursuit and never fail to catch him. He is then brought to the governor, who punishes him as he sees fit. The governor at the time of my passage treated me as a guest and showed me great kindness, and allowed all those who were with me to pass. From here we went on to Gaza, which is the first city of Syria on the side next to the Egyptian frontier.

From Gaza I traveled to the city of Abraham [Hebron], the mosque of which is of elegant, but substantial, construction, imposing and lofty, and built of squared stones. At one angle of it there is a stone, one of whose faces measures twenty-seven spans. It is said that Solomon commanded the *jinn* [spirits] to build it. Inside it is the sacred cave containing the graves of Abraham, Isaac, and Jacob, opposite which are three graves, which are those of their wives. I questioned the imam [leader of prayer], a man of great piety and learning, on the authenticity of these graves, and he replied: "All the scholars whom I have met hold these graves to be the very graves of Abraham, Isaac, Jacob, and their wives. No one questions this except introducers of false doctrines; it is a tradition which has passed from father to son for generations and admits of no doubt." This mosque contains also the grave of Joseph, and somewhat to the east of it lies the tomb of Lot, which is surmounted by an elegant building. In the neighborhood is Lot's lake [the Dead Sea], which is brackish and is said to cover the site of the settlements of Lot's people. On the way from Hebron to Jerusalem, I visited Bethlehem, the birthplace of Jesus. The site is covered by a large building; the Christians regard it with intense veneration and hospitably entertain all who dismount at it.

We then reached Jerusalem (may God ennoble her!), third in excellence after the two holy shrines of Mecca and Medina, and the place from where the Prophet was caught up into heaven. Its walls were destroyed by the illustrious King Saladin [r. 1174–1193] and his successors, for fear that the Christians should seize it and fortify themselves in it. The sacred mosque is a most beautiful building, and is said to be the largest mosque in the world. Its length from east to west is put at seven hundred fifty-two "royal" cubits and its breadth at four hundred thirty-five. On three sides it has many entrances, but on the south side I know of one only, which is that by which the imam enters. The entire mosque is an open court and unroofed, except the mosque al-Aqsa, which has a roof of most excellent workmanship, embellished with gold and brilliant colors. Some other parts of the mosque are roofed as well. The Dome of the Rock is a building of extraordinary beauty, solidity, elegance, and singularity of shape. It stands on an elevation in the center of the mosque and is reached by a flight of marble steps. It has four doors. The space round it is also paved with marble, excellently done, and the interior likewise. Both outside and inside the decoration is so magnificent and the workmanship so surpassing as to defy description. The greater part is covered with gold so that the eyes of one who gazes on its beauties are dazzled by its brilliance, now glowing like a mass of light, now flashing like lightning. In the center of the Dome is the blessed rock from which the Prophet ascended to heaven, a great rock projecting about a man's height, and underneath it there is a cave the size of a small room, also of a man's height, with steps leading down to it. Encircling the rock are two railings of excellent workmanship, the one nearer the rock being artistically constructed in iron, and the other of wood.

Among the grace-bestowing sanctuaries of Jerusalem is a building, situated on the farther side of the valley called the valley of Jahannam [Gehenna] to the east of the town, on a high hill. This building is said to mark the place from where Jesus ascended to heaven. In the bottom of the same valley is a church venerated by the Christians, who say that it contains the grave of Mary. In the same place there is another church which the Christians venerate and to which they come on pilgrimage. This is the church of which they are falsely persuaded to believe that it contains the grave of Jesus. All who come on pilgrimage to visit it pay a stipulated tax to the Muslims, and suffer very unwillingly various humiliations. Thereabouts also is the place of the cradle of Jesus, which is visited in order to obtain blessing.

I journeyed after that time from Jerusalem to the fortress of Ashkelon, which is a total ruin. Of the great mosque, known as the Mosque of Omar, nothing remains but its walls and some marble columns of matchless beauty, partly standing and partly fallen. Among them is a wonderful red column, of which the people tell that the Christians carried it off to their country but afterward lost it, when it was found in its place at Ashkelon. From there I went on to the city of Ramla, which is also called Filastin [Palestine], in the *qibla* [place of prayer] of those mosques they say three hundred of the prophets are buried. From Ramla I went to the town of Nablus, a city with an abundance of trees and perennial streams, and one of the richest in Syria for olives, the oil of which is exported from there to Cairo and Damascus. It is at Nablus that the carob sweet is manufactured and exported to Damascus and elsewhere. It is made in this way: the carobs are cooked and then pressed, the juice that runs out is gathered and the sweet is manufactured from it. The juice itself too is exported to Cairo and Damascus. Nablus has also a species of melon which is called by its name, a good and delicious fruit. From there I went to Ajloun making in the direction of Turkey, and passing through the Ghawr, followed the coast to Acre, which is in ruins. Acre was formerly the capital and port of the country of the Franks in Syria, and rivaled Constantinople itself.

I went on from here to Tyre, which is a ruin, though there is outside it an inhabited village, most of whose population belong to the sect called "Refusers." It is this city of Tyre which has become proverbial for impregnability, because the sea surrounds it on three sides and it has two gates, one on the landward side and one to the sea. That on the landward side is protected by four outer walls each with breastworks, while the sea gate stands between two great towers. There is no more marvelous or more remarkable piece of masonry in the world than this, for the sea surrounds it on three sides and on the fourth there is a wall under which the ships pass and come to anchor. In former times an iron chain was stretched between the two towers to form a barrier, so that there was no way in or out until it was lowered. It was placed under the charge of guards and trustworthy agents, and none might enter or leave without their knowledge. Acre also had a harbor resembling it, but it admitted only small ships. From Tyre I went on to Sidon, a pleasant town on the coast, and rich in fruit; it exports figs, raisins, and olive oil to Cairo.

Next I went on to the town of Tiberias. It was formerly a large and important city, of which nothing now remains but vestiges witnessing to its former greatness. It possesses wonderful baths with separate establishments for men and women, the water of which is very hot. At Tiberias is the famous lake [the Sea of Galilee], about eighteen miles long and more than nine in breadth. The town has a mosque known as the "Mosque of the Prophets," containing the graves of Shu'ayb [Jethro] and his daughter, the wife of Moses, as well as those of Solomon, Judah, and Reuben. From Tiberias we went to visit the well into which Joseph was cast, a large and deep well, in the courtyard of a small mosque, and drank some water from it. It was rain water, but the guardian told us that there is a spring in it as well. We went on from there to Beirut, a small town with fine markets and a beautiful mosque. Fruit and iron are exported from it to Egypt.

We set out from here to visit the tomb of Abu Ya'qub Yusuf, who, they say, was a king in northwest Africa. The tomb is at a place called Karak Nuh, and beside it is a religious house at which all travelers are entertained.

Some say that it was the Sultan Saladin who endowed it, others that it was the sultan Nur ad-Din [r. 1146–1174]. The story goes that Abu Ya'qub, after staying some time at Damascus with the sultan, who had been warned in a dream that Abu Ya'qub would bring him some advantage, left the town in solitary flight during a season of great coldness, and came to a village in its neighborhood. In this village there was a man of humble station who invited him to stay in his house, and on his consenting, made him soup and killed a chicken and brought it to him with barley bread. After his meal Abu Ya'qub prayed for a blessing on his host. Now this man had several children, one of them being a girl who was shortly to be escorted to her husband. It is a custom in that country that a girl's father gives her an outfit, the greater part of which consists in copper utensils. These are regarded by them with great pride and are made the subject of special stipulations in the marriage con-tract. Abu Ya'qub therefore said to the man, "Have you any copper utensils?" "Yes," he replied, "I have just bought some for my daughter's outfit." Abu Ya'qub told him to bring them and when he had brought them said, "Now borrow all that you can from your neighbors." So he did so and laid them all before him. He then lit fires round them, and taking out a purse which he had containing an elixir, threw some of it over the brass, and the whole array was changed into gold. Leaving these in a locked chamber, Abu Ya'qub wrote to Nur ad-Din at Damascus, telling him about them, and exhorting him to build and endow a hospital for sick strangers and to construct religious houses on the highways. He bade him also satisfy the owners of the copper vessels and provide for the maintenance of the owner of the house. The latter took the letter to the king, who came to the village and removed the gold, after satisfying the owners of the vessels and the man himself. He searched for Abu Ya'qub, but failing to find any trace or news of him, returned to Damascus, where he built the hospital which is known by his name and is the finest in the world.

I came next to the city of Tripoli, one of the principal towns in Syria. It lies two miles inland, and has only recently been built. The old town was right on the shore; the Christians held it for a time, and when it was recovered by Sultan Baybars [r. 1260–1277] it was pulled down and this new town built. There are some fine bathhouses in it, one of which is named after Sindamur, who was a former governor of the city. Many stories are told of his severity to evildoers. Here is one of them. A woman complained to him that one of the mamluks [slave soldiers] of his personal staff had seized some milk that she was selling and had drunk it. She had no evidence, but Sindamur sent for the man. He was cut in two, and the milk came out of his entrails. Similar stories are told of al-Atris at the time when he was governor of Aydhab under Sultan Qala'un, and of Kebek, the Sultan of Turkestan [central Asian territory].

From Tripoli I went by way of Hosn al-Akrad [Krak des Chevaliers] and Homs to Hama, another of the metropolitan cities of Syria. It is surrounded by orchards and gardens, in the midst of which there are waterwheels like revolving globes. From there to Maarat al-Numaan, which lies in a district inhabited by some sort of Shi'ites, abominable people who hate the Ten Companions and every person whose name is Omar. We went on from there to Sarmin, where brick soap is manufactured and exported to Cairo and Damascus. Besides this they manufacture perfumed soap, for washing hands, and color it red and yellow. These people too are revilers, who hate the Ten, and—an extraordinary thing—never mention the word *ten*. When their brokers are selling by auction in the markets and come to ten, they say "nine and one." One day a Turk happened to be there, and hearing a broker call "nine and one," he laid his club about his head, saying, "Say 'ten,'" immediately after which he said, "Ten with the club." We journeyed from there to Aleppo, which is the seat of the Malik al-Umara, who is the principal commander under the sultan of Egypt. He is a jurist and has a reputation for fair-dealing, but he is stingy.

I went on from there to Antioch, by way of Tayzin, a new town founded by the Turkmens. Antioch was protected formerly by a wall of unrivaled solidity among the cities of Syria, but al-Malik az-Zahir [Baybars] pulled it down when he captured the town. It is very densely populated and possesses beautiful buildings, with abundant trees and water. From there I visited the fortress of Baghras, at the entrance to the land of Sis, that is, the land of the Armenian infidels, and many other castles and fortresses, several of which belong to a sect called Ismailites or Fidawis and may be entered by none but members of the sect. They are the arrows of the sultan; by means of them he strikes those of his enemies who escape into Iraq and other lands. They receive fixed salaries, and when the sultan desires to send one of them to assassinate one of his enemies, he pays him his blood money. If after carrying out his allotted task he escapes with his life, the money is his, but if he is killed it goes to his sons. They carry poisoned daggers, with which they strike their victim, but sometimes their plans miscarry and they themselves are killed. . . .

We came next to the town of Baalbek, an old town and one of the finest in Syria, rivaling Damascus in its innumerable amenities. No other district has such an abundance of cherries, and many kinds of sweetmeats are manufactured in it, as well as textiles, and wooden vessels and spoons that cannot be equaled elsewhere. They make a series of plates one within the other to as many as ten in all, yet anyone looking at it would take them to be one plate. They do the same with spoons, and put them in a leather case. A man can carry this in his belt, and on joining in a meal with his friends take out what looks like one spoon and distribute nine others from within it. Baalbek is one day's journey from Damascus by hard going; caravans on leaving Baalbek spend a night at a small village called al-Zabadani and go on to Damascus the following morning. I reached Baalbek in the evening and left it next morning because of my eagerness to get to Damascus.

I entered Damascus on Thursday the ninth of Ramadan 726 [9 August 1326] and lodged at the Malikite college called ash-Sharabishiya. Damascus surpasses all other cities in beauty, and no description, however full, can do justice to its charms. Nothing, however, can better the words of Ibn Jubayr in describing it. The cathedral mosque, known as the Umayyad Mosque, is the most magnificent mosque in the world, the finest in construction and noblest in beauty, grace, and perfection; it is matchless and unequaled. The person who undertook its construction was the caliph Al-Walid I [r. 705–715]. He applied to the Roman [Byzantine] emperor at Constantinople ordering him to send craftsmen to him, and the emperor sent him twelve thousand of them. The site of the mosque was a church, and when the Muslims captured Damascus, one of their commanders entered from one side by the sword and reached as far as the middle of the church, while the other entered peaceably from the eastern side and reached the middle also. So the Muslims made the half of the church which they had entered by force into a mosque and the half which they had entered by peaceful agreement remained as a church. When Walid decided to extend the mosque over the entire church, he asked the Greeks to sell him their church for whatever equivalent they desired, but they refused, so he seized it. The Christians used to say that whoever destroyed the church would be stricken with madness and they told that to Walid. But he replied, "I will be the first to be stricken by madness in the service of God," and seizing an ax, he set to work to knock it down with his own hands. The Muslims on seeing that followed his example, and God proved false the assertion of the Christians.

This mosque has four doors. The southern door, called the "Door of Increase," is approached by a spacious passage where the dealers in second-hand goods and other commodities have their shops. Through it lies the way to the [former] cavalry house, and on the left as one emerges from it is the coppersmiths' gallery, a large bazaar, one of the finest in Damascus, extending along the south wall of the mosque. It also has a large passage, leading out to a large and extensive colonnade which is entered through a quintuple gateway between six tall columns. Along both sides of this passage are pillars, supporting circular galleries, where the cloth merchants among others have their shops; above these again are long galleries in which are the shops of the jewelers and booksellers and makers of admirable glassware. In the square adjoining the first door are the stalls of the principal notaries, in each of which there may be five or six witnesses in attendance and a person authorized by the qadi to perform marriage-ceremonies. The other notaries are scattered throughout the city. Near these stalls is the bazaar of the stationers, who sell paper, pens, and ink. In the middle of the passage there is a large round marble basin, surrounded by a pavilion supported on marble columns but lacking a roof. In the center of the basin is a copper pipe which forces out water under pressure so that it rises into the air more than a man's height. They call it "the Waterspout," and it is a fine sight. To the right as one comes out of the Jayrun door, which is called also the "Door of the Hours," is an upper gallery shaped like a large arch, within which there are small open arches furnished with doors, to the number of the hours of the day. These doors are painted green on the inside and yellow on the outside, and as each hour of the day passes the green inner side of the door is turned to the outside, and vice versa. They say that inside the gallery there is a person in the room who is responsible for turning them by hand as the hours pass. The western door is called the "Door of the Post." The passage outside it contains the shops of the candlemakers and a gallery for the sale of fruit. The northern door is called the "Door of the Confectioners"; it too has a large passageway, and on the right as one leaves it is a *khanqah*, which has a large basin of water in the center and lavatories supplied with running water. At each of the four doors of the mosque is a building for ritual ablutions, containing about a hundred rooms abundantly supplied with running water.

One of the principal Hanbalite doctors at Damascus was Taqi ad-Din Ibn Taymiya, a man of great ability and wide learning, but with some kink in his brain. The people of Damascus idolized him. He used to preach to them from the pulpit, and one day he made some statement that the other theologians disapproved; they carried the case to the sultan and in consequence Ibn Taymiya was imprisoned for some years. While he was in prison he wrote a commentary on the Qur'an, which he called *The Ocean*, in about forty volumes. Later on his mother presented herself before the sultan and interceded for him, so he was set at liberty, until he did the same thing again. I was in Damascus at the time and attended the service which he was conducting one Friday, as he was addressing and admonishing the people from the pulpit. In the midst of his discourse he said, "Truly God descends to the sky over our world [from heaven] in the same bodily fashion that I make this descent," and stepped down one step of the pulpit. A Malikite doctor present contradicted him and objected to his statement, but the common people rose up against this doctor, and beat him with their hands and their shoes so severely that his turban fell off and disclosed a silken skullcap on his head. Inveighing against him for wearing this, they dragged him before the qadi of the Hanbalites, who ordered him to be imprisoned and afterward had him beaten. The other doctors objected to this treatment and carried the matter before the principal emir [commander or ruler], who wrote to the sultan about the matter and at the same time drew up a legal attestation against Ibn Taymiya for various heretical pronouncements.

This deed was sent on to the sultan, who gave orders that Ibn Taymiya should be imprisoned in the citadel, and there he remained until his death.

One of the celebrated sanctuaries at Damascus is the Mosque of the Foot-prints [al-Aqdam], which lies two miles south of the city, alongside the main highway which leads to the Hejaz, Jerusalem, and Egypt. It is a large mosque, very blessed, richly endowed, and very highly venerated by the Damascenes. The footprints from which it derives its name are certain footprints impressed upon a rock there, which are said to be the mark of Moses' foot. In this mosque there is a small chamber containing a stone with the following inscription: "A certain pious man saw in his sleep the chosen one [Muhammad], who said to him 'Here is the grave of my brother Moses.'" I saw a remarkable instance of the veneration in which the Damascenes hold this mosque during the great pestilence, on my return journey through Damascus in the latter part of July 1348. The viceroy Arghun Shah ordered a crier to proclaim through Damas-cus that all the people should fast for three days and that no one should cook anything eatable in the market during the daytime. For most of the people there eat no food but what has been prepared in the market. So the people fasted for three successive days, the last of which was a Thursday, then they assembled in the Great Mosque, emirs, sharifs, qadis, theologians, and all the other classes of the people, until the place was filled to overflowing, and there they spent the Thursday night in prayers and litanies. After the dawn prayer next morning they all went out together on foot, holding Qur'ans in their hands, and the emirs barefoot. The procession was joined by the entire population of the town, men and women, small and large; the Jews came with their book of the law and the Christians with their Gospel, all of them with their women and children. The whole concourse, weeping and supplicating and seeking the favor of God through his books and his prophets, made their way to the Mosque of the Footprints, and there they remained in supplication and invocation until near midday. They then returned to the city and held the Friday service, and God lightened their affliction; for the number of deaths in a single day at Damascus did not attain two thousand, while in Cairo and Old Cairo it reached the figure of twenty-four thousand a day.

The variety and expenditure of the religious endowments at Damascus are beyond computation. There are endowments in aid of persons who cannot undertake the pilgrimage to Mecca, out of which are paid the expenses of those who go in their stead. There are other endowments for supplying wed-ding outfits to girls whose families are unable to provide them, and others for the freeing of prisoners. There are endowments for travelers, out of the revenues of which they are given food, clothing, and the expenses of convey-ance to their countries. Then there are endowments for the improvement and paving of the streets, because all the lanes in Damascus have pavements on either side, on which the foot passengers walk, while those who ride use the roadway in the center. Besides these there are endowments for other charitable purposes. One day as I went along a lane in Damascus I saw a small slave who had dropped a Chinese porcelain dish, which was broken to bits. A number of people collected around him and one of them said to him, "Gather up the pieces and take them to the custodian of the endowments for utensils." He did so, and the man went with him to the custodian, where the slave showed him the broken pieces and received a sum sufficient to buy a similar dish. This is an excellent institution, for the master of the slave would undoubtedly have beaten him, or at least scolded him, for breaking the dish, and the slave would have been heartbroken and upset at the accident. This benefaction is indeed a mender of hearts—may God richly reward him whose zeal for good works rose to such heights!

The people of Damascus vie with one another in building mosques, religious houses, colleges, and mausoleums. They have a high opinion of the North Africans, and freely entrust them with the care of their moneys, wives, and children. All strangers among them are handsomely treated, and care is taken that they are not forced to any action that might injure their self-respect. When I came to Damascus a firm friendship sprang up between the Malikite professor Nur ad-Din Sakhawi and me, and he besought me to breakfast at his house during the nights of Ramadan. After I had visited him for four nights I had a stroke of fever and absented myself. He sent in search of me, and although I pleaded my illness in excuse he refused to accept it. I went back to his house and spent the night there, and when I desired to take my leave the next morning he would not hear of it, but said to me, "Consider my house as your own or as your father's or brother's." He then had a doctor sent for, and gave orders that all the medicines and dishes that the doctor prescribed were to be made for me in his house. I stayed thus with him until the Fast-breaking [Eid al-Fitr], when I went to the festival prayers and God healed me of what had befallen me. Meanwhile all the money I had for my expenses was exhausted. Nur ad-Din, learning this, hired camels for me and gave me traveling and other provisions, and money in addition, saying, "It will come in for any serious matter that may land you in difficulties"—may God reward him!

The Damascenes observe an admirable order in funeral processions. They walk in front of the bier, while reciters intone the Qur'an in beautiful and affecting voices, and pray over it in the cathedral mosque. When the reading is completed the muezzins [reciters of the call for prayer] rise and say, "Reflect on your prayer for so-and-so, the pious and learned," describing him with good epithets, and having prayed over him they take him to his grave. The Indians have a funerary ceremony even more admirable than this. On the morning of the third day after the burial they assemble in the burial place of the deceased, which is spread with fine cloths, the grave being covered with magnificent hangings and surrounded by sweet-scented flowers, roses, sweetbriar, and jasmine, for these flowers are perennial with them. They bring lemon and citrus trees as well, tying on their fruits if they have none, and put up an awning to shade the mourning party. The qadis, emirs, and other persons of rank come and take their seats, and after recitation of the Qur'an, the qadi rises and delivers a set oration, speaking of the deceased, and mourning his death in an elegiac ode, then comforting his relatives, and praying for the sultan. When the sultan's name is mentioned the audience rise and bow their heads toward the quarter in which the sultan is. The qadi then resumes his seat, and rosewater is brought in and sprinkled on all the people, beginning with the qadi. After this syrup is brought in and served to everyone, beginning with the qadi. Finally the betel [a plant chewed as a stimulant] is brought. This they hold in high esteem, and give to their guests as a mark of respect; a gift of betel from the sultan is a greater honor than a gift of money or robes of honor. When a man dies, his family eat no betel until the day of this ceremony, when the qadi takes some leaves of it and gives them to the heir of the deceased, who eats them, after which the party disperses. . . .

From Tabuk the caravan travels with great speed night and day, for fear of this desert. Halfway through is the valley of al-Ukhaydir, which might well be the valley of hell (may God preserve us from it). One year the pilgrims suffered terribly here from the simoom wind [a hot, dry, violent wind]; the water supplies dried up and the price of a single drink rose to a thousand dinars, but both seller and buyer perished. Their story is written on a rock in the valley. Five days after leaving Tabuk they reach the well of al-Hijr, which has an abundance of water, but not a soul draws water there, however violent his thirst, following the example of the Prophet, who passed it on his expedition to Tabuk and drove on his camel, giving orders that none should drink of its waters. Here, in some hills of red rock, are the dwellings of Thamud. They are cut in the rock and have carved thresholds. Anyone seeing them would take them to be of recent construction. Their decayed bones are to be seen inside these houses. Al-'Ula, a large and pleasant village with palm-gardens and water-springs, lies half a day's journey or less from al-Hijr. The pilgrims halt there four days to provision themselves and wash their clothes. They leave behind them here any surplus of provisions they may have, taking with them nothing but what is strictly necessary. The people of the village are very trustworthy. The Christian merchants of Syria may come as far as this and no further, and they trade in provisions and other goods with the pilgrims here. On the third day after leaving Al-'Ula the caravan halts in the outskirts of the holy city of Medina.

That same evening we entered the holy sanctuary and reached the illustrious mosque, halting in salutation at the Gate of Peace; then we prayed in the illustrious "garden" between the tomb of the Prophet and the noble pulpit, and reverently touched the fragment that remains of the palm trunk against which the Prophet stood when he preached. Having paid our meed of salutation to the lord of men from first to last, the intercessor for sinners, the Prophet of Mecca, Muhammad, as well as to his two companions who share his grave, Abu Bakr and Omar, we returned to our camp, rejoicing at this great favor bestowed upon us, praising God for our having reached the former abodes and the magnificent sanctuaries of his holy Prophet, and praying him to grant that this visit should not be our last, and that we might be of those whose pilgrimage is accepted. On this journey our stay at Medina lasted four days. We used to spend every night in the illustrious mosque, where the people, after forming circles in the courtyard and lighting large numbers of candles, would pass the time either in reciting the Qur'an from volumes set on rests in front of them, or in intoning litanies, or in visiting the sanctuaries of the holy tomb.

We then set out from Medina toward Mecca, and halted near the mosque of Dhu'l-Hulayfa, five miles away. It was at this point that the Prophet assumed the pilgrim garb and obligations, and here too I divested myself of my tailored clothes, bathed, and putting on the pilgrim's garment I prayed and dedicated myself to the pilgrimage. Our fourth halt from here was at Badr, where God aided his Prophet and performed his promise. It is a village containing a series of palm gardens and a bubbling spring with a stream flowing from it. Our way lay from there through a frightful desert called the Valley of Bazwa for three days to the valley of Rabigh, where the rainwater forms pools which lie stagnant for a long time. From this point (which is just before Juhfah) the pilgrims from Egypt and northwest Africa put on the pilgrim garment. Three days after leaving Rabigh we reached the pool of Khulays, which lies in a plain and has many palm gardens. The Bedouin of that neighborhood hold a market there, to which they bring sheep, fruits, and condiments. From there we traveled through 'Usfan to the Bottom of Marr, a fertile valley with numerous palms and a spring supplying a stream from which the district is irrigated. From this valley fruit and vegetables are transported to Mecca. We set out at night from this blessed valley, with hearts full of joy at reaching the goal of our hopes, and in the morning arrived at the city of surety, Mecca (may God ennoble her!), where we immediately entered the holy sanctuary and began the rites of pilgrimage.

The inhabitants of Mecca are distinguished by many excellent and noble activities and qualities, by their beneficence to the humble and weak, and by their kindness to strangers. When any of them makes a feast, he begins by giving food to the religious devotees who are poor and without resources, inviting them first with kindness and delicacy. The majority of these unfortunates are to be found by the public bakehouses, and when anyone has his bread baked and takes it away to his house, they follow him and he gives each one of them some share of it, sending away none disappointed. Even if he has but a single loaf, he gives away a third or a half of it, cheerfully and without any grudgingness. Another good habit of theirs is this. The orphan children sit in the bazaar, each with two baskets, one large and one small. When one of the townspeople comes to the bazaar and buys cereals, meat and vegetables, he hands them to one of these boys, who puts the cereals in one basket and the meat and vegetables in the other and takes them to the man's house, so that his meal may be prepared. Meanwhile the man goes about his devotions and his business. There is no instance of any of the boys having ever abused this matter, and they are given a fixed fee of a few coppers. The Meccans are very elegant and clean in their dress, and most of them wear white garments, which you always see fresh and snowy. They use a great deal of perfume and kohl and make free use of toothpicks of green arak wood. The Meccan women are extraordinarily beautiful and very pious and modest. They too make great use of perfumes to such a degree that they will spend the night hungry in order to buy perfumes with the price of their food. They visit the mosque every Thursday night, wearing their finest apparel; and the whole sanctuary is saturated with the smell of their perfume. When one of these women goes away the odor of the perfume clings to the place after she has gone.

Among the personages who were living in religious retirement at Mecca was a pious and ascetic doctor who had a long-standing friendship with my father, and who used to stay with us when he came to our town of Tangier. In the daytime he taught at the Muzaffariya college, but at night he retired to his dwelling in the convent of Rabi'. This convent is one of the finest in Mecca; it has in its precincts a well of sweet water which has no equal in Mecca, and its inhabitants are all men of great piety. It is highly venerated by the people of the Hejaz, who bring votive offerings to it, and the people of Ta'if supply it with fruit. Their custom is that all those who possess a palm garden, or orchard of vines, peaches, or figs, give the alms tithe from its produce to this convent, and fetch it on their own camels. It is two days' journey from Ta'if to Mecca. If any person fails to do this, his crop is diminished and dearth stricken in the following year. One day the retainers of the governor of Mecca came to this convent, led in the governor's horses, and watered them at the well mentioned above. After the horses had been taken back to their stables, they were seized with colic and threw themselves to the ground, beating it with their heads and legs. On hearing of this the governor went in person to the gate of the convent and after apologizing to the poor recluses there, took one of them back with him. This man rubbed the beasts' bellies with his hand, when they expelled all the water that they had drunk, and were cured. After that the retainers never presented themselves at the convent except for good purposes. . . .

From Marrakesh I traveled with the suite of our master [the sultan] to Fez, where I took leave of our master and set out for the Country of the Blacks. I reached the town of Sijilmasa, a very fine town, with quantities of excellent dates. The city of Basra rivals it in abundance of dates, but the Sijilmasa dates are better, and the kind called *irar* has no equal in the world. I stayed there with the learned Abu Muhammad al-Bushri, the man whose brother I met in the city of Fuzhou [?] in China. How strangely separated they are! He showed me the utmost honor.

At Sijilmasa I bought camels and a four months' supply of forage for them. Shortly afterward I set out on the first of Muharram of the year [seven hundred and] fifty-three [18 February 1352] with a caravan including, among others, a number of the merchants of Sijilmasa. After twenty-five days we reached Taghaza, an unattractive village, with the curious feature that its houses and mosques are built of blocks of salt, roofed with camel skins. There are no trees there, nothing but sand. In the sand is a salt mine; they dig for the salt, and find it in thick slabs, lying one on top of the other, as though they had been tool-squared and laid under the surface of the earth. A camel will carry two of these slabs. No one lives at Taghaza except the slaves of the Masufa tribe, who dig for the salt; they subsist on dates imported from Dar'a and Sijilmasa, camels' flesh, and millet imported from the Country of the Blacks. The blacks come up from their country and take away the salt from there. At Oualata a load of salt brings eight to ten mithqals [gold coins]; in the town of Mali it sells for twenty to thirty, and sometimes as much as forty. The blacks use salt as a medium of exchange, just as gold and silver is used [elsewhere]; they cut it up into pieces and buy and sell with it. The business done at Taghaza, for all its meanness, amounts to an enormous figure in terms of hundredweights of gold dust.

We passed ten days of discomfort there, because the water is brackish and the place is plagued with flies. Water supplies are laid in at Taghaza for the crossing of the desert which lies beyond it, which is a ten nights' journey with no water on the way except on rare occasions. We indeed had the good fortune to find water in plenty, in pools left by the rain. One day we found a pool of sweet water between two rocky prominences. We quenched our thirst at it and then washed our clothes. Truffles are plentiful in this desert and it swarms with lice, so that people wear string necklaces containing mercury, which kills them. At that time we used to go ahead of the caravan, and when we found a place suitable for pasturage we would graze our beasts. We went on doing this until one of our party was lost in the desert; after that I neither went ahead nor lagged behind. We passed a caravan on the way and they told us that some of their party had become separated from them. We found one of them dead under a shrub, of the sort that grows in the sand, with his clothes on and a whip in his hand. The water was only about a mile away from him.

We came next to Tasarahla [Bir al-Ksaib?], a place of subterranean water-beds, where the caravans halt. They stay there three days to rest, mend their waterskins, fill them with water, and sew on them covers of sackcloth as a precaution against the wind. From this point the *takshif* is dispatched. The *takshif* is a name given to any man of the Masufa tribe who is hired by the persons in the caravan to go ahead to Oualata, carrying letters from them to their friends there, so that they may take lodgings for them. These persons then come out a distance of four nights' journey to meet the caravan, and bring water with them. Anyone who has no friend in Oualata writes to some merchant well known for his worthy character, who then undertakes the same services for him. It often happens that the *takshif* perishes in this desert, with the result that the people of Oualata know nothing about the caravan, and all or most of those who are with it perish. That desert is haunted by demons; if the *takshif* be alone, they make sport of him and disorder his mind, so that he loses his way and perishes. For there is no visible road or track in these parts—nothing but sand blown this way and that by the wind. You see hills of sand in one place, and afterward you will see them moved to quite another place. The guide there is one who has made the journey frequently in both directions, and who is gifted with a quick intelligence. I remarked, as a strange thing, that the guide whom we had was blind in one eye, and diseased in the other, yet he had the best knowledge of the road of any man. We hired the *takshif* on this journey for a hundred gold mithqals; he was a man of the Masufa. On the night of the seventh day [from Tasarahla] we saw with joy the fires of the party who had come out to meet us.

Thus we reached the town of Oualata after a journey from Sijilmasa of two months to a day. Oualata is the northernmost province of the blacks, and the sultan's representative there was one Farba Husayn, *farba* meaning deputy. When we arrived there, the merchants deposited their goods in an open square, where the blacks undertook to guard them, and went to the *farba*. He was sitting on a carpet under an archway, with his guards before him carrying lances and bows in their hands, and the headmen of the Masufa behind him. The merchants remained standing in front of him while he spoke to them through an interpreter, although they were close to him, to show his contempt for them. It was then that I repented of having come to their country, because of their lack of manners and their contempt for the whites.

I went to visit Ibn Badda, a worthy man of Sale to whom I had written requesting him to hire a house for me, and who had done so. Later on the *mushrif* [inspector] of Oualata, whose name was Mansha Ju, invited all those who had come on the caravan to partake of his hospitality. At first I refused to attend, but my companions urged me very strongly, so I went with the rest. The repast was served—some pounded millet mixed with a little honey and milk, put in a half calabash shaped like a large bowl. The guests drank and retired. I said to them, "Was it for this that the black invited us?" They answered, "Yes; and it is in their opinion the highest form of hospitality." This convinced me that there was no good to be hoped for from these people, and I made up my mind to travel with the pilgrim caravan from Oualata. Afterward, however, I thought it best to go to see the capital of their king.

My stay at Oualata lasted about fifty days; and I was shown honor and entertained by its inhabitants. It is an excessively hot place, and boasts a few small date palms, in the shade of which they sow watermelons. Its water comes from underground water-beds at that point, and there is plenty of mutton to be had. The garments of its inhabitants, most of whom belong to the Masufa tribe, are of fine Egyptian fabrics. Their women are of surpassing beauty, and are shown more respect than the men. The state of affairs among these people is indeed extraordinary. Their men show no signs of jealousy whatsoever; no one claims descent from his father, but on the contrary from his mother's brother. A person's heirs are his sister's sons, not his own sons. This is a thing which I have seen nowhere in the world except among the Indians of Malabar. But those are heathens; *these* people are Muslims, punctilious in observing the hours of prayer, studying books of law, and memorizing the Qur'an. Yet their women show no bashfulness before men and do not veil themselves, though they are assiduous in attending the prayers. Any man who wishes to marry one of them may do so, but they do not travel with their husbands, and even if one desired to do so her family would not allow her to go.

The women there have "friends" and "companions" among the men outside their own families, and the men in the same way have "companions" among the women of other families. A man may go into his house and find his wife entertaining her "companion" but he takes no objection to it. One day at Oualata I went into the qadi's house, after asking his permission to enter, and found with him a young woman of remarkable beauty. When I saw her, I was shocked and turned to go out, but she laughed at me, instead of being overcome by shame, and the qadi said to me, "Why are you going out? She is my companion." I was amazed at their conduct, for he was a theologian and a pilgrim to boot. I was told that he had asked the sultan's permission to make the pilgrimage that year with his "companion" (whether this one or not I cannot say) but the sultan would not grant it.

When I decided to make the journey to Mali, which is reached in twenty-four days from Oualata if the traveler pushes on rapidly, I hired a guide from the Masufa (for there is no necessity to travel in a company on account of the safety of that road), and set out with three of my companions. On the way there are many trees, and these trees are of great age and girth; a whole caravan may shelter in the shade of one of them. There are trees which have neither branches nor leaves, yet the shade cast by their trunks is sufficient to shelter a man. Some of these trees are rotted in the interior and the rainwater collects in them, so that they serve as wells and the people drink of the water inside them. In others there are bees and honey, which is collected by the people. I was surprised to find inside one tree, by which I passed, a man, a weaver, who had set up his loom in it and was actually weaving.

A traveler in this country carries no provisions, whether plain food or seasonings, and neither gold nor silver. He takes nothing but pieces of salt and glass ornaments, which the people call beads, and some aromatic goods. When he comes to a village the women of the blacks bring out millet, milk, chickens, pulped lotus fruit, rice, *funi* (a grain resembling mustard seed, from which couscous and gruel are made), and pounded haricot beans. The traveler buys what of these he wants, but their rice causes sickness to whites when it is eaten, and the *funi* is preferable to it.

Ten days after leaving Oualata we came to the village of Zaghari [Sokolo?], a large village, inhabited by black traders called *wanjarata*, along with whom live a community of whites of the Ibadite sect. It is from this village that millet is carried to Oualata. After leaving Zaghari we came to the great river, that is the Nile [actually the Niger], on which stands the town of Karsakhu [south of Sokolo?]. The Nile flows from there down to Kabara, and from there to Zagha [Dia?]. In both Kabara and Zagha there are sultans who owe allegiance to the king of Mali. The inhabitants of Zagha are of old standing in Islam; they show great devotion and zeal for study. From there the Nile descends to Timbuktu and Gao, both of which will be described later; then to the town of Muli [?] in the land of the Limiyes, which is the frontier province of [the kingdom of] Mali; from there to Yufi [Zimbabwe Plateau?], one of the largest towns of the blacks, whose ruler is one of the most considerable of the black rulers. It cannot be visited by any white man because they would kill him before he got there. From Yufi the Nile descends to the land of the Nubians, who profess the Christian faith, and from there to Dongola, which is their chief town. The sultan of Dongola is called Ibn Kanz ad-Din; he was converted to Islam in the days of [Sultan] al-Malik an-Nasir [of Egypt, 1293–1341]. From there it descends to the cataracts, which is the end of the black territories and the beginning of the province of Aswan in Upper Egypt. I saw a crocodile in this part of the Nile, close to the bank; it looked just like a small boat. One day I went down to the river to satisfy a need, and see, one of the blacks came and stood between me and the river. I was amazed at such lack of manners and decency on his part, and spoke of it to someone or other. He answered, "His purpose in doing that was solely to protect you from the crocodile, by placing himself between you and it."

We set out thereafter from Karsakhu and came to the river of Sansara [Sankarani?], which is about ten miles from Mali. It is their custom that no persons except those who have obtained permission are allowed to enter the city. I had already written to the white community [there] requesting them to hire a house for me, so when I arrived at this river, I crossed by the ferry with no interference. Thus I reached the city of Mali, the capital of the king of the blacks. I stopped at the cemetery and went to the quarter occupied by the whites, where I asked for Muhammad ibn al-Faqih. I found that he had hired a house for me and went there. His son-in-law brought me candles and food, and the next day Ibn al-Faqih himself came to visit me; he is a black, a pilgrim, and a man of fine character. I met also the interpreter Dugha, who is one of the principal men among the blacks. All these persons sent me hospitality gifts of food and treated me with the utmost generosity—may God reward them for their kindnesses! Ten days after our arrival we ate a gruel made of a root resembling colocasia, which is preferred by them to all other dishes. We all fell ill—there were six of us—and one of our number died. I for my part went to the morning prayer and fainted there. I asked a certain Egyptian for a loosening remedy and he gave me a thing called *baydar*, made of vegetable roots, which he mixed with anise and sugar, and stirred in water. I drank it off and vomited what I had eaten, together with a large quantity of bile. God preserved me from death but I was ill for two months.

The sultan of Mali is Mansa Suleyman [Keita, r. 1341–1360], *mansa* meaning sultan, and Suleyman being his proper name. He is a miserly king, not a man from whom one might hope for a rich present. It happened that I spent these two months without seeing him, on account of my illness. Later on he held a banquet in commemoration of our master [the late sultan of Morocco] Abu 'l-Hasan, to which the commanders, doctors, qadi, and preacher were invited, and I went along with them. Reading desks [were] brought in, and the Qur'an was read through, then they prayed for our master Abu 'l Hasan and also for Mansa Suleyman. When the ceremony was over I went forward and saluted Mansa Suleyman. The qadi, the preacher, and Ibn al-Faqih told him who I was, and he answered them in their tongue. They said to me, "The sultan says to you 'Give thanks to God,'" so I said, "Praise be to God and thanks under all circumstances."

When I withdrew the [sultan's] hospitality gift was sent to me. It was taken first to the qadi's house, and the qadi sent it on with his men to Ibn al-Faqih's house. Ibn al-Faqih came hurrying out of his house barefoot, and entered my room, saying, "Stand up; here comes the sultan's stuff and gift to you." So I stood up thinking that it consisted of robes of honor and money, and see! it was three cakes of bread, and a piece of beef fried in native oil, and a calabash of sour curds. When I saw this I burst out laughing, and thought it a most amazing thing that they could be so foolish and make so much of such a paltry matter.

For two months after this hospitality gift was sent to me I received nothing further from the sultan, and then followed the month of Ramadan. Meanwhile I used to go frequently to the palace where I would salute him and sit alongside the qadi and the preacher. I had a conversation with Dugha the interpreter, and he said, "Speak in his presence, and I will express on your behalf what is necessary." When the sultan held an audience early in Ramadan, I rose and stood before him and said to him, "I have traveled through the countries of the world and have met their kings. Here I have been four months in your country, yet you have neither shown me hospitality, nor given me anything. What am I to say of you in front of rulers?" The sultan replied, "I have not seen you, and have not been told about you." The qadi and Ibn al-Faqih rose and replied to him, saying, "He has already saluted you, and you have sent him food." Soon afterward he gave orders to set apart a house for my lodging and to pay me a daily sum for my expenses. Later on, on the night of the twenty-seventh of Ramadan, he distributed a sum of money which they call the zakat [alms] between the qadi, the preachers, and the doctors. He gave me a portion along with them of thirty-three and a third mithqals, and on my departure from Mali he bestowed on me a gift of a hundred gold mithqals.

On certain days the sultan holds audiences in the palace yard, where there is a platform under a tree, with three steps; this they call the *pempi*. It is carpeted with silk and has cushions placed on it. [Over it] is raised the umbrella, which is a sort of pavilion made of silk, surmounted by a bird in gold, about the size of a falcon. The sultan comes out of a door in a corner of the palace, carrying a bow in his hand and a quiver on his back. On his head he has a golden skullcap, bound with a gold band which has narrow ends shaped like knives, more than a span in length. His usual dress is a velvety red tunic, made of the European fabrics called *mutanfas*. The sultan is preceded by his musicians, who carry gold and silver guimbris [two-stringed guitars], and behind him come three hundred armed slaves. He walks in a leisurely fashion, affecting a very slow movement, and even stops from time to time. On reaching the *pempi* he stops and looks round the assembly, then ascends it in the sedate manner of a preacher ascending a mosque pulpit. As he takes his seat the drums, trumpets, and bugles are sounded. Three slaves go out at a run to summon the sovereign's deputy and the military commanders, who enter and sit down. Two saddled and bridled horses are brought, along with two goats, which they hold to serve as a protection against the evil eye. Dugha stands at the gate and the rest of the people remain in the street, under the trees.

The blacks are of all people the most submissive to their king and the most abject in their behavior before him. They swear by his name, saying, "Mansa Suleyman ki." If he summons any of them while he is holding an audience in his pavilion, the person summoned takes off his clothes and puts on worn garments, removes his turban and dons a dirty skullcap, and enters with his garments and trousers raised knee-high. He goes forward in an attitude of humility and dejection, and knocks the ground hard with his elbows, then stands with bowed head and bent back listening to what he says. If anyone addresses the king and receives a reply from him, he uncovers his back and throws dust over his head and back, for all the world like a bather splashing himself with water. I used to wonder how it was they did not blind themselves. If the sultan delivers any remarks during his audience, those present take off their turbans and put them down, and listen in silence to what he says. Sometimes one of them stands up before him and recalls his deeds in the sultan's service, saying, "I did so-and-so on such a day" or "I killed so-and-so on such a day." Those who have knowledge of this confirm his words, which they do by plucking the cord of the bow and releasing it, just as an archer does when shooting an arrow. If the sultan says "Truly spoken" or thanks him, he removes his clothes and "dusts." That is their idea of good manners.

Ibn Juzayy adds: "I have been told that when the pilgrim Musa al-Wanjarati came to our master Abu 'l-Hasan as envoy from Mansa Suleyman, one of his suite carried with him a basketful of dust when he entered the noble audience-hall, and the envoy 'dusted' whenever our master spoke a gracious word to him, just as he would do in his own country."

I was at Mali during the two festivals of the sacrifice and the fast-breaking. On these days the sultan takes his seat on the *pempi* after the midafternoon prayer. The armor bearers bring in magnificent arms—quivers of gold and silver, swords ornamented with gold and with golden scabbards, gold and silver lances, and crystal maces. At his head stand four emirs driving off the flies, having in their hands silver ornaments resembling saddle-stirrups. The commanders, qadi, and preacher sit in their usual places. The interpreter Dugha comes with his four wives and his slave girls, who are about a hundred in number. They are wearing beautiful robes, and on their heads they have gold and silver fillets, with gold and silver balls attached. A chair is placed for Dugha to sit on. He plays on an instrument made of reeds, with some small calabashes at its lower end, and chants a poem in praise of the sultan, recalling his battles and deeds of valor. The women and girls sing along with him and play with bows. Accompanying them are about thirty youths, wearing red woolen tunics and white skullcaps; each of them has his drum slung from his shoulder and beats it. Afterward come his boy pupils who play and turn wheels in the air, like the natives of Sind. They show a marvelous nimbleness and agility in these exercises and play most cleverly with swords. Dugha also makes a fine play with the sword. Soon afterward the sultan orders a gift to be presented to Dugha and he is given a purse containing two hundred mithqals of gold dust, and is informed of the contents of the purse before all the people. The commanders rise and twang their bows in thanks to the sultan. The next day each one of them gives Dugha a gift, every man according to his rank. Every Friday after the Asr prayer, Dugha carries out a similar ceremony to this that we have described.

On feast days, after Dugha has finished his display, the poets come in. Each of them is inside a figure resembling a thrush, made of feathers, and provided with a wooden head with a red beak, to look like a thrush's head. They stand in front of the sultan in this ridiculous makeup and recite their poems. I was told that their poetry is a kind of sermonizing in which they say to the sultan: "This *pempi* that you occupy was that where sat this king and that king, and such and such were this one's noble actions and such and such the other's. So do you too do good deeds whose memory will outlive you." After that, the chief of the poets mounts the steps of the *pempi* and lays his head on the sultan's lap, then climbs to the top of the *pempi* and lays his head first on the sultan's right shoulder and then on his left, speaking all the while in their tongue, and finally he comes down again. I was told that this practice is a very old custom among them, prior to the introduction of Islam, and that they have kept it up.

The blacks disliked Mansa Suleyman because of his avarice. His predecessor was Mansa Maghan [r. 1337–1341], and before him reigned Mansa Musa [r. 1312–1337], a generous and virtuous prince, who loved the whites and made gifts to them. It was he who gave Abu Ishaq as-Sahili four thousand mithqals in the course of a single day. I heard from a trustworthy source that he gave three thousand mithqals on one day to Mudrik ibn Faqqus, by whose grandfather his own grandfather, Saraq Jata, had been converted to Islam.

The blacks possess some admirable qualities. They are seldom unjust, and have a greater abhorrence of injustice than do any other people. Their sultan shows no mercy to anyone who is guilty of the least act of it. There is complete security in their country. Neither traveler nor inhabitant in it has anything to fear from robbers or men of violence. They do not confiscate the property of any white man who dies in their country, even if it be uncounted wealth. On the contrary, they give it into the charge of some trustworthy person among the whites, until the rightful heir takes possession of it. They are careful to observe the hours of prayer, and assiduous in attending them in congregations, and in bringing up their children to them. On Fridays, if a man does not go early to the mosque, he cannot find a corner to pray in, on account of the crowd. It is a custom of theirs to send each man his boy with his prayer mat; the boy spreads it out for his master in a place befitting him until he comes to the mosque. Their prayer mats are made of the leaves of a tree resembling a date palm, but without fruit.

Another of their good qualities is their habit of wearing clean white garments on Fridays. Even if a man has nothing but an old worn shirt, he washes it and cleans it, and wears it to the Friday service. Yet another is their zeal for knowing the Qur'an by heart. They put their children in chains if they show any backwardness in memorizing it, and they are not set free until they have it by heart. I visited the qadi in his house on the day of the festival. His children were chained up, so I said to him, "Will you not let them loose?" He replied, "I will not do so until they learn the Qur'an by heart." Among their bad qualities are the following. The woman servants, slave girls, and young girls go about in front of everyone naked, without a stitch of clothing on them. Women go into the sultan's presence naked and without coverings, and his daughters also go about naked. Then there is their custom of putting dust and ashes on their heads, as a mark of respect, and the grotesque ceremonies we have described when the poets recite their verses. Another reprehensible practice among many of them is the eating of carrion, dogs, and asses.

The date of my arrival at Mali was the fourteenth of Jumada I, [seven hundred and] fifty-three [28 June 1352] and of my departure from it the twenty-second of Muharram of the year fifty-four [27 February 1353]. I was accompanied by a merchant called Abu Bakr ibn Ya'qub. We took the Mema road. I had a camel which I was riding, because horses are expensive, and cost a hundred mithqals each. We came to a wide channel which flows out of the Nile and can only be crossed in boats. The place is infested with mosquitoes, and no one can pass that way except by night. We reached the channel three or four hours after nightfall on a moonlit night. On reaching it I saw sixteen beasts with enormous bodies, and marveled at them, taking them to be elephants, of which there are many in that country. Afterward I saw that they had gone into the river, so I said to Abu Bakr, "What kind of animals are these?" He replied, "They are hippopotami which have come out to pasture ashore." They are bulkier than horses, have manes and tails, and their heads are like horses' heads, but their feet like elephants' feet. I saw these hippopotami again when we sailed down the Nile from Timbuktu to Gao. They were swimming in the water, and lifting their heads and blowing. The men in the boat were afraid of them and kept close to the bank in case the hippopotami should sink them.

They have a cunning method of capturing these hippopotami. They use spears with a hole bored in them, through which strong cords are passed. The spear is thrown at one of the animals, and if it strikes its leg or neck it goes right through it. Then they pull on the rope until the beast is brought to the bank, kill it, and eat its flesh. Along the bank there are quantities of hippopotamus bones.

We halted near this channel at a large village, which had as governor a black, a pilgrim, and a man of fine character, named Farba Magha. He was one of the blacks who made the pilgrimage in the company of Sultan Mansa Musa. Farba Magha told me that when Mansa Musa came to this channel, he had with him a qadi, a white man. This qadi attempted to make away with four thousand mithqals and the sultan, on learning of it, was enraged at him and exiled him to the country of heathen cannibals. He lived among them for four years, at the end of which the sultan sent him back to his own country. The reason why the heathens did not eat him was that he was white, for they saw that the white is indigestible because he is not "ripe," whereas the black man is "ripe" in their opinion.

Sultan Mansa Suleyman was visited by a party of these black cannibals, including one of their emirs. They have a custom of wearing in their ears large pendants, each pendant having an opening of half a span. They wrap themselves in silk mantles, and in their country there is a gold mine. The sultan received them with honor, and gave them as his hospitality gift a servant, a black woman. They killed and ate her, and having smeared their faces and hands with her blood, came to the sultan to thank him. I was informed that this is their regular custom whenever they visit his court. Someone told me about them that they say that the choicest parts of women's flesh are the palm of the hand and the breast.

We continued our journey from this village which is by the channel, and came to the town of Quri Mansa [?]. At this point the camel which I was riding died. Its keeper informed me of its death, but when I went out to see it, I found that the blacks had already eaten it, according to their usual custom of eating carrion. I sent two lads whom I had hired for my service to buy me a camel at Zaghari, and waited at Quri Mansa for six days until they returned with it. I traveled next to the town of Mema and halted by some wells in its outskirts. From there we went on to Timbuktu, which stands four miles from the river. Most of its inhabitants are of the Masufa tribe, wearers of the face veil. Its governor is called Farba Musa. I was present with him one day when he had just appointed one of the Masufa to be emir of a section. He assigned to him a robe, a turban, and trousers, all of them of dyed cloth, and bade him sit upon a shield, and the chiefs of his tribe raised him on their heads. In this town is the grave of the meritorious poet Abu Ishaq as-Sahili, of Granada, who is known in his own land as at-Tuwayjin ["Little Saucepan"].

From Timbuktu I sailed down the Nile on a small boat, hollowed out of a single piece of wood. We used to go ashore every night at the villages and buy whatever we needed in the way of meat and butter in exchange for salt, spices, and glass beads. I then came to a place the name of which I have forgotten, where there was an excellent governor, a pilgrim, called Farba Suleyman. He is famous for his courage and strength, and none ventures to pluck his bow. I have not seen anyone among the blacks taller or more bulkier than him. At this town I was in need of some millet, so I visited him (it was on the Prophet's birthday) and saluted him. He took me by the hand, and led me into his audience hall. We were served with a drink of theirs called *daqnu*, which is water containing some pounded millet mixed with a little honey or milk. They drink this in place of water, because if they drink plain water it upsets them. If they have no millet they mix the water with honey or milk. Afterward a green melon was brought in and we ate some of it.

A young boy, not yet full-grown, came in, and Farba Suleyman, calling him, said to me, "Here is your hospitality gift; keep an eye on him in case he escapes." So I took the [slave] boy and prepared to withdraw, but he said, "Wait until the food comes." A slave girl of his joined us; she was an Arab girl, of Damascus, and she spoke to me in Arabic. While this was going on we heard cries in his house, so he sent the girl to find out what had happened. She returned to him and told him that a daughter of his had just died. He said, "I do not like crying, come, we will walk to the river," meaning the Nile, on which he has some houses. A horse was brought, and he told me to ride, but I said, "I will not ride if you are walking," so we walked together. We came to his houses by the Nile, where food was served, and after we had eaten I took leave of him and withdrew. I met no one among the blacks more generous or upright than him. The boy whom he gave me is still with me.

I went on from there to Gao, which is a large city on the Nile, and one of the finest towns in the Country of the Blacks. It is also one of their biggest and best-provisioned towns, with rice in plenty, milk, and fish, and there is a species of cucumber there called 'inani which has no equal. The buying and selling of its inhabitants is done with cowrie shells, and the same is the case at Mali. I stayed there about a month, and then set out in the direction of Takedda by land with a large caravan of merchants from Ghadames. Their guide and leader was the pilgrim Wuchin, which means "wolf" in the language of the blacks. I had a riding camel and a she-camel to carry my provisions, but when we had traveled the first stage, the she-camel would go no farther. So the pilgrim Wuchin took what was on it and distributed it among his party, each of whom undertook to carry a part of it. There was in the company a Maghrabin belonging to Tadala, who refused to carry any of it at all, as the rest had done. My boy was thirsty one day, and I asked this man for water, but he would not give it.

We now entered the territory of the Bardama, who are a tribe of Berbers. No caravan can travel [through their country] without a guarantee of their protection, and for this purpose a woman's guarantee is of more value than a man's. Their women are the most perfect in beauty and the most shapely in the figure of all women, of a pure white color and very stout; nowhere in the world have I seen any who equal them in stoutness. I fell ill in this country on account of the extreme heat, and a surplus of bile. We pushed on rapidly with our journey until we reached Tagadda. The houses at Tagadda are built of red stone, and its water runs by the copper mines, so that both its color and taste are affected. There are no grain crops there except a little wheat, which is consumed by merchants and strangers. The inhabitants of Taggada have no occupation except trade. They travel to Egypt every year, and import quantities of all the fine fabrics to be had there and of other Egyptian wares. They live in luxury and ease, and vie with one another in regard to the number of their slaves and serving women. The people of Mali and Oualata do the same. They never sell the educated female slaves, or but rarely and at a high price.

Questions: Which areas and which customs impressed Ibn Battuta most in his travels? What evidence is there in this source that Ibn Battuta took religion seriously? What kind of hospitality did Ibn Battuta expect to receive, and why was this so important to him? How does he think his own practice of Islam differs from Christianity and from the practices of other Muslim groups? How does Ibn Battuta describe the response of people in Damascus to the Black Death? Do Ibn Battuta's comments on blacks in West Africa reveal him as racist? What were his attitudes toward women? What do we learn about his wife?

38. PETRARCH, *ASCENT OF MT. VENTOUX*

Francesco Petrarca, called Petrarch in English (1304–1374), was one of the foremost authors of the Italian Renaissance. The occasion of this composition was his hike up Mt. Ventoux in Provence, France, on 26 April 1336, although the letter itself was not written until years later. The letter was addressed to Dionigi da Borgo, a priest and theologian, who had given Petrarch a copy of Augustine's Confessions. *Previous interpretations have seen this climb as embodying the spirit of the Renaissance, especially the decision to hike for the sake of the experience. More recent critics have questioned if the hike ever happened, or if it was a literary invention.*

Source: Henry Reeve, *Petrarch* (Edinburgh; London: William Blackwood and Sons, 1879), pp. 84–89. Latin. Revised.

I have this day ascended the highest mountain in this district, which is very deservedly called Le Ventoux [the windy one], for the sake of seeing the remarkable altitude of the place. I have cherished this project for many years. You know that from my boyhood, while fate has been disposing of the affairs of men, I have been passing my time here. This mountain, which is visible from a great distance, was always before my eyes, but it was long before I could find anyone to accompany me, until I opened the matter to my only younger brother, whom you know; and he was very delighted at my proposal, so I was pleased to have a friend and a brother for my companion.

On the appointed day we left home, and we got to Malaucène in the evening. This place is at the foot of the mountain toward the north. We stayed there one day, and this morning we started, with some servants, on our ascent, which we did not complete without much difficulty, for the mountain is extremely steep, and an almost inaccessible mass of rock. The poet, however, says rightly, "Dogged labor conquers all" [Vergil, *Georgics*]. The day was long, the air balmy, we were supported by the vigor of our minds, and such bodily strength and activity as we possess, so that the nature of the place was the only obstacle.

We met with an old shepherd in one of the dells of the mountain, who did all he could to dissuade us from our attempt, telling us that some fifty years before he had been invited to go to the summit by the ardor of youth, that he had got nothing by it but discouragement and fatigue, and that his body as well as his cloak were torn by the rocks and brambles; he added that he never heard of any similar enterprise being undertaken either before or since. While he was shouting all this, our desire to proceed (for thus it is with the incredulous minds of young men) increased with the objections he made. When the old man perceived that all his remarks were in vain, he accompanied us a little way among the rocks, and pointed out a made path, giving us at the time a vast deal of good advice, and making repeated signs to us after we were gone. We threw off such of our garments as might have encumbered us, and began the ascent with great vigor and happiness.

But, as usually happens, fatigue very soon follows great efforts. We soon sat down upon a rock, from where we again started at a more moderate pace, I more especially lessened my mountaineering enthusiasm, and while my brother was seeking for shortcuts over the steepest parts of the mountain, I more warily kept below, and when he pointed out the path to me, I answered that I hoped to find an easier access, and that I willingly went round in order to advance on more level ground. But while I was alleging this excuse for my laziness, the others got far above me, and I was wandering in the gullies of the mountain, where my path was far from being easier, so that the way was lengthened, and my useless labor became more and more irksome. As it was too late to repent of my error, I determined to go straight up, and I at last rejoined my brother, whom I had lost from sight, and who had been quietly resting on a rock, after much toil and anxiety, so that we again started together.

The same thing, however, happened again and again in a few hours, and I began to find that human ingenuity was not a match for the nature of things, and that it was impossible to gain heights by moving downwards. Passing, however, with the readiness of thought from corporeal to incorporeal things, I could not help addressing myself in the following words: "The very thing which has happened to you in the ascent of this mountain happens to you and to many of those who seek to arrive at final blessedness, though it is less evident, because the motions of the body are palpable and open, those of the mind are invisible and concealed. The life of the blessed is indeed set on a high place, straight is the path which leads to it, many are the hills which intervene, and the pilgrim must advance with great strides from virtue to virtue. Lofty is the end of all things, the termination of life, to which our journey tends. We all wish to arrive there, but, as Naso has it—'To wish is not enough; to gain your end you must ardently earn' [Ovid, *Ex Ponto*]. But you, certainly, unless in this as many things you are self-deceived—not only wish, but deserve. What, then, keeps you back? Nothing, indeed, but the apparent ease and advantage of that path which lies through earthly and low pleasures, in which when you have gone astray, you must either mount straight to the summit under all the weight of your misspent toil, or you must lie down in the trenched valleys of your sins to be haunted by the shadows and darkness of death, and to pass an eternal night in perpetual torture."

This reflection seemed to reanimate my sinking vigor, and enabled me to complete my ascent. I only wish that I may accomplish that journey of the soul, for which I daily and nightly sigh, as well as I have done this day's journey of the feet, after having overcome so many difficulties. And I do not know whether that pilgrimage, which is performed by an active and immortal soul, in the twinkling of an eye, without any local motion, is not easier than that which is carried on in a body worn out by the attacks of death and of decay, and laden with the weight of heavy members.

The highest peak of all is called *Le petit-fils* [Little Son] by a sense opposite to its meaning, for it seems rather to be the father of all the mountains in the neighborhood. There is a little plot upon the summit, where we were all very glad to sit down.

Since, father, you have read of all the perils of our ascent, I beg you to listen to the rest, and to the remaining occurrences of this one day of my life.

At first, I was so affected by the unaccustomed spirit of the air, and by the free prospect, that I stood as one stupefied. I look back; clouds were beneath my feet. I began to understand Athos and Olympus [Greek mountains], since I found that what I heard and read of them was true of a mountain of far less celebrity. I turn my eyes to that Italian region to which my soul most inclines, and the great rugged Alps (through which, we are told, that the greatest enemy of Rome made his way with vinegar) seemed quite close to me, though they really were at a great distance. I confess that I sighed for that Italian air, more sensible to the soul than to the eyes, and an intense longing came upon me, to behold my friends and my country once more.

Then a new reflection arose in my mind, I passed from place to time. I recollected that on this day ten years had elapsed since I ended my youthful studies in Bologna, and, O immortal God, O immutable wisdom, how many changes has that interval witnessed! . . . I wished to recollect my past uncleanness, and the carnal corruptions of my soul, not because I love them, but because I love you, O my God. . . . While I was rejoicing in my heart, father, at my advancement in years, I wept over my imperfections, I mourned the fickleness of human actions, I forgot the place I was in and the reason of my coming there, until, deferring my meditations to a fitter opportunity, I looked about to discern that which I came to see. The frontier of France, and the Pyrenees of Spain were not to be made out (though nothing, that I know of, intervened) by reason of the weakness of mortal sight. But I could very clearly see the mountains about Lyons on the right, and on the left the Bay of Marseilles, which is distant some days' journey. The Rhône flowed beneath our eyes.

But while I was admiring so many individual objects of the earth, and that my soul rose to lofty contemplations, by the example of the body, it occurred to me that I would look into the book of Augustine's *Confessions*, which I owe to your kindness, and which I generally carry about with me, and it is a volume of small dimensions, though of great sweetness. I open it randomly meaning to read whatever might present itself [a form of bibliomancy]—for what could have presented itself that was not pious and devout? The volume opened at the tenth book. My brother was expecting to hear the words of Augustine from my lips, and he can testify that in the first place I fixed my eyes, it was thus written: "There are men who go to admire the high places of mountains, the great waves of the sea, the wide currents of rivers, the circuit of the ocean, and the orbits of the stars—and who neglect themselves."

I confess that I was amazed; I begged my brother, who was anxious to hear more, not to interrupt me, and I shut the book half angry with myself, that I, who was even now admiring terrestrial things, ought already to have learned from the philosophers that nothing is truly great except the soul.

I was sufficiently satisfied with what I had seen upon the mountain, and turned my eyes back into myself, so that from that hour until we came to the bottom, no one heard me speak. The words I had read bruised me deeply, for I could scarcely imagine that they had occurred fortuitously, or that they were addressed to anyone but myself. You may imagine how often on that day I looked back to the summit of the mountain, which seemed but a cubit high in comparison with the height of human contemplation, were it not too often merged in the corruptions of the earth. At every step I thought if it cost so much sweat and toil to bring the body a little nearer to heaven, great indeed must be the cross, the dungeon, and the sting which should terrify the soul as it draws near to God, and crush the turgid height of insolence and the fate of man. Who will not be drawn aside from this path by the fear of trial or the desire of enjoyment? Happy, oh happy is he, of whom I think the poet spoke:

> Happy the man who is skilled to understand
> Nature's hidden causes; who beneath his feet
> All terrors casts, and death's relentless doom,
> And the loud roar of greedy Acheron [river leading
>   to the underworld]!
>
> [Vergil, *Georgics*]

How steadily must we labor, to put under our feet, not a speck of elevated earth, but the proud appetites of our terrestrial impulses!

In these undisguised reflections, I felt not the stones upon the path, and I returned to the rustic cottage which I had left before the dawn, at an advanced hour of the night; the constant moon offered sweet service to us as we walked; and now while the servants are busy preparing supper, I have stolen aside to write you these lines on the spur of the moment, that with change of scene and the variety of impressions the thoughts I have penned should not have deserted me.

You see, most beloved father, that there is nothing in me which I desire to conceal from your eyes, since I not only disclose to you my whole life, but even my individual reflections. Father, I crave your prayers, that whatever in me is vague and unstable may be strengthened, and that the thoughts I waste abroad on many things, may be turned to that one thing, which is true, good, and secure. Farewell.

Questions: Why did the old man attempt to dissuade Petrarch and his companions from traveling up the mountain, and why did they not listen to him? In what way did Petrarch view the climbing of the mountain as a metaphor for the ascent of his soul? Why did he consult Augustine's Confessions, and how did he then interpret his climb? Why did Petrarch want to ascend Mt. Ventoux, and what did he do when he reached its peak?

39. PERO TAFUR, *VOYAGES AND ADVENTURES*

Pero Tafur (c. 1410–c. 1484) was a Spanish nobleman who between 1435 and 1439 traveled extensively throughout the Mediterranean, central Europe, and the Middle East; he did not write down his account of the journey until the mid-fifteenth century. While Tafur seemed to travel largely out of a personal interest, he also served as a diplomat to the sultan of Egypt and he went on pilgrimage to Jerusalem. Tafur's book preserves a wealth of observations about his period, including the tumultuous state of both the Byzantine Empire and the papacy.

Source: trans. Malcolm Letts, Pero Tafur, *Travels and Adventures, 1435–1439* (London: G. Routledge, 1926), pp. 21–26, 81–95. Spanish. Revised.

1. We set sail and left the harbor of Sanlúcar de Barrameda. I traveled in a ship of Galicia, as I had already made preparations for my departure and had no horses and other things necessary for a land journey. That day and the night following we sailed on, and doubling Cape Trafalgar we entered the Straits, and at daylight we reached the promontory of Carnero at the entrance to Gibraltar. We anchored close to the town and saw there a great number of ships and a galley of the king, all of which had come with the count of Niebla [Enrique Pérez de Guzmán]. We found that the count was encamped about half a league from Gibraltar with 1,200 horsemen and 5,000 foot soldiers, and his son was there with him. I disembarked and went to see the count, and he was delighted to meet me, and marveled how I had been able to come, in view of my recent illness. He took counsel with his knights and told them the reason for his being there, which before had been kept secret. The undertaking was to be as follows. He had been told that in Gibraltar there were not ten Moors who were fighting men, whereas to defend so great a fortress not even a thousand would be sufficient, and that it could be taken by assault. He proposed to muster his horsemen at the entrance which is on land, while he with his men-at-arms launched an attack close to the dockyard, on the side of the mountain where King Alfonso [XI, r. 1312–1350] entered. His son Don Juan was to march against the tower of Tuerto, which is on the mountain. This was to be from the sea. Meanwhile the Biscayans with their ships and the galley were to attack the Casal de Ginoveses which is at the very summit of the mountain.

So he ordered everything, and the next day after Mass each one went to his station. We then set out and drew near to the town, and at low water we all disembarked and moved toward the wall, but that day we did not carry up our artillery, because this was only a test to see how many men were there to defend the place. Nevertheless, as soon as we came up to the wall, 15 or 20 of our men were killed at once. And we were so occupied that we did not observe how the tide was rising, and we were soon up to our knees in water. As we could do nothing, not having brought our artillery, the count gave orders to sound the retreat to the sea. The men retired to the boats, but the count remained behind collecting the others. As he was making for the last boat, with ten or twelve knights who had remained on shore with him, it became clear to the enemy that only a small party was left, and that the others had withdrawn without any orders having been given to cover the retreat with crossbows and artillery, and that all were taking to the water, and that the last boat was leaving. The Moors soon afterward dashed out with horsemen to the number of 20, with as many foot soldiers, and as they came up at a gallop, the boat, which was small and heavily laden, capsized, and the count and all those with him were drowned. Meanwhile the other engagements were proceeding, and the rest of the men had as much work as they could do, except the horsemen on the shore who had no one to fight with. So very sadly, with the loss of so noble a leader both on sea and land, we returned to Castile to Sanlúcar from which place we had set out.

Gibraltar is a very strong fortress and famous all the world over. It stands at the mouth of the Straits where the Atlantic Ocean joins the Mediterranean Sea, and it is a very fruitful place. The town commands the entrance to the mainland which is very narrow, and it is about a league from there to the top of the rock. It is very well walled, with orchards, vines, and excellent water, and it lies very low on the edge of the sea. Behind it stands the rock which is so high that it seems to reach to the clouds. It rises straight up, and although it looks formidable from the west, it is seen to greater advantage from the east. The harbor, which is very secure, is made by an arm of the sea which runs inland as far as Algeciras, three leagues distant, and the whole way is good anchorage. Leaving there, we sailed through the Straits in view of Cape Tarifa and past Cádiz and other places on the coast, and entered the harbor of Barrameda at Sanlúcar, where they received us with less lightness of heart than at our departure. I then collected the things I had prepared and put myself aboard a carrack [merchant ship] owned by Geronimo de Voltajo, who had come from Genoa with two other ships belonging to Esteban Doria and Geronimo Doria, and they had troops to defend them for fear of the Catalans, and most of the Genoese who were in Seville sailed in them, for they carried great riches.

We left the harbor of Cádiz and came to the coast of Barbary, to a town called Asilah, where we had to discharge and take fresh cargo. This town is close to the Cape of Spartel. It belongs to the king of Fez and had then as governor a Moorish knight, called Calabencala. It is a very fruitful place, but abounds more in animals and fowls than in anything else. We remained there three days. Then we set sail and entered the Straits of Gibraltar, and at the hour of vespers we espied two large ships which we took to be the Catalans, and we turned back and anchored off Tangier, but they passed by on their way to Cádiz. The next day we departed and came to Ceuta, where we learned from a Biscayan vessel that those two carracks belonged to the Genoese fleet, and that they came from Genoa to accompany the three of us. We anchored at Ceuta and disembarked, and hailed a sloop [sailboat] and sent letters to Cádiz saying that the carracks should await us there, or that at least they would find us at Málaga, where we had to discharge and take fresh cargoes. That day we remained at Ceuta, and I went about inspecting the city and its surroundings which appeared to me to be very excellent. It showed itself to have been a great place and, without doubt, if the king of Castile owned it and caused it to be embellished, it would, in view of its situation, be one of the most notable places in the world. The soil is generally fruitful, although it is rugged and the country mountainous, but there is a good harbor and much land, and fruit and water are abundant. What is left of the city is sufficiently strong. There is on one side on the mountain a rocky place surrounded by a wall, called *El Alminan,* which would be very remarkable if it were what it ought to be. In these mountains of Ceuta there are more lions than in any other part of the world, and porcupines, apes, panthers, bears, and pigs without number. They say that it is doubtful if there is any place so high and mountainous on the African side. This is said to arise from its nearness to the west side of the Straits.

We departed from Ceuta, and leaving Africa on the right hand, and having Europe on the left, we sailed through the Straits and entered the open sea, and continued along the coast until we anchored on the shore of Málaga, a city belonging to the king of Granada. There the merchants landed and discharged their cargoes and took others. We remained there nine days, and while we were there those carracks arrived which had passed us, and put their men on board our ships and took in merchandise, and returned to Cádiz for more to take to Flanders. During those nine days we had nothing to do but to admire the city of Málaga which impressed me favorably, both as regards its situation, though it has no port, and its soil, though there is a scarcity of bread; but what there is is good. And there is no shortage of orchards and fruit. The city is flat, for the most part walled, with a castle on either hand and a walled passage running from one to the other which they call Gibralfar. It is full of trade, and if it belonged to us it would be better. But all kinds of merchandise would have to go in from our country, which would never be suffered in any place held by the Moors. The sea flows up to the walls, in such wise that a fleet of galleys could throw out landing stages on to flat land. For the part toward the sea is very low-lying, although it is well defended on its landward side. There are many people there, but rather of the merchant class than skilled in war.

After nine days at Málaga the Genoese collected their goods and armed the ships and set them in order, for they had to coast from headland to headland along the country of the king of Aragon. Sailing onward, we followed the coast of Granada, past Salobreña, Almuñecar, and Almería, until we reached Cartagena which is in our country. We entered the harbor and remained there one day, awaiting news of the Catalans. It is one of the finest harbors, in my judgment, in the world, and the town is excellent. We departed and sailed along the coast of Aragon, by Elche and Alicante, until we came near to Valencia, and there we had advices to leave the coast and take to the open sea. The next day, leaving the coast, we came close to the island of Ibiza, belonging to the king of Aragon. So continuing our route, leaving Catalonia and Barcelona on the left hand, we passed the islands of Majorca and Minorca, which belong to the king of Aragon, and entered the Gulf of Lyons, which is so called as one goes out from it, but at the going in it is called the Gulf of Narbonne.

One day at vespers such a violent storm arose that we ran before it all that night, and the next day we were far away. The two large carracks were driven under bare poles toward Sardinia, and it was two months before we had news of them, but our ship, which still had its main sail, although but little of it remained, kept close to the island of Titan, as they call it, off the coast of Provence. This day and the following night we were in constant peril and had much labor, but we ran on and the next day we came to Nice. It was Christmas Eve, and we anchored there and repaired our sails. We then departed and came to Savona, a pleasant city, belonging to Genoa, and remained there for Christmas Day. The following day we set sail, and keeping close inland we passed along the seashore, 40 miles from Genoa, which is the most beautiful sight in the world. To one who does not know it, the whole coast from Savona to Genoa looks like one continuous city, so well inhabited is it, and so thickly studded with houses. . . .

9. That day I begged leave of the sultan [of Egypt] to go to Mount Sinai, and he consented, and ordered that one of his interpreters should go with me, and he provided three camels for me and mine, and would accept no payment. I then took my leave and departed in two days. In those two days, indeed, there was little leisure, since there were so many strange and remarkable things to see, and as the weather was very hot they brought me each morning a vase of water to drink, which was specially treated, and in it were certain seeds like hemp, and of a truth it was a very healthy drink. It is their custom to drink it fasting in the summer before dinner. The sultan's interpreter prepared everything that was necessary, and recommended me to the interpreter who was to go with me, and wrote himself to the patriarch of Alexandria who lived in Cairo (who selects the superior of the monastery of St-Catherine at Mount Sinai), to recommend me to him. We departed from Cairo, and crossed the lifeless desert of Egypt with much labor and in great peril. The heat was such that I was amazed that any man could withstand it. These deserts, they say, provide the mummies, which are the bodies of those who die there. For with the great dryness which is in those parts, the bodies do not decay, but the radical moisture is consumed, leaving the bodies entire and dried, so that they can be ground up. There is no road in the desert, for the wind effaces it and shifts the sands from one place to another and makes great hills, and people die there,

as I have related. They navigate here with the compass as at sea. There is no habitation between Babylonia [Old Cairo] and Mount Sinai, and the camels carry everything, as well for the travelers as for themselves.

The journey to Mount Sinai endured for 15 days. This mountain is very lofty and stands quite alone, about half a league from the Red Sea. On the summit of this mountain there was formerly a monastery, where the body of Saint Catherine was kept, and they say that one year, when there was great scarcity of bread, the monks, on that account, and also in view of the great labor in climbing those heights, went to Babylonia, leaving the monastery and the holy body unattended. Thereupon the blessed Saint Catherine appeared to them and told them to return, and that they would find provisions and a convenient place to live in, and that where they should find a great heap of wheat, there they should build their monastery and house her body. The monks soon afterward returned, and found at the foot of the mountain a great heap of wheat, and there, thanking God and the Virgin Saint Catherine for the blessings they had received, they erected their monastery which is still a most notable place. The monks ascended the mountain and brought down the body with great honor, and placed it in the monastery at the foot, where they now live, not, indeed, neglecting what is on the mountain itself, for there are many holy places there, it being the place where God gave the tables of the law to Moses, and where he appeared to him in the burning bush. Here also is the place where he commanded Moses strike the rock with his rod, and the water gushed forth, which to this day runs down to the foot.

The lower monastery is a fine building. There are in it about 50 or 60 persons, both monks and servants, and the church is well fashioned in the Greek manner. The body of Saint Catherine is beneath the chief altar. I did not see the body, because they are not accustomed to show it, and, indeed, the place is not convenient for seeing it, but it appeared to me, from its size, that the body must be greater by a span than the tallest women who could be found in the world today. There are in a house certain bodies of men embalmed. Some say they are the bodies of knights who visited that holy place and died there. Others say that some knights of Greece were carried there after death, and it is a place of great devotion. The monastery derives a large income from all Greece, and a great lord of Candia left to it, when he died, an income of 4,000 ducats [gold coins], but since the place is very remote, and the provisioning of it costs much money, part of the revenue is expended in maintaining an establishment at Babylonia, and the patriarch of Alexandria lives there. He provides for everything, and the revenues are paid to him. He also elects the patriarch who is sent to Greater India to Prester John, and while I was in Babylonia, the former patriarch being dead, he chose his successor and dispatched him there.

After spending three days at the monastery, I considered whether it would be possible to go to Greater India, and I spoke privately with the prior about the matter. He told me that a caravan, which was the means of communication with those parts, was due to arrive within two or three days, and that we could then obtain information as to the possibility of making the journey, but that he was altogether opposed to it. In four or five days the caravan duly arrived, bringing so many camels with it that I cannot give an account of them, as I do not wish to appear to speak extravagantly. This caravan carries all the spices, pearls, precious stones and gold, perfumes, and linen, and parrots, and cats from India, with many other things, which they distribute throughout the world. One half goes to Babylonia, and from there to Alexandria, and the rest to Damascus, and from there to the port of Beirut.

I went to the shore of the Red Sea, which is half a league from Mount Sinai, to see the arrival of the caravan, and I found that a Venetian had come with it, called Niccolò dei Conti, a gentleman of good birth who brought with him his wife and two sons and a daughter, all of whom had been born in India. It appeared that he and they had become Moors, having been forced to renounce their faith in Mecca, which is the Moors' holy place. As soon as he saw me he came up and inquired who I was, and what I did there, and what was my profession. I told him that I came from Italy, having been brought up at the court of the king of Cyprus, and that I was traveling on his affairs to the sultan who had given me license to come there, and that I intended to pass on to India. He told me at once that I ought not to attempt it, and that, however much I desired it, it could not be accomplished. As I seemed to be fixed in my determination, he begged and implored me to tell him truly who I was, and said that he could do me a great service, which was that he would tell me what I ought to do, and that I could trust him implicitly, since he was a Christian as I was. He also promised to relate the events of his life, and how he had come there. I, observing that he was a person both grave and discreet and of good address, told him that I was a noble of Spain, and had come to the Holy Sepulcher, and from there to Babylonia, with intent to see Mount Sinai and to go on to India.

On hearing this Niccolò dei Conti showed great pleasure and said as follows: "You must know that at the time when Timur Beg was ruling [1370–1405] I found myself in Alexandria with certain moneys of my father, and from there I had to go to Babylonia, and through bad management and youthful inexperience, for I was only 18 years of age, I lost what I had, and as I was desperate and ashamed to return home, I went to the place where Timur Beg was, and remained a year at his court. From there I sought the means to go into Greater India and learned that all was secure, for at that time the rule of Timur Beg extended from India to the Red Sea. When I arrived in India I was taken to see Prester John, who received me very graciously and showed me many favors, and married me to the woman I now have with me, and she bore me these children. I lived in India for 40 years, with a great longing to return to my country. I gained much wealth, and after Timur Beg had died, and the country was divided up, I arranged to journey to the Red Sea, and to go to Mecca, and to the place to which I am now come, and for this purpose I obtained a safe conduct from the sultan. I spent two years in procuring this, but at last he sent it to me. When I arrived with my wife and children at Mecca, they ordered us to abjure the faith or to be killed. I myself was ready to receive martyrdom, but I knew that my wife and children would rather renounce the faith than die, and I therefore decided to accept the alternative, hoping that God would save us in due time. But the sultan must have been a participant in all this, in order to have a share in that which they robbed me of. Now this is my life and the story of my past, and in what concerns you I pray you, in the name of God, and for the love which you bear him, and since you are a Christian and of my country, that you will not embark on such madness, for the way is very long and troublesome and perilous; the country is inhabited by strange races without king or laws or rulers; how can you expect to pass without a safe conduct, and whom will he fear who is minded to kill you? Further, the air is strange, and food and drink are different from those in your country. You will meet with bestial people. Unable to govern themselves, and although there are monstrous things to be seen they are not enough to give you satisfaction. You will see heaps of gold and pearls and precious stones, but what will they profit you since the people are beasts who wear them?"

These and other things were told me by Niccolò dei Conti, and finally I concluded that if I did not fly there it was impossible to make the journey. I saw clearly that it was his great affection and the kindness of his nature which moved him to counsel me thus, and as it well appeared that he told me the truth, I tired of my project, and we returned to the monastery and remained there three days, and the company prepared for the road, some, as I have said, to go to Babylonia, and the rest to Damascus. During those three days I did nothing but visit various places and the Red Sea, and the place where the Children of Israel entered the sea when pharaoh was following after them, and the sea became dry land and the waters were divided. From there we saw an island called Shushonah, whence, they say, the Jews came who are called in Castile Abens-susenes.

10. We departed from Mount Sinai, and I took my leave from the prior and the monks, and they gave me the device of Saint Catherine, which is a wheel with teeth of gold, and out of my own poverty I gave them money. I left my arms, and set out on my road with those of the caravan and with Niccolò dei Conti. During the journey I did little else except hear of his doings in India,

and he gave me many things written with his own hand. I asked him concerning Prester John and his authority, and he told me that he was a great lord,
and that he had 25 kings in his service, although they were not great rulers,
and also that many people who live without law, but follow heathen rites, are
in subjection to him.

They say that there is in India a very high mountain, the ascent of which
is exceedingly difficult, so much so that in ancient times those below knew
nothing about those above, and those above had no knowledge of those below,
and a road was made, and a chain was stretched from the top to the bottom, to
which those who ascended or descended could cling. On the top of the mountain is a great plain where they sow and reap wheat, and keep cattle and grain,
and where there are many orchards full of fruit, and much water; all things,
in short, necessary to the life of man. On one side is a very notable monastery,
to which it is the custom for those of fit rank to be prester to send 12 ancient
men, nobles by descent, and virtuous, to elect a new Prester John when the
office is vacant, and they do it in this manner. The chief sons and daughters
are sent there to serve, and they marry one with another and raise up children,
and they provide there all that is necessary for their existence, and give them
horses and arms, and bows and arrows, and they teach them warlike arts, and
the art of governing men. The electors who are there take counsel daily, and
observe that one which appears to them most fit to succeed to the government
when Prester John vacates it, and are already agreed as to the person to be
chosen. When the ruler is at last dead, his knights, as the custom is, carry him
to that mountain on a bier, covered in mourning, and the electors, beholding
them from the heights where they are, take the one who has been chosen, and
give him to the knights in exchange for the dead ruler. They then take up the
body and bury it in the mountain, with the honors due to it, while the others
go with their lord and, amid great feasts and rejoicings, make their submission to him. There come certain races, bringing presents. Some bring pearls
and others stones of great worth, or gold rods, each one according to the land
where he lives, or where he was born. Niccolò dei Conti told me also that in
the mountain of Ceylon [modern Sri Lanka] very fine cinnamon is grown. He
said, further, that there is a fruit there like a great round pumpkin, and inside
it are three separate fruits, each having its own taste.

He told me also of a seacoast where the crabs, on reaching land, and being
exposed to the air, turn to stone. He spoke, too, of a country belonging to the
heathen where there is a famous place of pilgrimage. Here a woman brought
forth two sons at one birth, and immediately they were born they covered
their eyes with their hands, and said that they did not intend to live in such a
wicked world, and they went to a mountain, and there they lived and died.
Where the one died there appeared a great lake of water, and where the other

died a great lake of mud, and the people throw themselves in and die, saying that they are going to glory. Others there are who, in order to leave behind them a reputation for strength, and that their sons may be known to be the sons of good men, make an apparatus like shears, and putting their heads between the blades they force them to shut with their feet, and so cut off their heads. Niccolò dei Conti told me also that he had seen people eating human flesh, the strangest thing he had ever seen. This, be it understood, is a heathen practice, but he had seen Christians eating the raw flesh of animals, after which it is necessary to eat of a very odoriferous herb within 15 to 20 days, but if they delay longer they become lepers.

I learned also that Prester John, desiring to know from where the Nile had its beginnings, prepared boats and sent men and provided much food, and ordered them to bring back news of its source, and they set out and saw so many strange countries and peoples and unfamiliar animals that it was a great marvel, but as they had eaten all their victuals they had to return without having found what they sought, and Prester John was much cast down. He then took counsel as to whether it was possible to send men who would not perish for lack of food, and he ordered them to take young children, and, depriving them of milk, he reared them on raw fish (which is no great marvel, for it is reported by those that go to Guinea that, in those parts, the heathens eat nothing but raw fish). After these children were grown up he prepared boats and nets, and ordered that they were in no wise to return without certain information concerning that which they sought. The departed and journeyed up the river, through diverse countries, but they communicated with no one for fear of being prevented, and they came to a great lake like the sea, and followed the shore, and went all round it to find out from where the water came which made that lake. They came at last to an opening where the water entered, and they proceeded until they came to a great mountain range which was very lofty and precipitous, and which seemed to be hewn out of the rock, and the top of it could not be seen. In it was a great opening through which the water poured, and close to that mountain range, and joined to it, was another as high as the former, and it could well be seen that the water came from it. The travelers decided to send up one of their party to report, but he that ascended, so they say, having beheld what was within, refused to come down or even to answer questions. Another of the party was then sent up, but it was with him as with the first. When the others saw this, and that there was no possibility of obtaining more information, they left those two on the mountain, being unable to recover them, and returned by the way they had come. They related to their master all that had befallen them, telling him that nothing further could be discovered, since it was clear that God did not desire that mortals should know more, and that he had therefore locked up the secret in that way.

Niccolò dei Conti also told me that he saw a heathen people who are not accustomed to take a dowry with their wives when they marry, but if the man dies first the woman has to burn herself, in the same way as the heathen burn dead bodies. But if the woman dies first the man does not have to burn himself, for they say that woman was made for the service of man, but not man for the woman; and if the principal should perish, the accessory is not worthy even of mention. This is what they do: when the man dies they put the corpse in the place where it is to be burnt. The woman then attires herself as finely as she can, saying that it is for nuptials better than the first, and that she is to accompany her husband for eternity in the place where he is. The people make merry and sing, both she and her kinsmen, and they inquire whether anyone desires to send a message to those on the other side, since she is about to depart there in company with her husband. Then they take off her clothes, and dress her in a sad robe, like a shroud, and sing dirges and sad songs the while. She then bids farewell to all and lies down beside her husband, placing her head on his right arm, and they say many things in conclusion, chiefly that the wife ought only to live so long as she is honored and defended by that arm, and they set fire to them, and thus, cheerfully and willingly, she goes to her death. In another place, where they have the same custom, there is this difference, that when the marriage is celebrated they ask the woman whether she wishes to be burnt or not. If she consents, she has to submit to the practice mentioned above, but if she declines, she has to provide a dowry. On the death of her husband the same ceremony is gone through, but when it comes to the burning, they put in her headdress in place of the woman, and she forfeits her dowry to the husband's heirs. Those that refuse to be burnt are looked upon as bad wives and not legitimate. It is said that there are very few such, and one of them, who did not elect to be burnt, left the country for shame and came to live in Babylonia, and Niccolò dei Conti saw her there.

Niccolò dei Conti told me that, although he had been plundered, he still had many things with him and much riches, such as pearls and precious stones. But he dwelled most upon the quantity of health-giving medicines which he had, so many, indeed, that their value was not to be estimated. He showed me a ruby of great worth, and also a round hat of grass, as delicate as the finest silk which could be found. He inquired of me where, if God brought him safely to Christian lands, his goods would have the best market. I told him that the emperor was at war with the king of Poland, and it was but a short time since he had come into his kingdom, and that he had little wealth, that there was less wealth in France on account of her longstanding wars, and that in Italy, as he knew better than I, they only bought to sell again. Further, that it appeared to me he would find the best market in Spain, chiefly on account of the great wealth of our king, but also because in all our wars we are always victorious, and have never been beaten. The people, I said, were very rich and valued such things more than anyone else. He, therefore, resolved to come to Spain.

I inquired whether he had ever seen monsters in human shape, such as some have reported, that is men with one leg and one eye, or but a cubit in height, or as tall as a lance. He replied that he had never met with such, but that he had seen beasts with very strange shapes. In a heathen land he had seen an elephant of great size and as white as snow, which is a very strange thing, since they are almost all black, and they kept it fastened to a column with chains of gold, and adored it as a god. He had seen also an ass which they brought to Prester John, not much larger than a hound, and of as many colors as it is possible to enumerate; also many unicorns and other animals, which it would take long to describe. He told me as well that he had seen them set up those castles upon the elephants, which they use when they go to fight. Prester John and his people are said to be as good Catholics and Christians as could be found anywhere, but they know nothing of our Roman Church, nor are governed by it. This lord is said to be held in such reverence that if the greatest of his subjects does anything worthy of death, he sends a servant with a letter ordering him to submit to execution by that servant, and in obedience to that letter, right away he lowers his head and suffers death. Niccolò dei Conti told me also that he saw a noble lord who brought a great present of gold to Prester John, and had so much glory in what he brought and said so much to him, bragging that no one had ever done him such service before, that Prester John immediately ordered him to be put to death, saying that it was the best service he could do him, which was no small one for that lord.

I learnt also that the people in those parts are very skilled in the black arts, and that when navigating in the Red Sea, dei Conti saw them consult with demons, and he told me that he could catch sight of a vague black shape moving up and down the mainmast. The sailors then implored it to keep still and demanded: "What of our voyage?" and the shape made answer: "You will have six days of dead calm when the sea will be like oil, but be prepared, for you will have as many days of very heavy storms." He described their ships as like great houses, and not fashioned at all like ours. They have ten or twelve sails, and great cisterns of water within, for there the winds are not very strong, and when at sea they have no dread of islands or rocks. These ships carry all the cargoes which the caravans receive from them at Mecca, which is the port where they unload. Dei Conti told me that Mecca is a great place, larger than Seville. It is in subjection to no ruler, except to the chief of their law, whom they regard as their pope, and they look on the sultan as emperor. There is a very rich mosque there where they keep the body of Muhammad, and certain Indians from Ethiopia [sub-Saharan Africa] who come there. . . . He said also that they could dam the water of the Nile, which runs from India to Ethiopia, and through all the land of Egypt to the Mediterranean Sea, and which divides itself into two arms, the one entering the sea close to Alexandria and the other by Damietta. If that water ceased to flow, the whole country would be depopulated.

I learned from Niccolò dei Conti that Prester John kept him continuously at his court, enquiring of him as to the Christian world, and concerning the princes and their estates, and the wars they were waging, and while he was there he saw Prester John on two occasions dispatch ambassadors to Christian princes, but he did not hear whether any news of them had been received. He saw, however, the preparations made by Prester John to come with his hosts to Jerusalem, which is much farther than the journey to Europe. He saw the church where lies the body of Saint Thomas, who converted the Indians. He mentioned also the drift which comes down, when the Nile rises, from the terrestrial paradise, which they call perfume of aloes, and in the time of Saint Thomas, when he went about preaching and the people would not be converted, there came down the Nile a great tree which was washed ashore in that place. The people went to their ruler and besought him to come and see the greatest marvel in the world, namely, an aloe tree, greater than had ever been seen, and he came at once, and when he saw it he ordered them to carry it away with oxen, but they could not move it. He then directed that it should be cut up, but the tools would not enter the wood. Saint Thomas the apostle, being there, told them that if they would be baptized and believe in God, who did these marvels, he alone with his hand would lift the tree and carry it to the desired place, and the ruler and his people replied that if he would do that they would believe. Saint Thomas then crossed himself and laid hold of the tree, and carried it to the place which they showed him. When the people saw that miracle, all were baptized and became Christians. The apostle then took that wood and had it sawed up, and made a chapel which he roofed with it, and there his body now lies. The Indians have today such devotion for the apostle, that they take earth from the place where he is buried, and make pellets, which they carry always in their breasts, saying that in the moment of death, if they cannot take communion, it suffices to eat one of these. Niccolò dei Conti gave me five or six of them, which I believe I have to this day.

The people of Greater India are a little darker in color than we are, but in Ethiopia they are much darker, and so on until you come to the blacks, who are at the equator, which they call the torrid zone.

Questions: Against whom were the Spaniards in Tafur's account fighting, and what did Tafur do in this battle? What did Tafur look for in places he visited, and what did he avoid? Who was Niccolò dei Conti, and what made him convert to Islam? What wonders of the east did Niccolò confirm or deny? Did Tafur believe his tales? What happened when men tried to find the origin of the Nile in sub-Saharan Africa, and what does this show about how this region was viewed?

40. JÖRG VON EHINGEN, *DIARY*

Jörg (or George) von Ehingen (1428–1508) was from an influential noble family from Swabia in modern southwestern Germany. Most of what we can reconstruct of his life comes from this autobiography, which he appears to have written over a period of years, causing uncertainties about its chronology and geography. At various points in his career he was a traveler, a knight, and a diplomat; as seen in the passage below, he also fought at the Seventh Siege of Gibraltar. Only one manuscript of this diary remains, which likely meant that the author did not intend it for wide dissemination.

Source: ed. and trans. Malcolm Letts, Jörg von Ehingen, *The Diary of Jörg von Ehingen* (London: Oxford University Press, 1929), pp. 19–40. German. Revised.

I, Jörg von Ehingen, knight, was sent in my youth as a page to the court at Innsbruck. At that time a young prince of Austria, Duke Sigismund, held his court there. He had married a queen of Scotland, and I was ordered to serve her. After a time I became carver and server of the dishes to this queen. But when I grew older and came to man's estate, and began to be conscious of my strength, I thought myself too lowly employed, and proposed to attach myself to some active prince, so that I might exercise myself in knightly matters and learn all the practices of knighthood, rather than remain in peace and pleasure at Innsbruck. Now, at that time, Duke Albert [VI] of Austria [r. 1424–1463], brother of the Roman emperor, Frederick [III, r. 1440–1452], had returned from the eastern countries to Swabia and upper Germany, and my late father assisted me with three horses to enter his service. This same duke, Albert, had many worthy people about him, and kept a costly, prince-like, and indeed, a royal court. After I had been some time at this court it happened on a time that Duke Sigismund of Austria was about to visit Duke Albert.

As I had then left Innsbruck in order to obtain service and experience with another prince, and was at that time only an ordinary attendant like any other nobleman, I was much perturbed that I might not seem to my former prince, Duke Sigismund, and his train to have lowered my condition. I therefore sought out my late father, who was an experienced courtier, to advise me how I might bring myself forward with the prince and his court, for there were so many good and diverse people there from all countries that none was regarded as of much account. When I spoke with him he desired to understand the matter further, and I knew that he had some excellent proposals to make. He considered for a while and then said to me: "Dear son, you are sufficiently strong and well grown to undertake all that is fitting to a young knight. I gather from your speech that you are ready to perform such duties and are content to bide your time. Now, all things must have a beginning. That you should desire a post, about the person of the prince is good, and you should prepare yourself for such a post with diligence, keeping aloof from worthless people, but not from nobles and persons of consequence, for it is in such matters that a young man becomes noticed and respected."

Soon afterward I asked my late father how I should labor to obtain such a position. He considered again for a while and said: "You departed from Innsbruck in some small disfavor, for young princes are generally disposed to think that they are all of princely estate, and that the best of everything in the world is to be had at their courts. Therefore you should approach the prince, Duke Albert, as a young courtier, taking care to choose an occasion when he is merry and not ill-disposed, and speak thus: 'Gracious prince. It is now some time since I was graciously accepted at your noble court, having come from my gracious lord, Duke Sigismund, and his noble lady whom I have served from youth upwards, my desire being, first of all, by good will to obtain your grace's favor, and to learn at your noble court such things as are fitting to the condition of a young knight. Now I have heard that my gracious lord, Duke Sigismund, is about to visit your court. If he were to see that I have deserved no post, be it however small, in your grace's service, I will be looked down upon as one of no account, and will be not a little shamed before him and his noble courtiers. Be pleased therefore to allot me as a young man some service about your grace's person, and I will seek only to do your grace's pleasure.'"

After that I parted from my late father and set about with particular diligence and preparation to do his bidding. And the time came when, as before mentioned, I was able to have speech with the prince. He regarded me with gentleness, laughed, and then said, speaking quickly and abruptly, with a familiar oath, "God's limping goose, so be it." And calling a nobleman to him, who was one of his chamberlains, he said, "Go and bring the keys of my apartments and give them to von Ehingen," which also happened. And thus was I attached with other gentlemen and nobles to the service of the bedchamber.

When my lord, Duke Sigismund, arrived I provided myself with a number of keys and waited diligently as a chamberlain on my gracious master, Duke Albert, so that Duke Sigismund and his train could see that I had earned a post at court. And when my master Duke Albert was alone in his chamber, and saw that his gracious plan had been successful, he laughed heartily with me and my companions who were present and we made merry together. So it fell out that, with the others who were about his grace, I rendered and received such services as were fitting to a young courtier, and I was able by careful attention to such matters to become the foremost among the duke's chamberlains.

In that year it fell out that King Ladislaus [r. 1440–1457], who was a prince of Austria and at the same time king of Hungary and Bohemia, caused himself to be crowned at Prague as king of Bohemia. Then my gracious master, Duke Albert, caused 500 horses to be equipped, and the margrave, Albert of Brandenburg, prepared himself also to accompany my master with 300 horses. I reported these matters to my late father, and acquainted him with the course I had followed in accordance with his counsel, and of my present position. At this he was much pleased and said: "Dear son, I will fit you out well and honorably for this expedition in such manner as becomes a knightly man, so that you may exercise yourself in all knightly matters and tournaments, and prepare to take your place among your equals and superiors who have been dubbed knights, and so will you return to your place."

Accordingly I was provided with armor and cuirass, with stallions, horses, pages, clothes, and other things, and fitted out as a knight, and my gracious master was much pleased with what had been done. His grace was attended by a well-equipped train of many distinguished people. So the two princes rode with each other to Vienna in Austria, where they found King Ladislaus, who received them honorably. From Vienna the princes traveled with the king, who was attended by many powerful men from Hungary, Austria, and other lands belonging to them, with a train of 10,000 horses, and thus he rode into Prague. But it would take too long to describe all the knightly sports and royal and costly displays which were seen at Vienna and on the road between that place and Prague. But King Ladislaus rode into Prague with many princes and lords, and his 10,000 horses, and was crowned king, and many counts, lords, and nobles were dubbed knights. Five members of my gracious master Duke Albert's train were knighted and accepted into the ranks of chivalry: lord Jörg, Truchsess of Waldsee, lord Bernhart of Bach, lord Conrad of Ramstein, lord Sigismund of Thun, and I, Jörg von Ehingen, knight.

Also, a queen rode into Prague in a golden litter, and four knights of Duke Albert's train were ordered to walk at the corners of the litter in full armor to carry it, of which I, Jörg von Ehingen, was one.

Also, after this we four knights engaged in a splendid tourney, the contest being waged beyond all measure fiercely.

Also, after these happenings my noble master and the margrave returned each to his home, and we arrived at Rottenburg am Neckar, where his grace remained with his court for a time.

At this time, when my late father heard of the arrival of my noble master, he came to Rottenburg, and after the entry, when each man went to his inn, my father came to me and welcomed me in God's name and wished me joy in my knighthood. He ordered me further, when a few days should have elapsed, to go to him at Kilchberg, as he desired to discuss certain matters with me.

Accordingly, after a few days, I went to Kilchberg. My father called me into his room, which still stands above the gate, and had long and agreeable speech with me concerning the state of knighthood, and in what matter I should comport myself, and presented me for my knighthood with 400 gulden [gold coins] which he had then by him in a bowl. He told me also that it was not his wish that I should from this time on spend my time in peace and useless-ness in the courts of princes, or in taverns, but that in the coming spring a splendid expedition under the command of the Knights of Saint John was set-ting out for Rhodes, since the Turkish ruler had allowed it to be known that he would attack Rhodes by sea and land with intent to conquer it. For this expedition I was to prepare myself as a young knight, and was to set out in the coming spring with the knights for Rhodes. And when the undertaking had been accomplished (if God the Lord had so long preserved my life) I was to proceed to the Holy Sepulcher of Christ and to the Holy Land. For my father had been possessed throughout his life with a great longing to see the Holy City and the land, but had been hindered by an abundance of weighty matters from accomplishing his purpose, and indeed he had told me many times. It would therefore give him great joy, he said, for me to visit the Holy Land and cities, for which purpose he would fit me out according to his means. This speech was very pleasing to me, and I gave my father to understand that it was my own wish and disposition to perform the obligations of knighthood in all earnestness. I proposed first of all to present the matter to my gracious master, and then prepare myself in accordance with his counsel. Now it had fallen out during my journey to Austria and Bohemia that certain of my stallions and horses had suffered injury. These and others I now sold to advantage to my gracious master, and to the gentlemen at court. I also informed my master of my determination, and received his gracious approval. But I retained my position at court, and his grace gave me his favor and leave of absence. I then took leave of my late father, who directed me among other things to leave a pledge and surety [so that his duties at court would be fulfilled] with Saint John, the holy apostle and evangelist, against my return, for this was always his custom when I left him.

Accordingly in the same spring I set forth alone at my own charges, with the associates of the Order of Saint John, toward Venice, but no one from my gracious master's court would travel with me. Nor did any gentleman or nobleman from upper Germany join the expedition, which later fell out to my benefit and advantage with the grand master. But many knightly persons and noblemen from France and Spain went with us. We left Venice on the outward journey, and many things happened to us before we reached Rhodes, which for the sake of brevity I omit. But when we arrived at Rhodes I was especially well and graciously received by the grand master, for the knights of the order with whom I traveled had informed his grace why and in what manner I had come there. The grand master was at that time fully mobilized, for he had received many and various warnings, and his preparations occupied some time. But there was little for us to do by sea or land, such as we had promised ourselves in a war with the Turks. I applied myself with the greatest diligence at all times with the captains to those knightly exercises which I had come there to perform. But the Turks delayed so long with their attack that in the meantime the Turkish ruler died, and the siege by the Turks did not take place, from which the grand master and many of the Christians assumed that it had been abandoned.

After these happenings, when I had been eleven months at Rhodes and about its seaboard, the grand master gave me leave and thanked me graciously. He honored me also with costly gifts, particularly certain relics, including a thorn from our Lord's crown. In such manner and with such honors I left Rhodes and took with me a safe conduct from the grand master to the king of Cyprus, in case, on my return journey from the Holy Land, I should come there, which also happened. And since I had learned that at Beirut the holy knight Saint George had slain the dreadful dragon, and also converted the king, his wife and daughter, and the whole land to Christianity, I was most desirous of going first to that place. So I came to Beirut and visited the town and the churches where so many marvelous things had happened.

I traveled there with an escort by land for eight days, and came to certain large towns, called Tyre, Safed, and Appollosso [?], and so to Nazareth and Jerusalem. We passed also the Sea of Galilee, from which the country is called Galilee. When I had visited the holy places and had seen the greater part of them, and had spent 15 days in Jerusalem, it was my desire to proceed to St-Catherine Monastery and to Babylonia [Old Cairo], and I thereupon attached myself to certain merchants and barefoot monks. I obtained in this manner an honest companion, an adroit man, called the monk of Basle, who was willing to travel with me to St-Catherine. We set out, therefore, with an escort and came to Damascus. Here we were to be joined by other pilgrims, as the merchants and barefoot monks had told us. The town of Damascus is large and well built. We were shown the house in which the apostle Paul had lodged, with many other places, and heard stories of many holy men and prophets. After we had spent some days in Damascus and were preparing ourselves for the lengthy journey to St-Catherine, I and my companion were seized and closely imprisoned. We finally obtained our liberty, but it cost us as much as 30 ducats. Our journey, therefore, was abandoned, for we did not desire to know more of the heathens and Arabs.

We came now to Alexandria, where the holy virgin Saint Catherine was martyred. It is a seaport and is well defended by the sultan with many soldiers and mamluks. Here the great river Nile, which flows through Babylonia and Egypt, enters the sea. As soon as we could find a ship we sailed to the kingdom of Cyprus, but before we came there my companion, the one called the monk of Basle, died. He was thrown from the galley into the sea. I was much downcast at his death. May God be gracious and merciful to his soul.

I traveled on to Cyprus to acquaint myself with the king's court and his kingdom. At this time King Philip [John II?, r. 1432–1458] was reigning. I was traveling with certain Venetian merchants from Cyprus who were intending to return there, and thus I came to the kingdom, to the town of Rhodes [Nicosia]. I presented the safe conduct from the grand master, and was most graciously received by the king. He caused me to be carried about to see his kingdom, and honored me with his royal company, and I then took leave of him and returned to Rhodes. When I arrived there I was very graciously received and entertained by the grand master. But I became somewhat ill and had to lie still for some weeks, and the grand master sent me his own physician and everything I had need of until I recovered. Soon afterward I left him once more and traveled to Venice, and from there to my fatherland. When I reached home and came to my father's castle of Kilchberg, I was received by him with great joy, and I carried the relics to his chapel, which gave him special pleasure. I remained thus some days at Kilchberg, and procured fresh clothes for myself and certain of my servants. This happened in the year 1454.

At this time my gracious master, Duke Albert, was with his court at Rottenburg am Neckar. I presented myself to his grace and was very graciously and well received by him, as well as by the courtiers and all the nobles and knights. The duke presented me also with the princely order of the Salamander, and I remained a whole year with his grace at court, but my desire still was to follow the profession of knighthood. I was preferred by his grace above all other lords and nobles, and became his chief chamberlain. It happened in that year that his grace spoke frequently with me on many matters touching my sea journeys, and I made his grace aware of my desire, that as soon as I heard of a worthy expedition of knights to attach myself to them, with his gracious consent, and to follow their fortunes, carrying myself therein in such a way as to bring distinction to his grace's name. With this the duke was well content. But at that time there were, so far as I could learn, no warlike disturbances in the country of any king or prince, for peace prevailed in all the kingdoms of the Christian world. And I began to think that it was useless for me to waste my time thus sitting still, for my gracious master also had then no particular business in hand, and spent the time at his court in Rottenburg or at Freiburg very pleasantly in racing, tourneys, and dancing, and similar pastimes, in which I also took part as best I could, and applied myself very diligently to them. For my late father said always that sloth was a great vice in young and old. I hoped also by such exercises to obtain practice and facility which would profit me in my knightly undertakings and be very useful to me, for I contemplated visiting the most famous kingdoms of Christendom, intending to wander from one country to another until I met with serious and important affairs.

Now, at that time, there was a young and sturdy nobleman at my gracious master's court called Jörg von Ramsyden. He came from the Salzburg Mountains, where he had a castle and estates. He sought my company at all times, and begged me, if I were traveling into foreign countries, to allow him to accompany me. I found him to be of a ready and honest disposition; he was also well set up and very strong. He was also rich and owned many estates. I therefore told him, if it pleased him, and at his own request and desire, that I would gladly take him as a companion, for my mind was to set off very soon to distant kingdoms. At that he rejoiced greatly and told me that he would regard me as his father. And as I had seen more of the world and had greater experience, he begged me to advise and instruct him, for which he was prepared to lay down the whole of his fortune. We therefore agreed that we should obtain letters from his imperial majesty and from King Ladislaus, also from other noble personages to the kings next mentioned, and also to other Christian kings and mighty princes, so that we could visit them in case it should fall out that we could find no employment elsewhere. We asked our gracious master to procure us the letters, and he was pleased to consent and agreed to obtain them, and in order that we might have special praise and approval, since we came from his court, and from the most famous house of Austria, his grace sent personally to his imperial majesty and to King Ladislaus to obtain the letters and safe conducts. In these we were to be presented with high recommendations to the king of France, the king of Portugal (who was brother to the empress), the king of Spain, the king of England, and his grace proposed also to give us a general letter to all Christian kings and princes. These letters were accordingly procured. In addition my gracious master placed at our disposal an experienced herald, who spoke many languages, and arranged all things most graciously. We had between us eight horses, and in addition, a herald, and a sack or baggage servant who had charge of our clothes, so that we had altogether ten horses.

We traveled first of all to the king of France, King Charles [VII, r. 1422–1461], and when we arrived at his court we were greatly honored by the French lords and courtiers, and by virtue of the letter which we carried we were also specially honored and well treated by the king himself.

There were, however, no particular knightly pastimes at his court, since he was a solemn king, somewhat advanced in years. But when we had been six weeks there a splendid ambassador arrived from the king of Spain, who announced to the king that his master was about to undertake a mighty expedition against the infidel king of Granada, since this same infidel king, with help from the king of Tunis and other heathen kings of Africa, had threatened to overrun the whole of Spain. The messenger intimated that the king's undertaking was intended to prevent this, which might happen at any time, and under God, to render thus to his kingdom and to Christendom in general a profitable service. He begged the king to publish abroad throughout the whole kingdom of France the news of his king's most Christian determination, to the end that knightly persons might be moved to ride forth with him; which thing the French king commanded should be done in accord with the messenger's requests. Upon this we informed the king that we were desirous to undertake the journey and support the undertaking, and craved humbly that we might receive the necessary assistance. The king heard this with much pleasure and dispatched us most honorably. He presented to each of us a new suit of armor and a stallion, together with 300 crowns [gold coins], and gave us a letter to the king of Spain, and another also which would procure us honorable reception throughout the whole of France. We then traveled through the country and through Armagnac and Toulouse until we reached the kingdom of Navarre and came to the chief town of the king, called Pamplona. On our journey we were apprised that the king of Sicily held his court at Angers, in France. We therefore traveled there, since it was not far out of our way, it being our intention at the same time to let our stallions and horses stand and rest, and to remain some weeks with the king. This king's name was René, and he possessed many excellent estates, as well as towns and castles, in France. So we came to the court of King René of Sicily [r. 1435–1480] at Angers, where we were well and courteously received and honored by the king himself.

After some weeks we departed, but as we were traveling through France toward Pamplona in the kingdom of Navarre, as already reported, we were informed that the expedition to Granada had been abandoned, and we were advised to proceed to the king of Navarre and remain there for a while in order to accustom ourselves a little to the country, after which we could continue our journey to Portugal. We accordingly proceeded to the court of the king of Navarre, whose name was John [II, r. 1425–1479], where we remained for two months. The king received us courteously, and arranged many entertainments in our honor such as hunting, dancing, feasting, and other pastimes.

Among certain information which came to our ears at court was the news that the king of Portugal was engaged in serious warfare by land and at sea with the infidels of Africa, and especially with the heathen king of Fez, for the king of Portugal had taken from him some years before a great town across the sea in Africa called Ceuta, and we were advised to proceed with all speed to Portugal. We therefore begged leave of the king of Navarre, which was graciously granted, and departed in great honor with the assurance that we should be treated throughout his kingdom with great respect.

Thus we traveled through the kingdom of Spain, visiting several great towns, such as Burgos and others, until we reached Santiago de Compostela. Here we parted with certain of our heavy stallions, for the way is very long, and proposed to take ship at the seaport called Lagrunge [A Coruña?], which the peasants and Jacobsbrüder [pilgrims to Compostela] in our country call "at the dark star," and this we did. We took ship and sailed across the sea to the kingdom of Portugal, this distance being 120 miles by water, and we landed at the town of Lisbon, which is the chief town in Portugal. We caused the king to be informed of our arrival, and as soon as he understood that we had come from the emperor and from the House of Austria he sent to us in our inn and informed us that he had taken note of our arrival, but that after so long a journey by land and sea we must rest and refresh ourselves for a while, and that he would then grant us a speedy audience. He gave orders also that we should be well treated at the inn. Some days later the king sent for us to court, and several lords and noblemen came to escort us there. When we were presented to the king, who was splendidly attended in his royal chamber by numerous princes and marquesses and many lords and knights, he spoke graciously to us, but since we did not understand his language we could only make by gestures to the king and his attendants such reverence and honor as seemed fitting, and allowed our letters, which were in Latin, to speak for us. The king caused the letters to be read, and later conversed much with us through an interpreter on many subjects in the Dutch-Brabant speech. We informed the king that we understood that his majesty was waging war against the infidel king of Fez, and that we were willing to serve in this war by land or sea. The king heard this very graciously, and told us that he would rely on us, and that at the proper time he would make use of our services, but that we must first remain for some time longer with him at court in order to become acquainted with the lords and nobles, and to see something more of his country. He caused us to be escorted back to our inn, and commanded the lords and nobles to lend us their company, which also happened. And such were the honors and merrymakings that the like can never have been seen by any king or prince. We were also introduced frequently into the apartments of the queen's ladies, where many beautiful dances were held. Then to the chase, with jumping, wrestling, throwing, fencing, and racing with horses and jennets [small Spanish horses], and there was also much feasting. It was indeed delightful to be there. The king was named Alfonso [V, r. 1438–1481]. He was a handsome, well-grown prince, the most Christian, the worthiest, and most righteous king I have ever known. He kept also a regal court, and had with him two margraves and many counts and lords and knights, as well as beautiful women without number. We exercised ourselves in the same manner with knightly sports, on horseback and on foot, with jousting, and tourneys in full armor, since the king took great pleasure in such pastimes. My companion was the strongest in throwing the stone and iron bar, the latter being not light but very weighty, for he was a tall and powerful man, and no one could surpass him in throwing the great stone or at wrestling on horseback or on foot. I was particularly diligent in the combats in armor, for in these I was more skillful than my companion.

The kingdom is noted for its knighthood, which comprises many noble, worthy, and respected personages. The country is also well built, and the best and sweetest fruits grow there, grapes, grain, oil, sugar, and there is also much salt. We were carried about the kingdom, near and far, to beautiful towns, castles and monasteries, and particularly to one monastery, the most beautiful I have ever seen. It belongs to the Dominican Order, and the knights of Portugal are buried there. The monastery is called the Monastery of the Battle, since many years ago a king of Portugal won a battle there against the Spaniards.

About this time an urgent message arrived for the king from Africa, from the chief captain at Ceuta, reporting that the infidel king of Fez, assisted by other African kings, was mobilizing and preparing for war, and was intending to march against Ceuta with a great army, to the end that he might conquer it and take it again into his hands. The king sent for us and told us the news. Immediately afterward we begged his majesty to fit us out to fight against the infidel, which he did most graciously. He gave each of us a strong jennet, and to each of our attendants a suit of tilting armor called *brigandin*, and orders were given for a great company from the court and elsewhere to set out for Ceuta. When we were once on the sea we were shipped quickly from Portugal to Africa, for at that place the sea is narrow. On the night when we arrived at Ceuta in the great town, the whole company assembled in a vast square with armor and weapons at hand, and that night many messages were received, reporting that the infidels were approaching in great numbers. But although by day and night we heard the noise of many troops, and could see them before the town, the main army had not yet arrived. On the fourth day, when the commander and chief captain had manned the forts and divided the town into quarters, I was appointed by him to be captain over one quarter, and was given a company of able men, among whom were many who could speak and understand the Low German tongue.

Orders were given that each commander and captain of horse should fly a flag bearing his arms above his quarter of the town, and accordingly I gave the necessary directions and flew my flag. But on the fourth day, as before mentioned, the chief captain sent for me and my companions and asked us to sail with him and other experienced soldiers, and embark on the sea to spy out and take count of the infidel troops who were camped by the seashore.

We sailed accordingly and approached as near as might be to the infidels. But we beheld such a countless host of horsemen and footmen that the captain and the other lords were of opinion that we could not estimate the numbers to within 20,000. It was therefore resolved to count the tents and see how many there might be, so that those who were familiar with the habits of the infidels might judge of the size of the army. And it was resolved and considered that there were 10,000 tents, from which countless numbers might be estimated. We nevertheless decided that if all the infidels in the world were to march against us we would remain, dead or alive, in the town. We therefore returned to Ceuta, and agreed that next morning, very early, we would all assemble in the temple with our companies. This had been a fine, large heathen temple, but it was now a beautiful Christian cathedral, and we resolved to partake of the holy sacrament [communion], and the greater number among us did so.

Now it should be known that Ceuta is a great and broad town, and three parts of it face the land, and one part lies on the water, and in my judgment it is larger than Cologne. On the land side are dry ditches, in which a citadel had been erected with a number of separate towers, provided with embrasures below and protected above with tin, and surrounded on the town side by a wall. This citadel with its towers was well manned and divided into quarters, for it was very spacious. The captain was stationed there with a vast number of light horsemen, while a host of the ablest footmen had been placed between the citadel and the wall, with orders, if need arose, to spring mines and proceed as they might be directed, which indeed they did very well.

When we were all in church, as before mentioned, at sunrise, the watchers on the towers gave warning and cried aloud that the infidels were drawing near in great numbers. At this each man seized his weapon. Then we saw the infidels crossing a mountain which lay in front of the town, and, indeed, the whole mountain seemed to be covered with men. We shot at them with our bombards, which were the best we could employ at the moment. But they drew near to the ditches, being armed with handbows and curious long crossbows, and other weapons. They assailed us with these and with bombards, and shot at us all that day whenever one exposed himself, and while they engaged us, they set the main army in array. They had also many drums, great and small, and strange horns, and banners and flags without number. Thus we fought all day, and many of the infidels were shot, and we also had many wounded, for the enemy approached quite close to us into the ditches. The night was even more disturbed, for then they came closer still, with long wooden implements and spiked helmets, axes, lanterns, and shields, and bucklers called *rundella*.

When the Portuguese king was informed of the serious nature of the attack, he proposed to come in person and to ride into Ceuta with all his forces, with intent to attack the infidels from the town and to fall upon their armies, for it was not possible to engage them in any other way. When the infidels learned of this they stormed us for three days in succession, commencing at daybreak and continuing into the night. Then, indeed, there was much labor on both sides, and although countless numbers of infidels were shot and thrown down about the town, in the ditches and by the walls, it happened also frequently that the Christians were repulsed by the attacks when the captain was not ready with his counterattack, and we were therefore in difficulties. But when the infidels had assailed us for three days, as before mentioned, and had lost an extraordinary number of men, an evil stink arose from the dead bodies, and they ceased their attacks and withdrew.

Then we prepared ourselves with 400 horses and 1,000 footmen, the best that we had, and followed after them. The infidels turned frequently and skirmished with us for so long until we had seized one of the mountains. The infidels then occupied another mountain, and between us there was a fine level plain. And when evening came on, certain of our men drew near and reported that a mighty man among the infidels desired to engage in combat with a Christian in the plain between the two hills. Then I begged the captain that he would send me, for I was well arrayed and very apt in tilting armor. I had also a strong jennet which the king had presented to me. The captain consented and caused the signal to be blown to cease fighting, and the hosts reassembled. Then I made a cross with my spear, and holding it in front of me I rode from our army toward the infidels across the valley, and when the infidels saw this they returned also to their armies. Our captain also sent out a trumpeter toward the infidels, who blew a blast and gave the signal. Then, very speedily, one of the infidels appeared, riding across the plain on a fine Barbary steed. I did not delay, but rode at once to meet him. The infidel threw his shield in front of him, and laying his spear on his arm he ran swiftly at me, uttering a cry. I approached, having my spear at the thigh, but as I drew near I couched my spear and thrust at his shield, and although he struck me with his spear in the flank and forearm, I was able to give him such a mighty thrust that horse and man fell to the ground. But his spear hung in my armor and hindered me, and I had great difficulty in loosing it and dismounting from my horse. By this time he also was dismounted. I had my sword in my hand; he likewise seized his sword, and we advanced and gave each other a mighty blow. The infidel had excellent armor, and although I struck him by the shield he received no injury. Nor did his blows injure me. We then gripped each other and wrestled so long that we fell to the ground side by side. But the infidel was a man of amazing strength. He tore himself from my grasp, and we both raised our bodies until we were kneeling side by side. I then thrust him from me with my left hand in order to be able to strike at him with my sword, and this I was able to do, for with the thrust his body was so far removed that I was able to cut at his face, and although the blow was not wholly successful, I wounded him so that he swayed and was half blinded. I then struck him a direct blow in the face and hurled him to the ground, and falling upon him I thrust my sword through his throat, after which I rose to my feet, took his sword, and returned to my horse. The two beasts were standing side by side. They had been worked hard the whole day, and were quite quiet.

When the infidels saw that I had conquered, they drew off their forces. But the Portuguese and Christians approached and cut off the infidel's head, and took his spear, and placed the head upon it, and removed his armor. It was a costly suit, made in the heathen fashion, very strong and richly ornamented. They took also his shield and horse, and carried me back to the captain, who was beyond all measure delighted, and clasped me in his arms, and there was great joy throughout the whole army. But on that day great numbers of men and horses on both sides were wounded and shot down. The captain commanded that the infidel's head, his horse, shield, and sword should be carried before me, and that the most famous lords and knights with their attendants should follow after. I had to ride with them preceded by a trumpeter, and so they carried me in triumph through the great town of Ceuta. The Christians were all greatly rejoiced, and more honor was shown me than was my due. Almighty God fought for me in that hour, for I was never in greater danger, since the infidel was a very mighty man, and I was conscious that his strength far exceeded my own. God, the Lord, be praised in eternity.

The captain wrote an account of this affair to the king, who received it with particular pleasure. And since there was no more anxiety on account of the infidels, the king desired that I and my companion should return to his court, and we accordingly crossed the sea again to Portugal. We were received by the king beyond all measure well. He presented me with a bowl filled with Portuguese gulden, which bowl I brought back with me to my fatherland. I and my companion had been seven months in the town of Ceuta before we returned to the king in Portugal. During this time there were many knightly enterprises in Africa, in which I and my companion did our best against the infidels and Moors. When we had remained for a time with the king, and had been much honored, we traveled to the court of the king's brother. He was a mighty prince and kept a princely court, and his name was Infante Don Fernando. We visited also an elderly prince, who was uncle to both, called Infante Don Aweikusz [?], and he likewise kept his own princely court. We were received by these two princes beyond all measure well, and when we were about to return to the king's court we were most honorably provided for by each of them.

It now happened that King Henry [IV, r. 1454–1474] of Spain was about to undertake another expedition against the infidel king of Granada, as had been proposed when we were at the court of the king of France, but the business had been hindered by the plague. We therefore begged leave of the king of Portugal to depart, and informed him that, if God spared our lives, we would return to his court when our mission had been accomplished, which the king also desired of us. He gave us his leave, and we set off for Spain, where we were most courteously received, carrying with us letters from the king of Portugal. These we produced to the king so that he readily understood in what manner we had come. The king was preparing actively for war, and although there was much urgent business at court, certain knightly person-ages were assigned to us who bore us company and entertained us well. A great company of people on horse and foot had assembled, for trustworthy news had been received that the king of Tunis and other African kings had transported a great army of horsemen and footmen across the sea to Granada. The king of Spain had gathered together as many as 70,000 men under arms, and such an army had never been seen before by any Christian man, where-soever he may have lived. The knights of the Order of Saint James were also with the king, accompanied by an immense following. The Spaniards told us that there were 1,500 jennets or horses with his order alone. We then marched in good order into the kingdom of Granada, and wherever we came upon small towns or castles we had to take them by force, for the infidels made stalwart defense, relying on the mighty armies which were gathered together in the town of Granada. We had therefore to storm the majority of the towns and castles, and we slew all the infidels. The rank and file had orders also to kill the women and children, which was done. So we drew near to the town of Granada and made all things ready and prepared our armies, for we saw that the infidels, who were in great force in the town, would sally forth to meet us, which also happened. They did not suffer us to approach near to the town, but came out against us with a great host, nevertheless, without advantage to themselves, for we were better provided with artillery and were otherwise well prepared. But certain experienced men and captains of the king were commanded to take particular note of the infidel forces, and to advise themselves as to their condition, and we were both honored as friends, and attached to them. We had many heavy skirmishes with the infidels for two whole days until we had overthrown them. There were 50,000 infidels, among whom were 30,000 gunners.

When we returned to the main army we were attached to the royal stan-dard, and this was done to honor us. The infidels lay in a valley between us and the town of Granada, so that we could not engage them. We remained for several days thus over against each other, and night and day there were attacks and skirmishes, so that on both sides many were killed. We then passed by Granada through the kingdom, and destroyed and burnt and slew where we could, so that nothing remained standing as we passed, for everything was laid waste. We were a month and some days in the kingdom of Granada. My companion and I acquitted ourselves as best we could, until at last the whole army was gathered before a small town which was well defended and filled with troops. This we took by storm, but we lost many excellent men. I was badly wounded on the shin by an arrow from a sling, and although the wound healed subsequently, it broke out again when I returned to Swabia, and I retained until my old age a hole in the shin and discharge [from it].

After these happenings we all returned to Spain, and remained two months at the court of the king. We were much honored with feasting, dancing, hunting, horse racing, and similar pastimes. After two months we took leave of the king in order to return to the king of Portugal, and were most graciously dispatched. The king gave us both his orders, namely the Spanish Order, which is a broad collar overlapping like large fish scales, also the order of Castile, a scarlet cloak with a gold band, two thumbs breadth, over the left shoulder, running in front on the right side down to the bottom of the cloak, and then at the back of the cloak running up again to the left shoulder. The third order is that of Granada, a granite apple set on a club, with a stalk and some leaves upon it. The king gave us also 300 ducats, and to each of us a fine jennet. So we took our leave most honorably and usefully from the Christian King Henry, in the year, as one counts from the birth of our Lord, 1457.

Also, we came once more to Portugal.

Also, war then broke out in Germany.

Also, when the king [of Portugal] dismissed us he presented us with a cloth of gold worth 200 ducats. Also, a piece of crimson satin and 100 ells of black satin: also to each of us a Portuguese stallion and 300 ducats for the journey. He desired particularly that we should return to him.

Also, we traveled through Portugal and Spain, and when we came to a great town called Saragossa, we sold the gold cloth and some of the satin, which was not necessary to us for clothes, and 500 ducats were dispensed.

Also, we traveled through Spain and France, and on the way we sold certain of our heavy horses, for the way is long. In France we took ship and traveled to the king of England. The king gave us his order. My companion then left me, and I traveled to Scotland. The king was my gracious lady's brother, and he received me graciously and well. The queen was a duchess of Guelders, and a Low German.

Also, the king presented me with two tents and a cloth of black satin, and to each of my pages he gave ten ducats, there being four pages.

Also, the queen gave me a fine jewel worth 30 ducats, and a stallion worth quite 100 gulden, and much honor was shown me in hunting, dancing, and feasting.

Questions: How did the world of western European nobility work, according to this source? How did one advance one's career? How did one gain honor? How did noble connections facilitate travel? What was the impetus for the author to go on pilgrimage? Why did he wish to fight? Where was he frustrated in his attempts to fight, and where was he successful? How can one account for Jörg's unemotional description of sack and slaughter, and the slaying of women and children? What was the relationship between war and religion?

SOURCES

Abd-al-Razzaq Samarqandi. "Narrative of the Journey," in *India in the Fifteenth Century*. Ed. and trans. R.H. Major. London: Hakluyt Society, 1857.

Janet Bately, trans. "Account of Ohthere and Wulfstan," in *Ohthere's Voyages: A Late 9th-Century Account of Voyages Along the Coasts of Norway and Denmark and Its Cultural Context*. Ed. Janet Bately and Anton Englert. Roskilde: The Viking Ship Museum, © 2007. Reprinted with permission.

Benedict the Pole, "Narrative," in *The Mission to Asia: Narratives and Letters of the Franciscan Missionaries in Mongolia and China in the Thirteenth and Fourteenth Centuries*. Ed. Christopher Dawson. London: Sheed & Ward, an imprint of Bloomsbury Publishing Plc., 1980. © Christopher Dawson, 1980.

Benjamin of Tudela. *The Itinerary of Benjamin of Tudela: Critical Text, Translation and Commentary*. Ed. and trans. M.N. Adler. London: Henry Frowde, 1907.

Charles Stuart Boswell, trans. "The Vision of Adamnán," in *An Irish Precursor of Dante*. London: D. Nutt, 1908.

Wilhelm Braune, Karl Helm, and Ernst A. Ebbinghaus, eds. "Paris Conversations," in *Althochdeutsches Lesebuch: Zusammengestellt und mit Wörterbuch versehen*, 17th ed. Trans. John F. Romano. Tübingen: Max Niemeyer Verlag, 1994.

Samuel Hazzard Cross and Olgerd P. Sherbowitz-Wetzor, eds. and trans. *The Russian Primary Chronicle: Laurentian Text*. Cambridge: MA: Medieval Academy of America, 1953. Reprinted with permission.

B.F. DeCosta. "Saga of the Greenlanders," in *A Pre-Columbian Discovery of America by the Northmen: With Translations from the Icelandic Sagas*, 2nd ed. Albany: J. Munsell's Sons, 1890.

Stefano Del Lungo, ed. "Einsiedeln Itinerary," in *Roma in eta carolingia e gli scritti dell'Anonimo augiense*. Trans. John F. Romano. Rome: Presso la Società alla biblioteca Vallicelliana, 2004.

Charles Barbier de Meynard, ed. and trans. "Le livre des routes et des provinces, par Ibn Khordadbeh," in *Journal Asiatique*, sixth series, vol. 5 (1865): 5–127, 227–96, 446–527. Trans. John F. Romano.

Jean Deshusses, ed. *Le sacramentaire grégorien: Ses principales formes d'après les plus anciens manuscrits*, vol. 1. Trans. John F. Romano. Fribourg: Éditions universitaires, 1971–82.

Paul Edward Dutton, ed. and trans. "Life of Anskar," in *Carolingian Civilization: A Reader*, 2nd ed. Peterborough: Broadview Press, © 2004. Reprinted with permission.

Paul Edward Dutton, ed. and trans. "The Western European Monk Bernard's Journey to Jerusalem," in *Carolingian Civilization: A Reader*, 2nd ed. Peterborough: Broadview Press, © 2004. Reprinted with permission.

Einhard. "The Translation and Miracles of Marcellinus and Peter," in *Charlemagne's Courtier*. Ed. and trans. Paul Edward Dutton. Peterborough: Broadview Press, © 1998. Reprinted with permission of the translator.

S.D. Goitein, ed. and trans. *Letters of Medieval Jewish Traders*. Princeton: Princeton University Press, © 1973. Reprinted with permission.

R.K. Gordon, trans. "The Seafarer," in *Anglo-Saxon Poetry*. London: J.M. Dent & Sons, 1926.

Hafiz Abru. *A Persian Embassy to China*. Ed. and trans. K.M. Maitra. New York: Paragon Book Reprint Corp., 1970.

Ibn Battuta. *Ibn Battuta, Travels in Asia and Africa, 1325–1354*. Trans. H.A.R. Gibb. London: G. Routledge & Sons, Ltd., 1929.

Ibn Fadlan. *Mission to the Volga*, in *Two Arabic Travel Books: Accounts of China and India*. Ed. and trans. James E. Montgomery. New York: New York University Press, © 2014. Reprinted with permission.

Ibn Gubayr. *Viaggio in Ispagna, Sicilia, Siria e Palestina, Mesopotamia, Arabia, Egitto compiuto nel secolo XII*. Trans. Celestino Schiaparelli. Trans. John F. Romano. Rome: Casa editrice italiana, 1906.

Cosmas Indikopleustes. *The Christian Topography of Cosmas, an Egyptian Monk*. Trans. John W. McCrindle. London: Hakluyt Society, 1897.

Jacobus de Voragine. *Legenda aurea: Vulgo historia Lombardica dicta*. Ed. Johann Georg Theodor Graesse. Trans. John F. Romano. Dresden; Leipzig: Arnold, 1846.

Friar Jordanus. *Mirabilia descripta or the Wonders of the East*. Trans. Henry Yule. London: Hakluyt Society, 1863.

Liudprand of Cremona. "Retribution" and "The Embassy of Liutprand," in *The Complete Works of Liudprand of Cremona*. Trans. Paolo Squatrini. Washington, DC: Catholic University of America Press, © 2007. Reprinted with permission.

Clements Markham, trans. *Book of the Knowledge of All the Kingdoms, Lands, and Lordships That Are in the World, and the Arms and Devices of Each Land and Lordship, or of the Kings and Lords Who Possess Them*. London: Hakluyt Society, 1912.

Nasir-i Khusraw. *Nasir-i Khusraw's Book of Travels: Safarnamah*. Trans. Wheeler M. Thackston. Costa Mesa: Mazda Publishers, © 2001. Reprinted with permission.

Afanasy Nikitin. "Voyage beyond Three Seas," in *India in the Fifteenth Century*. Ed. and trans. Mikhail Wielhorski. London: Hakluyt Society, 1857.

Pascal de Vitoria. "Letter," in *Cathay and the Way Thither*, vol. 1. Trans. Henry Yule. London: Hakluyt Society, 1866.

Francesco Balducci Pegolotti. "Merchant Handbook," in *Cathay and the Way Thither*, vol. 3. Trans. Henry Yule. London: Hakluyt Society, 1914.

Marco Polo. *The Travels of Marco Polo*. Ed. and trans. H. Murray. Edinburgh: Oliver & Boyd, 1845.

Henry Reeve. *Petrarch*. Edinburgh; London: William Blackwood and Sons, 1879.

Richer of Saint-Rémi. *Histories*, vol. 2. Ed. and trans. Justin Lake. Dumbarton Oaks Medieval Library, vol. 11. Cambridge, MA: Harvard University Press, © 2011. Copyright © 2011 by the President.

Rabban Sauma. "Travelogue," in *The Monks of Kublai Khan*. Trans. E.A. Wallis Budge. London: Religious Tract Society, 1928.

J. Shinners, ed. and trans. "The Book of Margery Kempe," in *Medieval Popular Religion, 1000–1500: A Reader*, 2nd ed. Peterborough: Broadview, © 2007. Reprinted with permission.

Al-Tabari. "The Prophet Ascends to the Seventh Heaven," in *The History of Al-Ṭabarī*, vol. 6: *Muḥammad at Mecca*. Trans. W. Montgomery Watt and M.V. MacDonald. Albany: State University of New York Press, © 1987. Reprinted with permission.

Pero Tafur. *Travels and Adventures, 1435–1439*. Ed. and trans. Malcolm Letts. London: G. Routledge, © 1926.

Jörg von Ehingen. *The Diary of Jörg von Ehingen*. Ed. and trans. Malcolm Letts. London: Oxford University Press, 1929.

FIGURES

Figure 1.1: Isidorus Hispalensis, *Etymologiae* (Augsburg: Günther Zainer, 1472).

Figure 1.2: Konrad Miller, *Mappaemundi: Die ältesten Weltkarten*, vol. 1: *Die Weltkarte des Beatus* (776 n. Chr.) (Stuttgart: J. Roth, 1895–98).

Figure 1.3: Konrad Miller, *Mappaemundi: Die ältesten Weltkarten*, vol. 3: *Die kleineren Weltkarten* (Stuttgart: J. Roth, 1895–98).

Figure 1.4: William Vincent, *The Commerce and Navigation of the Ancients in the Indian Ocean* (London: T. Cadell and W. Davies, 1807).

Figure 1.5: M. Jomard, *Les monuments de la géographie; ou Recueil d'anciennes cartes européennes et orientales* (Paris: M. Duprat, 1862).

Figures 1.6–1.14: Bernhard von Breydenbach, *Peregrinatio in terram sanctam* (Mainz: Erhard Reuwich, 1486).

Figures 1.15–1.16: Hartmann Schedel, *Liber chronicarum* (Nuremberg: Anton Koberger, 1493).

INDEX OF TOPICS

Topics are listed by document number. Multiple documents under the same heading are identified by their order—a, b, c, etc. The index is intended to be used in tandem with the table of contents.

READINGS IN MEDIEVAL CIVILIZATIONS AND CULTURES
Series Editor: Paul Edward Dutton

"Readings in Medieval Civilizations and Cultures is in my opinion the most useful series being published today."
—William C. Jordan, Princeton University

I—Carolingian Civilization: A Reader, Second Edition
edited by Paul Edward Dutton

II—Medieval Popular Religion, 1000–1500: A Reader, Second Edition
edited by John Shinners

III—Charlemagne's Courtier: The Complete Einhard
translated & edited by Paul Edward Dutton

IV—Medieval Saints: A Reader
edited by Mary-Ann Stouck

V—From Roman to Merovingian Gaul: A Reader
translated & edited by Alexander Callander Murray

VI—Medieval England, 500–1500: A Reader, Second Edition
edited by Emilie Amt & Katherine Allen Smith

VII—Love, Marriage, and Family in the Middle Ages: A Reader
edited by Jacqueline Murray

VIII—The Crusades: A Reader, Second Edition
edited by S.J. Allen & Emilie Amt

IX—The Annals of Flodoard of Reims, 919–966
translated & edited by Bernard S. Bachrach & Steven Fanning

X—Gregory of Tours: The Merovingians
translated & edited by Alexander Callander Murray

XI—Medieval Towns: A Reader
edited by Maryanne Kowaleski

XII—A Short Reader of Medieval Saints
edited by Mary-Ann Stouck

XIII—Vengeance in Medieval Europe: A Reader
edited by Daniel Lord Smail & Kelly Gibson

XIV—The Viking Age: A Reader, Third Edition
edited by Angus A. Somerville & R. Andrew McDonald

XV—Medieval Medicine: A Reader
edited by Faith Wallis

XVI—Pilgrimage in the Middle Ages : A Reader
edited by Brett Edward Whalen

XVII—Prologues to Ancient and Medieval History: A Reader
edited by Justin Lake

Printed in the USA
CPSIA information can be obtained
at www.ICGtesting.com
LVHW012153240824
789201LV00009B/380

9 781487 588021